E X P L O R I N G

MOSCOW
& ST. PETERSBURG

FODOR'S TRAVEL PUBLICATIONS, INC.

NEW YORK • TORONTO • LONDON • SYDNEY • AUCKLAND

HTTP://WWW.FODORS.COM/

Copyright © The Automobile Association 1998
Maps copyright © The Automobile Association 1998

Published in the United States by Fodor's Travel Publications, Inc.
Published in the United Kingdom by AA Publishing.

Fodor's and Fodor's Exploring Guides are registered trademarks of Fodor's Travel Publications, Inc.

ISBN 0–679–03474–9
Second Edition

Fodor's Exploring Moscow & St Petersburg

Authors: **Christopher and Melanie Rice**
Joint Series Editor: **Susi Bailey**
Copy Editor: **Helen McCurdy**
Original Photography: **Ken Paterson**
Cartography: **The Automobile Association**
Cover Design: **Louise Fili, Fabrizio La Rocca**
Front Cover Silhouette: **Demetrio Carrasco/TSW**

Printed and bound in Italy by Printer Trento srl.
10 9 8 7 6 5 4 3 2 1

How to use this book

This book is divided into five main sections:

❏ Section 1
**Moscow and
St. Petersburg Are**
discusses life and living in
Russia's two greatest cities,
from the new economic order to
art and architecture

❏ Section 2:
**Moscow and
St. Petersburg Were**
places the cities in their historical
context and explores those past
events whose influences are felt
to this day

❏ Section 3:
A to Z Section
covers places to visit, with
suggested walks and excursions.
Within this section fall the Focus-
on articles, which consider a
variety of topics in greater detail

❏ Section 4:
Travel Facts
contains the strictly practical
information that is vital for a
successful trip

❏ Section 5:
Hotels and Restaurants
lists recommended
establishments in Moscow and
St. Petersburg, giving a brief
description of what they offer

How to use the star rating
Most places described in this book
have been given a separate rating:

▶▶▶ **Do not miss**

▶▶ **Highly recommended**

▶ **Worth seeing**

Not essential viewing

Map references
To make the location of a particular
place easier to find, every main entry
in this book is given a map
reference, such as 176B3. The first
number (176) indicates the page on
which the map can be found; the
letter (B) and the second number (3)
pinpoint the square in which the
main entry is located. The maps on
the inside front cover and inside
back cover are referred to as IFC and
IBC respectively.

Street name changes
Since 1991 the names of many
streets, metro stations, bridges,
canals, theaters, and institutions in
Moscow and St. Petersburg have
reverted to their prerevolutionary
names, a process that is ongoing.
Many Soviet-era street signs have
also yet to be replaced. This book
uses the post-Soviet names as far as
they were available at the time of
going to press.

Contents

Quick reference

This quick-reference guide high-lights the elements of the book you will use most often: the maps, the introductory features, the Focus-on articles, the walks and excursions

6

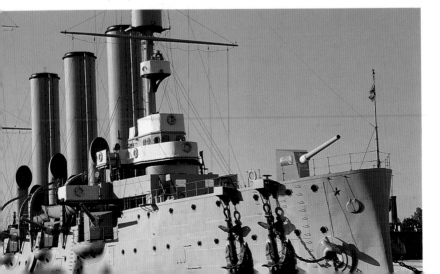

Quick reference

Our Moscow and St. Petersburg

by Christopher and Melanie Rice

Sated with palaces, monuments, and museums, we escape the dusty streets of St. Petersburg, and head for the pine-scented dunes of the Gulf of Finland. We visit Shalash, where Vladimir Ilych Lenin, founder of Russian Communism, once hid while on the run from the Provisional Government. Today, the enormous museum parking lot is deserted. When we arrive at the once resplendent pavilion, we find a solitary old woman making tea in the kitchen. "It's not safe here any more," explains Yelena Mikhailovna, "not since the hooligans started coming." Like many Russians of the older generation, Yelena believes that the decline started with Gorbachev, and she clearly yearns for a return to the old certainties.

Others, equally unsure about the future, have no inclination to return to the Communist past and are looking to capitalism and Western-style consumerism as a solution to their problems. The banks and insurance offices, the billboard advertising and fast-food restaurants, the stores selling mobile phones are all signs of how far Russia has already traveled down the capitalist road.

Yet, every visitor to Moscow or St. Petersburg will be struck by the hundreds of restored and newly reopened churches, filled to capacity every Sunday as the Orthodox Church makes a comeback. The sincerity of the worshippers is beyond doubt, and their religious fervor carries an almost Messianic zeal. Attending a service in St. Petersburg's Aleksandr Nevskiy Monastery, we were approached by a young man who presented us with a handwritten brochure that explained the significance to Russians of that famous warrior saint. Nicholas II, murdered by the Bolsheviks in Yekaterinburg in 1918, has had his proponents for canonisation, although their efforts have so far been frustrated by the authorities. A statue of the Tsar, erected by monarchists on the outskirts of Moscow, was blown up by saboteurs after just a few months.

Where is Russia heading? Clearly, a consensus of opinion is still eluding her complex and passionate people.

Christopher and Melanie Rice fell in love with Russia on their first visit more than 20 years ago, and have been returning regularly ever since. They have traveled extensively in Europe and the Near East, and enjoy sharing their experiences with others. Christopher holds a PhD in Russian history from Birmingham University, and writes regularly on Russia and Eastern Europe. Melanie is also a writer, and shares his fascination with Moscow and St. Petersburg. Together the Rices have written numerous guidebooks and travel articles.

MOSCOW AND ST. PETERSBURG ARE

■ **In June 1990 the largest city in Europe, already capital of the largest country on earth, became simultaneously the capital of a newly independent country. The city was Moscow, the country was Russia. Since then, the Soviet Union has disappeared. What else has changed?** ■

Two coups The first attempt at a *coup d'état* was the failed attempt to overthrow President Gorbachev in August 1991; the second, in October 1993, was the attempt by his erstwhile supporters, now in alliance with the right, to stop the clock of economic reform and revert to some kind of pseudo-Soviet regime. Both events brought the streets of Moscow to the television screens of millions around the world, as, true to its history, Moscow became the stage where the nation's great events were acted out. Westerners now became familiar not only with such traditional landmarks as the Kremlin and Red Square, but with the White House and the Ostankino TV Tower.

This second *coup* had been initiated after President Yeltsin had arbitrarily suspended the obstructive Congress of People's Deputies (the parliament) in favor of ruling by decree, with the promise of democratic elections in December 1993. But this move

backfired—the right, hitherto disorganized, emerged in the repackaged form of Vladimir Zhirinovsky's quaintly named Liberal Democrats and captured nearly a quarter of the vote. So it was that the new lower house, the State *Duma*, met for the first time amid scenes of near chaos.

Time for a change Much else has changed in Moscow since Russia became independent. The white, blue, and red tricolor, rather than the Red Flag with the hammer and sickle, flies over the Kremlin and other public buildings. Former President Gorbachev presides over the Gorbachev Foundation, an economics institute located in a Soviet classical building on the road in from Sheremetevo Airport. The old Communist statues of secret police chief Felix Dzerzhinskiy et al. have

Counting the ballot papers in Moscow during Russia's first free and fair parliamentary elections

❏ The Russian constitution of 1993 allows for a Federal Assembly, comprising a Federal Council (upper chamber) with 178 seats and a State *Duma* (lower house) with 450 seats. The head of state is the president, elected for a four-year term and barred from serving more than two terms consecutively. ❏

the Gothic skyscrapers of the old Ukraine Hotel and the Foreign Ministry looking contemptuously down on the modest Western-style shop fronts down below. Building after building, made redundant by the demise of Communism with its vastly over-swollen bureaucracy, and now taken over by the new organizations, refuses to budge. And the arteries of the crumbling capital are becoming increasingly clogged with traffic, thanks to efforts to humanize the central areas by introducing more pedestrian zones.

Today, although Moscow has much in common with its great Western counterparts— Paris, London, New York—it still has a stubbornly Russian stamp.

been consigned to a tawdry theme park at the House of Artists—modern politicians are now more likely to emerge in miniature form as the faces on *matryoshka* dolls. The central streets too have largely reverted to their old prerevolutionary names, while the number of places named after Lenin has been drastically reduced. And not all the changes are skin-deep. The new advertising billboards, many in English as well as Russian, point to real and profound economic change. Western investment and cooperative agreements have led to a rash of new buildings, notably hotels and business complexes.

City without parallel
Yet for all this, the face of Moscow appears curiously impervious to change. Its Stalinist physiognomy, born in the 1930s, continues to brazen it out,

The August 1991 coup: Boris Yeltsin faces the press (top) and (right) the Russian tricolor emerges as the national flag

■ **As Russia has become more materially impoverished, it has come to rely ever more on the riches of its cultural heritage. Anyone sampling the arts scene in these two great cities will be convinced of Russia's continuing creative vitality.** ■

12

Music Opera lovers still rightly regard a visit to Moscow's Bolshoy or St. Petersburg's Mariinskiy Theater as a treat. Both companies are finding it difficult to cope with recessionary times and tend to rely on standards like Tchaikovsky's *Eugene Onegin* and Moussorgsky's *Boris Godunov*. Nevertheless, the brilliant setting and the audience's infectious enthusiasm still make an evening at the opera an occasion to savor.

For concert lovers, the return from American exile of the great cellist Mstislav Rostropovich was a major event—as too was the return, in 1994, of another legendary exile, the writer Alexander Solzhenitsyn.

There are major orchestras in both cities, but for a real flavor of Russian music of the past, try to hear the old court choir, the St. Petersburg (Glinka) Kapella.

Jazz has a long and highly

Outlawed in the 1920s as an expression of bourgeois decadence, jazz has now reemerged with a vengeance

respectable tradition in Russia, surviving decades of Communist persecution to emerge as vibrant and challenging as ever. Rock music has received a great deal of publicity in recent years in the West, and the scene is as multifarious and fast-changing as anywhere else. Moscow's Rock and Jazz Laboratory and St. Petersburg's Rock Club are good starting points.

Dance Such is the reputation of the Bolshoy and Mariinskiy Ballet companies that visitors to Russia still gasp with pleasure when the tour representative announces that tickets are available for *Swan Lake*. Recent tours of the West suggest that nowadays that reputation is somewhat inflated. Nevertheless, the schools continue to produce dancers of supreme virtuosity, in spite of desperate shortages of funds, which limit the introduction of new, more experimental works into the repertoire.

Art St. Petersburg's Hermitage ranks with the Vatican and the Louvre in holding one of the world's finest international art collections. But Russian art itself also has a lot to offer, as visitors to St. Petersburg's Russian Museum and Moscow's Tretyakov Gallery soon realize. The socialist realist art of the Communist era has now been ousted by the work of previously banned artists with an international reputation like Malevich and Chagall. A thriving commercial art market provides a showcase for the work of young contemporary artists in private galleries in both cities.

Theater Theater continues to thrive with contemporary companies like St. Petersburg's Maly Theater, which toured Western Europe with a highly

Top, opposite: St. Petersburg's Kirov Ballet. Above: the world-famous Bolshoy Theater, Moscow

Nobel Prize-winning author Alexander Solzhenitsyn, now resettled in Moscow

acclaimed production of Anton Chekhov's *The Cherry Orchard*. A more unusual theatrical development was the opera singer Galina Vishnevskaya's triumphant return to the Russian stage—12 years after her retirement as a singer—in the acting role of Catherine the Great in Yelena Gremina's comedy *Behind the Mirror*.

Literature Russians revere their writers above other cultural figures, and in June 1994 an international festival, "Pushkin and St. Petersburg," heralded five years of festivities in the city of Pushkin's birth, which will culminate in his bicentennial year, 1999.

New writers are also given encouragement, with the creation of an annual—and lucrative—prize awarded for the best new work of fiction. Entries are judged by a distinguished panel, and the publicity which the short-listed novels receive gives them a good chance of future publication in the West.

■ **Moscow and St. Petersburg were once poles apart: one facing east, the other west, one homey and provincial, the other symbolizing Russia's wealth and power. But what divides the inhabitants today is not where they live, but their place in the economic pecking order, as the gap between rich and poor grows ever wider.** ■

Status symbols One noticeable trend in both cities is the growing number of foreign car showrooms and dealers. What is remarkable, however, is that the major purchasers are not foreign diplomats and Western businesspeople but top Russian executives, for whom ownership of a quality car is the ultimate status symbol.

Everything is possible for the new élite. They can buy a house in the leafy Moscow suburbs, an old *dacha* on one of the fashionable St. Petersburg islands, or a downtown apartment, remodeled by one of the many Western firms dealing in real estate. They can vacation in luxury hotels on the Crimea or travel to foreign destinations by booking through the new private operators. They can dance the night away in the most exclusive restaurants and nightspots or gamble in casinos, where they rub shoulders with wealthy Arabs and Western businesspeople. They can even send their children to private schools.

Western-style fashion promotions have little relevance for the average Russian woman

The new élite Who make up this new wealthy class? Some are former Communist officials, late converts to capitalism, but well placed to steer the levers of power and influence in their direction. Some are economic whiz kids not yet out of their twenties, who have made a killing on the stock exchange or from buying and reselling computers and hi-fi equipment. Then there are the gangsters from the southern republics, accompanied by the high-class prostitutes who bribe their way into the large hotels and charge a small fortune for their favors.

Standing slightly apart from this caste is the equally privileged new intelligentsia—actresses, artists, fashion designers, rock musicians etc., whose careers, outlandish tastes, and mannered opinions are featured in the pages of the new glossies.

Making ends meet For the majority of Muscovites and Petersburgers, inhabiting grim apartment blocks and satellite towns of the outer city, life

is increasingly a hand-to-mouth existence. Everyone has been affected, whether it is the nuclear scientist, tempted to sell his expertise abroad because he is making only $100 a month at home, or the doctor trying to cope with conditions in the ramshackle health service, the young graduate who turns to prostitution because she does not have a job, or the pensioner who sells his apartment to a private marketeer for the price of a few groceries or a bottle of vodka.

For the average family, adjusting to the new economic order means having to take a second job—driving taxis, selling candy and cigarettes, sewing clothes, cleaning offices, carrying out house repairs. To travel on the increasingly overloaded metro system is uncomfortable and inconvenient, but necessary when

even Russian makes of car are now beyond the reach of the average budget and the cost of gas has risen astronomically. Shopping is no longer a matter of waiting in line but a dispiriting search for goods and fresh produce at affordable prices.

But the most pressing problem is housing. In central St. Petersburg, behind many of the ornate, even stately 19th-century façades, up to 15 families can be found living in communal apartments, sharing a single bathroom, toilet, and kitchen. No repairs have been undertaken for decades so roofs leak, walls crack, and floors collapse as the inhabitants try to go about their daily lives.

While some Russians still line up for bare necessities, the new rich have both time and money to shop in GUM's new Western stores

■ In 1979 a Soviet guidebook promised that over the ensuing 25 years "Moscow will become even more beautiful and modern, reflecting in its appearance the lofty concepts of the age of Socialism and Communism." ■

This is far from the Moscow that visitors at the time of Karl Baedeker's 1914 guide would have been familiar with, the city known to Russians as *matyushka Moskva* (little mother Moscow), the homey town to which Chekhov's *Three Sisters* yearned to return. That Moscow was all but obliterated by Stalin's planners in the 1930s, when they began the wholesale destruction of monasteries and churches, of ancient gateways and city walls. Nineteenth-century Moscow can never be re-created, but many Muscovites are now keen both to preserve what has not been destroyed and to restore

Demolished in the 1930s to allow greater access to Red Square, Kazan Cathedral is now rebuilt

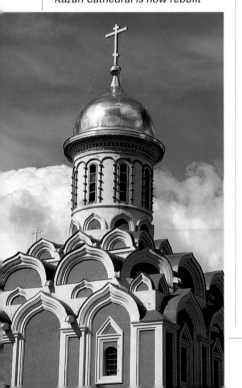

buildings that have fallen into disrepair and ruin.

Echoes from the past A start was made with the renaming of streets. Back came the reminders of Moscow's picturesque past— Povarskaya Ulitsa (Cooks' Street), Vetoshniy Pereulok (Old Clothes Lane), Okhotniy Ryad (Hunter's Row), Patriarshiy Prud (Patriarch's Pond), and so on. The pedestrianization of Ulitsa Arbat is a belated but nonetheless welcome attempt to re-create the easygoing atmosphere of this once fashionable, semirural district. Demands for this principle to be extended to other parts of the center of the city have been received sympathetically by the authorities; so far, however, the attempts to outlaw motor traffic have resulted in atrocious snarl-ups on the already overused Garden Beltway (Sadovaya).

Restoration Moscow once boasted more than 500 churches and, though many were closed and destroyed following the Revolution, about half survived after being converted to secular uses. The restoration of the Danilovskiy Monastery in the 1980s paved the way for work to begin on other religious foundations throughout the capital. In 1994, the decision was made to rebuild one of Moscow's most famous prerevolutionary religious monuments, to be completed in time for the 850th anniversary of the founding of Moscow in 1997. The Cathedral of Christ the Savior was blown up by Stalin's workmen in 1931 to make way for a Palace of Soviets which was never actually built. The staggering cost of the reconstruction (at least $150 million) has been widely criticized.

Digging for history The most promising site from an archaeological point of view is that of Manezhnaya Ploshchad, just outside the Kremlin walls. The findings have revealed much about the fascinating history of the Kremlin and also life in old Moscow, when the area around Okhotniy Ryad was once occupied by shops and merchants' houses. Archeologists collaborated with a team of amateur divers who explored the honeycomb of sewers and tunnels beneath Red Square. Many artifacts were recovered, including a tsarist sword and a revolver thought to have been dropped down a drain during the Moscow uprising in December 1905. These and other items will eventually be exhibited in the Moscow History

Above: the hidden secrets of 500 years were unearthed during excavations on Red Square
Top opposite: detail, Metropol Hotel, Moscow

Museum, which already boasts a fascinating collection including treasure buried at the time of the Mongol invasions in 1237. The noticeable increase in interest in Moscow's past can also be seen in the growing number of antiquarian bookstores and in the sale of Russian-language postcard sets of old Moscow. Commercial interest in the past has also been quick to respond, with the building of night-clubs in the old style within the sadly neglected, but potentially beautiful Hermitage Gardens.

■ **The city of St. Petersburg is itself a unique architectural monument, a visionary parade of ensembles and majestic set-pieces: palaces and cathedrals, rivers and canals, public squares and sweeping perspectives, all described with unerring, Euclidian precision.** ■

The façades follow seamlessly and without apparent interruption, the colors—greens, blues, ochers, and yellows—never quite defined as they adjust subtly to the vagaries of the northern light. Two architectural styles prevail: the baroque, exuberant and delicate; and the neoclassical, its pillars, columns, and entablatures gentle but firm reminders of the sober Roman virtues. St. Petersburg presents an architectural paradox which, tantalizingly for the visitor, is never quite resolved.

The architects

Domenico Trezzini (1670–1734) Recruited by Peter the Great to work on the founding of St. Petersburg, this Italian assumed overall charge with special responsibility for the Peter-Paul fortress and the Summer Palace. Trezzini also had a hand in the Twelve Colleges and an early version of the Winter Palace.

Bartolommeo Rastrelli (1700–1771) Rastrelli came to St. Petersburg from Italy aged 16, with his sculptor father. A great favorite of the Empress Elizabeth, he is most famous as the architect of the baroque Winter Palace. Among a host of other commissions were the Catherine Palace at Tsarskoe Selo, the Peterhof Palace, and the Smolniy Cathedral.

Andrei Zakharov's gilded spire crowns the Admiralty building

J. Vallin de la Mothe (1729–1800) Of the many French architects who worked in St. Petersburg, de la Mothe is probably the most distinguished. His commissions include the Small Hermitage and the Academy of Arts, but he is best known for creating the elegant façade of Gostiniy Dvor (the covered market). De la Mothe taught a generation of Russian architects, the most gifted of whom was Vasily Bazhenov.

Charles Cameron (1743–1812) Cameron became obsessed with the architecture of the classical world after leaving Scotland to study in Rome. He was invited to St. Petersburg by Catherine the Great to decorate the interiors of the Catherine Palace at Tsarskoe Selo. Catherine also commissioned him to build Pavlovsk Palace for her son, Paul.

Carlo Rossi (1775–1849) The son of a ballerina, Rossi was rumored to have been fathered by Tsar Paul I. Appointed court architect in 1816, the Italian imposed a neo-classical stamp on much of St. Petersburg. Among his superb creations are the Arch and General Staff building on Palace Square, the Pushkin Theater and Ostrovskiy Square, Arts Square, the Senate and Synod buildings on Decembrists' Square, and Yelagin Palace.

Andrei Nikiforovich Voronykin (1760–1814) Born a serf, this Russian was almost certainly the illegitimate son of Count A. S. Stroganov, who paid for his education as an architect. After traveling in Europe he returned in 1790 to decorate the interior of Stroganov's palace in St. Petersburg. He is best known for the Kazan Cathedral on Nevskiy Prospekt.

Heritage The visit, in 1994, of the heir to the British throne, Prince Charles, drew the world's attention to the sorry plight of St. Petersburg's dazzling architectural heritage. Unfortunately the problem is not confined merely to the flaking plaster of the façades but includes the structural underpinnings of their

St. Petersburg is almost over-endowed with out-of-town palaces. Yelagin Palace is one of many in need of restoration

foundations. The money has been found for some restoration work, most recently the Cathedral of the Savior "on the Blood," but the scale of the problem is daunting. The State Inspectorate for the Protection of Monuments is responsible for the maintenance of 8,000 historic buildings, including 400 palaces. And the fact that many of these structures are in daily use does not make matters easier. It will probably need a major rescue mission on the scale of "Venice in Peril" to save St. Petersburg.

■ **Moscow has not always been a gourmet's paradise, but in recent years there has been a culinary revolution. Nowadays you can eat out as well in the Russian capital as in any European city. Even if funds are limited, this can still be a pleasurable experience.** ■

Etiquette For Russians, eating out is a celebration. They arrive early, expect the meal to last well into the night, and tend to be noisy and boisterous, enjoying music and dancing. After a few drinks Russians will often invite strangers to join them at their table, or, more commonly, to partner them in a dance. In the old Communist days Westerners frequently complained about the slow service. This criticism owed something to the natural rhythm of the Russian meal, which prolongs the first course of *zakuski* or hors d'oeuvres, often for a couple of hours. The main course, however, tends to be something of an afterthought, although this does not mean that Russians are undiscriminating. The average Russian has a sweet tooth so dessert is *de rigueur*. Vodka is consumed steadily throughout the evening, though many Russians accompany it with *shampanskoe* (Russian champagne), a sweeter and lighter version of the French equivalent.

Black caviar, the slated roe of sturgeon, is preferred to red, extracted from salmon

Typical foods
Zakuski On most menus it is possible to choose from among the following: *икра* (*ikra*) caviar—the black (*чёрная, chernaya*) is considered more of a delicacy than the red (*красная, krasnaya*); *блины* (*bliny*) pancakes—these are generally served either *с икрой* (*s ikroi*) with caviar or, *с сметаной* (*s smetanoy*) with sour cream; *столичный салат* (*stolichniy salat*) chicken and potato salad; *салат из крабов* (*salat iz krabov*) crab salad; *салат из огурцов / помидоров* (*salat iz ogurtsov/pomidorov*) cucumber/tomato salad; *маринованные грибы* (*marinovannye griby*) marinated mushrooms; *осетрина* (*osetrina*) sturgeon, *селъд* (*seld*) herring, and *копченая семга* (*kopchenaya semga*) smoked salmon. You can also choose from *мясная закуска* (*myasnaya zakuska*) cold cuts, like *ветчина* (*vetchina*) ham and *колбаса* (*kolbasa*) sausage.

Soups There is a large variety of Russian soups, such as the traditional peasant dishes, *борщ* (*borshch*) and щи (shchi). *Borshch* is almost a meal in itself, a hot soup comprising shin of beef, beet, potatoes, cabbage, tomatoes, and onions. *Shchi* is cabbage soup with ham, salami, and mixed vegetables. The most common cold soup is **окрошка** *(okroshka),* made with cucumbers.

Main courses The Russian diet is still heavily meat-based: **бэф–строганов** *(bef-stroganov)* beef stroganoff, **гуляш** *(gulyash)* goulash, **свинина** *(svinina)* pork, **курица** *(kuritsa)* chicken, and **котлеты по–киевски** *(kotlety po-Kievski)* chicken Kiev are common dishes; however, fish, especially **осетрина** *(osetrina)* sturgeon and **судак** *(sudak)* pike-perch, will often be served.

Desserts мороженое *(morozhenoe)* Ice cream is the favorite but you may also find **блинчики с вареньем** *(blinchiki s varenem)* jam pancakes.

Moscow is international
The first private restaurant, Kropotkinskaya 36, opened in Moscow in 1987, and has now been joined by nearly 200 others, serving not only quality Russian food but also international cuisine: there are fish restaurants, bistros, pizza parlors, but as yet nothing purely vegetarian. The private-sector restaurants pride themselves on Western-style service and presentation and generally live up to the standards they set.

You can also choose your own ambience, dining in a 19th-century banqueting hall (the Budapest Hotel), in an 18th-century mansion (Glazur), on board ship (the cruiser *Alexander Blok*), or in the intimacy of Emily's (Stanislavskovo 2). Entertainment ranges from classical piano and violin to jazz, gypsy music, folk ensembles, and bands.

Kebabs, like shashliks, originated in the Southern Republics

21

ВЫПУСК

■ "Organized crime has the country by the throat," declared President Boris Yeltsin in 1994, as he justified a crackdown on crime and lawlessness that gave the police and the authorities sweeping powers of investigation and arrest. **■**

Everyone, it seems, is being deployed in the fight against crime: the Interior Ministry, the Federal Counterintelligence Service, the prosecutor's office, specialized crime units, the OMON (special troops), and even the American FBI. There are plenty of policemen in the cities, but despite getting new Western patrol cars, they lack the computers and surveillance equipment taken for granted in the West.

Roots of corruption Organized crime has its roots in the Brezhnev era, when the creaking Soviet economy was propped up by an alternative black market to which practically all Russians had to resort for everyday goods and services; this was known as *na levo* (literally "on the left").

Despite an anticorruption drive in the mid-1980s, which purged Communist parties across the Soviet Union, the newly organized crime gangs were already becoming established, many in regions like Georgia, Chechnya, Azerbaijan, and Daghestan.

Russia's *Cosa Nostra* Moscow's crime wave has been blamed on gangs from the Volga city of Kazan, although this is certainly a simplification. What is indisputable is that there are now at least 100 gangs operating in the city, half a dozen powerful enough to control their own turf. One runs the neighborhood of

Below: nerve center of law and order, Moscow's Petrovka police barracks. Top: headline news

Izmailovskiy Park, for example, another downtown Tverskaya, and so on. The core membership of each gang is said to be about 300. The activities of Russia's Mafia, with its own organizational structures and conventions, cover the whole gamut of organized crime: tax scams and money laundering, extortion, drugs, prostitution, racketeering, contract killings.

Protection Protection rackets are the bread-and-butter of the Mafia businesses. Any new firm opening up premises on Moscow's Tverskaya or St. Petersburg's Nevskiy Prospekt is likely to receive a visit from gentlemen in Armani suits offering to "help out" with security or even to buy into the business. The British shopping chain of Littlewoods, which opened a department store in St. Petersburg's premier shopping mall, Gostiniy Dvor, became the focus of Mafia attention after the management refused to pay protection money. In this case, revenge was confined to assaults on staff; other firms, especially Russian ones, have not been so lucky—kidnappings and contract killings are currently running at 500 a year, and there have been several car bomb attacks on the streets of Moscow.

A shortage of patrol cars is just one problem the police have to face

Guns for sale The Russian Mafia can count on an almost limitless supply of arms—not only handguns and the regulation Kalashnikovs but mortars, grenades, rocket launchers, and bombs. It is the simplest thing in the world nowadays to acquire a pistol: in St. Petersburg prospective buyers head for the Apraksin Dvor market where dealers openly wave advertisements offering the sale of weapons and ammunition.

Force breeds force, and most international businesses now hire their own private security (Russian firms advertise quite openly in directories and newspapers). Most of the employees are Afghan veterans, former servicemen, and ex-KGB personnel—other ex-KGB men work for the Mafia as contract killers and technical advisors.

No easy solutions That organized crime is at last being tackled comes as a great relief to ordinary Russians. Whether the government's draconian solution, which involves bending the law to bring the law breakers to justice, will ultimately do more harm than good remains to be seen.

■ **Before the Revolution (according to Baedeker) Moscow time was 29 minutes ahead of St. Petersburg time. Perhaps this gave Moscow an advantage that explains its undeniable lead over its rival in business today. For under Communism, Moscow became the capital of a highly centralized state and of a planned economy where every decision emanated from that city. Until recently, a certain wariness of St. Petersburg existed among Western businesspeople, as the Mafia exerted a tighter grip on commerce there.** ■

A question of temperament There is no inherent difference in entrepreneurial acumen or enterprise where the two business communities are concerned. By common consent the Russian character has certain drawbacks when it comes to business—Russians are garrulous and easygoing, inclined to be careless and wary of accepting responsibility. More seriously, the collective mentality, partly deep-rooted in the Russian psyche and the nation's history, partly imposed by 70 years of Communist indoctrination, has led to a widespread suspicion of individual enterprise. On the other hand, many Western businesspeople have found that in general Russians also have a number of characteristics that are ideally suited to the world of commerce: they are bright and self-confident, adaptable, eager to question and to learn, not afraid of making mistakes.

Adapting to change For a country with only a few years' experience of capitalism to draw on, management training is a high priority. Western-initiated programs now in place in Moscow and St. Petersburg have attracted a great deal of interest from professors, translators, engineers, and scientists, disillusioned with their former careers and anxious to "seize the day." Lectures in corporate finance, marketing, contractual negotiations, and accounting are intended to prepare the Russian business-person to make his own well-judged commercial decisions.

Joint ventures Visitors to Russia will quickly realize that the economy is highly dependent on Western capital, much of it invested in joint ventures with Russian businesses; hence the large number of new hotels, shopping malls, airport improvements, business and information centers, and developments in telecommunications and the media. The problems begin when the parties disagree, as happened recently in one of Moscow's most prestigious joint ventures, the Radisson Slavyanskaya Hotel. The dispute arose when Radisson, which runs the hotel, Americom, which manages the business center, and the Russian partner, Mosintour, couldn't agree about privatization and the payment of debts amounting to some $8 million. The Russian Mafia became involved, and in November 1996 the director of the hotel, Paul Tatum, was gunned down outside the entrance of a nearby metro station.

Free enterprise The recent privatization law has led to an astonishing increase in small-scale private trading. The kiosks that abound in Moscow and St. Petersburg offer the best opportunity for the enterprising young Russian to go into *biznis*. Operating in cash, the kiosks trade mainly in Western goods with a high turnover—soft drinks, chocolate, small items of clothing, sunglasses, CDs, toys, toiletries. Many stallholders, though, have cast any notion of trading standards to the winds; others are downright unscrupulous. This has led to a

rash of complaints in the press about contaminated foodstuffs and counterfeit or bootleg liquor. In a recent spotcheck of a thousand Moscow kiosks, 800 were found to be operating without the approval of the city's sanitation office. Not a single kiosk possessed a refrigeration unit, even though many of the goods on sale were perishables. Moscow's mayor has declared all-out war on the kiosk traders, but until the banking system becomes more supportive of small businesses, it is unlikely that the economy can survive without them.

Top: T-shirt kiosk. Below: Moscow is going out of its way to provide up-to-date communications facilities for Western businesspeople

■ **Like all Russians, Muscovites and Petersburgers love to party. Their enthusiasm is infectious, so why not join them in their celebrations? Here is a selection of some of the events and festivals you can enjoy with them throughout the year.** ■

Winter The "Russian Winter" festival traditionally begins on December 25 and is a secular celebration involving family parties, concerts, New Year trees, fireworks, and the Russian Santa Claus—*Ded-Moroz* (Grandfather Frost). Nowadays Christmas is also a religious celebration, marked on the Orthodox calendar as January 7. In February and March there is a folklore festival, "Farewell to the Russian Winter," with concerts and troika rides.

Spring The long hard winter ends dramatically in April with the cracking of the ice and the appearance of the first spring flowers. During the spring there are several public holidays: March 8—International Women's Day; May 1 and 2—Labor Day/Spring Holiday; May 9—Victory Day (end of World War II). The Spring Music

Top: in Gorky Park, Moscow Below: rock music—part protest, part entertainment—has a surprisingly long pedigree in Russia

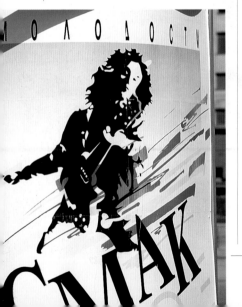

❑ **Nevskiy Prospekt**
"Of an evening the Prospect is flooded with fiery obfuscation. Down the middle, at regular intervals, hang the apples of electric lights. While along the sides plays the changeable glitter of shop signs. Here the sudden flare of ruby lights, there the flare of emeralds. A moment later the rubies are there and the emeralds are here."
—Andrei Bely *St. Petersburg*
"Pavel Nikolaevich Yablochkov was responsible for the illumination (name formed from the diminutive of apple [*yabloko*])."
—Footnote in Penguin edition ❑

Festival held in April focuses on Russian classical music, ancient and modern. Easter is a solemn religious occasion in the Orthodox Church and is celebrated in April, but rarely on the same date as in the West.

Summer The summer months in Moscow and St. Petersburg are generally sunny and hot: bands play in the public parks and outside palaces. It is the season of outdoor rock concerts and boat parties. A new public holiday is Russian Independence Day, June 12. Also in June, St. Petersburg celebrates the White Nights. For a week or so, when the sun dips below the horizon for no more than 40 minutes in every 24 hours, the city doesn't sleep: the place to be is on the river, where special boat parties and celebrations are organized by the major hotels.

Fall This season tends to be short, and by the Day of National Reconciliation on November 7, temperatures are already near freezing.

MOSCOW AND ST. PETERSBURG WERE

■ **Yuri Dolgorukiy (literally, "George the long-armed") is still honored today as the founder of Moscow. A statue of the helmeted warrior on horseback occupies a prime site on Tverskaya Ulitsa opposite City Hall.** ■

According to tradition, Moscow was founded in 1147, when, as the Russian *Chronicles* tell us, Prince Yuri of Suzdal invited a neighboring Prince from Novgorod-Seversky to a "mighty dinner in Moscow." At that time Moscow was no more than one of a number of military outposts in the northern principality of Vladimir-Suzdal, but by 1156 Prince Yuri had commenced the building of the fortifications which would eventually become the Kremlin.

Top: Russia's traditional emblem, the two-headed eagle. Below: the arms of the Muscovy Company

Mongol invasion Moscow rapidly developed as a trading settlement until disaster struck in 1237, when Batu, grandson of Genghis Khan, unleashed his ferocious Mongol hordes on Russia. Crossing the Volga with lightening speed, Batu laid waste everything before him. Moscow was burned to the ground a year later and the population was massacred. But thereafter the city fared better, its deeply forested environs offering some protection against the enemy.

Money bags Under Mongol rule the Russian princes became glorified tax collectors, each suffering the humiliation of having to dress in Mongol clothes and travel to Saray on the Volga, where Batu Khan had established his capital, in order to swear allegiance to the khan.

It was in these circumstances that the princes of Moscow emerged as the most powerful in the region. Strengthening their kingdom by building a ring of fortified monasteries around it, they exploited their allegiance to the khan by carrying out punitive raids against any principality that dared to rebel against the authority of the Golden Horde. This policy was doubly self-serving: winning Moscow the approbation of the khans while simultaneously rubbing out potential rivals in the locality.

The highpoint of the strategy came in 1328 when the most zealous tax collector of all, Ivan "Kalita" ("money-bags"), was awarded the title of Grand Prince of Muscovy for his pains.

Two-headed eagle When Ivan III came to the throne in 1462 he inherited territories eight times greater than they had been a century before. By the time of his death in 1505 Muscovy had become the largest state in Europe with an area of nearly half a million square miles: Yaroslavl, Rostov, Tver, and Novgorod, all proud and once independent princedoms, were each in turn swallowed up by their insatiable neighbor. Ivan's writ now ran from the Ural Mountains in the east to the Arctic Ocean in the north. At the same time, he strengthened his dynastic

It took three sculptors to design the statue of Moscow's founder, Prince Yuri of Suzdal, unveiled in 1954

position by marrying Zoe (or Sophia), niece of the last emperor of Constantinople. With Zoe came not only Italian builders and craftsmen, but mint masters, engineers, and diplomats—Russia had arrived on the European scene. Very much conscious of his status, Ivan borrowed the two-headed eagle of Byzantium for his seal and began using the title "tsar" or "caesar" which had previously been reserved for the eastern emperor. To further stake out his claim to the mantle of Byzantium, he declared Moscow to be the third Rome, the new center of the Eastern Orthodox Church. His authority was now absolute, as he revealed to all in 1480 when he ceased paying tribute to the khan.

❏ Life under the khans was "nasty, brutish, and short," which explains why so many Russian words dealing with repression have a Mongol derivation: *kandaly* (chains), *nagayka* (a horsewhip later used by Cossack troops), and *katorga* (hard labor). The single best attested example of Tatar cruelty was the occasion when they held a victory banquet on a heavy wooden platform balanced on the writhing bodies of their prisoners. ❏

■ **Ivan the Terrible has exercised a powerful influence over Russian as well as Western minds. Certainly, as his sobriquet "the dread" or "awesome" implies, he was a striking personality.** ■

During the first part of his reign, which technically began at the age of three in 1533, Ivan was almost universally praised for ruling firmly but without undue show of force. He consulted with church leaders, introduced a new legal code curbing the power of provincial governors, clarified the civic duties of the gentry, and modernized the army. In 1552–1556 Ivan conquered the khanates of Kazan and Astrakhan, effectively opening the way to Siberia.

Mental decline Then everything began to go wrong. In 1560 his first, much-loved wife Anastasia Romanova died. Ivan suspected that she had been poisoned, and the first of his retaliatory purges followed. More serious, however, was the defection of his friend, the general

The benign appearance of Ivan the Terrible in this engraving belies the dreadful reality

Prince Andrei Kurbsky, to the rival state of Poland–Lithuania. Stricken with paranoia, Ivan left Moscow and, from monastic retreat, sent a letter to the Metropolitan of the Orthodox Church accusing the *boyars* (Russia's nobility) of insubordination. When a deputation of ministers set out to meet him, they found a changed man—his eyes staring out of his head, his hair and beard in shreds and completely white. This was the prelude to the first Russian terror.

The *oprichniki* Under Ivan's instructions, a band of trusted henchmen known as the *oprichniki* roamed the land hunting for "subversives." The *boyars* suffered exile, seizure of property, torture, and execution. Then, in 1570, Ivan launched an attack on Novgorod, massacring its inhabitants. To raise taxes for his increasingly unsuccessful military campaigns, he imposed harsh taxes on the peasantry and, to make collection easier, limited their legal right to move—the first step on the road to serfdom.

Ivan alternated between moods of profound and exceptional cruelty and extravagant contrition, sending lists of his victims to monasteries so that Masses could be offered for their souls. Then in 1581 in a fit of rage, he struck down his son and heir Ivan with his staff, paving the way for a crisis in the succession.

False Dmitris When Ivan died in 1584 his kingdom lay devastated. A period of unrest followed, when Boris Godunov took over as regent in place of the mentally feeble heir Fedor, who died in 1598. On his election to the throne in that year, Boris was suspected of having murdered Ivan the Terrible's other son, Dmitri, who had died in 1591. Most modern historians are now

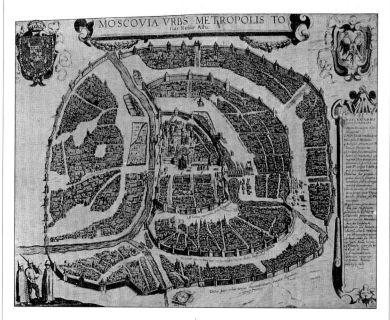

MOSCOVIA VRBS METROPOLIS TO
tius Russiæ Albæ.

By the 16th century Moscow was firmly on the itinerary of Europe's merchant class

convinced that Dmitri died of natural causes, but at the time, Boris was vulnerable to allegations that undermined the legitimacy of his claim to the throne. When he died in 1605, a reign of great promise had been shattered by paranoid obsessions not unlike Ivan the Terrible's own; by natural calamity (the terrible famine of 1601–1603); and by the appearance of a pretender to the throne claiming to be the "murdered" Dmitri. After Boris's death the Russian state slid rapidly into anarchy. No sooner had the first "false Dmitri" been murdered in the Kremlin, his ashes shot into the air from a large cannon, than several more appeared on the scene. In 1610 the Poles, Russia's great enemy, occupied Moscow. It was two years before patriotic forces under the leadership of Kuzma Minin, a butcher from Nizhny-Novgorod, and Prince Dmitri Pozharskiy ejected them amidst great national rejoicing. In 1613 a national assembly unanimously acclaimed Ivan the Terrible's great-nephew Mikhail

Romanov as tsar, launching a dynasty of rulers which would survive for more than 300 years.

Ilya Repin's mesmerizing portrayal of Ivan the Terrible and his dying son

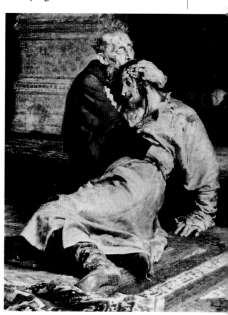

■ **Like Ivan the Terrible, Peter the Great grew up in an atmosphere of nightmarish insecurity and intrigue. Technically Peter ruled from the age of nine in 1682, but even when the élite military corps, the *Streltsy*, deposed the regent Sofia seven years later, he was still not master of his own fate.** ■

War games Peter was a highly original individual. He spent his childhood in the "German suburb" of Moscow. Here, he enjoyed the company of foreigners—English, Dutch, and German merchants—and was eager to learn about everything that was happening in the "mysterious West." He studied mathematics, learned to sail, and took a serious interest in the conduct and mechanics of modern warfare.

Overseas tour In 1697 Peter conceived the idea, extraordinary for a Russian monarch, of undertaking the Grand Tour, but with a typically idiosyncratic emphasis on science and technology. For four months he worked incognito as a ship's carpenter in Holland. Then, with the assistance of William of Orange (also King of England), he went to England,

touring the dockyards at Deptford and visiting the Woolwich Arsenal, the Royal Observatory at Greenwich, the Mint, and the University of Oxford. While in Venice, he learned of another *Streltsy* revolt in Moscow. On his return, Peter was ruthless in his punishment of the rebels, putting to death as many as 2,000 subjects over the next two years.

Lookout on the Baltic It was the onset of war with Sweden in 1700 that decided the site of Peter's future capital to which he assigned the foreign name of Sankt Peterburg. The Swedes were so dominant in the Baltic that for several years after the founding of the city in 1703, Peter's

Top: detail, Petrodvorets fountain
Below: a cartographer's nightmare, a city built amid swamp and forest

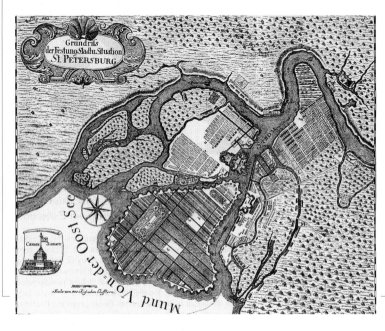

Grundriß der Festung, Stadt u. Situation ST. PETERSBURG

> ❏ "And he thought: From here we will outface the Swede;
> To spite our haughty neighbor I shall found
> A city here. By nature we are fated
> To cut a window through to Europe, To stand with a firm foothold on the sea."
> —Alexander Pushkin, *The Bronze Horseman,* translated by D. M. Thomas ❏

The complex of palaces, parks, and fountains at Peterhof was initially planned by Peter the Great (seen below) after a visit to Versailles

of the tsar's boundless ambition.

To populate the new capital, Peter issued decree after decree summoning nobles, merchants, and artisans to build their homes on designated sites, at their own expense and in conformity with his tastes and specifications. (They even had to bring their own stone.) They came unwillingly, protesting at the rigors of the climate, the dreariness of the landscape, and the measureless gloom of the northern winter; but when Peter died, his new capital had more than 40,000 permanent inhabitants.

architects and builders were working in virtual siege conditions. However, Peter's investment in Western technological know-how and personnel to create a new army and navy paid handsome dividends—in 1709 he inflicted a decisive defeat on Charles XII of Sweden at Poltava. By the time of Peter's death in 1725 Russia had acquired control of the Baltic shoreline as well as the neighboring territories of Estonia and Livonia.

The first Petersburgers In the early 1700s St. Petersburg resembled a gigantic building site, worked by thousands of serfs drafted from all over Russia, and Swedish prisoners of war. There was a shortage of wheelbarrows, so the laborers carried the earth in the skirts of their clothes or in bags of rough matting. Due to persistent shortages of food and shelter untold thousands died of exhaustion and disease in the service

■ **"The public buildings, churches, monasteries, and private palaces of the nobility are of an immense size and seem as if designed for creatures of a superior height and dimensions to man,"** wrote Sir Nicholas Wraxall after a visit to St. Petersburg in 1775. But the luxury and ostentation of the imperial capital did not reflect the poverty of the mass of the Russian population. ■

Voice of reason In 1790 a young nobleman, Alexander Radishchev, wrote a book called *Journey from St. Petersburg to Moscow* which revealed in brutally vivid terms the evils of serfdom and the lack of all notions of human rights in Russia under Catherine the Great. Theoretically Catherine was an enlightened ruler, who corresponded with the French philosophers Voltaire and Diderot and had drawn up, on the French model, a new legal code condemning serfdom—at least in principle. Advocating basic rights for the individual, Catherine had even convened a representative assembly which collected and discussed grievances and the shortcomings of government throughout the country. Unfortunately, Catherine had failed to match good intentions with appropriate actions.

Potemkin villages Catherine once boasted to Voltaire: "There are no shortages of any kind [in Russia]; people spend their time in singing thanksgiving Masses, in dancing and rejoicing." This myth was perpetuated by her loyal ministers, such as her favorite Prince Grigori Potemkin, who pandered to Catherine's wishful thinking. When Catherine visited him at his base on the Black Sea coast, Potemkin carefully arranged for her route to be lined with idyllic artificial settlements known thereafter as "Potemkin villages."

Rumblings of revolution Never had the gulf between the ruling privileged classes and the common people been greater. In a country where more than 90 percent of the population lived in abject poverty, Catherine expended huge sums on her favorites—50 million rubles on Potemkin alone. When the empress conferred vast tracts of crown land on the likes of Count Orlov, at the stroke of a pen she also made a gift of the thousands of peasants who lived on that land.

Before judging Catherine too harshly, however, one should recall that the last years of her reign coincided with the turmoil of the French Revolution and that she herself had been confronted with the most severe challenge to her authority with the Pugachev rebellion of 1773–1774. This popular revolt, on a truly frightening scale, had at one point threatened to topple Catherine from her throne.

Despairing voice At least Catherine was capable of comprehending the potential benefits of a humanitarian philosophy. Compare this attitude with that of Empress Elizabeth, whose achievements are confined to advances in palace architecture, or to

❏ Yemelyan Pugachev, a Don Cossack, claimed to be the murdered tsar, Peter III. Starting in the south, his rebellion spread like wildfire to the Volga and Ural regions, as his call for the seizure of the landowners' estates struck a common chord with the disaffected population. He was captured in September 1774, brought to Moscow in an iron cage, and beheaded on January 10, 1775. ❏

the even more frivolous Anna, whose predilection for dwarfs, hunchbacks, and performing animals culminated in the bizarre mock wedding of the aristocratic Prince A. M. Golitsyn to a notoriously ugly Mongolian woman in a mansion built entirely of ice.

In some ways, St. Petersburg itself was developing into a kind of national Potemkin village; the imperial edifices, with their pretentious façades, barely concealing a bleak landscape of wooden huts, swamp, and forest.

As for Radishchev, the "enlightened" Catherine II condemned him to death for treason. The sentence was later commuted to ten years' exile in Siberia, but he committed suicide in 1802.

Enlightened ruler? Westernizing Catherine the Great Top: scene at her court

■ **"Are we to abandon Russia's ancient and sacred capital without a struggle, or are we to defend it?"**
This, according to Tolstoy in the epic novel *War and Peace*, was the question that preoccupied Russia's generals on September 13, 1812, as they gathered for a council of war in a peasant's hut outside Moscow. ■

Borodino It was less than three months since, without warning, Napoleon had led his *Grande Armée* of more than 500,000 men across the Niemen River into Russia. Instinctively the emperor realized that the key to this vast country was not the new northern capital of St. Petersburg, but "Holy Moscow." Heavily outnumbered, the Russian forces had little option but to retreat.

Most of the Russian nobility, and none more so than Alexander I, were scandalized at their generals' decision not to stand and fight. In August, the tsar reluctantly appointed 67-year-old Prince Mikhail Kutuzov, "the old fox of the north," commander-in-chief, but the strategy remained unchanged. Eventually the clamor for battle was such that the Russian army about-faced to take on the French at Borodino, 72 miles southwest of Moscow, on September 7, 1812. The encounter was a bloody stalemate—30,000 French dead against 45,000 Russian.

Firefighting equipment was removed to guarantee a conflagration Napoleon would never forget Top: his retreat from Moscow

This 19th-century artist cleverly disguises the fact that Field Marshal Kutuzov was blind in his right eye

The burning of Moscow Borodino stiffened the Russians' resolve. Kutuzov's generals—Barclay de Tolly and Bennigsen—both argued for another stand before Moscow, but the obstinate Kutuzov refused: "You fear a retreat through Moscow," he told his officers, "but I regard it as farsighted because it will save the army. Napoleon is like a stormy torrent which we are as yet unable to stop. Moscow will be the sponge that will suck him in."

Napoleon looked down on Moscow's golden cupolas from Poklonnaya Gora (Hill of Greeting) on the morning of September 14, 1812, waiting in vain for someone to meet him with a formal surrender. But no one came, for Moscow was all but deserted.

Fighting back By the time Napoleon arrived at the Kremlin, fires had already broken out in the city. For five days the conflagration raged out of control, devouring more than 80 percent of the houses, which were still mainly built of timber. So bright were the flames in the night sky that it was light enough to read by, but still there was no word of surrender from Tsar Alexander; nor would there be. Fast running out of supplies, Napoleon was forced to think the unthinkable: on October 19 the *Grande Armée* began the long retreat from Moscow. The Russian winter, particularly savage in 1812, did its worst. By the time Napoleon abandoned the tattered remnants of his army, only 25,000 men remained.

A triumphant Alexander proclaimed to his people: "He fled from Moscow with humiliation and fear equal only to the pride and vanity with which he had approached it ... In the name of the fatherland we express our thanks and gratitude to all our loyal subjects, true sons of Russia."

❏ In 1839 work began in Moscow on the Cathedral of Christ the Savior—the site, on the right bank of the Moskva River between the old Smolensk and Kaluga roads was quite deliberate: Napoleon had entered the city by the former route and left it by the latter. The interior walls were decorated with 177 marble tablets bearing the names of the battles of the War of Liberation and of the officers who fell in them. ❏

■ **Nicholas II's first major speech as tsar, delivered in January 1895, set the tone for the rest of his reign. Dismissing the ambitions of would-be reformers as "senseless dreams," he ended his address with the ringing declaration: "Let it be known to all ... that I shall uphold the principle of autocracy as firmly and as unflinchingly as did my ever-lamented father."** ■

The tsar, and the conservative advisers who wrote his speeches for him, believed in an almost mystical union of church, monarch, and people. Nicholas preferred traditional Muscovite values over those of his westernizing predecessor, Peter the Great, and he had no compunction in imposing those values on an empire with many different nationalities and traditions. It was symbolic of Nicholas's distaste for the modern world that at the very beginning of his reign he moved from the Anichkov Palace in the heart of St. Petersburg to the peace of Tsarskoe Selo 15 miles away.

Changing times By 1890 Moscow and St. Petersburg had changed beyond all recognition. The population of both cities had trebled since 1850. Nearly one and a half million people now lived in St. Petersburg. Smokestacks were encroaching on the splendid vistas and landmarks; industrial effluent was corrupting the canals; layers of soot blackened the façades of the palaces. The face of Moscow was also changing as a new bourgeoisie oversaw improvements in sanitation, street paving and lighting, the introduction of electric trams, as well as the opening of municipal schools, galleries, and hospitals.

Strike! At about the time Nicholas II was referring to the "senseless dreams" of reformers, young students were making their first contacts with the factory workers of St. Petersburg. Brought up on the heroes of the "People's Will" movement of the 1870s (members

This lithograph shows Russian washerwomen from a textile mill cleaning bales of cloth by the frozen Moskva River

Opposite: prerevolutionary currency. Above: Moscow's ever growing army of poor line up for a bed outside a municipal shelter

of which had assassinated Alexander II in 1881), Russia's educated young people were coming under the influence of Karl Marx, whose theories seemed to offer the most satisfying explanation of the political changes that were needed in Russia.

Some of these students, among them Lenin's future wife, focused their attention on women workers whom they met in voluntary Sunday schools and clandestinely in private houses. Their mission was twofold—to increase the women's revolutionary consciousness and to help them formulate their grievances in an organized way. The women indeed had many legitimate complaints, including long hours, low wages, lack of child-care facilities, and fines for imperfect work. But the most frequent complaint concerned sexual harassment: "Specifically, a foreman—or even just a worker—would push a girl into a corner and demand favors from her."

Political consciousness-raising appeared to pay off only a year later, when about 30,000 workers in St. Petersburg's predominantly female textile industry went on strike and won a shorter working day.

Bloody Sunday Strikes became contagious. In January 1905 the country was plunged into revolutionary chaos when a former port chaplain, Father Georgiy Gapon, led 200,000 workers on a procession to the Winter Palace to present a petition to the sovereign. Singing hymns and carrying icons as well as portraits of the tsar and tsarina, they were confronted by massed ranks of troops who opened fire without warning, killing over a hundred. The day became known as "Bloody Sunday," and for most workers it ended any notions of the tsar as "the little father of his people."

❑ "Consequently ... we have judged it right to abdicate the throne of the Russian state and to lay down supreme power ... may the Lord God help Russia!" —Order of abdication, Pskov, March 2, 1917, 3 PM ❑

■ As American journalist John Reed emerged bleary-eyed from St. Petersburg's Astoria Hotel on the morning of November 7, 1917, he heard the twelve o'clock gun resound from the Peter-Paul Fortress across the river. ■

Making his way to Nevskiy Prospekt, Reed was told by some soldiers standing guard outside the state bank that there was "no more government, *Slava Bogu!* (Glory to God)." Another soldier sold Reed a copy of the newspaper *Den*, "The Day." In the "Stop Press" section he read about the events of the night before—that the Bolsheviks (Communists) had captured the telephone exchange, the Baltic railroad station, the telegraph agency; that some ministers had been arrested; that there had been isolated skirmishes between Red Guards and soldiers loyal to the Provisional Government. Outside the Mariinskiy Palace an armored car trailing a red flag, its guns trained on St. Isaac's Cathedral, stood beside makeshift barricades of barrels, boxes, bedsprings, and logs.

Looking for action Anxious to witness the unfolding of events, Reed made his way to the Winter Palace where he encountered a surreal scene: on the one hand, uniformed court lackeys were dutifully taking the visitors' coats; while inside, the stuccoed and gilded halls had been converted into a military camp—the floors littered with mattresses, some occupied by lounging soldiers. These were the *Yunkers* (tsarist cadets) still nervously awaiting an assault by Bolshevik troops.

On the eve That same evening, as the street lights came on along Nevskiy Prospekt, streams of workers went home as usual, packing the grimy trams. An hour or two later, the city streets filled up again with their customary evening traffic. Elegantly dressed music lovers began arriving at the Mariinskiy Theater where Chaliapin was appearing in *Boris Godunov*. The fashionable Restaurant de Paris and the A l'Ours began serving dinner. Everything was unremarkable.

A new dawn The final act of this complex drama was about to be played out in the refined classical surroundings of the Smolniy Institute. Lenin's Bolsheviks had timed their *coup* to coincide with the opening of the Second All-Russian Congress of Soviets, to which they were planning to transfer power. But earlier that morning, in a room at the Smolniy, the Central Committee of Lenin's party had met to appoint their own

Top: the battleship Aurora. *Below: Bolsheviks in power; Stalin, Lenin, and Kalinin (Soviet President)*

41

Revolutionaries in 1917, anxious to remove all traces of Tsar Alexander III from Petrograd

government, at Trotsky's suggestion naming their new ministers "People's Commissars." Lenin liked the name: "That's very good, it smells of revolution," he said, and suggested calling the government itself "the Council of People's Commissars." Shortly afterwards he drafted his first manifesto, "To the Citizens of Russia," informing the population that the Provisional Government had been overthrown.

Lenin's *coup* When the Congress of Soviets finally convened at 11 PM on November 7, uproar quickly broke out as the delegates realized that the executive was to be dominated by the Bolsheviks. Menshevik and Socialist Revolutionary supporters of Kerensky's Provisional Government began shouting out demands for a coalition and for a peaceful settlement

that would avert civil war. When these delegates began to walk out of the hall in protest, Trotsky stood up and delivered his famous interjection: "To those who have left ... we must say: you are miserable bankrupts, your role is played out; go where you ought to go into the dustbin of history!"

❑ Born in Oregon in 1887, John Reed was educated at Harvard before becoming a war correspondent in Mexico in 1916. A supporter of Communism, he traveled to Russia in 1917 to cover the Revolution. About a year after Lenin's seizure of power he completed his vivid account of that time, *Ten Days That Shook the World*. When he died in Russia of typhoid in 1920, Reed was accorded the rare honor of being buried in the Kremlin Wall. ❑

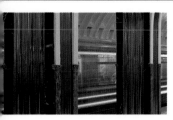

■ **In 1918, while civil war was raging across the former empire, Lenin defiantly approved two new emblems for the Soviet state: the five-pointed red star, the points symbolizing the union of workers of each of the five continents, and the crossed hammer and sickle, representing the indissoluble ties of worker and peasant.** ■

The shock of the new Lenin's optimism in the face of all the odds proved contagious, inspiring all kinds of futuristic experiments over the next few years, especially in the arts: mass pageants and street festivals, utopian novels, "proletarian" choirs and orchestras, agitational theater trains, trolleys bearing revolutionary slogans, constructivist sculptures, musical compositions incorporating factory whistles, and settings of Lenin's speeches. The embodiment of the new cult of progress was the outlandish but gifted poet Vladimir Mayakovsky.

Leftward march Mayakovsky was one of only a handful of writers to sign up with the new regime, writing verse that was brutal, dissonant, provocative, and bristling with revolutionary slogans. The titles of the poems speak for themselves: *Leftward March*, *1 May*, *Our God is Speed*, *The Heart is our Drum*. His plays were equally unconventional: on the first anniversary of the Revolution, Mayakovsky's *Mystery-Bouffe* was described by one critic as "the civil war in theater."

Store-window Communism
During the civil war, Mayakovsky was commissioned by the Russian Press Agency (ROSTA) to design posters on political themes to replace store advertising and to disguise the all too obvious absence of food and other consumer goods in the windows. They were intended to

appeal particularly to workers and peasants as part of the government's literacy campaign.

State capitalism With the end of the civil war came the New Economic Policy (NEP) which confined state intervention in industry to the "commanding heights." Elsewhere free enterprise was encouraged in the need to regenerate an economy that, as a result of the civil war, was in tatters. Mayakovsky now became a design consultant to the government, charged with creating a new commercial art that would help state-owned businesses to fend off competition from the private sector. Together with his main collaborator in this venture, the painter and

The ruby stars on the Kremlin Towers signaled hope, replacing the blackened imperial eagles of the tsars

Top: the metro station named after poet/designer Mayakovsky and (above) an example of his collaborator Rodchenko's graphics

sculptor Alexander Rodchenko, he set up a business in Moscow under the name of "Advertisement-Constructor." The Mayakovsky–Rodchenko team designed everything from candy wrappers—Red Star caramels told the story of the civil war—to cigarette advertising—"Smoke Klads and win a horse absolutely free."

Mayakovsky once wrote that "the work of the artist is a branch of engineering." His posters reflect the Communist worship of science and technology and the contemporary obsession with speed and the machine—passenger liners, airplanes, trains in motion, belching smokestacks, conveyer belts; one of

the first illuminated signs on Pushkin Square was of a gigantic set of cog wheels.

Disillusionment In 1928 and 1929 Mayakovsky wrote two plays for the Moscow stage, *The Bed Bug* and *The Bathhouse*. But, to the surprise of the establishment, these savage satires attacked not the old regime, as was customary, but corrupt elements in the new—pen-pushing yes-men and, more controversially, tainted proletarians interested only in the good life. Mayakovsky's frustration with himself and his disillusionment with the way the Revolution was going are vividly expressed in his last major poem: "At the top of my voice I subdued myself, setting a heel on the throat of my own song." His suicide in 1930 at the age of only 37 signaled the end of an era.

■ **At noon on June 22, 1941, workers in Moscow were summoned to factory meetings to hear the devastating announcement that in the early hours of that morning, Nazi Germany had launched a massive, unprovoked offensive against the Soviet Union.** ■

Brothers and sisters In fact Stalin had had good warning of Hitler's intentions but preferred to believe his own propaganda. As a result, the partially demobilized Soviet army was taken completely by surprise. Reality broke in with such force that Stalin suffered a kind of nervous breakdown, and by the time he recovered, the Germans were already in Minsk. Stalin realized that he must now appeal to the people in the name of the Motherland. In a low, hesitant voice he recalled the heroes of Russia's distant past—Alexander Nevskiy, Dmitri Donskoy, General Suvorov—before comparing the country's plight with the situation in 1812, the time of the first "patriotic war." But privately the Soviet leader was doubtful about the possibility of defending Moscow. As a precaution he ordered the evacuation not only of the government but of whole industries to the relative safety of Kuibishev, beyond the Ural Mountains.

Backs to the wall Every available soldier and every piece of equipment was mobilized in the defense of the capital; even civilians were ordered to dig antitank defenses. Barrage balloons were floated above strategic points, barricades erected near major highways. Citizens sheltered from the nightly bombardment in the opulent surroundings of the metro stations. To raise morale, a captured German airplane was displayed on Theater Square. On the anniversary of the Revolution, November 7, 1941, Stalin took the salute from the reviewing stand on the Lenin Mausoleum as the soldiers of the Red Army marched off to the front.

During World War II, newsreel footage was eagerly seized on by the Soviet propaganda machine

Stalin with U.S. President Franklin D. Roosevelt and British premier Winston Churchill at Yalta in 1945

Aided once again by Russia's old ally—the bitter cold of winter—Soviet troops succeeded in stemming the Nazi tide, but only just. Some German detachments got as far as Moscow's suburbs.

Hero city Just as the German army was being rolled back from Moscow, Leningrad was enduring its first winter under the encirclement which later came to be known as the 900-Day Siege. Like so much else in the war, the German offensive that began in September 1941 caught the Soviet authorities by surprise. Stalin quickly abandoned Leningrad to its fate. Such food as had been stockpiled in the city's Badaevskiy warehouses was captured by the Germans and destroyed in full view of the residents. The Siege lasted for 17 months until February 1943, when the first food supplies arrived at the Finland station. The winter of 1941–1942 was the most terrible. Starvation claimed the lives of more than 53,000 people in December alone, as the bread ration was reduced from 400 grams a day to just 125 grams.

But food shortages were not the only hardship Leningraders had to endure: enemy bombing destroyed the water supply, while the power stations quickly ran out of fuel so that homes were left without heating or lighting in a season when temperatures hovered around −13°F and daylight was confined to about six hours in 24. Of the 670,000 Leningraders who lost their lives in the Siege, only 17,000 were the victims of enemy bombardment.

❑ The composer Dmitri Shostakovich served in the Leningrad civil defense force as a fireman during the Siege, while working on his Seventh Symphony. In August 1942, front-line units were ordered to release every available instrumentalist for a broadcast performance of this, the so-called "Leningrad" Symphony, at the city's Philharmonic Hall. The work was broadcast live over the radio, and many of the besieged citizens later testified to the role it played in holding body and soul together. ❑

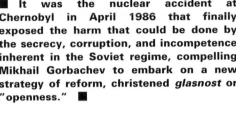

■ It was the nuclear accident at Chernobyl in April 1986 that finally exposed the harm that could be done by the secrecy, corruption, and incompetence inherent in the Soviet regime, compelling Mikhail Gorbachev to embark on a new strategy of reform, christened *glasnost* or "openness." ■

Glasnost By practically abolishing censorship, *glasnost* gave the green light to the media to raise issues about the Communist past that were judged to be impeding progress. Facing up to Stalinism had already been attempted in the 1950s and early 1960s, but halfheartedly. *Glasnost* now remorselessly uncovered the darker secrets of the Communist past: the brutal herding of the peasantry into collective farms, the slave labor ingredient in Stalin's industrial planning, a deliberately induced famine in Ukraine in the 1930s, among other horrors.

In this cathartic climate, the release in 1986 of the banned film *Repentance*, directed by Tengis

Military parades became increasingly anachronistic in the era of glasnost

Abuladze, concerning the evil doings of a Georgian dictator, had a charged, symbolic significance, as did the publication for the first time in the Soviet Union of Lenin's *Testament*, which belatedly warned of the danger of Stalin overreaching himself. The rehabilitation of Stalin's disgraced Communist rivals killed in the purges, notably Nikolai Bukharin, further helped in the creation of a climate of questioning and fundamental reappraisal.

Memorial It was one thing to raise criticisms in the newspapers and on television, quite another for the Communist leadership to acknowledge the imputed guilt in public. In November 1987, on the 70th anniversary of the Revolution, Gorbachev delivered an address which condemned Stalin's crimes as "enormous

and unforgivable" and implied that the great Soviet achievements in building Socialism and in overcoming Fascism happened despite Stalin and not because of him. The following year, a campaign was launched to build a monument and research center in Moscow dedicated to the memory of Stalin's victims. *Memorial* immediately sponsored archeological investigations that led to a discovery of mass graves all over the Soviet Union, notably Chelyabinsk in Siberia (80,000 victims) and Kuropatiy Forest near Minsk (75,000 victims).

Burying Lenin Political democratization led, in May 1989, to the convening of the first elected parliament since the Revolution, the Congress of Peoples' Deputies. The decision to televise the sessions meant that millions of Soviet citizens were able to watch, fascinated, as one delegate called for the removal of Lenin's body from the mausoleum; another denounced the KGB as an "underground empire," while a third criticized by name members of the Politburo sitting on the podium. This parliament brought to the fore a new generation of radical reformers. It also witnessed the astonishing comeback of former Politburo member and Moscow party chief Boris Yeltsin, disgraced in 1987 for his relentless opposition to Gorbachev, yet soon to be president of Russia.

The scene was now set for the demise of Communism itself—the disappearance of Eastern Europe from the Soviet orbit, the abolition of the Communist party following the failed *coup* against President Gorbachev in August 1991, and the breakup of the former Soviet Union.

Last to go was the cult of Lenin, although the mausoleum in Red Square, under threat of closure, remains open at the present time.

Under Mikhail Gorbachev the Soviet Union finally turned its back on the era of Stalinism

❑ The publication, in 1994, of the long-suppressed 1939 census led Russian statisticians to confirm Western estimates of a population shortfall, from the Terror, famine, and war, of about 40 million in the Stalin era—about a quarter of the Soviet population. ❑

MOSCOW

Introduction Think of Moscow as a wheel. The hub is the Kremlin and Red Square (Krasnaya Ploshchad). The spokes radiating from here are the city's main streets, the most important of which is the principal shopping street, Tverskaya Ulitsa. The outer rim is the Garden Beltway (Sadovaya), once idyllically suburban, but now sadly overloaded with traffic. The inner rim is the decaying but much more picturesque Boulevard Ring.

Most of the main sights are located between the hub and the inner rim of the wheel.

It is also handy to know that the Circle Line of the Moscow metro (still probably the most efficient subway of its size in the world) follows the southern section of the Garden Beltway (Koltsevaya). For how to use the metro see page 268.

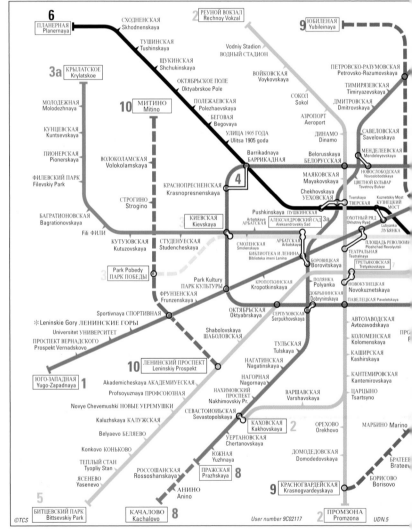

The gazetteer for Moscow, which follows, is divided into areas that, roughly speaking, emanate from the Kremlin outward.

Moscow's timekeeper: the Savior's Tower stands vigil over Red Square

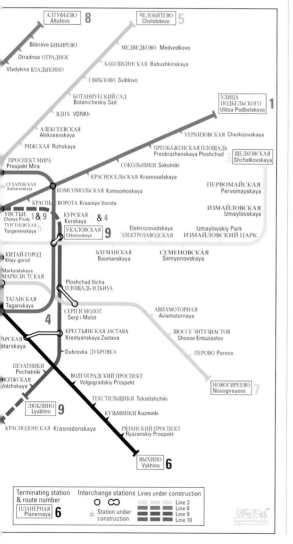

Kreml (The Kremlin)

Introduction The Kremlin►►► is still very much the heart of Moscow: as well as being Russia's most famous landmark, it is instantly recognizable from the pages of travel brochures and as a backdrop to foreign news broadcasts. To Muscovites the famous towers and spires are so familiar that they are frequently overlooked, although the clock on the Savior Tower, which keeps time for radio and television, is a constant reminder that the old guardian of the city is alive and well. The Kremlin is also Russia's most popular tourist attraction, with up to 60,000 visitors a day. And no wonder, with its towers and gates, churches, cathedrals, and palaces, and the magnificent treasure house of the Armory thrown in for good measure.

Practical points You can visit the Kremlin independently, or you can join a guided tour organized by Intourist. The latter option is expensive but the advantages include

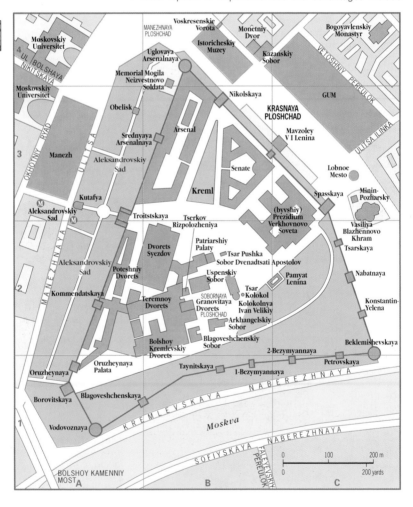

immediate access to all buildings open to the public, the services of a knowledgable guide, and, most importantly, entry to the Armory and the Diamond Fund which can only be seen on group tours. The disadvantage is the relentless and sometimes deadening thoroughness of the commentary, which can all too easily induce the slightly shaming feeling of "not another glass case/fresco." However, the riches of the Armory collection are such that you might feel, in retrospect, it has all been worth it. Entry to several areas is by special permission only and must be prearranged, including Lenin's former office and apartment, the Great Kremlin Palace, the medieval Terem Palace, and the Palace of Facets. Visitors may be allowed greater access to these sites in the future, so it's worth making inquiries.

The Kremlin churches, the Armory and Diamond Fund, and the Museum of 17th-Century Life (Patriarch's Palace) are open daily 10–5 except Thursday. As parts of the Kremlin are still sometimes used for official functions and for religious services, the entire site may be closed for whole days, so *do* check before setting out.

The main entrance to the Kremlin is through the Kutafya Tower leading to the Trinity Gate. Charges for foreigners, which are 10 times the cost for Russians, are displayed at the ticket office (*kassa*) in English as well as Russian. You can pay to see each site individually, so if you do not have enough time to visit, say, the Cathedral of the Annunciation one day, you can come back on another without having to pay the price of a complete tour all over again.

Readopting old images
Moscow has recently adopted the great warrior hero—St. George slaying the dragon—as its new city emblem, an image which has long been popular in Russian iconography. Another potent symbol that is also reappearing is the two-headed eagle—symbol of the tsars and now being revived as the emblem of the Party of the Majority, Russia's monarchist party, which would like to see a tsar back on the throne again. The image of Nicholas II is increasingly becoming associated with the neofascist political tendency.

Orthodox return
In October 1989, for the first time in more than 70 years, the Soviet government allowed the Assumption Cathedral in the Kremlin to be used for a Russian Orthodox service. This act signified a long-overdue relaxation of religious repression. The Khrushchev era in particular witnessed some of the most vigorous persecution: during the early 1960s some 10,000 churches were closed, monasteries and their buildings requisitioned by local soviets, and priests, pilgrims, and believers of all kinds harassed and beaten up.

The Kutafya watchtower was once joined to the Kremlin by a bridge across Neglinnaya River

MOSCOW: KREML

Terrible
According to Prince Kurbsky, Ivan IV's sadistic leanings began as a child when he used to throw cats and other animals from the tops of towers. Later, as a teenager, he graduated to roaming the streets of Moscow with a gang of youths, robbing and beating people indiscriminately.

Public restrooms
For visitors to the Kremlin, cloakroom and toilet facilities are available in the Alexandrov Gardens near the Trinity Gate (52A2) and toilets can also be found on the north side of the Cathedral of the Assumption (52B2).

The Cathedral of the Assumption: gilded domes help to give the Kremlin its distinctly Russian character

The word *kreml* means "citadel" or "fortress," although the origins of the word are obscure. In 1156 Prince Yuri Dolgorukiy laid the foundations of the first wooden fortress on Borovitskiy or Pine Hill, at the confluence of the Moscow and Neglinnaya rivers. This first Kremlin was roughly triangular in shape but occupied only about one-sixth of the present site. A tall wooden palisade encompassed a small trading settlement as well as the princely residence, but housing spilled over along the riverbank and there was a marketplace immediately outside the walls. In 1960 archeologists provided important clues to what this first settlement looked like when they discovered the well-preserved remains of sturdy log cabins with massively proportioned timbers. To speak of "a" Kremlin is perhaps misleading; in reality there was a succession of wooden fortresses, each ravaged by fire after an incursion by one of Moscow's numerous enemies, such as that by the armies of the Mongol Khan in 1240.

During the reign of Ivan Kalita (1328–1340) the Kremlin doubled in size, but it was Ivan Kalita's grandson, Dmitri Donskoy, who ordered the building of the first stone castle in 1367. The walls were now extended to roughly their present limits and strengthened by eight massive towers, battlements, and a moat.

By the reign of Ivan III (*c.* 1462–1505) the white stone Kremlin had fallen into disrepair and it was decided to rebuild from scratch in a manner that would symbolize Moscow's predominance and the new preeminence of her rulers. Italian military engineers were invited to Ivan's court to work alongside Russian master builders—which is why the Kremlin visitor today sees much that is akin to Renaissance fortresses. From an architectural point of view it was a perfect meeting of Russian and Italian minds and from a military-strategic perspective a masterpiece, for the new Kremlin was virtually impregnable. To add to the city's security, two outer walls were constructed to embrace the suburbs of Kitay Gorod and Beliy Gorod, while a ring of fortified monasteries guarded the outskirts.

Following the Time of Troubles (1605–1613) Moscow enjoyed an unprecedented period of peace. As the Kremlin's military significance diminished, its appearance altered. Elaborate tent roofs were added to the towers and graced with playful ornamentation—weathervanes, gryphons, clocks, and spires—so that the formidable fortress began to take on the characteristics of a fantasy castle.

With the transfer of the capital to St. Petersburg in the 18th century, Moscow and its Kremlin went into decline. Russia's rulers, now looking westward, were increasingly uncomfortable with reminders of a "barbaric" past. In 1775 Catherine the Great, herself a German by origin, ordered Vasiliy Bazhenov to design an enormous neo-classical palace fronting the river, to replace the Kremlin as part of a wholesale rebuilding program. Fortunately this project ran out of funds before it left the drawing board. The Kremlin had an even narrower escape in 1812, when Napoleon ordered its complete destruction on the eve of his retreat. Charges were laid and primed to explode, but a heavy downpour coupled with the prompt arrival of Russian troops prevented disaster by extinguishing the fuses.

The character of the Kremlin changed once again when Moscow became the center of the Soviet government in 1918. Its role as a bulwark against imperialism was symbolized, in 1935, by the removal of the imperial eagles from the towers and their replacement by glowing red stars. Closed to the public in the 1930s, the Kremlin underwent various changes to accommodate new admin-istrative buildings. The culmination of this program of reconstruction was the building of the Palace of Congresses in the early 1960s. In recent years a less ideologically inspired appreciation of the Kremlin's architectural heritage has led to a more consistent approach to its preservation.

A 19th-century view of the Kremlin. Many of the domes and spires belonged to buildings demolished in the 1930s, but the Bell Tower of Ivan the Great is still a landmark

Hidden wealth
In May 1988 a workman digging a hole in the basement of a Kremlin canteen near the Savior Gate found a hoard of 299 pieces of 13th-century silver jewelry and other precious objects.

Moscow architect Osip Bove allowed his imagination to run away with him when he designed a classical folly in the Alexander Gardens

Obelisk for all seasons
When the Communists came to power they altered the design of the obelisk commemorating the Romanovs in Aleksandrovskiy Sad to reflect their own ideological preferences. The imperial eagles were removed and the monument rededicated to revolutionary thinkers—watch this space!

► **Aleksandrovskiy Sad (Alexander Gardens)** 52A2–A3

These gardens were named after Alexander I and were laid out in 1821–1823 as part of the restoration of the Kremlin after the Napoleonic Wars. The architect, Osip Bove, also carried out repairs to several of the Kremlin Towers. Beneath the gardens flows the Neglinnaya River, which once formed part of the Kremlin moat (a stone bridge still links the Kutafya Tower and Trinity Gate). The obelisk was erected in 1913 to celebrate the 300th anniversary of the Romanov dynasty. A later addition is the Tomb of the Unknown Soldier with its eternal flame. The inscription, surrounded by tablets commemorating the various battles of World War II, reads: "Your name is unknown, your deeds immortal." It is still customary for a newly married couple to lay flowers here immediately after their wedding.

► **Arsenal** 52B3

The original Arsenal was commissioned by Peter the Great in 1701 for the manufacture of weapons and the storage of military hardware. It was not completed until 1736, and only a year later a devastating fire left it severely damaged. The present building is an assemblage of the original 1736 construction and later restoration work dating from 1817 by Osip Bove and Fedor Zolokov. Its most interesting feature is the untidy rows of cannons captured during Napoleon's retreat from Moscow in 1812. There are 800 cannon in all, the barrels cast in bronze in Paris, Lyon, and Wroclaw. Thrown in for good measure are a number of guns manufactured in Russian workshops, one of which, the Troilus, dates from 1590. The Arsenal was the scene of bloody skirmishes during the October Revolution—a marble plaque in the wall commemorates those on the Soviet side killed by counterinsurgents (mainly young cadets).

■ In 1474 Ivan III sent one of his most trusted boyars, Simeon Tolbuzin, to Italy on a vital mission—to entice architects of world renown to come to Russia and oversee the rebuilding of the Kremlin. Tolbuzin was advised to make contact with Aristotele Fioravanti—architect, engineer, and (according to rumor) alchemist. ■

Rare as gold dust Fioravanti already had an established reputation, having worked in Rome, Milan, and Venice. On his arrival in Moscow, Tsar Ivan immediately sent him on a journey to Vladimir to study the Uspenskiy Cathedral, which he was to use as his model for the new Moscow church. Fioravanti was impressed but not intimidated, succeeding in the space of only four years in creating a well-nigh miraculous fusion of Renaissance and Russian styles. Amazingly he had also found time to accompany Ivan himself on a campaign against Novgorod, where he had used his skills as a military engineer to construct a crossing of the Volkhov River. Clearly, this sort of man was as rare as gold dust, so it came as a great shock to Ivan when, in 1479, Fioravanti asked for permission to return to Bologna. Ivan refused point blank, eventually compelling him to live out the remainder of his days in enforced exile, training Moscow blacksmiths to make cannon.

Quattrocento Moscow In 1485 Marco Ruffo, Pietro Solario, and the brothers Antonio and Marco Friazin began work on the reconstruction of the Kremlin walls using brick instead of stone and an ingenious system of moats, drawbridges, secret passageways, and portcullises which made the fortress virtually impregnable. Between 1487 and 1491 Ruffo and Solario constructed the magnificent Palace of Facets, the most explicit manifestation of the north Italian Quattrocento in Russia, modeled on the Palazzo dei Diamanti in Ferrara. In 1499, a fifth Italian, Alevisio da Carcanno, oversaw the laying of the foundations of a second palace, the Terem.

Conjurer
When Tolbuzin first met Fioravanti, so the story goes, the latter impressed him with his sleight of hand, conjuring water, then wine from an empty pewter vessel into a copper dish. "Whatever was requested," Tolbuzin reported back to his superiors, "began to flow." The credulous Muscovites, believing every word, venerated Fioravanti for his supernatural powers.

Top: detail, Palace of Facets, the Kremlin Below: the scallop-shell motif on the Cathedral of the Archangel Michael in the Kremlin is puzzling until you know that the architect was a Venetian

MOSCOW: KREML

The Great Kremlin Palace. The architect K. A. Ton also designed Moscow's Nikolayevskiy (Leningrad) Station

► **Bolshoy Kremlevskiy Dvorets (Great Kremlin Palace)**   *52B2*

The Great Kremlin Palace is the last in a long line of impos-ing royal residences belonging to the Muscovite princes and Russian tsars.

The first palace built on the site of Borovitskiy Hill was made of wood. In the second half of the 14th century Prince Dmitri Donskoy commissioned a more ambitious residence, known as the "Riverside Chambers" because of its orientation toward the Moscow River. The Palace of Facets (see page 62) created by the Italian architects Marco Ruffo and Pietro Solario was Ivan III's contribution. By the 17th century, the palace complexes had become a labyrinth of passageways, staircases, and connecting galleries which linked state apartments, sprawling living quarters, and churches. The medieval buildings were neglected during the 18th century, causing Catherine the Great to commission a new palace in the classical style from the outstanding Russian architect Bazhenov. This was never built, but the Great Kremlin Palace, the final realization of Catherine's dream, adopted Bazhenov's pro-posal of incorporating the surviving palaces within the overall design. A team of Russian architects, under the supervision of K. A. Ton, collaborated on the present building, which was completed in 1849. The façade skill-fully integrates Russian elements into the overall neo-classical design, but it is unfortunate that the older palaces are now, to varying degrees, obscured from view.

The interior of the palace is now a jumble of styles, reflecting all too accurately the taste of the unimaginative

Tsar Nicholas I who commissioned it. The centerpiece is the St. George's Hall, consisting of a cloister vault 200 feet long, more than 60 feet wide, and 58 feet high, supported by arches so thickly encrusted with white stucco as to resemble the decoration on a wedding cake. Sometimes a ballroom, it was subsequently adapted to more somber ceremonial uses. Two other halls, the St. Andrew and St. Alexander, were combined to create a large venue in the 1930s for meetings of the Supreme Soviet and Party Congresses. The remainder of the Great Palace is divided up into ceremonial halls, state chambers, and the former private apartments of the imperial family, all uniformly sumptuous with their malachite, marble, jasper, gold, and bronze. The palace is not usually open to the public.

Reconciled
The Church of the Deposition was built to celebrate the reconciliation of Ivan III and the Metropolitan Geronti who had clashed over the unlikely issue of whether religious processions should move in the direction of the rising sun!

▶   **Lesser Kremlin churches**   *52B2*

A number of historic churches were incorporated into the Great Kremlin Palace in the 19th century. The colorful cluster of domes topped by elaborate gilded crosses (clearly visible beside the Palace of Facets) conceals four churches and chapels all brought together under one roof in 1681: the Upper Cathedral of the Savior (the tsar's private chapel) and, beneath it, the Church of St. Catherine; the Church of the Crucifixion; and the Church of the Resurrection. To the rear, even more hidden from view, are the Church of the Raising of Lazarus, whose 14th-century crypt makes it the oldest surviving church in the Kremlin, and the Church of Nativity of the Virgin Mary. Between the Cathedral of the Assumption and the Palace of Facets is the exquisitely proportioned, golden-domed Church of the Deposition of the Robe (open to the public) built in 1484–1485 on the site of an earlier church destroyed by fire. The architects were from the same workshop in Pskov as the builders of the Cathedral of the Annunciation (see page 73). A gallery linked the church—which once served the Patriarch as his private chapel—with the Palace next door. The Pskov trademark, the octagonal pedestal supporting the drum of the cupola, rests on tall slender pillars, drawing the eye toward the vertical and giving the impression of additional height without losing the feeling of intimacy. The wall paintings, dating from 1643–1644, are perfectly integrated into the overall design; they were fully rediscovered only in 1956 when restorers removed overpainting from the 19th century. The magnificent iconostasis was painted in 1627 in the workshop of the artist Nazari Istomin.

A confusion of cupolas creates problems for the visitor in identifying all the Kremlin churches. Some churches are not visible from the outside at all!

59

FOCUS ON *The Kremlin Towers*

■ Since the 15th century, the Kremlin Towers have been witness to many dramatic events—insurrection, assassination, murder, sieges, victory parades, and religious processions. Each name tells its own story and reveals something of the daily life of a working fortress. ■

Rehabilitation?
In 1993 an exhibition was held in the Manege to mark the 125th anniversary of the birth of Tsar Nicholas II. Encouraged by the climate of Romanov nostalgia that accompanied it, some right-wing patriots suggested the reerection of the memorial to the Grand Duke Sergei Alexandrovich—despite his reputation as a reactionary and notorious anti-Semite.

Top: detail, Trinity Gate Tower
Below: the Beklemishev Tower. The ornate decoration on the Kremlin Towers is a 17th-century afterthought

Beklemishevskaya Built by Antonio Friazin in 1487, the tower takes its name from the family whose estate once adjoined it. It is said that the original boyar Beklemishev still haunts the tower.

Borovitskaya The tower was built in 1490 on the hilltop where the original Kremlin was founded in the 12th century. The Borovitskaya was traditionally the "tradesmen's entrance," but is now the formal entrance for members of the government and official guests.

Konstantin-Yelena Named after a nearby church dedicated to these two saints, this tower was used as a prison and torture chamber. The thick walls were ideal for stifling the cries of protesting traitors!

Nabatnaya The name means "alarm," and a bell was installed for the purpose soon after the tower was built. It was rung in earnest during the Pugachev rebellion in 1773; afterward Catherine the Great ordered its "tongue" to be removed and it remained silent from that time on.

Nikolskaya This unassuming tower with an unusual Gothic spire has had a turbulent history. It was built by Pietro Solario in 1491 and commemorates St. Nicholas the Miracle Worker. The Neglinnaya River was diverted here via a system of dams and locks to feed the Kremlin moat. In 1612 two Russian patriots, Minin and Pozharskiy, led their forces through this gate to retake the Kremlin after expelling the Polish occupants. Exactly two centuries later it suffered serious damage at the hands of another foreign invader, Napoleon Bonaparte. Here also, in February 1905, a revolutionary terrorist, Ivan Kalyaev, lobbed a bomb through the carriage window of the tsar's uncle, Grand Duke Sergei Alexandrovich, killing him instantly. The government later erected a monument on the site: an obelisk surmounted by a Russian cross. The tower was again severely damaged by Bolshevik insurgents in November 1917 and the monument to the grand duke was removed.

Spasskaya The Savior's Tower, built in 1491, was originally called the Frolovskaya. It was renamed in the 17th century when an icon of the Savior was placed over the entrance. From earliest times the Savior Gate was the official processional route into the Kremlin and everyone, even the Tsar, was obliged to remove his headgear before passing through. The white slab containing inscriptions in Russian and Latin, as well as the name of the

builder, Pietro Solario, is part of the original structure, but the elaborate tent roof was not added until 1625, when an Englishman, Christopher Holloway, installed the first clock. As late as the 19th century the arched bridge, which once spanned the moat, was favored by tradesmen selling antiques and rare books.

Taynitskaya Named from the Russian word for secret, *tayna*, this, the oldest Kremlin tower, has an underground passage which once led to the Moskva River, an essential source of fresh water in time of siege.

Troitskaya This tower is named after the Trinity-Sergius monastery in Sergiev-Zagorsk, which owned property nearby. Traditionally, this was the entrance where patriarchs and priests greeted the tsar on his return from military campaigns, and it is where Napoleon entered the Kremlin in September 1812.

Tsarskaya The original wooden tower is said to have been the favorite of Ivan the Terrible, because from here he could secretly watch his victims suffering the agonies of long-drawn-out execution on Red Square.

Vodovoznaya This tower was built at the point where the Neglinnaya flowed into the Moskva River. A waterwheel pumped water through a lead pipe from here to the gardens of the upper Kremlin—hence the name meaning "water-pumping tower."

Tourists approach the Kremlin from the Trinity Gate Tower

Change of tune
Before the Revolution the clock in the Savior Tower was programmed to play the national anthem "God Save the Tsar." When the clock was repaired in 1918, on Lenin's personal order the tune was changed to the socialist hymn "The Internationale"!

Movie première
One of the world's first movies captures the coronation of Tsar Nicholas II and his wife Alexandra in May 1896. They can clearly be seen descending the Red Staircase beside the Palace of Facets. The movie was first shown in St. Petersburg by an operator from the Lumière Brothers.

The interior decoration of the Palace of Facets, though still impressive, has been much altered over the centuries

► Granovitaya Dvorets (Palace of Facets)   *52B2*

Situated between the Cathedrals of the Assumption and Annunciation, this noble Renaissance palace was designed by the Italian architects Marco Ruffo and Pietro Solario in 1487 and completed four years later. It has become known as the Palace of Facets from the distinctive limestone rustications that decorate the eastern side. Unfortunately the original Venetian-style windows have not survived, but the delicate tracery and columns carved in stone by Osip Startsev in 1682 are a generous compensation. Originally the roof was much steeper and decorated with gilt and gaudily painted tin. Inside, the walls of the great vaulted chamber, supported by a single, central pier, are covered with paintings of religious subjects—19th-century copies of the originals which Peter the Great had concealed with designs of his own. In this chamber Ivan the Terrible celebrated his victory over the Tatars at Kazan in 1552 with a banquet. Here too the tsar's advisers met in conference, patriarchs were nominated, and foreign dignitaries received. Outside the palace, adjoining the southern wall, is the famous Red Staircase (destroyed in the 1930s, rebuilt 1994) from where the tsar's coronation procession made its way in state to the Cathedral of the Assumption. During the revolt of the *Streltsy* in 1682, members of the overbearing Naryshkin family were hurled from the staircase and impaled on the pikes of their persecutors below. Here too Napoleon watched the great blaze which destroyed much of Moscow in 1812.

The Palace of Facets is not at present open to the public.

▶▶▶ **Oruzheynaya Palata (The Armory)** *52A1*

One of the greatest museums of its kind in the world, the Armory is a storehouse of treasures accumulated by the Russian tsars and princes of Muscovy from the 13th century onward. First mentioned in *The Chronicles* in 1547, the Armory was originally a center of manufacture for the accoutrements of war: cut-and-thrust weapons, firearms, and suits of armor. The regalia of state and other valuables were stored in a separate building, commissioned by Ivan III in 1485. As the armory developed, several new workshops were established—the Office of Stables, for the manufacture of riding equipment and bridles; the Chamber of the Tsaritsa, specializing in sewing, embroidery, and the overseeing of the royal wardrobes; the Hall of Gold and Silver; and the Office of Icons, which called on the most skillful painters in Russia to decorate cathedrals and palaces. This accumulation of riches dazzled the increasing number of visiting European delegations, surprised to find their own exquisite gifts matched by superb Russian craftsmanship. The Armory flourished until the time of Peter the Great, at which point the Kremlin ceased to be the center of the Russian state and the treasure house became a museum. The Armory that visitors see today was commissioned from the architect K. A. Ton by Nicholas I in 1851 as an extension of the Great Kremlin Palace.

The collection is arranged chronologically and is spread over two floors.

Rooms One and **Two** hold a dazzling collection of Russian gold and silver work dating from the 12th to the 17th centuries. The local craftsmen (artists would be a more appropriate term) were masters of filigree, enameling, and *niello* (a technique used for carving inscriptions in metal). The Ryazan Treasure (case 9), consisting of earrings, bracelets, collars, and rings, must be seen, as should the beautifully enameled chalice (case 13) presented to the Monastery of the Miracles by the *boyarina*, Anna Morozova in 1664. The feast continues with bejeweled Gospel covers, gilt reliquaries, diptychs, and folding icons, all reflecting the high point of Russian gold- and silversmithery.

The pleasing rhythms of the façade of K. A. Ton's Armory building are best appreciated from the riverside

Winter's victory
Over the centuries, military leaders have discovered to their cost that invading Russia is no piece of cake. As Field Marshal Montgomery put it in 1962: "Rule 1, on page 1 of the book of war, is: 'Do not march on Moscow.' Various people have tried it, Napoleon and Hitler, and it is no good."

In the case of both Napoleon in 1812 and Hitler (in particular at Stalingrad) Russia's age-old ally, the cold, saved the day. Tsar Nicholas I aptly summed it up in 1855: "Russia has two generals in whom she can confide—Generals Janvier (January) and Février (February)."

MOSCOW: KREML

This 12th-century Kolt pendant from Ryazan was originally part of a high Russian headdress known as a kokoshnik

A perennial favorite with the public in **Room Two** is the display of jewelry from the House of Fabergé. Typical are the intricate toys such as the Heliotrope Egg (1891), decorated with diamonds and containing a gold and platinum replica of the cruiser *Pamyat Azova*, on which Nicholas II sailed to Japan while tsarevich, and the miniature clockwork model of the Trans-Siberian Express, complete with ruby headlamp, rock crystal windows, and tiny *nielloed* inscriptions, which was originally enclosed in one of Fabergé's famous Easter eggs. (See page 202.)

Rooms Three and **Four** contain a display of arms and armor dating back to the medieval era. The oldest exhibit (case 1) is the iron helmet of Yaroslav, father of Alexander Nevskiy. The reason for its badly weathered appearance is that it lay undiscovered on the site of a medieval battlefield until 1808. Other interesting items include a small spiked helmet commissioned by Ivan the Terrible for his three-year-old son—the same son he later murdered; the sabers of Minin and Pozharskiy, who led the Russian armies to victory over the Poles during the Time of Troubles; and a suit of mail belonging to Tsar Boris Godunov, each iron ring of which is inscribed with the words "God with us and none against us."

Room Five reflects the growing importance of Russia as a center of European trade and commerce. In the 16th and 17th centuries foreign envoys from England, Holland, Scandinavia, Poland, and the Holy Roman Empire lined up to present lavish gifts, mainly gold and silver, to the tsar and his court. Most noteworthy are the host of items from a variety of German craft schools—more than 450 from Augsburg alone—including a silver eagle presented to Tsar Alexei Mikhailovich by King John Sobieski of Poland in 1671 (case 32). The Armory also boasts one of the finest collections of English silver in the world, dating from the 16th and 17th centuries (case 30). In presenting these exquisite pieces to the Russian court, English merchants were performing an unwitting service—much of the silverware left behind in England was melted down by Oliver Cromwell after the English Civil War.

Room Six is devoted to vestments and fabrics across the centuries. Pride of place belongs to the silk *sakkos*, or chasuble, embroidered for the Patriarch Nikon in 1654. Much of the great weight of the garment (53 lb.)

Еженедельный
публицистический
литературно-художественный
иллюстрированный журнал
Индекс 70663

comprised the array of pearls and precious stones attached to the sleeves, front, and hems (case 28).

Room Seven is resplendent with thrones and imperial regalia. Among the most spectacular items are the intricately carved ivory throne of Ivan the Terrible (case 48) and the throne presented to Boris Godunov by the Shah of Persia in 1604, decorated with gold leaf, turquoises, and more than 2,000 other precious stones (case 49). The most impressive and the most famous piece of headgear is the ancient Cap or Crown of Monomakh, made in the late 13th or early 14th century from gold plate, decorated with precious stones, and trimmed with sable. This was used in coronations from the end of the 15th century to 1682 (case 58). Catherine the Great's Western-style silver wedding dress, with wide paniers and embroidered with imperial eagles, is in marked contrast to the straight gown in the traditional Russian style worn by the last Romanov empress, Alexandra, at her coronation in 1896.

Some idea of the splendor of state processions can be gleaned from the regalia in **Room Eight**, including dress harnesses, embroidered coach rugs, and saddles. The tour of the Armory then concludes in **Room Nine** with a review of imperial equipages from the 16th to the end of the 18th century. The scaled-down coaches made for the child Pyotr Alexeevich in 1675 were drawn by small ponies and had dwarves to serve as coachmen.

Good intentions
Ivan the Terrible celebrated the birth of his son, also called Ivan, with the Measure Icon, a representation of the child's patron saint, John (Ivan) of the Ladder, made to the exact length of the newborn. Twenty-seven years later, Ivan senior murdered his son in a fit of rage.

By skillfully combining classical with traditional Russian motifs, the architect of the Armory is alluding to the continuity of the imperial regime

65

Patriarch Nikon, who commissioned this beautiful palace, is better known for presiding over a schism in the Orthodox Church

▶▶▶ Patriarshiy Palaty (Patriarch's Palace)   52B2

The four-story palace and the adjoining Cathedral of the Twelve Apostles (recognizable by its five silver domes) is most closely associated with the reforming Patriarch Nikon. When Nikon became head of the Russian church in 1652, he insisted that the design conform to his conservative architectural tastes. This accounts for the building's resemblance to the Cathedral of the Annunciation. The Chamber of the Cross created a sensation on its completion because of the magnificent vault, which is entirely unsupported by columns. Its dimensions are equally impressive, the total area being 3,000 square feet. Councils of the Orthodox Church were held here until the secularization of 1721, when the building became the Moscow headquarters of the Holy Synod.

The entrance is on the south side of the palace. The Museum of 17th-Century Applied Arts is not as stuffy as it sounds and consists of more than a thousand exhibits from the Armory collection, relating to many aspects of 17th-century life. The cases are labeled in Russian, but a taped commentary in English is available for an additional charge. The display begins with a collection of liturgical vestments brought here from the sacristies of various churches in the Moscow region; pride of place belongs to Patriarch Nikon's own dazzling set of robes. Other precious objects include jeweled crucifixes and communion cups, liturgical books, altar cloths, incense burners, and plate. A delightful, diminutive stone gateway leads to two rooms laid out in the style of a rich boyar's house of the period. The basic furnishings are solid and utilitarian—

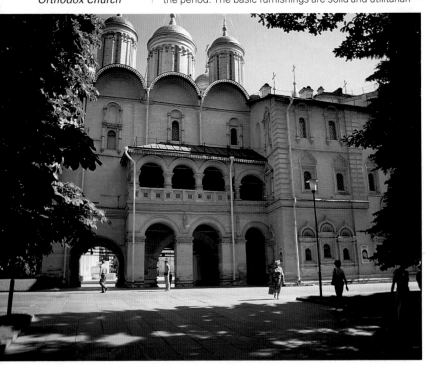

The Patriarch's Palace is seen here dazzled by the golden domes of the Cathedral of the Assumption

67

massive wooden chests, a wooden table, and an attractive tiled stove. By mid-century, however, the typical nobleman's tastes were increasingly influenced by the West—finely carved chairs imported from Holland and Germany, luxuries like a clock, candle holders, an astrological globe, and a delicate silver and wood chess set made in Frankfurt. Also noteworthy is a tutor's book dating from 1693, and a Russian grammar. The Cathedral contains an exhibition of Russian icon painting and features work by such masters as Simon Ushakov, Fedor Zubov, Kirill Ulanov, and Ivan Saltanov. Many of these icons were removed from some of the Kremlin cathedrals and churches which were demolished by the Communists. The enormous golden iconostasis, for example, dating from about 1700, was actually created for the long-demolished Convent of the Ascension.

The most eye-catching exhibits in the Chamber of the Cross are the enormous silver vats and stoves used after 1763 for manufacturing holy oil (*miro*) for use in churches throughout Russia—from which time the Chamber became known as the *miro* brewery. The accent on the ecclesiastical is offset by arresting collections of riding and hunting equipment, chain mail, clothing, buttons, jewelry, and clocks—including a model of an elephant hauling a carriage.

►   **Poteshniy Dvorets**
       (Amusement Palace)   *52A2*

The Amusement Palace, situated on the west side of the Kremlin near the Trinity Gate, is so called because when the state acquired it from the estate of a prominent boyar in 1652, it was used for theatrical productions and other entertainment. There have been numerous alterations in the design, most notably by K. A. Ton in the 19th century, who adapted it to suit the look of the Great Kremlin Palace. Stalin had an apartment here in the 1920s and 1930s, and his archrival Trotsky was a close neighbor before his fall from power.

The Moscow metro

■ **Not many subway systems in the world can claim to be tourist attractions and artistic monuments in their own right. The Moscow metro is an outstanding exception. It was built as a glorification of proletarian labor and had comfort, convenience, and, above all, speed in mind.** ■

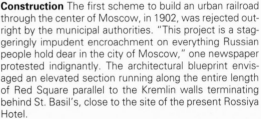

Grand prix
The design for Mayakovskaya metro station won the grand prize at the International Exposition held in New York in 1938; 20 years later Komsomolskaya station won an identical award.

68

Above: historical allusions abound in the decorations of Komsomolskaya metro station
Top: detail, Arbatskaya metro station

Construction The first scheme to build an urban railroad through the center of Moscow, in 1902, was rejected outright by the municipal authorities. "This project is a staggeringly impudent encroachment on everything Russian people hold dear in the city of Moscow," one newspaper protested indignantly. The architectural blueprint envisaged an elevated section running along the entire length of Red Square parallel to the Kremlin walls terminating behind St. Basil's, close to the site of the present Rossiya Hotel.

By the early 1930s, however, the Soviet government saw the metro as an opportunity for a propaganda *coup*: an underground network that was built in record time and designed to celebrate socialist achievements. Construction workers were drafted in from every Soviet republic, while soldiers of the Red Army and members of the Communist Youth League labored for the love of it. The materials and the technology too came from all over the country: shielding for the tunnels from Moscow, escalators from Leningrad, rails from the steelworks of Kuznetsk, granite from Ukraine, and marble from the Caucasus. "Shock" workers were awarded with medals and other blandishments for overfulfilling the plan, while distinguished artists were invited to design the stations. No expense was spared on this showcase construction project, at a time when living conditions for the much-lauded working classes were appalling. The first stretch, from Sokolniki to Park Kultury (a distance of 7.2 miles) was opened to the public on May 15, 1935.

Facts and statistics More than six million passengers use the metro daily. Already the system extends over 150 miles and is projected to reach 250 miles by the year 2000. There are more than 120 stations at present. Some 763,000 square feet of mosiacs, marbles, precious metals, gold, and glass were lavished on the thirteen stations of the original line. While the fabric of the metro has deteriorated noticeably over the last decade or so, its efficiency has been little impaired. No passenger is expected to wait more than three minutes for trains which hurtle through the tunnels at speeds of up to 55 mph. Even taking into account recent price hikes, the Moscow metro is still one of the cheapest systems of its kind in the world.

Tour of stations
Ploshchad Revolyutsii "The Great October Revolution" of 1917 is the theme of this station. Under each of the 40 arches is a pair of heroic bronze figures symbolizing a key group in the Bolshevik conquest of power and the

building of the Soviet state: sailors, young pioneers, frontier guards, mothers and children, architects, and sportsmen.

Komsomolskaya Most people's favorite, this palatial hallway of gold and florid stucco, supported on squat neo-classical marble piers and lit by elaborate chandeliers, honors the Communist Youth Organization which played more than an ornamental role in the building of the metro. The mosaics depict famous scenes from Russian history.

Mayakovskaya The station is named after the poet and playwright Vladimir Mayakovsky (1893–1930). The fluorescent mosaics were designed by one of the few truly talented exponents of Socialist Realism in art, Alexander Deyneka.

Kievskaya The theme, appropriately, harps on the achievements of the Ukrainian people. It is worth reflecting, while studying the joyous peasant faces and muscular figures, that a famine induced by Stalin in 1932–1934, as a result of collectivization, killed five million in Ukraine.

Park Kultury The original terminus of the metro, the Park of Culture and Rest is celebrated by the sculptural 1930s-style figures on the interior walls of the platforms playing all kinds of sports.

When Stalin ordered the building of the palatial Moscow metro in the 1930s, no one dared raise the question of the cost of its upkeep. Now the Moscow authorities are paying the price for their faint-heartedness. Above: Komsomolskaya metro station

Restoration of the monarchy?

There are plans to erect a statue of Nicholas II outside the Kremlin's Trinity Gate, and Russia's monarchists are currently debating the contentious issue of who should sit on a new Russian throne, should the monarchy be restored. There are four claimants, all direct descendants of Nicholas II's uncle Vladimir Alexandrovich: Leonida Georgievna, her daughter Maria Vladimirova, and (the favorite) her teenage son Prince Georgy Mikhailovich. The fourth claimant, Princess Vera Constantinova, lives in the United States.

Only VIPs travel in Zil limousines. Communist **apparatchiks** *avoided publicity by drawing the curtains*

 Senate and Seat of Government *52B3*

Familiar from photographs and TV news broadcasts, the green, domed roof of the handsome Senate building was commissioned by Catherine the Great in 1776 from Matvei Kazakov. Its design was skillfully adapted to the requirements of the site, made irregular by existing buildings, some of which have since been demolished. Although the headquarters of the Senate was in St. Petersburg, the Moscow branch dispensed justice well into the 19th century, when it was converted into court offices. When the threat of invasion compelled the Soviet government to evacuate Petrograd (St. Petersburg) in March 1918, the Senate was chosen as a convenient new location. At that time the Kremlin had fallen into a state of disrepair, and Lenin had to stay at the National Hotel while suitable accommodations and office space were made ready. (His first action is said to have been to order the raising of the Red Flag on the dome, where it remained until it was replaced by the Russian national flag in 1991.)

The Council of People's Commissars (later Ministers) was allocated a room on the top floor of the Senate; the Party politburo continued to meet in this part of the building until the 1950s, while early party congresses were held in the beautiful Catherine Hall (Sverdlov in the Soviet period), which was directly beneath the dome. Adjoining the ministerial conference room was Lenin's office. It was here that he entertained sympathetic foreign guests, including the American businessman Armand Hammer and the British novelist H. G. Wells. Lenin's own private apartment consisted of four simply furnished rooms, which he shared with his wife and his unmarried sister. It was here that Lenin was brought following the attempt on his life on August 31, 1918. Shortly afterward a cameraman confirmed that the great man was still alive and well by filming him strolling through the Kremlin grounds in the company of a friend, Vladimir Bonch-Bruevich—an early example of the photo opportunity. When Lenin suffered a second, debilitating stroke on

December 13, 1922, he was moved out of the Kremlin to convalesce in Gorky Leninskiye, where he died on January 21, 1924.

The Kremlin remained the center of government under Stalin. His office on the first floor of the Senate acquired even greater importance during World War II, when it became the headquarters of the Supreme Command of the Red Army. The massive bureaucratic expansion of the Soviet state put space in the Kremlin at a premium. In 1932 work began on the building adjacent to the Senate, which eventually became the offices of the Presidium of the Supreme Soviet (the rubber-stamp parliament). Several monuments of major historic and architectural importance were torn down to make way for this building (see page 16). In the late 1950s further demolition work on the opposite side of the Kremlin was undertaken to make way for the Palace of Congresses. The main assembly hall can accommodate up to 6,000, while the absence of pillars allows an uninterrupted view of the proceedings—no longer party congresses, of course, but opera or ballet performances. (If the Bolshoy Theater closes as expected for a serious structural overhaul, the Palace of Congresses will be the alternative venue.) With the close of the Gorbachev era in 1991, government functions began to be dispersed to alternative centers like the White House, on the Smolenskaya Embankment. However, some parts of the Kremlin, most notably the sumptuous St. George's Hall in the Great Kremlin Palace, are still used to receive foreign dignitaries and to mark the signing of international treaties. It would be unthinkable for the Kremlin to lose its administrative significance altogether.

The huge auditorium in the Palace of Congresses—once a favorite venue for Communist Party conferences and other gatherings of the faithful

The constitution
The Russian constitution of 1993 provides for a president, elected for a four-year term, who is not allowed to serve more than two terms consecutively. It guarantees the right to private ownership of land and other property, free enterprise, individual privacy, freedom of movement, and religion. It also outlaws censorship and torture but provides for emergency rule by decree in exceptional circumstances, during which the president can temporarily restrict certain civil freedoms.

Sobornaya Ploshchad (Cathedral Square) 52B2

Christian worship has been practiced on or near the site of Cathedral Square since the founding of the Kremlin in the 12th century. The first stone churches were constructed in the reign of Ivan Kalita, but the present appearance of the square is the result of the inspired rebuilding program started by Ivan III (the Great) in about 1470. The Kremlin cathedrals have been the scene of all the great ceremonial occasions of state from the Middle Ages until the demise of the tsarist monarchy in 1917. Under the Communists they were converted to museums.

The Cathedral of the Annunciation. In this instance Ivan III relied on Russian master craftsmen from Pskov instead of his favorite Italian architects

▶▶▶ Arkhangelskiy Sobor (Cathedral of the Archangel) 52B2

The Cathedral of the Archangel Michael was built by an Italian known as Aleviz Noviy in 1505–1508. He was instructed to base his design on the Uspenskiy Cathedral in Vladimir. His main departure in style lies in the exuberant richness of the external decoration: arches, pilasters,

paneling, and scallop shells immediately beneath the roof. All the tsars and princes of Muscovy, from 1340 to the beginning of the 18th century, are buried in the Archangel Cathedral, with the exception of Boris Godunov, whose body lies in Sergiev Posad (Zagorsk). The tomb of Ivan the Terrible is situated in the sanctuary near the high altar; the sarcophagus was opened during excavations in the 1960s and from the remains a Soviet anthropologist reconstructed the tsar's likeness—the bust is now on display. Frescos dating mainly from the late 17th century decorate the walls and gallery, where there are more than 60 idealized portraits of Russian rulers.

▶▶▶ Blagoveshchenskiy Sobor (Cathedral of the Annunciation)   52B2

The Cathedral of the Annunciation was used as a private place of worship by the tsar and his family, and is where royal marriages and christenings were celebrated. It was built by a team of architects from Pskov in 1484–1489. After a fire, Ivan the Terrible added four more chapels and a number of domes, before giving orders for the entire roof to be covered with gold. Forbidden by church law to use the main entrance following his fourth marriage in 1572, he built a staircase, porch, and chapel of his own and watched the services from behind a screen. The Cathedral of the Annunciation contains some of the finest artwork in the Kremlin, with frescoes dating from around 1508 by Theodosius, son of the famous icon painter Dionysius. Biblical scenes alternate with solemn figures of the saints, prophets, apostles, the Pantocrator (Our Lord), and the Mother of God. The iconostasis includes work by the masters Andrei Rublev, Theophanes the Greek, and Prokhor of Gorodets. Also remarkable are the interior portals, supported by Corinthian columns and richly decorated with plantlike ornamentation.

▶▶▶ Kolokolnya Ivan Velikiy (Bell Tower of Ivan the Great)   52B2

At 267 feet, the Bell Tower of Ivan the Great is the highest point in the Kremlin and was completed in its present form by Boris Godunov in 1600. It is said that Tsar Boris's motivation in beautifying the tower was remorse over his supposed part in the death of the heir apparent, Prince Dmitri, but the additional height made it ideal as a lookout tower. The inscription immediately beneath the cupola reads: "By the Grace of the Holy Trinity and by order of the Tsar and Grand Prince Boris Fedorovich, Autocrat of all Russia, this temple was finished and gilded in the second year of their reign." The largest of the 21 bells in the belfry is the 70-ton "Resurrection," which by tradition tolled three times to announce the death of a tsar.

▶▶▶ Tsar Kolokol (The Tsar's Bell)   52B2

Resting at the foot of the Bell Tower of Ivan the Great is the world's largest, and most useless bell. The Tsar's Bell was cast in 1735 in the workshop of Ivan Motorin, but during a fire in the Kremlin in 1737 a large section broke off when it was doused with water. The bell was never repaired and is now more famous for its vital statistics: height 20 feet, weight 230 tons, diameter 21 feet 7 inches.

Spiritual inspiration
The work of the great icon painter Andrei Rublev has always held pride of place in the history of this art form. Yet very little is known about the life of the man who created these enduring spiritual images. Born sometime around 1360, he learned his skills from another legendary icon painter, Theophanes the Greek. Rublev later became a monk, at the Trinity-St. Sergius Monastery at Zagorsk, before moving to Moscow, where he died in 1430. Although few of his works have survived, the beauty and serenity of those that have attest to his deep religiosity and unrivaled skill.

The Bell Tower of Ivan the Great. The name refers not to the Tsar, as many people suppose, but to St. Ivan (John) of the Ladder

►►► Tsar Pushka
(The Tsar's Cannon)
52B2

The world's largest and most useless cannon was cast in 1586 for the feeble-minded Tsar Fedor, son of Ivan the Terrible, and although it was never intended to be fired in anger, several cannon balls were manufactured just in case. This gargantuan artillery piece weighs nearly 44 tons and the barrel is over 16 feet long.

►►► Uspenskiy Sobor
(Cathedral of the Assumption)
52B2

The Cathedral of the Assumption, sometimes known as the Dormition, was designed by Aristotele Fioravanti of Bologna in 1475 and took only four years to complete. Although based on various traditional Russian models, most notably the Uspenskiy Cathedral in Vladimir, the Italian architect extended the cathedral's length by adding two extra sets of piers to the usual four, and created five apses, so that the church has a much greater feeling of space than its Russian-designed counterparts. The largest and most important of the Kremlin churches, this is where the tsars were crowned and the patriarchs and metropolitans of the Orthodox Church laid to rest. Although most of the original frescos have been lost or painted over, the overall impression of the interior is still quite breathtaking. The walls and pillars are covered in highly schematized artwork of the finest quality, dating mainly from the 17th century, and there are at least two icons said to be by Dionysius (15th century). The lower section of the iconostasis also contains some very old paintings, including a 12th-century St. George, probably from Novgorod. The cathedral also contains the throne of Ivan the Terrible, a magnificent piece of woodcarving dating from 1551.

► Teremnoy Dvorets
(Terem Palace)
52B2

The Terem Palace is one of the hidden jewels of the Kremlin. Sadly, it is not open to the public. In the 19th

Missing treasures
When the French occupied Moscow in 1812, they turned the Cathedral of the Assumption into a stable, plundering the treasures in the process. Huge amounts of silver and gold were hauled away as booty. Much of the silver was later recovered by the Cossacks, who presented the chandelier which now hangs from the dome.

One important icon is also missing from the Cathedral's interior: the 12th-century *Virgin of Vladimir*, brought here by Basil III in 1395 and revered throughout Russia. When Lenin came to power and closed the Kremlin churches, the icon was removed to the Tretyakov Art Gallery, where it can still be seen.

74

The magnificent north portal of the Cathedral of the Assumption

century K. A. Ton incorporated the building into the Grand Kremlin Palace, redesigning the two arcaded lower floors, which date from the early 16th century. The upper stories, painted red and with fancifully embellished windows, rise toward a checkerboard roof. They were built for Tsar Mikhail Fedorovich in 1635–1636 by Bazhen Ogurtsev. Unfortunately the Terem Palace is visible only from a distance (the best view is from the river). This was the oldest part of the tsar's residence and was designed with luxury in mind. Despite this, the tsar's private apartments on the fourth floor, while breathtakingly beautiful in their decoration, are modest in size, a fact accentuated by the low, vaulted roofs. They include the Chamber of the Cross, used for small assemblies, a throne room, prayer room, and bedchamber. Next door is an antechamber, where the most elevated boyars traditionally greeted their lord each morning. At the eastern end of the palace is the Golden Tsaritsa Chamber, constructed for Irina Godunova, wife of Tsar Fedor Ivanovich, in the 16th century and, again, beautifully decorated with a tiled stove, stained-glass windows, and wall paintings that allude to the tsaritsa's Byzantine ancestry.

The Chamber of the Cross, Terem Palace

Coronation
Ivan IV was the first tsar to have himself crowned in the Assumption Cathedral in the Kremlin in a ceremony which revived the awe-inspiring splendor of the crowning of the Byzantine Emperors. He was also the first monarch to proclaim himself "Tsar of all Russia" and he took for his wife (the first of seven) a boyar's daughter, Anastasia Romanov, whose great nephew, Michael Romanov, gave his name to the subsequent dynasty.

Basketball first
In June 1994 a crowd of 5,000 spectators saw the former Soviet Olympic gold-medal winners of 1988 play an American all-star team on a special court only 100 feet from the Lenin Mausoleum.

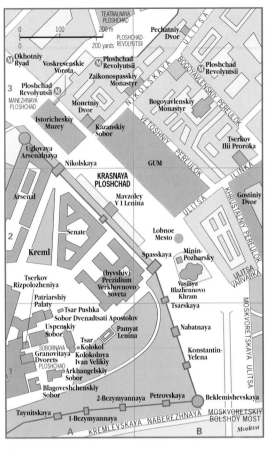

The magnificent glass roof of GUM spans the shopping arcade like an enormous spiderweb

Krasnaya Ploshchad (Red Square)

Red Square►►► was originally known more prosaically as the *torg* or marketplace. The present name dates from the 17th century, when the word *krasniy* meant "beautiful" as well as "red." Before the November Revolution, Red Square was the scene of markets, fairs, and religious festivals, most colorfully on Palm Sunday when the patriarch rode through the Savior's Gate to St. Basil's on a donkey to commemorate Christ's entry into Jerusalem. The Palm Sunday bazaar was equally famous, and the square would fill with wandering holy men, beggars, errand boys, and peasants visiting from the countryside. Tents, booths, and stalls proliferated, while hawkers, itinerant craftsmen, and traders sold everything from children's toys, balloons, and flowers to illustrated papers, sweetmeats, and icon lamps.

Red Square was also a famous place of execution. Here rebels met their deaths beside the raised circular dais called the *Lobnoe Mesto* from which state decrees were also read out.

Red Square still holds a fascination for visitors to Moscow

Fallen idols
In 1996, to coincide with the centennial of Nicholas II's coronation, Russian monarchists called for a 16-foot bronze statue of the Tsar by the sculptor Vyacheslav Klykov to be erected outside the Kremlin on Teatralnaya Ploshchad. It would share the same spot where, in Communist times, there had been a monument to the first Soviet president, Yakov Sverdlov. Anxious about the impending presidential election, the authorities refused, but instead gave permission for the statue to be erected beyond the city limits in the village of Tayninskoe. Less than a year later, in April 1997, the monument was blown up by unidentified saboteurs in an explosion that could be heard 2½ miles away.

Under the Communists a military parade was held in Red Square every year on November 7 to mark the anniversary of the Revolution. This procession of tanks and military hardware past the members of the Politburo became a distorted echo of the religious processions of old and dates back to the days when War Commissar Leon Trotsky harangued raw recruits of the Red Army before sending them off to battle against the counter-revolutionaries. The square was briefly reclaimed as a genuine public forum in 1989 when protestors broke up the traditional May Day celebrations, forcing Mikhail Gorbachev and the other Soviet leaders to leave the square in embarrassment.

The appearance of Red Square has changed little over the centuries, with the exception of the demolition of the Iberian Gate which used to dominate the approach to the Square from Okhotniy Ryad. The monument to Minin and Pozharsky, now outside St. Basil's, originally stood in front of GUM; it was moved so as not to deflect attention from the Lenin Mausoleum. Already two old landmarks, the Kazan Cathedral and the Iberian Gate, have been rebuilt; the cathedral is now open to the public (see page 78).

▶▶▶ GUM   *76B3*

The initials stand for **Gosudarstvenniy Universalniy Magazin** (State Universal Store). This magnificent building dates from 1888–1893, when it was known as the Upper Trading Rows, a reference to some earlier market stalls destroyed during the brief French occupation of 1812. The design, by A. N. Pomerantsev, draws on motifs from traditional Russian architectural styles then in vogue. The interior, with its galleries punctuated with stuccoed archways, ornate iron railings, and bridges, surmounted by a spectacular glass roof, can hardly fail to impress. Originally there were more than 1,000 separate outlets in the Upper Trading Rows, but the Communists reduced the number to 150. Economic reforms have enabled Western firms to use GUM as a showcase for their own products.

Ice cream
Before buying the expensive Italian ice cream on sale at GUM, remember the Russian stallholders outside, who sell the same product, without the frills, at a fraction of the price. Russians love ice cream even in the dead of winter, and more than 170 tons of it are consumed in Moscow and St. Petersburg each day.

MOSCOW

The architect of the Historical Museum wanted to use multi-colored tiles for the exterior to contrast with the fantastic patterning of St. Basil's Cathedral opposite, but in the end he had to settle for red brick

Lights out
Starved of funds, an increasing number of Russian museums are being forced to close temporarily because they are unable to pay outstanding lighting and heating bills. The most recent casualty was the Stanislavsky Museum, dedicated to the founder of the Moscow Arts Theater and located in his former apartment. When the hot water was turned off after the director fell behind in his payments, the pipes burst, causing untold damage to the precious costume collection and the original set of Chekhov's *Three Sisters.*

► **Istoricheskiy Muzey (Historical Museum)** 76A3

Krasnaya Ploshchad 1/2
Metro: Okhotniy Ryad
The Historical Museum was designed by Vladimir Sherwood in 1878 and stands on the original site of Moscow University. The heavily ornamented red-brick building is a rather overwrought example of the neo-Russian style popular toward the end of the 19th century. The theme of the museum is the history of the peoples of the former USSR. There are said to be more than four million items on display, but few visitors will relish the grueling trek through 48 halls to see everything. Some of the more colorful items include Peter the Great's sleigh, the cage in which Yemelyan Pugachev, leader of the Peasant's Revolt against Catherine the Great, was brought to Moscow for execution, clothing belonging to Ivan the Terrible, and Napoleon's saber and field kitchen. The museum has been closed for some time for repairs but will reopen soon.

Adjacent to the Historical Museum is the splendid Iberian Gate, a pair of matching white towers capped by green tent spires. Originally built in the 17th century, the gateway was called after the tiny chapel dedicated to the Iberian Virgin which stood between its twin arches. Whenever the tsar came to Moscow, it was customary for him to visit the shrine before entering the Kremlin.

►► **Kazanskiy Sobor (Kazan Cathedral)** 76A3

Krasnaya Ploshchad
The Kazan Cathedral was dedicated in October 1636 in the presence of Tsar Mikhail Fedorovich. It was named in honor of the Kazan icon of the Virgin which Prince Pozharskiy carried before him during the storming of the walls of the Kitay Gorod in 1612. The cathedral's importance declined after the icon was moved to the new Kazan Cathedral in St. Petersburg early in the 19th century (see page 180). The Moscow cathedral was demolished in 1936 in line with the Stalinist plan for the reconstruction of the city, but fortunately the site had already been carefully documented and photographed by the architect P. D. Baranovsky, and this facilitated the reconstruction of the building following excavations on the site of the old bell tower in 1989. In 1990 a historic

Defiance
The Kazan icon assumed great political significance in the summer of 1687 when Peter the Great's sister, Sofia, insisted on carrying it in procession through the city—a privilege traditionally accorded to the tsar. This act of defiance was a signal to the *Streltsy* to launch a rebellion against him.

procession, led by Patriarch Alexis II, Boris Yeltsin, and the then mayor of Moscow, Gavriil Popov, left the Kremlin to lay the foundation stone of the new cathedral here, which is now open once again for worship.

►   Lobnoe Mesto (Place of the Skulls)   *76B2*

The "Place of the Skulls" was where state decrees were issued and, as the macabre name implies, where criminals were executed—the gallows stood alongside the stone dais. The leader of one of Russia's most famous peasant revolts, Stenka Razin, was led to execution here in 1671. Jacob Reitenfels, the nephew of the court doctor, witnessed the event: "In prison, Stenka Razin had been flogged with the knout, tortured by fire, undergone the water torture, and other more extraordinary horrors. All his body was a living sore, so that the knout fell on raw bones. After having heard the death sentence pronounced by the judge in a loud voice, Razin made the sign of the cross and lay down on the scaffold. A hatchet severed his legs and arms, followed by his head."

►   Mavzoley V. I. Lenina
(Lenin Mausoleum)   *76A2*

Since November 1917, when victims of revolutionary clashes were buried here in two common graves, the Kremlin Wall has served as a Communist shrine. After Lenin's death on January 21, 1924, his successors put the body on public display. A frequent topic of discussion is the removal of Lenin's body for reburial with other members of his family in St. Petersburg. Other Communist worthies, including Josef Stalin, are buried behind the mausoleum under the Kremlin wall.

►   Monetniy Dvor (The Mint)   *76A3*

The old baroque Mint of 1697 is hidden within the courtyard of the later, ornate building built by Empress Anna in 1733 next to the Kazan Cathedral, which now houses an exclusive jewelry and folk-art store.

Lenin
The embalming of Lenin's body was undertaken by Professor Vorobev in March 1924 after other experts had pronounced it impossible. By 1939 a special "Preservation Institute" with a staff of 20, including 13 doctors, had been created to look after Lenin's corpse. The mausoleum was regularly closed at 18-month intervals for retouching, while there were twice-weekly inspections of hands and feet. Rumors of the substitution of plastic ears were strenuously denied! It has, however, recently been admitted that the corpse has turned bright auburn—the special glass case protecting it filters the light to make it seem a more reasonable color!

79

A. V. Shchusev's red granite mausoleum replaced the wooden original in 1930

One of Moscow's best-known landmarks—St. Basil's Cathedral in Red Square

Religious persecution
Priests were among the early victims of the Soviet regime, with thousands being subjected to torture and execution. For example, the last incumbent of St. Basil's Cathedral, Ioann Vostorgov, a well-known preacher and missionary, was shot by the Communists on August 23, 1918. In the same month, British diplomat Robert Bruce Lockhart, himself in custody in the Lubyanka, recalled looking down into the prison yard and seeing a prominent bishop being dragged away to his death.

►►► Vasiliya Blazhennovo Khram (Cathedral of Basil the Blessed) 76B2

Krasnaya Ploshchad
Metro: Ploshchad Revolyutsii
Open: Wed–Mon 9:30–5

The Cathedral of Basil the Blessed was commissioned by Ivan the Terrible to commemorate victory over the Tatars on the feast day of the Holy Virgin's Veil and was completed in 1560. After the Tsar's death, the remains of the holy fool Basil the Blessed (one of Ivan's most outspoken critics) were brought here in 1588 and reinterred in a specially constructed chapel. The cathedral's external appearance—a riot of pinnacles, tent roofs, onion domes, and spade-shaped gables—was inspired by traditional Russian timber architecture and, unlike the Kremlin cathedrals, owes very little to foreign influences. The garish color scheme dates only from 1670; the cathedral was originally painted red with white details. At one time it was entirely white with gilded domes.

The interior is an architectural sleight of hand. The ground plan resembles an eight-pointed star, but the symmetry is obscured by the disorienting maze of corridors, vestibules, and twisting staircases which link the eight highly individual chapels to the central church. Carefully restored painted ceilings and floral-patterned wall decorations are the most arresting features, though difficult to see in the dim light. The icon screens are copies, but many of the icons themselves are genuine.

St. Basil's was damaged by fire in 1739 and restored in the reign of Catherine II. According to legend, during the Napoleonic invasion of 1812 the cathedral was used to stable horses. After the Revolution St. Basil's was designated a museum. The present exhibition traces the progress of archeological investigations undertaken in the 1920s, as well as the history of the cathedral itself, using models, sketches, plans, lithographs, and photographs. There is a small display of vestments, Bibles, and other sacred objects dating from the 16th century and armor and weapons illustrating Ivan's campaigns against the Tatars.

Folk art

The painted lacquer boxes known as *palekh* actually originate in the neighboring village of Fedoskino, where the first one was produced in 1796. The lacquer is painted over papier-mâché and decorated with scenes from traditional fairy tales such as *The Frog Princess*, *The Tale of Tsar Saltan* and *The Golden Cockerel*. Equally familiar is the set of wooden nest dolls known as a *matryoshka*.

Souvenir-seekers are also likely to see the blue and white pottery that is the trademark of Gzhel village, carved wooden toys from Sergiev-Zagorsk, samovars from Tula, as well as carved bird feathers from the northern port of Archangel.

Modern crafts Three thousand Russian folk artists lay out their wares for sale in the former churches of St. George's and St. Maxim's (Varvarka Ulitsa 6 and 12). These are the showcases for everything from pottery and ceramics to balalaikas, rag dolls, puppets, icons, wood carvings, embroidery, and jewelry.

Folk museums The biggest collection of folk art in Russia is owned by Moscow's Museum of Applied Folk Art (Delegatskaya Ulitsa 3. *Open* Tue–Sat 10–6; closed last Thu in the month). Pride of place belongs to the display of embroidery, dating back to the 18th century, including court dresses in brocaded silks, traditional peasant headdresses (*kokoshniki*), and embroidered shawls. Also entertaining is the samovar exhibition tracing the history of the art from its birth in Tula in 1778. By the end of the 19th century there were more than 150 different types of tea urns made by craftsmen in the local villages.

The Moscow region's huge folk art output is now wholly geared to the tourist market. The matryoshka *above and the lacquer boxes shown in the foreground of the display below are perennial favorites with visitors*

The secret police

■ **The long reign of the KGB finally came to an end in December 1993 when President Boris Yeltsin, concerned about the organization's ambiguous role in the attempted *coup* two months earlier and the unexpectedly strong showing of the right in the December elections, abolished the "unreformable" Security Ministry and replaced it with a federal counterintelligence service. ■**

The infamous Lubyanka prison and KGB headquarters

Lax security
When General Mezentsov, head of the Third (Security) Section of the Russian police, was assassinated in broad daylight on Italianskaya Ulitsa, St. Petersburg, in 1878, his bodyguard was armed only with an umbrella!

Lavrentiy Beria, the notorious head of the KGB under Stalin, was secretly executed (exact date unknown) on the orders of a fearful Politburo headed by Nikita S. Khrushchev

Sniffing out treason Ivan the Terrible was the first Russian ruler to feel the need for a secret police force. In 1565 he founded the *Oprichnina*, a force of 6,000 men who rode on black horses and carried on their saddles the dreaded emblem of a dog's head and a broom, symbolizing the sniffing out and the sweeping away of treason. Peter the Great had his own version, the *Preobrazhenskiy Prikaz*, so secret that no one knows the date of its founding and so deadly that by the end of his reign no one dared even make a joke about the ruler for fear that it would be misconstrued as conspiracy. The 19th-century successor to this, the *Okhrana*, was set up in 1881 in response to the assassination of Tsar Alexander II. With a staff which eventually numbered more than 10,000, and sweeping powers of search, arrest, imprisonment, and "administrative exile" (banishment without trial to Siberia), the *Okhrana* was a secret police force without parallel in Europe at that time.

Red Terror Not surprisingly Lenin's Bolsheviks were among the most vociferous opponents of such repressive tsarist organizations, but within three months of coming to power in November 1917 they had set up their own machinery which would far outstrip its predecessors. This was the All-Russian Extraordinary Commission for Combating Counterrevolution and Sabotage (known universally by the abbreviation *Cheka*). After an attempt on Lenin's life in 1918, the *Cheka* increased its activities. By 1922, it was a force totaling 260,000 and had carried out an estimated 250,000 executions. In addition, in April 1919 Lenin had sanctioned the setting up of a new network of more than 80 forced labor camps with a floating population of about 50,000.

The ruthless efficiency of the *Cheka* under Lenin paved the way for the monstrous actions of his successor, Joseph Stalin. The Great Terror was launched in 1934 using the time-honored precedent of assassination, the difference being that in this case the victim, Sergei Kirov, was almost certainly killed on Stalin's orders. During the next five years, one citizen in 20 was "purged" by the secret police (then known as the NKVD) and there were at least one million executions over the same period.

The climate of fear, at its worst in the late 1930s, was all-pervasive. By day people pretended to go about their business as if nothing was happening. At night came the dreaded knock on the door. The accused were taken away in blue-painted bread vans to the various interrogation

centers—most people kept a suitcase packed for just such an event. The most feared destinations were the torture cells in the basement of the Lubyanka or at Moscow's Lefortovo prison. For the overwhelming majority, the final destination was the Gulag—the vast network of Soviet slave labor camps, concentrated mainly in the wastelands of Siberia.

Can a leopard change its spots? The nightmare only came to an end with the death of Stalin in 1953. Yet the KGB was hardly apologetic; its members continued to call themselves *chekisty* and to wear the *Cheka* emblem of shield and sword with pride, while devotion to the memory of their founder, Felix Dzerzhinsky ("Iron Felix"), attained the status of a cult.

During the Gorbachev era the first Western journalists were allowed into the Lubyanka. When interviewed, KGB chief Vladimir Kryuchkov assured the press of his support for *perestroika*; a year later he was arrested for his part in the *coup* which tried to topple Gorbachev from power.

Off to obscurity: the statue of Felix Dzerzhinsky is removed from its plinth on Ploshchad Lubyanka

Insecure times
In 1937–1938 employees were being denounced and arrested at such a rate that journalists in the Moscow offices of *Izvestiya* gave up changing the nameplates on doors.

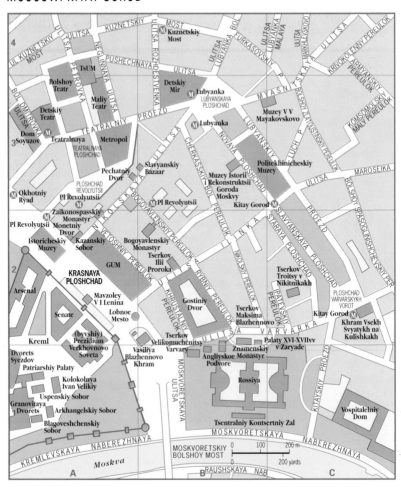

84

Kitay Gorod

By the end of the 12th century, Moscow had outgrown the Kremlin as far as the three streets just beyond Red Square: Nikolskaya, Ilinka, and Varvarka. Around these arteries there developed a thriving merchants' quarter of shops and stalls, solid timber houses, churches, monasteries, and noblemen's estates with enclosed gardens. The origin of the district's name is obscure—*kitay* might refer to the wooden palisade (*kiti*) which once gave it protection; *gorod* means town. Between 1534 and 1538 the original earth fortifications were replaced by a brick wall, about 9 feet high with 12 towers, which was built around the settlement to strengthen the Kremlin's defenses. This was demolished by the Soviets when it was found to interfere with "progressive" socialist planning, but a surprising number of the old buildings remain and parts of the wall can still be seen in the vicinity of the Rossiya Hotel and near the Metropol Hotel on Teatralniy Proezd.

► Angliyskoe Podvore
(The English Residence)
84B1

Open: Tue, Sat and Sun 10–6, Wed–Fri 11–7

The large whitewashed building on Ulitsa Varvarka (see page 87), next to the Church of St. Barbara, was originally the property of a Russian merchant. It was handed over to the English merchant adventurer Richard Chancellor in 1556, after which it became a trade center for visiting delegations from England.

Gostinitsa Rossiya
(Hotel Rossiya)
84B1

Dominating the skyline behind St. Basil's is one of Moscow's great architectural eyesores, the Hotel Russia. It was opened in 1971 and claimed the dubious distinction of being the largest hotel in the world. Capable of accommodating up to 6,000 guests, it was used by the Communists as an enormous hold-all for foreign tourists; nowadays it is forced to compete on the open market and is finding life a lot harder.

►► Ulitsa Ilinka (Ilinka Street)
84B2

In the 19th century, this, the main street of the Kitay Gorod, contained many warehouses and banks. Known in the Soviet era as Kuybyshev Street after one of Stalin's cronies, it has recently reverted to its old name, which refers to the Church of St. Elijah, part of a 19th-century building. At No. 6 is the Stock Exchange or *birzha* which first opened in 1839.

The imposing building on Rybniy Pereulok is the Gostiniy Dvor or Merchant's Yard, designed in the classical style by the famous St. Petersburg architect Giacomo Quarenghi and completed in 1805. Although the building is now used for offices, this magnificent arcade with its unrivaled outlook on the Kremlin is still worth exploring.

►► Nikolskaya Ulitsa
(Nikolskaya Street)
84B3

Known in the Soviet era as 25 October Street to commemorate the Revolution, Nikolskaya is regaining its reputation for thriving petty commerce, not all of it legal. There are a number of interesting buildings on this street: the Zaikonospasskiy Monastery (No. 7) takes its name from the trade in icons which once flourished here; the red and white church with its robust, tiered tower is all that survives of the monastery today. These used to be the premises of Moscow's first institution of higher education, the Slavic-Greek-Latin Academy, which operated from 1687 to 1814. A detour to the right at Bogoyavlenskiy Pereulok leads to the Bogoyavlenskiy (Epiphany) Monastery founded by Prince Daniil in the 1290s. The red brick baroque cathedral with its massive but refined tower, dating from the late 17th century, survives. Back on Nikolskaya, at No. 15, are the spires of the green and white Synodal Printing House. The original chambers of 1679 survive in the courtyard, but the street façade dates from 1815. The plaque explains that Russia's first book, the Acts of the Apostles, was printed here in 1564 by Ivan Fedorov. The most famous building on Nikolskaya Ulitsa is the Slavyanskiy Bazaar Restaurant (No. 19). One of Chekhov's favorite haunts, it suffered serious damage in a fire in 1993.

The playful ornamentation on this beautiful building is typical of the 19th-century architecture on Ilinka Street

Long lunch
At 2 PM on the afternoon of June 22, 1897, the actor and impresario Konstantin Stanislavskiy and the dramatist Vladimir Nemirovich-Danchenko sat down to lunch at the Slavyanskiy Bazaar Restaurant to work out the details of a new theatrical venture which was to result in the Moscow Arts Theater. The discussions continued until 8:00 the following morning.

MOSCOW

The Synodal Printing House on Nikolskaya Street. Russia's first printing press was founded by Ivan the Terrible, but this typically Muscovite flight of fancy is 19th-century

Royal refusal
Diplomatic relations between England and Russia go back a long way. Ivan the Terrible went to great lengths to court the various trading missions from England that visited him in the 16th century. He even offered to marry Queen Elizabeth I, an offer she wisely declined. Perhaps aware of his reputation among his own subjects, Elizabeth promised him a place of asylum in England if he should ever be in need of it.

Tragic muse
In November 1996, a precious trawl of love letters from the writer Boris Pasternak to Olga Ivinskaya (the inspiration for the character of Lara in *Dr. Zhivago*) went on sale at Christies, the London auction house. Ivinskaya's relationship with Pasternak began in 1946 and continued until his death 14 years later. When Pasternak was awarded the Nobel Prize for literature in 1958—after smuggling the manuscript of his novel out of the country—the authorities hit back at him through his lover, who was sentenced to eight years in a labor camp. Ivinskaya is said to have approved of Julie Christie's portrayal of her in the 1965 film of the novel.

▶▶ **Palaty XVI–XVII vv. v Zaryade
(Palace of the 16th–17th C. in Zaryad)** *84C1*

Ulitsa Varvarka 10
Open: Thu–Mon 10–6, Wed 11–7
Beyond the white, two-domed church of St. Maxim the Blessed (17th century) is the Romanov House, later part of the Znamenskiy Monastyr (Monastery of the Sign). The monastery was founded in 1631 by Tsar Mikhail Romanov, the founder of Russia's last ruling dynasty, on the family estate where he was born. The buildings comprise a church, monks' cells, and the former Romanov palace, now a museum. The exhibition consists of clothes and furniture from the period and a reconstruction of a boyar's study as it would have appeared in the 17th century, complete with wooden chests, trunks, kitchen equipment, money, and other furnishings.

▶ **Lubyanskaya Ploshchad
(Lubyanka Square)** *84B3*

For centuries, Lubyanka Square was approached from Nikolskaya Ulitsa via the magnificent Vladimir Gate. This was demolished in the 1930s to give greater access to modern through-traffic. The Lubyanka's more sinister reputation dates from 1918, when the Communist secret police moved its headquarters here from Leningrad (St. Petersburg), choosing the former premises of the Rossiya Insurance Company. One of the first "guests" of the Soviet government was the British diplomat Robert Bruce Lockhart, arrested for his part in the conspiracy against Lenin's life in August 1918. After a fairly gentlemanly interrogation, Lockhart was removed to the Kremlin and, though under sentence of death, was eventually released. In 1926 the square was renamed after the founder of the KGB, Felix Dzerzhinsky, who died that year. The statue of "Iron Felix," as the implacable and incorruptible Dzerzhinsky was known to his admirers, was removed in 1991 and replaced for a time by a plain wooden cross in memory of his countless victims. Just down the road from Lubyanka Square is the famous children's store Detskiy Mir (Children's World), which is now privatized.

►► Tserkov Troitsy v Nikitnikakh (Church of the Trinity in Nikitniki) 84C2

Nikitnikov Pereulok 3
Metro: Kitay Gorod
Open: Wed–Mon 10–6

Situated just off Ipatevskiy Pereulok, between Ulitsa Varvarka and Staraya Ploshchad, this fine church was built for the merchant Grigori Nikitnikov in 1635–1653. The red-brick building is surmounted by five domes and tiers of gables and has a tent-roofed belfry. The church is now a museum. The Nikitnikov family is buried in the small chapel, accessible through a splendid carved portal. The superb iconostasis dates from the 1640s and includes work by the 17th-century master Simon Ushakov.

►► Ulitsa Varvarka (Varvarka Street) 84B2–C2

Now renamed after the Church of St. Barbara the Martyr, which stands on the corner at No. 6, the Varvarka is the old trade route to Vladimir. Prince Dmitri Donskoy is said to have taken this road on his way to fight the Mongols at Kulikovo Field in 1380. The Communists subsequently renamed it after the rebel leader Stenka Razin, who was led to execution along this street in 1671. The small peach and white classical Church of St. Barbara was built in 1795–1804 on the site of a 16th-century predecessor. The area occupied by the Rossiya Hotel was once known as the *Zaryade* ("beyond the trading rows"). Until at least the 1870s, there were no Western-style shops in Moscow, with the exception of provision stores. Instead, Muscovites frequented the lines of market stalls which stretched all the way from Red Square to Lubyanskaya Ploshchad and along Novaya Ploshchad down to the river. Especially famous before the Revolution was the *tolkuchiy rynok* (second-hand market) which sold cheap clothes, shoes, and meals. The market was a lifeline for Moscow's poor, with its rows of trestle tables resembling a permanent soup kitchen.

> **Reluctant soldiers**
> The Russian army is currently facing a crisis with almost 40 percent of eligible conscripts in Moscow alone failing to report for service.
> Many manage to gain exemption for medical reasons or because they are full-time students. Elsewhere, reluctant recruits are being virtually press-ganged into service in an army which is often drafted into civilian tasks like picking potatoes.

The Foundling Home on the Moskva embankment. In the 18th century consciences were troubled by the huge numbers of orphans on the streets of Moscow. Here they were given an education which, for some at least, led to fame and fortune

Boat trip **The Moskva River**

If you are finding the Moscow summer heat oppressive (and it can get very humid) or you are becoming footsore from sightseeing, or you are simply at a loss for what to do next, why not join Muscovites for a couple of hours cruising the Moskva River? The boat trip is also an excellent way to get to know this very large city and is much less stuffy than the Intourist coach.

The boat trip downstream is not only extremely good value, it also offers views of the Kremlin which simply cannot be bettered—don't forget your camera. Company boat tours with bar and restaurant facilities can be chartered for special occasions but don't come cheap (contact: Charter Boat Tours, tel: 459 74 76; River Boat Tickets, tel: 257 71 09). There are piers at regular intervals on either bank of the river, but the most useful embarkation points are the Ustinskiy Bolshoy Bridge near the Rossiya Hotel and the pier near the Kiev station.

Sparrow Hills and the Kremlin

Boats leave from the pier near the Kiev station and travel downstream from the Kremlin as far as the Novospasskiy Monastery. The full trip, paid for in rubles, takes about two hours but can be interrupted at any point. Boats leave approximately every half hour, and snacks including beer are available on board.

From Kievskaya to the Novodevichiy Convent

As the boat moves downstream, it leaves behind two typical examples of the "wedding cake" architecture of the Stalin period—the **Ukraine Hotel** and the **Ministry of Foreign Affairs**. In the distance is the **Ostankino television tower**, while on the left the spires and onion domes of the **Novodevichiy Convent** (see page 122) are already coming into view.

From the Krasnoluzhskiy Most to the Sparrow Hills

On the right, beyond the cantilevered railroad bridge, are the Sparrow Hills (see page 122). The floodlights of the **Lenin Stadium** and the bulky presence of **MGU (Moscow State University)** are clearly visible. After the boat passes under a blue two-tiered bridge (Luzhnikovskiy Most), the river makes a 90-degree turn. The tiny church peeping through the trees on the right is **St. Andrew's**

Opposite : the Krymskiy Most or Crimean Bridge

Monastery, dating from the 17th century and now holding religious services again.

From Gorky Park to Krymskiy Most

At this point the natural landscape of the Sparrow Hills yields to the more formal but equally verdant **Gorky Park**. The domed pavilions by M. F. Kazakov (18th-century) mark the site of a former pleasure ground once visited by Pushkin, who now gives his name to the embankment. A block of show apartments, completed after World War II and decorated with a mural showing a happy Soviet family, can be seen on the opposite bank. The next main bridge is the **Krymskiy (Crimean) Most**, which carries the heavy road traffic from the Garden Ring across the river.

From Park Iskusstv to the Rossiya Hotel

The modern concrete building dominating **Arts Park** is the former Picture Gallery of the U.S.S.R., now known as the **New Tretyakov** (see pages 128–129), but a better example of 20th-century design is the art nouveau **Pertsov House** of 1905–1907 with attractive mosaics by the artist Sergei Malyutin. Beyond the **Bolshoy Kamenniy Most** (Great Stone Bridge)

a magnificent view of the **Kremlin Towers** opens up, with, on the opposite bank, the stately residence and offices of the **British Embassy**, formerly the mansion of a wealthy merchant. Past **Red Square** and **St. Basil's Cathedral** is the **Rossiya Hotel** and the tiny single dome of the **Church of St. Anna**. This may be a convenient point to disembark.

From Ustinskiy Bolshoy Most to Novospasskiy Monastery

If you are staying on board you will pass on the left an enormous yellow classical building—this is the **Foundling Home**, dating from the 18th century (see page 117). A tributary of the Moskva River, the Yauza, flows in from the left. Being in the 19th century a byword for pollution (caused by effluent from the textile factories which hugged its banks), the Yauza now carries barge traffic at a leisurely pace. Looming into view is an extravagantly grotesque apartment block in Stalinist Gothic, once heralded as Moscow's first skyscraper and considered at the time to be a triumph of socialist architectural planning. The cruise ends at the **Novospasskiy Most**, which refers to the **New Monastery of the Savior** with its impressive fortified walls.

Gorky Park—Moscow's most famous green space

89

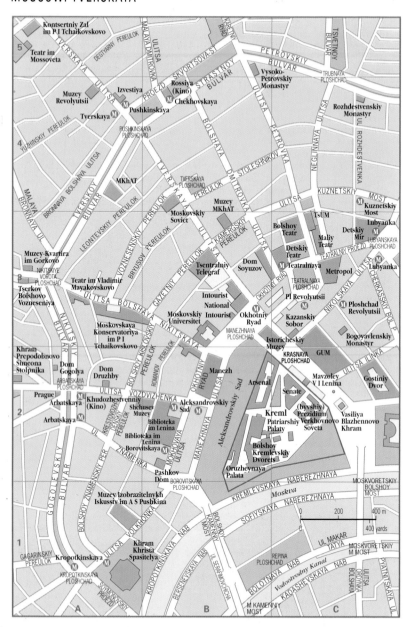

Tverskaya

Tverskaya Ulitsa, the northern road to St. Petersburg via the town of Tver, became Moscow's main street in the 18th century. Here stood imposing government offices and, later, fashionable French stores. Despite the depredations of the 1930s, a surprising amount of old, historic Moscow is still preserved, hidden away in the numerous twisting alleys and side streets off the Tverskaya.

►► Hotels Metropol and National *90C3/B3*

Two of Moscow's grandest hotels occupy prime sites in central Moscow. The National, on the corner of Tverskaya Ulitsa, was built by A. I. Ivanov in 1903; the Metropol, on Teatralniy Proezd, was designed by a British architect, W. F. Walcott, in 1899. This outstanding example of art nouveau *stil modern* contains colorful mosaics, some by the distinguished Russian artist Mikhail Vrubel, which are perfectly complemented by the delicately wrought balconies and classical friezes.

►► Manezh (Manège) *90B2*

The Central Exhibition Hall, which stages events ranging from motor shows to art exhibitions, was originally a military riding school (*manège*). It was completed in 1825 by Alexander I's most favored Moscow architect, Osip Bove, to a design by Augustine Betancourt. The roof span of 160 feet was until Soviet times held up by wooden girders without any intermediate supports.

► Mokhovaya Ulitsa (Mokhovaya Street) *90B2*

Moss for insulation was sold here in the 18th century, hence the name. However, the character of the Mokhovaya changed forever in the early 1930s, when many old buildings were bulldozed as part of a Soviet plan to build a grand highway. Excavations are now going on around Manezhnaya Ploshchad in an effort to salvage something of the Mokhovaya's past. One building which did survive is the 18th-century Pashkov Dom, situated just opposite the Alexander Gardens (see page 56).

Higher up, on either side of Bolshaya Nikolskaya Ulitsa, are the old premises of **Moscow University►**. The columned "new building" at No. 20 was completed in 1836 to a design by Tyurin and now serves as the student union (the main faculty buildings are at Sparrow Hills; see page 118). In the courtyard is a statue of one of Russia's great "Renaissance men," M. V. Lomonosov, who founded the university in 1755. Few foreigners are aware that the headquarters of Russia's first secret police, Ivan the Terrible's notorious *Oprichnina*, was located on this site. The "old building," distinguished by a shallow dome which rests on a columned portico, is also in the classical style and was designed by M. F. Kazakov in 1793.

Exhibitions

In 1962 Soviet leader Nikita Khrushchev was invited to visit an exhibition given by Russian artists in the Manezh. Scandalized by examples of nonfigurative art which contradicted the official doctrine of Socialist Realism, he stormed out, criticizing the work as "donkey shit."

More recently, in May 1993, the Manezh mounted an exhibition of photographs and other mementoes of the last tsar, Nicholas II, and his family. To many Russians these photos, some seen for the first time, came as a revelation and showed a touching, human side to the old autocracy.

Moscow's newly refurbished National Hotel

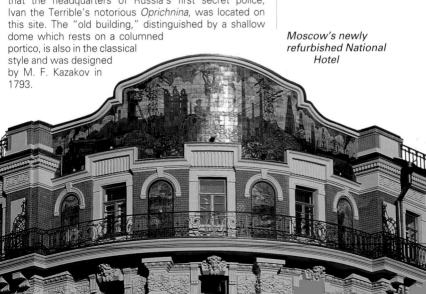

Originally named after Tsar Alexander III, the Museum of Fine Arts became the Pushkin in the poet's centenary year, 1937

▶▶▶ **Muzey Izobrazitelnykh Iskusstv im A. S. Pushkina (Pushkin Fine Arts Museum)** 90A1

Ulitsa Volkhonka 12
Metro: Kropotkinskaya
Open: Tue–Fri 10–4, weekends noon–6

The Pushkin Fine Arts Museum is renowned for its collection of French painting, especially of the Impressionist and Post-Impressionist Schools. In 1918 the canvases belonging to two great private collectors, S. I. Shchukin and I. A. Morozov, were nationalized. For a time they were housed together in Morozov's former mansion, rechristened the Museum of Modern Western Art. Then, in the 1930s, part of the collection was presented to the Hermitage in St. Petersburg. When the Museum of Modern Western Art was closed for ideological reasons in 1948 (modern painting outside the narrow confines of Socialist Realism being regarded as decadent), the French collection was moved to the Pushkin Museum, but for many years the paintings were kept from the public gaze. With the death of Stalin in 1953, favored *cognoscenti* and reliable party stalwarts were allowed into a back room at the museum to see the forbidden fruits: half a dozen paintings by Matisse and Picasso.

The ground floor is devoted mainly to the Pushkin's other strong suit, its collection of Old Masters. A total of 460 Western paintings were transferred here from the Hermitage Gallery during the 1920s in exchange for the share of the Shchukin and Morozov collections. They include a Botticelli *Annunciation*, a *Madonna and Child* by Perugino, and a *Holy Family* by Veronese. Paintings by Canaletto and Tiepolo can be found in **Room 12**. The Pushkin is well endowed with art of the Flemish and Dutch schools. There are several portraits by van Dyck, landscapes by van Ruisdael and van Goyen, and charming studies of peasant life by Jacob Jordaens. But pride of

place belongs to the magnificent collection of Rembrandts, which include biblical scenes and portraits.

The Pushkin's French collection also begins on this floor (**Room 13**), with examples from the work of the 17th- and 18th-century artists Poussin, Lorrain, Watteau, Chardin, Greuze, and Fragonard. The upper floor begins with Ingres and Delacroix and landscape artists from the Barbizon school, including Courbet and Millet (**Room 23**). Then come the Impressionists: in **Room 21** there are 11 works by Monet, including the superbly lit *Déjeuner sur l'herbe* and two canvases from the Rouen Cathedral sequence; several works by Manet (*Au café,* for example) and some outstanding Renoirs, among them *La grenouil-lère* (Bathing on the Seine), *Au moulin de la galette,* and the stunning portrait of *Jeanne Samary.* Degas is represented by landscapes such as *Paysage de Sainte-Victoire* and the memorable study *Danseuses en bleu.* **Room 18** has a marvelous exhibition of Cézannes, for example, *Pierrot et Arlequin* and *La Montagne Sainte-Victoire*; Van Gogh's turbulent *La Merau Saintes-Maries* and the haunting scene in a prison exercise yard, *La ronde des prisonniers.*

One of Morozov's favorite painters was the lesser-known Impressionist Pierre Bonnard, which explains the prominence of this artist in **Room 17**. But Shchukin showed far more foresight in collecting works by Henri Matisse at a time when the painter was little known, even in France. There are some outstanding paintings by this great artist here, including *L'atelier du peintre*, *Les poissons rouges* and *Les capucines à "la dance."* Shchukin was also interested in Matisse's friend, Pablo Picasso, and acquired more than 50 works by this 20th-century master, among them *Two saltimbanques*, *Acrobat on a ball* and *Portrait of Sabartès*.

Designed by R. I. Klein, the Pushkin Fine Arts Museum was founded in 1912 by I. V. Tsvetaev, professor of Art History at Moscow University and father of the poet Marina Tsvetaeva. It originally housed a large collection of plaster casts and copies of great classical sculptures. These, and antiquities from Egypt, the Near East, Rome, and Byzantium, can still be seen on the ground floor.

The Pushkin Museum is renowned for its collection of 20th-century French paintings

Counterfeit money
Two or three items of forged currency appear every day on the streets of Moscow, mostly masquerading as US dollars. The problem is made particularly difficult because Russia is still so much a cash-based society. It is by no means uncommon, for example, for Russian "businessmen" to deposit suitcases containing hundreds of thousands of dollars in cash in local banks.

► **Muzey Revolyutsii (Museum of the Revolution)** 90A4

Tverskaya Ulitsa 21
Metro: Tverskaya
Open: Tue, Thu–Sun 10–6, Wed 11–7

The stone lions guarding the entrance to the Museum of the Revolution are mentioned by Pushkin in his famous poem *Eugene Onegin*. The handsome red building with its white columned portico dates from 1780. The exhibition now consists of a somewhat overwhelming array of documents, photos, paintings, and objects relating to the Revolution of 1905, the Revolutions of 1917, and the attempted *coups* of 1991 and 1993.

► **Okhotniy Ryad (Hunter's Row)** 90B3

Metro: Okhotniy Ryad

Hunter's Row was the principal game market of old Moscow. In the late 1930s it became part of the thoroughfare known as Prospekt Marksa. The green-painted House of Trade Unions (Dom Soyuzov) at No. 10 is sadly overshadowed by the former offices of Gosplan, the State Planning Institute, now the *Duma* (parliament), next door. In the 19th century the House of Trade Unions was the Noblemen's Club, and its ballroom was the place to be seen. The building, a fine example of Russian classical architecture, was designed by M. F. Kazakov in the 1780s. A number of important historical events have taken place here. In 1856 Alexander II addressed the Russian nobility on the need to abolish serfdom. In 1924, more than a million people lined up in temperatures of –17°F to pay their last respects to Lenin, whose body lay in state in the Hall of Columns. Many of his closest colleagues who took their place in the guard of honor on that occasion later found themselves in the dock here during the great Show Trials of 1936–1938. Their persecutor, Stalin, also lay in state here on his death in 1953.

► **Pashkov Dom (Pashkov House)** 90B2

Metro: Okhotniy Ryad

Like many of Moscow's historic buildings, the Pashkov House—named after its original owner, the governor of Siberia, P. Ye Pashkov—has been sadly let down by subsequent architectural developments. The neoclassical building was erected in 1784–1786 to a design by Vasiliy Bazhenov. In 1861 the famous Rumyantsev Museum was housed here. The Soviet government inherited the library collection of more than a million volumes, and in 1925 the library was renamed after V. I. Lenin. The ugly duckling next door is the modern extension, completed in the 1950s.

►► **Petrovskiy Bulvar (Petrovskiy Boulevard)** 90B5–C5

Metro: Chekhovskaya

Petrovskiy, a delightful boulevard with unassuming 19th-century houses, takes its name from the Vysoko-Petrovskiy Monastery nearby, easily distinguishable by its tall red-brick tower and gleaming cupola. It was founded in the 1380s and soon afterward became a fortified monastery on the lines and scale of the Novodevichiy Convent (see page 122). In 1782 Peter the Great was

Class
There is a saying, "Children are the only privileged class in our country"—quote from Soviet era guidebook (Progress Publishers, 1979). In the Soviet era, Progress Publishers was in the vanguard of the Communist propaganda machine. Their guidebooks, which were translated into Western languages, were heavily laced with bold and futuristic statements alluding to Soviet achievements which did not reflect the reality.

ОДЕЖДА

95

forced to take refuge here during the revolt of the *Streltsy*. Nowadays the buildings, which mostly date from the 17th century, are all but inaccessible, but it is possible to glimpse the cluster of small churches and the rows of windows which once belonged to the monastic cells.

Strastnoy Bulvar (Strastnoy Boulevard) 90B5

Metro: Chekhovskaya
The Boulevard Ring which girdles the inner districts of northern Moscow follows the line of a fortified wall erected in the 16th century. These boulevards date from the 18th century; a surprisingly restful atmosphere still prevails here, thanks to the shady pathways and strategically placed park benches. Strastnoy Bulvar is named after the Monastery of the Savior which used to stand at the western end. Tsvetnoy Bulvar (a reference to the local flower market) was a favorite haunt of prostitutes in the 19th century, who picked up clients emerging from the Hermitage Restaurant nearby. The street running north between Strastnoy Bulvar and Petrovskiy Bulvar is Karetniy Ryad, a reference to the coachmakers who once worked here. Sadly, the Hermitage Gardens are now overgrown, but the designers of the Penthouse nightclub have tried surprisingly hard to re-create the appearance of a 19th-century suburban restaurant.

Every visitor knows the GUM shopping arcade, but many Muscovites prefer to shop in the equally stylish Petrovskiy Passage

Gridlock
According to GAI (Russian traffic police), 25 serious and 230 minor car accidents occur in Moscow each day. During 1992 the number of cars in Moscow increased by 120,000, in 1993 (the most recent year for which figures are currently available) by 230,000; similar increases are expected in the future. Moscow now has more than 1,000,000 cars on the roads (120 percent overcapacity).

MOSCOW: TVERSKAYA

Political platform

In August 1917, the Bolshoy was the scene of a state conference called by Prime Minister Kerensky in order to rally support for his ailing government. After making an impassioned two-hour speech Kerensky was given a standing ovation. This rise of the Bolshoy as a political forum continued into the 1930s, when it became customary to precede performances at the theater with political harangues which might go on for the better part of two hours. One visitor recalls that the subject of one of these agitational lectures was a transportation strike—in London!

The Chariot of Apollo, designed by Kavos, was a feature of the original Bolshoy Theater which was destroyed by fire

 ►► **Teatralnaya Ploshchad (Theater Square)** *90C3*

Metro: Teatralnaya Ploshchad

There are three theaters in the square, the Maliy (or Small) Theater, the Bolshoy (*bolshoy* means big) and, opposite the Maliy, the Children's Theater. The Maliy's heyday was in the second half of the 19th century when it was closely associated with the distinguished playwright Alexander Ostrovsky. The Children's Theater was founded in 1921.

Presiding over Theater Square, which was laid out at the beginning of the 19th century, is the majestic **Bolshoy Theater**►►►. The first theater on this site, known as the Petrovskiy, was opened in 1780. A new theater, designed by Osip Bove and Alexander Mikhailov in 1824, was destroyed by fire in 1853 and immediately rebuilt by Albert Kavos in the neoclassical style.

The opera and ballet tradition began in the 18th century, but for most of the 19th century the Bolshoy opera and ballet companies were very much in the shadow of the Mariinskiy Teatr in St. Petersburg. However, the most famous ballet of all, Tchaikovsky's *Swan Lake*, was premiered here by the Bolshoy company in 1877.

During and after the Revolution, the Bolshoy was used for political assemblies. On the first anniversary of the Revolution (November 7, 1918) Lenin unveiled a temporary statue to Marx and Engels in front of the theater. The present granite statue of Marx was not unveiled until 1961.

Anyone passing the theater will be struck by the way the building has been allowed to fall into disrepair. More serious, however, is the undermining of the foundations by the Neglinnaya River, which flows beneath the square. So far commercial pressures have prevented the administration closing the theater for much-needed capital repairs. However, it is possible that the Bolshoy may close at some point—if it does, performances will probably take place at the Palace of Congresses in the Kremlin.

Anton Chekhov

■ **In 1879, a 19-year-old youth from Taganrog, a provincial backwater near the Sea of Azov (southern Russia), came to Moscow to study medicine at the university. He was eventually to find fame there, but not as a doctor. His name was Anton Chekhov.** ■

шара пролетит в пространстве как
дит только глину и голые утесы. В
вственный закон — пропадет и да
. Что же значат стыд перед лавочн
отов, тяжелая дружба Михаила Ав
р и пустяки.
кие рассуждения уже не помогали.
мной шар через миллион лет, как из

By 1886, Chekhov was managing to supplement his income as a medical practitioner by selling humorous stories and sketches to contemporary periodicals. He was now able to support his impoverished family, including his elderly father who had been forced to flee Taganrog after being declared bankrupt. These years marked the start of his literary success.

Triumph Sadly, Chekhov's health deteriorated alarmingly during the following decade. Other family members had developed tuberculosis, and in 1897 Chekhov suffered a massive hemorrhage. At his doctor's insistence, he moved to Yalta in the Crimea. The following year his new play, *The Seagull*, flopped disastrously at its premiere in St. Petersburg. Reluctant to have anything more to do with the stage, Chekhov was persuaded to change his mind by the actor-impresario Konstantin Stanislavsky. Together with his partner, the critic Vladimir Nemirovich-Danchenko, Stanislavsky had recently founded a new theater in Moscow dedicated to the promotion of new dramatic works by the likes of Hauptmann, Ibsen, and Gorky. The Moscow premiere of *The Seagull* on December 17, 1898, was a triumph, restoring Chekhov's confidence in his own talent.

Cherry Orchard One of the leading actresses in the company was the effervescent and highly talented Olga Knipper. She and Chekhov fell in love and were married in 1901. The prolonged separations resulting from Chekhov's enforced exile in the south for the sake of his health were frustrating to both partners and necessitated the exchange of flurries of letters between Moscow and Yalta. Chekhov was able to oversee the rehearsals of his next two plays: *Three Sisters* and *The Cherry Orchard*, and was present at the premiere of the latter on his birthday, January 17, 1904. This was to be his last appearance in public: by now Chekhov's health had broken down irrevocably, and he died in Badenweiler in the Black Forest in July 1904.

Medicine and literature
Although Chekhov earned his medical degree in 1884, his literary career rapidly took over and he only practiced medicine intermittently for a few years after this. His interest in medicine and science never left him though, and his medical background had a strong influence on much of his writing. As he once explained to his publisher Alexei Suvorin: "Medicine is my lawful wife and literature is my mistress. When I get tired of one I spend the night with the other."

A portrait of the young Anton Chekhov

French fashion became a Muscovite fad in the 18th century. Today Christian Dior is building on the tradition

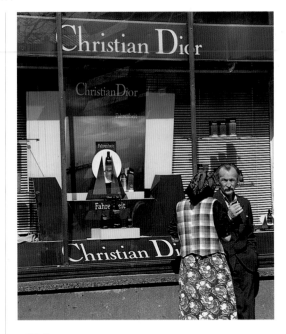

Holiday to remember
The status of the former Soviet Union's most sacrosanct public holiday, the "Anniversary of the Great October Socialist Revolution" on November 7, has been in doubt ever since the disappearance of the Communist order in 1991. It was not until October 1996 that President Boris Yeltsin, then recovering from a heart bypass operation, announced that in the future November 7 would be known as the "Day of National Reconciliation." Russia currently has 11 public holidays, including Independence Day (June 12) and Constitution Day (December 12).

Yesterday's Yar
A little way beyond Tverskaya Ulitsa, on what was once the edge of open country, stood Moscow's Yar restaurant. An ornate wooden building in the traditional Russian style, Yar was famous for its gypsy dancers and singers. On one occasion during World War I, Rasputin was ejected from the restaurant after becoming involved in a brawl. The site is now occupied by the modern Sovetskaya Hotel, and the present Yar restaurant bears no resemblance to the original.

▶▶▶ **Tverskaya Ulitsa (Tver Street)**   *90B4*

Metro: Okhotniy Ryad

From 1935 to 1990 Moscow's main shopping street was named after the "proletarian" writer Maxim Gorky, who actually hailed from Nizhniy-Novgorod. The appearance of the street dates from the late 1930s when the narrow arterial road, with a quaint, almost provincial character, was turned into a highway (the street was widened from about 60 feet to nearly 180 feet). At the same time, many two- and three-story buildings were demolished to make way for ten- to 12-story monoliths, envisioned as being suitably grandiose apartment blocks for the Soviet élite (these still dominate one end of the street). The feel of the neighborhood as it once was can best be gauged by exploring the side streets, many of which were left largely untouched.

Today foreign outlets like Dior, Yves Rocher, McDonald's, and Pizza Hut (pronounced "khat" by Russians) have taken over from the old state stores. There are cafés, expensive clothing shops (well beyond the pockets of most Muscovites), and even nightclubs. The Soviet enterprises with their blunt signs ("Fish," "Milk") are as uninviting as ever, but lines no longer form for food. Most visitors to Moscow soon come to know the Intourist Hotel, a 1960s high-rise on the left-hand side (No. 3). The large gray building with the revolving globe (No. 7) has a more distinguished pedigree. It was designed by the architect Ivan Rerberg in 1927 to house the Central Telegraph Office.

The familiar features of Anton Chekhov, complete with pince-nez, look down benevolently from a wall on the opposite side of the street. **The Moscow Arts Theater▶**, where three of Chekhov's plays, *The Three Sisters*, *Uncle Vanya*, and *The Cherry Orchard*, received their first performances, is a stroll down the street called Kamergerskiy Pereulok. (The new Moscow Arts Theater on Tverskoy Bulvar is under different management.) Farther along Tverskaya Ulitsa is Tverskaya Ploshchad. On the right is the equestrian statue of Prince Yuri Dolgorukiy, the founder of Moscow, and opposite is the building of the Moscow City Hall. In tsarist times this was the residence of the governor-general. The entire building was later moved (!) nearly 50 feet to allow for the widening of the road. Unfortunately, when it was reconstructed, M. F. Kazakov's elegant design of 1782 was "improved," greatly to its detriment.

Beyond the Central Hotel, at No. 14, is the famous food store known popularly as "Yeliseev's" and more prosaically as "Gastronom No. 1." Visitors may admire the luxurious late 19th-century décor, complete with glittering chandeliers, marble counters, and stained glass. The food, too, is an improvement on the standard fare.

A little farther on is **Pushkin Square▶**. Once known as Strastnaya or Passion Square after the 17th-century monastery that used to dominate its northern side, it now honors the famous writer Alexander Pushkin. The statue, by Alexander Opekushin, was erected in 1880, and the unveiling ceremony was attended by two other great writers, Ivan Turgenev and Fedor Dostoevsky. (In the 1960s and 1970s the statue was a favorite assembly point for Soviet dissidents, who were routinely filmed by agents of the KGB.) Also in the neighborhood of the square are the gargantuan Rossiya Cinema and the offices of *Izvestiya*. Beyond the metro station (Pushkinskaya), the handsome red classical building is the Museum of the Revolution, formerly the aristocratic English Club (see page 94). Tverskaya Ulitsa continues to Triumfalnaya Ploshchad (see page 108) as Tverskaya Yamskaya Ulitsa—Triumfalnaya because temporary triumphal arches used to be erected here to welcome visiting tsars and victorious armies.

Exotic ancestry
Alexander Pushkin was descended from an old aristocratic Russian family. His great-grandfather on his mother's side was an African slave named Hannibal, who had been presented to Peter the Great by the Sultan of Turkey. One of Pushkin's first attempts at writing fiction was a historical novel about this ancestor, *The Negro of Peter the Great*, which he began in 1828 but never finished.

The Moscow Arts Theater was converted by the highly innovative architect Fedor Shekhtel in 1902 at the height of Chekhov's dramatic successes. But the theater had been operating earlier and was used for opera performances as well as plays

Playboy
Nikolai, brother of notable icon collector and art patron Stepan Ryabushinsky, was born into a family of wealthy Russian industrialists. In 1906 he founded the influential but short-lived avant-garde arts magazine *Golden Fleece*, which promoted the work of Symbolist writers like Blok, Bely, and Remizov.

Four-times married, Ryabushinsky was a notorious playboy and high lifer. He once spent the enormous sum of 32,000 rubles entertaining guests at Moscow's Strelnya restaurant. The tables were decorated with a profusion of forget-me-nots, and oysters were served from the paws of an enormous bear sculpted from blocks of ice.

▶▶　**Ulitsa Bolshaya Nikitskaya
(Bolshaya Nikitskaya Street)**　　*90A3–B3*

The street was formerly named after a 19th-century radical thinker, Alexander Herzen. Traditionally this was an aristocratic neighborhood: the Naryshkins, Orlovs, and Menshikovs all built palaces here in the 18th century. The beautiful Empire-style former residence of Prince S. A. Menshikov (No. 12, accessible via Ulitsa Ogareva) was completed shortly after the great fire of 1812. The yellow building at No. 13 also began life as a palace, but is better known today as the **Moscow Conservatory of Music▶**, founded in 1866 by Nikolai Rubinstein. Famous alumni include the pianist-composers Sergei Rachmaninov and Alexander Scriabin, while one of the founding professors was Pyotr Ilych Tchaikovsky. The ugly, russet-colored building on the left-hand side of Ulitsa Bolshaya Nikitskaya, near the corner of Sobinovskiy Pereulok, is the **Mayakovsky Theater▶**, famous in the 1920s for its association with the experimental theater director Vsevolod Meyerhold. Meyerhold staged Mayakovsky's most famous play *The Bedbug* here in 1929. The green-domed Church of the Great Ascension (Tserkov Bolshovo Vozneseniya) was built 1798–1848 and is currently being restored. On the other side of Ulitsa Kachalova (No. 6/2) is a later architectural monument, the former home of wealthy icon collector Stepan Ryabushinsky, which is now the **Gorky Museum▶**. This boldly unconventional brick villa, decorated with exquisite mosaic friezes and windows patterned with wrought iron, was designed for the merchant millionaire in 1900 by Fedor Shekhtel, then Russia's most innovative architect. It's worth popping in to see the interior, including the highly unusual staircase.

The fine detail of the Vysoko-Petrovskiy Monastery is still hidden from public view

▶　　**Ulitsa Petrovka (Petrovka Street)**　　*90C4*

Petrovka Street takes its name from the Vysoko-Petrovskiy Monastery. Across the road from the Bolshoy Theater is the gray, neogothic façade of TsUM (Central Universal Store) but familiar to locals by its prerevolutionary name of Muir and Mirrielees (the original British owners). Mention the Petrovka to Muscovites and they are more likely to think of police headquarters. The enormous classical mansion, just past the intersection with Petrovskiy Bulvar, was taken over by the tsarist Corps of Gendarmes as its barracks in the 19th century. In the 1930s it was used by Stalin's notorious secret police, the NKVD.

The distinctive gables of the Convent of the Nativity, now once again functioning as a monastic building

101

Monumental folly?
The growing number of monuments appearing on the streets of Moscow is good news for one of Russia's most controversial artists, Zurab Tsereteli. His most recent commission is a 300-foot bronze statue of Peter the Great, which will tower over an artificial island in the Moskva River (Tseretelli also has plans for a yacht club, a Peter the Great Museum, and a Petrovskiy restaurant). Tsereteli's other commissions have included a portrait of Margaret Thatcher and a statue of St. George for the United Nations in New York City. He created a furor when his plans for landscaping the giant Manège shopping complex beside the Kremlin walls led to the destruction of the wrought-iron railings of the Aleksandrovskiy Gardens, a UNESCO world heritage site.

► **Ulitsa Rozhdestvenka (Rozhdestvenka Street)** *90C4*

The Convent of the Nativity of the Virgin, from which the street takes its name, is on the corner of Rozhdestvenskiy Bulvar. It was founded in 1386 by the wife of Prince Andrei Serphukhovskiy, son of Ivan Kalita, and grew into one of the chain of fortified monasteries which protected the city. The small white cathedral with the single dome and remarkable tiered gabling dates from 1501–1505; there is also a church, dedicated to St. John of Zlatoust, and some monastic cells.

►► **Ulitsa Vozdvizhenka (Vozdvizhenka Street)** *90B2*

This is the best-preserved stretch of the former Prospekt Kalinina. The building with the semicircular colonnade at the corner of Ulitsa Granovskovo is the former home of the fabulously wealthy Count Sheremetev, whose family once owned 200,000 serfs. Across the street, at No. 5, is a mansion by the School of M. F. Kazakov, now the **Shchusev Museum of Architecture►**. But the most spectacular building on the Vozdvizhenka is at No. 16. This **moorish-style castle►** was built for the merchant A. A. Morozov by V. A. Mazyrin in 1894–1898 and is modeled on a castle in Sintra, Portugal, which took Morozov's fancy while on vacation. In Communist times it was the House of Friendship, where young people from the West were introduced to officially approved Soviet youngsters over tea and cakes. (The street continues into Noviy Arbat, see page 108.)

Money no object
It is said that when the architect Mazyrin first asked Morozov in what style he would like his house built, he replied: "In all styles, I have the money."
One of Morozov's relatives once lost a million rubles in a single evening of gambling at Moscow's English Club and later inspired a popular play called *The Gentleman* (his nickname).

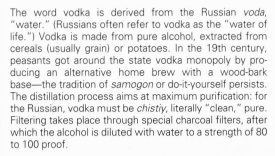

■ In terms of the number of bottles consumed annually, vodka is the world's most popular drink. This is strange when one considers that it is colorless, flavorless, and burns the throat. This "water of life" is consumed with a passion by hardened Russian drinkers, who claim that it can be consumed without the dreaded hangover. ■

The Russian national drink is still sold at bargain-basement prices—but study labels carefully

Supply and demand
The state-run Liviz factory in St. Petersburg produces 200,000 liters of vodka a day, many for export, and more than 50 different types, including Stolichnaya.

The word vodka is derived from the Russian *voda*, "water." (Russians often refer to vodka as the "water of life.") Vodka is made from pure alcohol, extracted from cereals (usually grain) or potatoes. In the 19th century, peasants got around the state vodka monopoly by producing an alternative home brew with a wood-bark base—the tradition of *samogon* or do-it-yourself persists. The distillation process aims at maximum purification: for the Russian, vodka must be *chistiy*, literally "clean," pure. Filtering takes place through special charcoal filters, after which the alcohol is diluted with water to a strength of 80 to 100 proof.

Scientific discovery Not for nothing do the Russians refer to their national drink as the demon vodka. The 17th-century German traveler Olearius once observed that Russians "are more addicted to drunkenness than any nation in the world." In 1865, concern about the level of alcohol abuse led the government to commission a report from the famous Russian scientist Dmitri Mendeleev, who found that the body could best assimilate alcohol in the proportion 40 percent spirit to 60 percent water. From that time on, the imperial vodka factories followed Mendeleev's recommendations—but without curing the nation's passion for vodka.

President Gorbachev, himself a teetotaller, waged his own war on alcoholism in the mid-1980s. The drinking age was increased from 18 to 21, vodka rationed to two bottles a month, and state factories ordered to produce more fruit juices. The campaign fizzled out after little more than two years. Boris Yeltsin's well-known preference for the hard stuff is more in keeping with the Russian character, although his vodka tax puts the more expensive brands beyond the pockets of most Russians who earn their living honestly. There are now plans to restore the vodka monopoly.

Vodka tips Normally nestled in an ice bucket, vodka is drunk neat in one gulp and chased with a mouthful of food. It goes down particularly well with *zakuski* (hors d'oeuvres)—smoked salmon, salted herring, marinated mushrooms, salami, caviar, etc. To quell the fiery taste, some Russians advise exhaling before gulping, while others recommend deep inhalation. Many Russians swear by a shot of vodka with a dash of pepper as a cure for the common cold. Victims of the 1986 Chernobyl nuclear plant disaster drank copious amounts of vodka because rumor had it that the vodka would neutralize any

nuclear particles absorbed into the body. Whatever its therapeutic effects may be, vodka breaks down inhibitions and produces a state of conviviality which the Russians refer to as *dusha-dushe* (heart-to-heart). When a Russian taps his throat it means "it's time to start drinking." It's impossible to refuse this invitation to conviviality. You may wish to sidestep the offer, but you can be sure you are in for a lively evening.

Best buys The most popular Russian brands of vodka are Stolichnaya, Pshenichnaya, Russkaya, and Moskovskaya. These brands are often counterfeited nowadays and sold at street kiosks. (One survey discovered that as many as eight bottles out of ten are not genuine.) To be on the safe side look for imported brands like Rasputin, Derzhavnaya (Autocrat)—the label carries a portrait of Nicholas II—and of course Smirnoff; also the high-quality Russian brand *Pyotr Veliki* (distinguished by a picture of Peter the Great).

In hard-currency shops and bars you will also see flavored vodkas such as Pertsovka (hot peppered vodka); Limonaya with lemon; Okhotnichnaya with juniper berries, ginger, and cloves; and Starka with apple and pear leaf. To the Russian, however, flavored vodka is sacrilegious.

How to tell fake vodka
Tried and tested methods of spotting an impostor include: checking that the label has been applied evenly by machine and not glued on by hand; tilting the bottle upside down and shaking—if genuine, a mass of tiny bubbles will rise to the surface; finally, checking the seal, which should fit tightly and not break easily.

A vodka vendor in a street kiosk

Arbatskaya

The name Arbat is derived from a Tatar word meaning "suburb." In the 16th century this area was the servants' quarters of the imperial household, the atmosphere of which is still preserved in the names of the side streets—Silver Lane, Carpenters' Lane, Old Stables Lane, and Pastry Cook Lane. Like neighboring Prechistenka, the Arbat became an aristocratic neighborhood in the early 1800s, and by the turn of the century had become a popular place to shop. Much of the area's more picturesque sights were destroyed when Khrushchev ordered the building of Kalinin Prospekt. But the tourist potential of this atmospheric neighborhood is now being belatedly exploited. The main street has been prettified and pedestrianized as a cobbled area and is now the haunt of artists, poets, street entertainers, and souvenir sellers, all vying with each other for much-sought-after foreign currency.

The stained-glass window is an unusual feature of the Glinka Museum of Musical Culture

Souvenirs
The Arbat is well known for its great number of gift shops. Here, you can buy fur coats, lacquer boxes, Lenin memorabilia, face masks of political leaders, and some of the huge surplus of ex-Soviet military gear like army belts, buckles, and uniforms. There may be pickpockets operating in this area though, so be sure to watch wallets and purses.

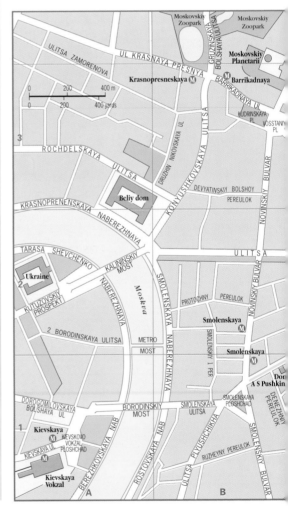

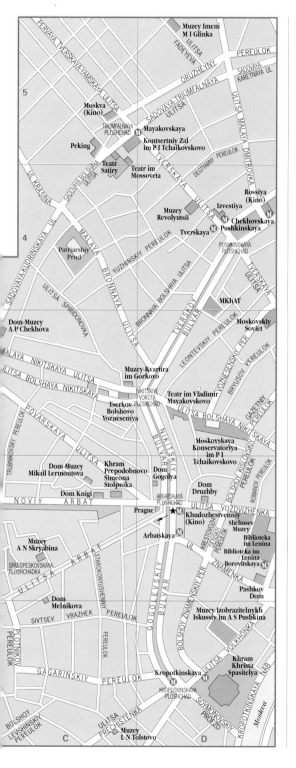

Inducements

President Yeltsin once offered to build a new parliamentary complex beside the White House on the site of a soccer field. The deputies were more impressed when he announced that each of them would receive a four-bedroom apartment in the complex (at an estimated cost of $500 million).

Some 2,000 Turkish workers were employed to repair the White House in double-quick time after the 1993 *coup*. Many were accommodated in the Ukraine Hotel, opposite, where they were to be seen making the most of the bars and the prostitutes, whom not even the severest of Moscow's doormen could keep at bay.

Modern symbol of the embattled Russian democracy—the distinctive tower of the White House

Politics

"Stalinism was positive in that we avoided venereal disease."

"Japan, China, and the West should understand that they can torture Russia for a long time, but when Russia rises there will be nothing left of Japan or Europe."

—Vladimir Zhirinovsky, leader of Russia's Liberal Democrats.

Rough justice

Record crime levels and an increasing recourse to violence by members of the public are imposing an impossible strain on Russia's creaking legal system. This was highlighted recently when Valery Ivankov was fined for illegal street trading, and his stock of children's clothing confiscated. Ivankov's response was to buy a knife with which he entered the courtroom in Ostankino the following day and stabbed the judge, who later died. The profession of judge has become so dangerous and so poorly paid that currently 95 out of 450 posts remain vacant.

Chekhov House Museum—the writer's home in the 1880s

► ► **Beliy Dom (White House)**   *104A3*

Konyushkovskaya Ulitsa

The "White House" is the ironic popular name for the functional modern building across the river from the Ukraine Hotel that was once the administrative headquarters of the Russian Republic of the USSR. It first shot to notoriety in August 1991 when a group of conservative plotters opposed to Soviet President Mikhail Gorbachev staged a *coup* while he was on vacation in the Crimea. Opposition to the *coup* centered on the White House, by now headquarters of the Russian parliament and of its President Boris Yeltsin. In a moment of high drama, Yeltsin clambered onto a tank in order to stir up popular indignation and rally thousands of demonstrators to head for parliament and defend it against the conspirators. In the end the *coup* collapsed because of the hopeless incompetence of its instigators and because crucial sections of the armed forces and even the KGB remained loyal to Yeltsin. The events of August 1991 proved to be a turning point, leading not only to the demise of the Communist Party but of the Soviet Union itself.

Yet within two years of Yeltsin's election as president, disillusionment had become widespread, as the promised reforms stagnated and inflation soared to the accompaniment of a frightening breakdown in law and order. In September 1993, when Yeltsin issued a decree suspending the constitution for three months, Parliament mutinied and Yeltsin's deputy, Alexander Rutskoy, declared himself "acting president." Once again, action centered on the White House as Yeltsin lay siege to parliament, a state of affairs which lasted 11 days. Finally, on October 4, after the recapture of the television station at Ostankino and other strategic points, army tanks shelled Yeltsin's opponents into submission. Television cameras from around the world captured the dramatic events as the upper stories were subsumed by flames and the 300 defendants of the White House surrendered. The institutions of government are now dispersed around Moscow, but the restored White House, now called Government House, is no longer the presidential office.

► ► **Dom-Muzey A. P. Chekhova**
(Chekhov House Museum)   *105C3*

Sadovaya-Kudrinskaya Ulitsa 6
Metro: Barrikadnaya
Open: Tue, Thu, Sat, and Sun 11–5, Wed and Fri 2–7

The Chekhov House Museum was the author's home from 1886 to 1890, the period when he finally abandoned practicing medicine to become a full-time writer. Chekhov nicknamed the modest but charming two-story building "the commode." The museum is all but obscured by other buildings, but when Chekhov lived here the Garden Ring was a quiet suburban road lined with trees. The brass nameplate on the door is still inscribed Doctor A. P. Chekhov. The furnishings and study where Chekhov worked on his first major play, *Ivanov*, and many of his short stories are as they would have been in the 1880s, authenticity being guaranteed by the writer's wife, the actress Olga Knipper, who was present at the opening of the museum in 1954.

Muzey A. N. Skryabina (Scriabin Museum) 105C2

Ulitsa Vakhtangova 11
Metro: Arbatskaya
Open: Tue–Sun 10–6; closed last Fri of the month

This museum is the former apartment of the eminent Russian composer Alexander Scriabin (1872–1915). A contemporary of Rachmaninov's at the Moscow Conservatory, Scriabin established an international reputation as a concert pianist but was also a highly original and distinctly Russian composer who is best known for his mystical orchestral works, including *Prometheus* and *Poema Ekstaza*. Scriabin spent much of the latter part of his life giving concerts abroad. The house-museum has been preserved as it was in his lifetime. Regular concerts of Scriabin's music are given here on Sundays, and the works of other composers on weekdays.

▶ Muzey Imeni M. I. Glinka (Glinka Museum) 105D5

Ulitsa Fadeyeva 4
Metro: Mayakovskaya
Open: Wed–Mon noon–7; closed last Fri of the month

The Glinka Museum of Musical Culture is named after the founder of modern Russian music, Mikhail Glinka (1804–1857). As well as its displays of musical instruments, scores, letters, and other items relating to the great Russian composers of the 18th and 19th centuries, it is also a good place to enjoy concerts and temporary exhibitions.

▶ Patriarshiy Prud (Patriarch's Pond) 105C4

The small but delightful park running alongside Malaya Bronnaya Ulitsa and known as Patriarch's Pond was a favorite with one of the great satirists of the Soviet period, Mikhail Bulgakov (1891–1940), who lived nearby. The reference to the Patriarch dates back to a time when the area belonged to the Orthodox Church. This beautifully secluded garden, with the pond as its central feature, also contains a statue of the 19th-century poet and satirist I. A. Krylov (1768–1844).

Harsh truths
"People have been fed on sweets for too long," wrote the Russian poet Mikhail Lermontov. "Bitter medicines and harsh truths are needed now." Among these "harsh truths" was the poet's belief that many members of Russia's ruling class were leading "superfluous" and useless lives, much of which he reflected in his most successful work, the novel *A Hero of Our Time*.

107

Moscow's homey 19th-century character is preserved at Patriarch's Pond

MOSCOW: ARBATSKAYA

The pedestrianization of Ulitsa Arbat which allowed musicians and other street performers to entertain around the clock was one of the first signs of a more welcoming attitude to Western visitors

► **Triumfalnaya Ploshchad (Triumfalnaya Square)**   *105C5*

The square is named after the triumphal arches that were erected on this site in the 18th century to welcome visiting tsars and victorious armies. For a time it was renamed after the Futurist poet Vladimir Mayakovsky (1893–1930)—the metro station still bears his name and his defiant statue stands by the Tverskaya Ulitsa underpass. The square intersects with the frantically busy Garden Beltway. The most important building here is the Tchaikovsky Concert Hall, built 1938–1940, with its ten-columned portico, now rather the worse for wear. The wedding-cake style skyscraper with the spire and clock is the Peking Hotel. Also on the square are the Moskva Cinema and the Mossoviet and Satire Theaters.

► **Ulitsa Noviy Arbat (New Arbat Street)**   *105C2*

New Arbat Street is a continuation of Ulitsa Vozdvizhenka (see page 101). Dating from the 1960s when it was known as Prospekt Kalinina, this "Brave New World" of a street is an uncomfortable mix of shops and apartments, housed in a series of identical high-rise blocks. Opposite Arbatskaya metro station and the Prague Restaurant (see page 108) is the 17th–century church of St. Simon Stylites, slightly out of place in the modernistic surroundings. Occupying the ground floor of the first high-rise on the right is Dom Knigi (the House of Books).

A small detour along Malaya Molchanovka Ulitsa leads, on the right, to the house of the 19th-century poet **Mikhail Lermontov** (1814–1841)► (*Open* Wed and Fri 2–9, Tue, Sat, and Sun 11–7) who was an exact contemporary of Pushkin. Much of Lermontov's life mirrored that of his literary peer: his work also fell foul of the censors and, like Pushkin, he died young in an unnecessary duel. Take the metro to Arbatskaya and from there to Malaya Molchanovka Ulitsa 2.

The premises opposite the House of Books are among the many, such as the Cherry Casino Club, which are now privatized.

Bulgakov
Mikhail Bulgakov, like Anton Chekhov a doctor by profession, leapt to fame with his novel about the Civil War, *The White Guard*, which he adapted for the stage in 1926 as *The Days of the Turbins*. Between 1926 and 1929 he wrote several successful stage plays, but his highly satirical style provoked atttacks in the Soviet press and his work was subsequently suppressed as Bulgakov fell from favor. While awaiting permission to emigrate, Bulgakov worked on his masterpiece, the novel *The Master and Margarita*, which he completed in 1938, a year before going blind. He died in 1940.

Walk Exploring the Arbat

The Arbat is an area for strolling in, either during the day or in the evening. The easiest way to approach this delightful part of old Moscow is to walk up **Ulitsa Vozdvizhenka** and **Novy Arbat**, turning left just after the overpass near the **Prague Restaurant**. Alternatively, take the metro and alight at Arbatskaya.

Begin at **Arbatskaya Ploshchad** (Arbat Square). The building of a concrete underpass here involved the demolition of two historic churches and changed the once secluded character of the square forever. Two lone survivors from earlier days are the **Khudozhestvenniy Cinema**, one of Russia's first, designed by Shekhtel in 1912 (on the corner of Novy Arbat, near the metro station) and the **Prague Restaurant** opposite. Before the Revolution this was known to Moscow cab drivers as the *braga* or brewery. Once a small pub, it was transformed into a restaurant on the eve of World War I.

Take the turning by the restaurant into **Ulitsa Arbat**. This quaint street is popular with tourists, although Muscovites frequent it too. It was once Moscow's leading shopping street, but now it's a haunt of sidewalk artists, street poets, and musicians. The lower section is particularly attractive with its bookstores, antique shops, and cafés, among them Ogni Arbata (Lights of Arbat), Skazki Starovo Arbata (Tales of Old Arbat), and Russkiy Traktir (*traktir* is the old word for inn or pub). There is also a fresh fruit shop, a post office, and a McDonald's.

Literary Arbat This little neck of the woods has a number of literary associations. The poet Alexander Pushkin lived in the blue building at **No. 53 Ulitsa Arbat** for a short period not long after his marriage to Natalia Goncharova in 1831. The novelist and story writer Nikolai Gogol spent his final years in a house on **Nikitskiy**

Bulvar on the far side of Arbat Square, which contains a small museum. This is where Gogol completed the novel *Dead Souls,* the manuscript of which he later burned in a state of dementia.

The 1920s satirist Mikhail Bulgakov lived on **Furmanova Ulitsa**, while Boris Pasternak set several of the episodes in *Doctor Zhivago* on **Sivtsev Vrazhek Pereulok**. More recently, the novelist Anatoly Rybakov had an immense success with his novel *Deti Arbata* (available in English as *Children of the Arbat*).

Rural Arbat Nineteenth-century guidebooks unfailingly comment on the idyllic, almost bucolic character of the Arbat. At the time, it was still a maze of rambling lanes, country cottages, flowerbeds, and stables.

Aristocratic Arbat Traces of this old area can be found down neighboring streets and alleyways like **Starokonyushenniy Pereulok**. The walk finishes at the southern end of **Ulitsa Arbat**, near **Smolenskaya** metro station.

Street artists ply their trade in the Arbat

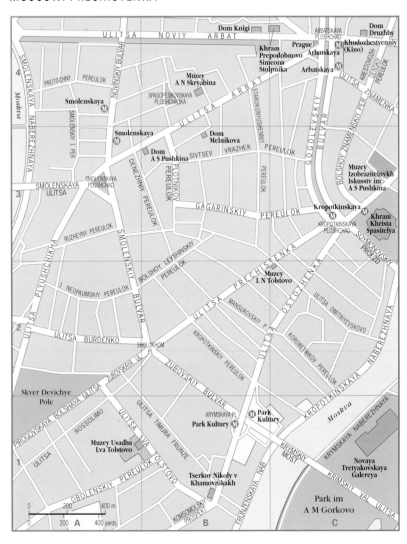

Prechistenka

The name means "most pure," from the Novodevichiy Convent at the end of the road, where the icon of the Most Pure Virgin was venerated. By the 18th century, it was a residential area for families of noble pedigree like the Orlovs and Dolgorukovs. Prince Peter Kropotkin, the famous anarchist, was born near here and Ulitsa Prechistenka was once called after him—the metro station still bears his name. Later, the area was occupied by professionals and businessmen, like the merchant millionaire Sergei Tretyakov, brother of the famous art patron Pavel, and by writers and members of the intelligentsia, among them Ivan Turgenev and Russia's most famous author, Count Lev Tolstoy. Parts of the area that still have wooden houses are akin to neighboring Arbatskaya and retain a rural feel.

► **Dom Melnikova (Melnikov House)** *110B3*

Krivoarbatskiy Pereulok 10
Metro: Kropotkinskaya

The Melnikov house was designed by the remarkable Constructivist architect Konstantin Melnikov for his own family in 1927. Honeycombed and cylindrical, the building was to have been a prototype for Moscow housing development built on the basis of the single family unit. Melnikov's originality and vision are preserved here, with the emphasis on light and unity—the various living quarters, linked by a spiral staircase, are divided only by partial screens. In 1987, the house was declared a historic monument, and there are plans to open it as a museum in the future.

► **Khram Khrista Spasitelya**
   (Cathedral of Christ the Savior) *110C3*

Ulitsa Volkhonka
Metro: Kropotkinskaya

The original Cathedral of Christ the Savior, designed by Konstantin Ton in 1883, was demolished in 1931 to make way for a colossal Palace of Soviets which was never actually built—the Moskva Swimming Pool later occupied the site. In 1994 the decision was made to reconstruct the cathedral in time for Moscow's 850th anniversary in 1997. The cost, in excess of $150 million, has been the subject of fierce controversy.

► **Muzey L. N. Tolstovo**
   (Tolstoy Museum) *110C2*

Ulitsa Prechistenka 11
Metro: Kropotkinskaya
Open: Tue and weekends 10–6, Wed and Fri 12–7

This museum, devoted to the life and work of novelist Count Lev Tolstoy, has no historical connection with the writer and should be seen as complementing, and on no account replacing, the Tolstoy Estate-Museum (see page 112). Housed in an Empire-style building once owned by one of Russia's oldest aristocratic families, the Lopukhins, the exhibition consists chiefly of first editions, manuscripts, photographs, paintings, and portraits. The ideological slant of the museum, emphasizing Tolstoy's role as would-be social reformer, has been somewhat watered down.

The son of award-winning architect Konstantin Melnikov at work in the house built by his father

Old Prechistenka
"A few yards farther on we turned down what might be a lane in a country village... There are trees, two or three small laburnums or acacias and a flowerbed, and cocks and hens are walking about on a grass plot; there is perhaps a cow and a stable and a coachhouse."
—G. T. Lowth, *Around the Kremlin,* 1868

Peasants
"The shock heads of matted hair and full, unkempt beards of the peasants, combined with the low foreheads and often brutish countenances, gave some of them the appearance of huge Skye terriers, rather than human beings. In cheap bazaars and at crowded church services, sheepskin-clad individuals should be given a wide berth by the tourist, as close contact is by no means pleasant."'
—Curtis Guild, *Britons and Muscovites,* 1888

Museum guides
On entering any of Moscow's literary museums, be ready to don the obligatory overshoes: the authorities do not like wear and tear on the nice parquet flooring.

Also be prepared to be accosted by the enthusiastic old ladies on duty there, who are always eager to reveal the museum's hidden secrets, but in Russian only. Although some of the venues provide typewritten guides in English, there is an official guide at Pushkin's house and a recorded commentary featuring some of his poetry.

▶▶▶ **Muzey-Usadba Lva Tolstovo
(Lev Tolstoy Estate-Museum)** *110A1*

Ulitsa Lva Tolstova 21
Metro: Kropotkinskaya
Open: Tue–Sun 10–6; closed Mon and the last day of the month

The Tolstoy Estate-Museum is one of the most interesting in Russia and should not be missed. It is both an evocative monument to Russia's greatest and most famous novelist, and a wonderful window onto the world of the late 19th century and life as it was lived by a member of the privileged classes. The building is a fine example of a Russian timberhouse and a reminder that even in Tolstoy's lifetime 90 percent of Moscow's buildings were constructed of wood.

The ticket office (*kassa*) for the Tolstoy Estate-Museum is at the side of the main house. Photography is permitted inside but it is necessary to buy a special, though inexpensive, entry ticket beforehand. The entrance to each room has a placard explaining its purpose and contents in several languages, including a rather quirky but serviceable English. Count Lev Tolstoy (1828–1910) bought this house in 1882 and wintered here until 1901—his summers were spent at his birthplace, Yasnaya Polyana, an estate about 120 miles south of Moscow (see page 114).

By the time he moved in here, Tolstoy was already an established author, having written his two masterpieces, *War and Peace* and *Anna Karenina*, as well as *A Confession*, a work which describes his religious conversion following a profound spiritual crisis. While living in Moscow he wrote another novel, *Resurrection,* and two of his finest short stories, *The Death of Ivan Ilych* and *The Kreutzer Sonata.*

It is worth exploring the estate outbuildings which comprise: the caretaker's house; an additional wing dating from the 1830s that contained a publishing office for Tolstoy's works, as well as rooms on the third floor where he lived while the main house was being rebuilt; a barn for horses, cows, and a carriage; an outside kitchen.

Sixteen rooms in the house have been preserved as Tolstoy left them. A table in the dining room is still laid for dinner, which was heralded by the cuckoo on the German grandfather clock summoning each member of the family to their preassigned place (Tolstoy's long-suffering wife, Sofia, sat at the head). Marital relations between the couple were often strained, not least on account of the author's conversion to total sexual abstinence, the consequences of which are hinted at in the bedroom, complete with dividing screen. The bedcover was knitted by Sofia for her husband. The children's wing contains a playroom, a classroom, a corner for the family's German nanny, and bedrooms for the 13 children—abstinence evidently came rather late in the day!

Rubinstein, Rimsky-Korsakov, and Rachmaninov all played on the piano in the hall, sometimes accompanying the great bass Chaliapin. Other distinguished visitors to the house included the playwrights Chekhov, Gorky, and Ostrovsky. The tiny housekeeper's room has its own icon corner, a feature of every Russian home. Tolstoy's valet also had his own room, close to the writer's surprisingly modest working quarters, which include not only expected items like desk, pens, and paperweights, but also dumbbells, a shoemaking kit, and a bicycle, all testifying to a decidedly eccentric lifestyle.

Among the delightful period pieces are a Chinese billiard table, numerous embroidered cloths and fabrics (one bearing the signatures of family and friends), some children's drawings, copybooks and toys (including a wooden rocking horse), paintings by eminent artists such as Ilya Repin, beautifully crafted samovars and oil lamps, a Turkish ottoman, a stuffed bear, and a chess set. Tolstoy's personal effects include his overcoat and boots.

As you leave, look for other surviving remnants of Prechistenka on this street, including more houses in the log cabin style, the whitewashed communal house (No. 10) belonging to the Weavers' Guild (see below), and some stone houses of the 19th century, richly ornamented with stucco.

▶▶▶ Tserkov Nikoly v Khamovnikakh
(Church of St. Nicholas of the Weavers) *110B1*

Ulitsa Lva Tolstovo 2
Metro: Park Kultury. Trolleybus: 28

The Church of St. Nicholas of the Weavers is one of the heartwarming sights of Moscow. The Weavers moved into this quarter of the city and commissioned this beautiful church in 1676. It was completed six years later. Rising proudly at the western end is the bell tower with a decorated baroque tent roof. The hall-like refectory links it with the church proper, an exuberant structure ornamented with dark green and brick-red stucco and surmounted by five golden cupolas that shimmer brilliantly in the sunlight. Visit the church on a Sunday and there's the opportunity to observe or take part in an Orthodox service, a quite breathtaking experience for the uninitiated. Ancients begging for alms at the gate complete a scene redolent of Russia's past.

Unlikely relationship
The famous American dancer Isadora Duncan, an ardent pro-Bolshevik who had danced in Moscow after the Revolution, opened a dance school at Ulitsa Prechistenka No. 20 in 1921. At about the same time, she met and fell madly in love with the mentally unstable poet Sergei Yesenin. Despite the fact that she spoke no Russian, and he no English, they married in 1922. Their brief, stormy relationship was the source of much scandal and gossip. In 1925, not long after their divorce, Yesenin committed suicide in a Leningrad (St. Petersburg) hotel room after writing a final poem in his own blood.

113

The stunning decoration of the Church of St. Nicholas of the Weavers was inspired by the embroidery of the weavers who commissioned it

Tolstoy's country estate

■ **For more than 60 years Russia's most famous novelist, Lev Tolstoy, lived on his beloved country estate of Yasnaya Polyana, one of the most beautiful country houses in Russia, near the town of Tula, about 120 miles south of Moscow. The name means "Clear Glade."** ■

Tolstoy memorabilia at the house-museum

Tolstoy's tipple?
At Yasnaya Polyana they are selling something that sounds very Russian—Tolstoy vodka. The label shows a picture of the great man and is on sale for 3,300 rubles (about $2) at the gate to the estate. Unfortunately it is manufactured in Germany. "It is blasphemy," says descendant Vladimir Tolstoy, who has threatened to sue the manufacturer.

Anna Karenina
Hollywood came to St. Petersburg for a few weeks in 1996 when movie director Bernard Rose shot several scenes from *Anna Karenina* on location here. All the film's stars—including French actress Sophie Marceau who plays Anna, Sean Bean (Vronsky), James Fox (Karenin), and Alfred Molina (Levin)—were in town, to the delight of autograph hunters who had been led to believe that the relevant scenes would be shot in Prague to save money. Now St. Petersburg's movie-goers—as well as its visitors—can have fun identifying the locations.

The aristocratic Tolstoy family had lived on the estate at Yasnaya Polyana since the late 17th century, and Lev Nikolaevich was born in the manor house here on August 28, 1828. It was here too that he eventually settled, returning with his bride, Sofia Andreevna, in 1862. In his diary he wrote of "immense happiness ... it is impossible that all this should end, except with life itself."

Fertile territory Yasnaya Polyana was to prove fertile ground in more ways than one—apart from fathering 13 children by his wife and at least as many out of wedlock, Tolstoy was to write his two greatest novels here: *War and Peace*, an astonishing panorama of Russian life set in the Napoleonic era which expounds Tolstoy's thesis that history is made not by the grandiose scheming of great men, but by the chance actions of ordinary people; and *Anna Karenina*, the study of a "fallen woman" whose plight Tolstoy describes without sentimentality or passing moral judgment. Life at Yasnaya Polyana was anything but dull. Tolstoy founded a village school for local peasant children, devising the curriculum from his own highly individual educational theories, based on fairness, understanding, and mutual respect.

Convention to the winds The writer's unconventional attitudes and behavior became more marked after a mid-life crisis in the 1870s. He developed his own form of Christianity, preaching pacifism, nonviolence, and the precepts of Jesus's Sermon on the Mount. He became a vegetarian, worked in the fields, and wore simple peasant smocks. He even set up his own printing press to propagate his beliefs. In time Tolstoy became a cult figure, as thousands of ardent young people came to Yasnaya Polyana to sit at his feet. One of these disciples, V. G. Chertkov, caused a rift between Tolstoy and his wife, who was jealous of Chertkov's influence and increasingly antagonized by what she saw as eccentric and dangerous tendencies in her husband's behavior. After waking to find his wife going through papers in his study one morning in October 1910, Tolstoy left Yasnaya Polyana, taking his youngest daughter Alexandra and his doctor with him. He drove to the nearest train station, but was forced to leave the train at the tiny halt at Astapovo when he was taken ill with influenza. As disciples, family, well-wishers, and the press converged on the station waiting room, Tolstoy lay dying, his wife shut outside and forced to peep in at him through a window. Tolstoy died on November 7, 1910. His last words were: "To seek, always to seek."

Master portraitist Ilya Repin chose to paint Tolstoy wearing a traditional peasant smock, in his favorite pose as a simple man of the people

Descendants
Vladimir Tolstoy, the writer's great-grandson, was chosen by 150 descendants in 1992 to take charge of the Yasnaya Polyana Estate. But he has no legal claim to ownership and is paid a salary of only $160 per month.

House-museum Today Yasnaya Polyana is open to the public as a house-museum (*Open* Wed–Sun 10–5:30), and Intourist runs regular bus trips here. Tolstoy spent most of his idyllic childhood exploring the rambling country park, and visitors too will enjoy following pathways overhung with dappled birch, or wandering through woodland and meadows strewn with flowers and punctuated with ponds and streams. Tolstoy's younger brother once told him: "Happiness is to be found in the place of the green stick." The author is buried on that very spot, beneath a simple mound of earth.

The manor house has been preserved exactly as Tolstoy left it. There are portraits of Lev, by Ilya Repin, of Sofia, by Valentin Serov, and of their daughter Tatiana by her friend Yulia Igumnova. By the washstand in Tolstoy's bedroom are his dumbbells, riding crop, and walking sticks—exercise played an important role in the writer's daily life. The library contains more than 22,000 books written not only in Russian, but also in French and English, in which Tolstoy was fluent.

Old aristocracy
In 1995 London's Dorchester Hotel was the venue for the seventh War and Peace ball, organized by members of the Tolstoy family to raise money for the Russian and Greek Orthodox churches. The ball was attended by many White Russian aristocrats. Legendary names like Tolstoy, Galitzyn, and Obolensky mingled with Russia's new rich, who had flown in specially for the occasion along with their bodyguards.

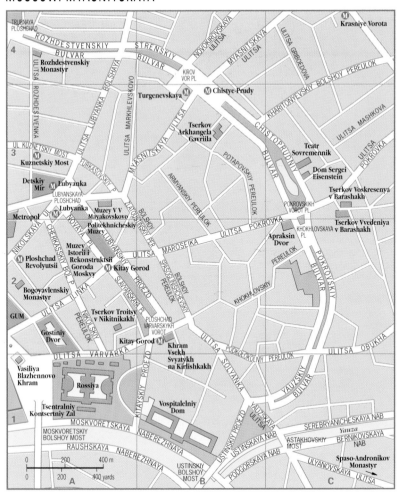

Myasnitskaya

This eastern neighborhood of central Moscow was one of the poorest parts of the city. It is known as "the Butchers"—after the meat market that was once here. At the intersection of Podkolokolniy Pereulok and Solyanka Ulitsa was the notorious Khitrov market, once the haunt of criminals and prostitutes. The market, Moscow's Skid Row, was covered by a latticed iron canopy called a *balagan* and sold secondhand clothes, paper flowers, stale bread, - omelets made from rotten eggs, not to mention passports for men and women on the run. The Khitrov was also a labor market for artisans and casual workers—carpenters, painters, laborers, and draymen. The neighborhood was a warren of narrow, twisting streets lit only by kerosene lamps and punctuated by taverns, brothels, and cheap lodging houses. The area was visited by Tolstoy and chronicled by Gorky in his play *The Lower Depths*. The actors even visited Khitrov to study conditions at first hand.

▶▶ **Chistoprudniy Bulvar
(Chistoprudniy Boulevard)** *116C3*

Metro: Chistye-Prudy

The name comes from a pond where butchers' waste was once dumped. In 1703 it was cleaned of effluent and renamed "Clean Ponds." There are several handsome buildings on the square, among them the old hotel Gostinitsa u Pokrovskikh Vorot, built in 1799–1802 to a design by Stasov. Just off the boulevard, along Arkhangelskiy Pereulok, is the Tserkov Arkhangela Gavriila (Church of the Archangel Gabriel), better known as the Menshikov Tower after Aleksandr Menshikov, an adviser of Peter the Great, who built it in 1704–1707. The white classical building at Chistoprudniy Bulvar No. 19a is the Sovremennik (Contemporary) Theater. Originally built as a movie theater in 1914, the Sovremennik flourished famously in the 1960s under the direction of Oleg Yefremov. Nearby, on Ulitsa Makarenko No. 23, is the former home of film director Sergei Eisenstein, director of *October* and *The Battleship Potemkin*.

On the corner of Ulitsa Pokrovka is the Apraksin Mansion dating from 1766, once a beautiful baroque residence but now unfortunately in need of restoration. The two churches near here are the Church of the Resurrection and the Church of the Presentation.

▶ **Khram Vsekh Svyatykh na Kulishkakh
(Church of All Saints "Na Kulishkakh")** *116B2*

Ploshchad Varvarskykh Vorot 2
Metro: Kitay Gorod

Tradition has it that Prince Dmitri Donskoy came to pray here on the eve of the Battle of Kulikovo Field in 1380, at which the Russians defeated the Mongols. The present Church of All Saints, which is now open for worship, dates from the 16th and 17th centuries.

▶▶ **Spaso-Andronikov Monastyr
(Andronikov Monastery, incorporating
Rublev Museum of Old Russian Art)** *116C1*

Ploshchad Pryamikova 10
Metro: Ploshchad Ilycha
Open: daily 11–5; closed Wed

The Andronikov was founded by the Metropolitan Alexei in 1359 as a thank offering for his safe return voyage to Moscow. The white stone building is the Cathedral of the Savior, dating from 1427. Other buildings worthy of note are the refectory (early 16th century) and the Church of the Archangel Michael and St. Alexius (1694–1739). Andrei Rublev, one of the greatest Russian icon painters, was a monk here. Most of his finest work is now in the Tretyakov Gallery (see page 128), but the museum does contain some splendid icons, including a work by another master icon painter, Dionysius.

▶ **Vospitatelniy Dom (Foundling Home)** *116B1*

South of Ulitsa Solyanka is the splendid Foundling Home. Some of the thousands of orphans who once lived here were trained as dancers for the Bolshoy Theater. The home was built by Karl Blank in 1764–1770; the scale is best appreciated from the river. Under the Communists it became a military academy.

Lost market
The 19th-century journalist Vladimir Gilyarovsky described the Khitrov market as "a big square in the center of the capital, near the Yauza River, surrounded by peeling stone houses. It lies in a low place into which lead several side streets like streams into a swamp. It's always bursting, especially toward evening. When it's a little foggy, or just after a rain, standing at the top of one of the side streets, you can barely make out the figures below you descending into a crawling, putrid pit."

117

The portico of the Menshikov Tower. The architect was ordered to build a spire which would be taller than the bell tower in the Kremlin. The spire was later destroyed by lightning

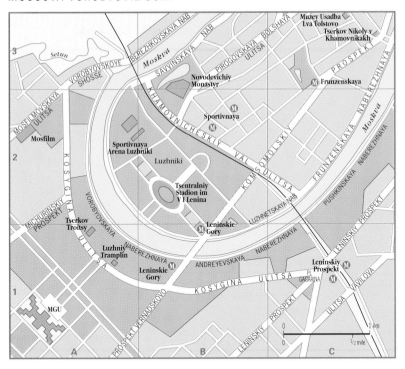

Vorobyovie Gory
(Sparrow Hills)

Sparrow Hills▶▶▶, a wooded area in the southwest of the city, occupies a marked bend in the Moskva River and offers unparalleled views of the Kremlin and the Moscow skyline. There is a viewing platform about 15 to 20 minutes' walk from Leninskie Gory metro station—which retains the Communist name for the area but is currently closed for repairs—along Vorobyovkskoye Shosse. A glass-covered escalator about 50 yards from the station is also a good viewing point. Known from 1935 to 1992 as Lenin Hills, Sparrow Hills is a favorite recreational spot for Muscovites, a place for walking in the woods, swimming, rowing, skating, tobogganing, or even skiing. The hills also have a long-standing connection with the revolutionary movement: revolutionary groups of students and workers came here for clandestine meetings at the end of the 19th century, away from the steady gaze of the secret police. During the Revolution of 1917 gun placements were set up here to bombard the doomed forces of the Provisional Government. Today Sparrow Hills retains its relaxed atmosphere—quite a surprise given its proximity to the center of a city as industrialized as Moscow—and offers a pleasant break from sightseeing.

▶　　　**Luzhniki**　　　　　　　　　　　*118B2*

Sportivnaya metro station is a natural stopping-off point for the sports complex, built at huge cost to host the ill-fated Olympic Games of 1980, which were boycotted by Western countries in protest against the Soviet invasion of Afghanistan. The former Olympic village occupies a 250-acre site at the far end of Prospekt Vernadskovo. Now a conventional housing estate, it is still known as Olympic Village. Occupying center stage and flanked by a smaller sports arena, a swimming pool, and a gymnasium, is the 100,000-seater Lenin Stadium, built originally in the 1950s and reconstructed for the Games. It stands on meadowland highly susceptible to flooding (*Luzhniki*—from *lug*, meadow). The stadium forecourt is now a huge fleamarket. Soccer (in summer) and ice hockey (in winter) are played at the Luzhniki Sports Hall. The outdoor tennis courts at the Luzhniki Sports Complex are also open to foreigners (see page 209).

Also to be seen on Prospekt Vernadskovo are the Palace of Young Pioneers and, near the Universitet metro stop, the new building that houses the Moscow Circus.

MGU (Moscow State University)   *118A1*

The 787-foot-high, 36-story building of Moscow State University is the tallest of the seven "wedding-cake" skyscrapers built in the twilight of the Stalin era (1949–1953). The students' rooms are cramped, poorly lit, and gloomy in the extreme; the corridors used to be patrolled by a voluntary student militia charged with enforcing curfews and generally keeping everyone on the straight and narrow. The campus incorporates, to the right of the main building, the green-domed Church of the Trinity, dating from 1811.

Mosfilm   *118A2*

Mosfilmovskaya Ulitsa

Parallel to Prospekt Vernadskovo are the film studios of Mosfilm, dating from 1927. It was here that such famed Soviet directors as Eisenstein, Pudovkin, Dovzhenko, and Tarkovsky worked.

Great minds
One of the most extraordinary collaborations in the history of Soviet moviemaking was that between the outstanding director Sergei Eisenstein and the composer Sergei Prokofiev. In 1938, Eisenstein asked Prokofiev to compose the soundtrack for *Alexander Nevskiy*, and from the outset the two men worked together with an instinctive rapport. So great was the trust between them that, instead of composing immediately after seeing the rushes, Prokofiev was allowed to write music for scenes that were not yet filmed, relying only on Eisenstein's sketches and suggestions.

119

Peace and friendship
A guidebook, published by the state-run Progress Publishers to coincide with the Moscow Olympics in 1980, proclaimed: "Soviet athletes first took part in the Olympic Games in Helsinki in 1952, since when they have brought in the spirit and principles of the policy of peaceful coexistence, true friendship, and peace among nations affiliated to the Olympic Movement."

Moscow State University in Sparrow Hills—a typical example of the architectural hybrid sometimes referred to as Stalinist Gothic

The Orthodox Church

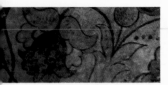

■ **More than 150 Moscow churches are now open for worship again as the Orthodox Church reestablishes itself with renewed vigor and confidence after 70 years of state-sponsored atheism and the destruction of many beautiful historic buildings.** ■

Consecrating parliament
"We pray for the Lord's blessing to accompany those who will work here for the good of the motherland." With these words the restored White House was blessed by Bishop Arseniy of Istra, who presented Prime Minister Victor Chernomyrdin with an icon to commemorate the event. In return Chernomyrdin promised to hand back to the Orthodox Church nearly a thousand icons which had been confiscated at the Russian Customs from traffickers dealing in the illegal icon trade.

Women were the mainstay of the Russian Orthodox Church during its years of persecution

Religious persecution began almost immediately after the Communists came to power. In 1918 Church was separated from State, priests and monks were outlawed, church buildings were closed and their furnishings and ornaments looted or desecrated. Religious instruction was strictly forbidden, as were pastoral visits and even charitable work.

The worst decade was the 1930s: by 1939 only 4,000 of the 50,000 churches in Russia remained open, and the number of bishops was reduced from 163 to just four. Tens of thousands of priests were arrested and sent to labor camps. Then came a great blessing in disguise. In June 1941 the acting head of the Church, Metropolitan Sergei, called on the people to defend the Motherland against the Fascist aggressor. Stalin was forced to recognize that the Church was a more powerful unifying factor than devotion to the Party. When a second wave of persecution swept over the Church in the Khrushchev era, the wanton destruction of religious buildings led to an outcry from architects and heritage experts, and the policy was quietly dropped. The authorities had to content themselves with using the Church as an instrument of propaganda. Religious leaders were expected to endorse all aspects of Soviet foreign policy, with its emphasis on peace and internationalism; some churchmen went further and all but granted the Soviet system full legitimacy.

Glasnost and sobornost Then came *glasnost* and with it a wholesale reevaluation of Church–State relations, timed to coincide with the celebrations, in 1988, of the 1,000th anniversary of the coming of Christianity to Russia. Legislation was passed to give the Church greater rights, while a great symbolic advance was the return to the Church of the Danilovskiy Monastery in Moscow as its new headquarters.

According to the Moscow Diocesan Directory, published for the first time in 1993, there were more than 300 diocesan priests and 100 deacons serving the capital. The Church owns property, runs seminaries and training colleges, schools and hospitals, publishing houses and printing works, icon workshops and shops selling books and religious objects. Most importantly, Christians can now meet, discuss, and profess their faith in a true spirit of *sobornost* or "togetherness."

Ritual and etiquette Attendance at an Orthodox service is a deeply moving experience, even for a nonbeliever. Both the liturgy and the accompanying ceremonial are unhurried and enhanced by the performance of sacred music. The composers Tchaikovsky and Rachmaninov both wrote magnificent settings for the Church: Rachmaninov's *Vespers* are well known nowadays in the West, Tchaikovsky's *Liturgy of St. John Chrysostom* less so. Ancient chants have recently been rediscovered and reinterpreted by groups like Anatoly Grindenko's Moscow Orthodox Male Choir and the Glinka Capella of St. Petersburg (the former court chapel choir).

The Sunday liturgy normally lasts for about two hours. It is customary to light a candle (on sale near the main door) and for women to cover their heads and men to remove their hats. The congregation in a Russian church stands throughout the service, but people move around freely at the periphery to pray at the various shrines or before their favorite icon.

The body of the church is divided into two halves; the narthex represents earth, the sanctuary, heaven; between the two is the screen known as the iconostasis. The holy doors, decorated with the Annunciation, are opened at the beginning of each day, an act which symbolizes the opening of the gates of Paradise to sinful Adam (Man). The form of service will be familiar enough to those acquainted either with the Roman Catholic Mass or the Episcopal rite of Holy Communion. The distinctive element is the insertion at the Offertory of a Cherubic Hymn, sung by the choir, while the clergy go in procession with the bread and wine from the offertory table to the sanctuary.

Detail, St. Basil's Cathedral

Easter service in Moscow
"The church is crowded to suffocation. Everybody is standing up, as there would be no room to kneel. The church is lit with countless small wax tapers. The priests are clothed in white and silver. The singing of the noble plain chant without any accompaniment ebbs and flows in perfectly disciplined cadences; the bass voices are unequalled in the world. Every class of the population is represented in the church ... There is a smell of incense and a still stronger smell of poor people, without which, someone said, a church is not a church."
—Maurice Baring, *What I Saw in Russia, 1905–1906*

A familiar figure in Moscow today—the Patriarch of all Russia, Alexey II

Nightmare
As a punishment for his half-sister, Sofia's part in leading the revolt of the *Streltsy* against him in 1698, Peter the Great incarcerated her in the Convent until her death. As an additional punishment, Peter ordered the bodies of the *Streltsy* to be strung up directly outside her cell—so closely that their boots thudded against the window panes, no doubt the cause of many a sleepless night thereafter for Sofia.

The towering north gate of the Novodevichiy Convent

▶▶▶ Novodevichiy Monastyr (Novodevichiy Convent/Convent of the New Maidens) 118B3

Novodevichiy Proezd 1
Metro: Sportivnaya
Open: May–Oct, Wed–Mon 10–6; Nov–Apr, 10–5; closed last day of the month (may vary)

The Convent of the New Maidens is a dazzling architectural gem, with crenellated walls of white brick, red-capped towers, and gleaming onion domes. Founded by Grand Prince Basil III in 1524 to commemorate the capture of Smolensk from the Lithuanians, the convent also served as an important link in the chain of fortified monasteries that surrounded Moscow. It was staffed almost exclusively by daughters of the nobility and even by members of the royal family. Boris Godunov was proclaimed tsar here in 1598, after his sister, Irina, took the veil following the death of her husband, Tsar Fedor. After the Time of Troubles when it was severely damaged, Peter the Great's half-sister, Sofia, presided over the convent's restoration. It was also in the late 17th century that the plain towers were decorated with arcades, gables, and pinnacles, giving them a fairy-tale appearance. When Napoleon arrived in Moscow in 1812 he gave orders for

the now dilapidated building to be blown up, but at the last moment an unknown hero managed to extinguish the fuses. Under the Communists, the complex was converted into a museum. However, these days the Church of the Assumption is possibly the best place in Moscow to hear divine service—the singing of the choir is superb, so try to schedule a visit for Sunday.

Rising majestically above the main entrance is the Gate Church of the Transfiguration, built in the baroque style in 1687–1689. The long two-story building nearby, broken up with white pillars, is the Lopukhin Chamber, residence of yet another of Peter's victims, his former wife Yevdokiya. The attention to detail in the external decoration, with pilasters, carved window surrounds, and gables, has to be admired and is a common feature of the convent buildings. In contrast, the ground-floor windows lack all decoration—these were the servants' quarters.

The white stone Virgin of Smolensk Cathedral, the oldest part of the convent, lies at the center of the complex. Dating from 1524–1525, it was clearly inspired by the Cathedral of the Assumption in the Kremlin. The walls are decorated with frescos from the late 16th century which provide a magnificent backdrop for the five-tier iconostasis presented by Sofia in 1686. Bibles, vestments, silver, and other religious treasures are also on view here. Behind the apse of the cathedral is an octagonal bell tower—six tiers, each ornamented in a style of its own, rising with effortless grace to a golden onion dome surmounted by a tall cross.

The strangely elongated Church of the Assumption (sometimes called the Dormition) is to the west of the Smolensk Cathedral. Both the church and the adjoining refectory were built in 1685–1687.

Beyond the refectory is the 16th-century Church of St. Ambrose, and almost hugging the southern wall of the fortress is the Chamber of Irina Godunova. Another Gate Church, called the Pokrov or Intercession, rounds off the architectural masterpiece.

Just outside the southern walls is the cemetery, final resting place of numerous illustrious Russians, including the writers Gogol and Chekhov, the film director Eisenstein, the composer Prokofiev, the theater director Stanislavsky, former Soviet leader Nikita Khrushchev, and Stalin's ill-fated wife, Nadezhda Alliluyeva. Some of Moscow's more enthusiastic entrepreneurs set out their wares in the convent's precincts, so prepare to be hassled in a good-natured way.

123

Prophet of doom
In 1994, arriving in Russia after 20 years' exile in the United States, writer Alexander Solzhenitsyn embarked on a grueling four-month tour of his homeland. With his striking Old Testament prophet stance and his powers of oratory, Solzhenitsyn quickly stepped back into the limelight by haranguing the State *Duma* as "Russia's sham democracy" and accusing Russia's new government of being nothing but an oligarchy. As he saw it, it was once again a case of the old tsarist system of rule by the few: " Ordinary people are in practice excluded from life. It passes them by, leaving them with an ugly choice between eking out a shameful beggar's existence or deceiving the state and each other."

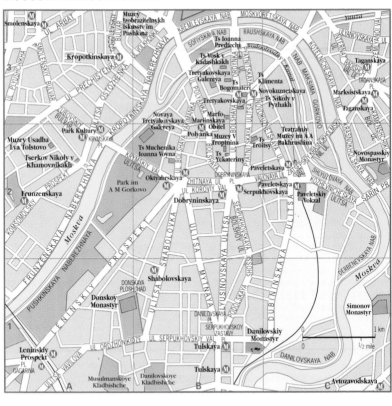

Zamoskvoreche

Zamoskvoreche means literally "beyond the Moskva River" and applies to the southern area of the old city opposite the Kremlin. Until modern times Zamoskvoreche had a sleepy rural feel—even today the old twisting streets give it a character all but obliterated in other parts of the city. By the 17th century Zamoskvoreche was well settled by a population of artisans serving the Court as well as being the first line of defense against the Tatars—even in the reign of Tsar Alexei there were more than 20 companies of *Streltsy* guards quartered here. In the 19th century members of that most distinctive of classes, the Moscow merchants, built their homes in Zamoskvoreche. Almost a separate caste, with flowing beards, kaftans, and patriarchal ways, they kept themselves to themselves, venturing out only to visit their businesses across the river in the Kitay Gorod. The smokestacks that still discolor and corrupt the air in this part of Moscow date from the same period, when almost one-third of the city's workers lived here.

Cool recommendation
In 1868 the Russian guidebook writer M. Zakharov described Zamoskvoreche (south Moscow) as "a dreadful, provincial Godforsaken place." In those days the fringes of the city more closely resembled American frontier towns than a European capital city. It was common for roads to trail off into rainsoaked fields in which isolated cabins, stores, and factories were dotted about without any thought for planning.

Danilovskiy Monastyr
(Danilov Monastery)   124B1

Danilovskiy Val 22
Metro: Tulskaya
The monastery, the oldest in Moscow, was founded in 1282 by the Orthodox Prince-Saint Daniil of Moscow

(son of Alexander Nevsky) and served as part of the southern defenses of the city. The present ensemble of buildings dates mainly from the 17th to the 19th centuries. The tiered gate tower was erected in 1730–1732 and contains the belfried Church of St. Simeon Stylites. The oldest of the three monastery churches can easily be recognized by its squat white tower, green dome, and simple neoclassical lines. On the second floor, the Church of the Holy Fathers of the Seven Ecumenical Councils has recently been restored: the iconostasis dates mainly from the 17th century. On the first floor is the Church of the Protecting Veil of the Most Holy Mother of God and the northern chapel of Saint Daniel. The icons here are modern, produced in the monastery workshop. The largest building in the complex is the orange Trinity Cathedral, erected in 1833–1838 to a late classical design by the famous Moscow architect Osip Bove. The interior is gorgeously decorated in the appropriate 19th-century style.

In 1930 the monastery was closed and allowed to fall into serious disrepair. The buildings were used variously as an electronics factory and a home for juvenile delinquents. Restoration work began after the complex was handed back to the Moscow Patriarchate in 1983; the churches were reconsecrated two years later, and today the monastery is the headquarters of the Russian Orthodox Church.

Opening times vary, as this is a working church. Divine services are held daily at 6 AM and 5 PM. Individual visitors may attend services but are otherwise confined to the courtyard and outbuildings; only the guided tour (by arrangement) guarantees access to all the main buildings.

Strongholds
The famous 19th-century Russian critic Vissarion Belinsky compared the merchants' houses of Zamoskvoreche to miniature fortresses "preparing to endure a lengthy siege. The windows are hung with curtains and the gates are under lock and key. A knock on them starts an expensive dog barking."

125

During the 18th century the Don Monastery became one of the most prosperous in Russia, owning 7,000 serfs

▶ **Donskoy Monastyr (Don Monastery)**   *124A1*
Donskaya Ploshchad 1
Metro: Shabolovskaya
Open: Tue–Fri and Sun 11–6

The Don Monastery is no longer a museum but an operational monastery again. It was founded by Boris Godunov in 1591 on the site of Russia's victory over the Tatars, her success attributed to a miraculous icon of the Virgin of the Don. The original is now displayed in the Tretyakov Gallery. The New Cathedral and the defensive walls which surround it were added by Peter the Great's half-sister, Sofia, in the late 17th century. The church contains an impressive iconostasis and frescos by Antonio Claudio painted to the design of Vasiliy Bazhenov. The monastery is also the resting place of many of Moscow's aristocrats. Situated within its grounds are the Church of the Archangel Michael, where members of the powerful Golitsyn family lie buried, and the Gate Church of the Virgin of Tikhvin.

▶▶ **Muzey V. Tropinina**
(Tropinin Museum)   124B2

Shchetininskiy Pereulok 10
Metro: Novokuznetskaya
Open: Wed, Fri–Sun 10–5, Tue and Thu 1–8

Vasily Tropinin was a serf artist working in the late 18th and early 19th centuries, but the museum includes portraits and miniatures by various artists of the same period and some fascinating landscapes of old Moscow. Together with his contemporary, Orest Kiprensky, Tropinin was a student at the Academy of Arts. The characters in their portraits could have come straight from the pages of Tolstoy's *War and Peace.*

▶▶ **Park im A. M. Gorkovo**
(Gorky Park)   124A2

Trolleybus: 4, 7, 62
Open: daily 9 AM–midnight

Gorky Park lies across the Moskva River from the metro station, Park Kultury. It can also be reached via Oktyabrskaya metro station. A large colonnaded archway marks the entrance on Krymskiy Val Ulitsa.

Named after the Soviet writer Maxim Gorky, the park was laid out as a Park of Culture and Rest in the late 1920s. The central area was once the Golitsyn Gardens, laid out for Prince Golitsyn by M. F. Kazakov in the late 18th century as an adjunct to a local hospital that the prince had endowed. Before the Revolution, the southwestern section of the park was known as the Neskuchniy ("not boring") Pleasure Gardens. This was once the estate of the aristocratic Trubetskoy family, but was purchased in 1826 by Nicholas I, who built a large Empire-style house on the land. Later the Soviet Academy of Sciences adopted the garden site as its headquarters. The estate was once part of the Botanical Gardens, which stretch all the way to the river. It is well provided with recreational and entertainment facilities. Plays are performed in the 10,000-seat open-air Zelyoniy ("Green") Theater in the summer, while the ice-

Fame
Gorky Park gained dubious international fame in 1983 from the movie of the same name, which was a bleak, contemporary thriller set in and around the area. Directed by Michael Apted and starring Lee Marvin and William Hurt, the story was adapted by Dennis Potter from the novel by Martin Cruz Smith. At that time, the political climate prevented the film being made in Moscow, and the Russian locations had to be recreated in Finland.

126

Leisure for the masses was the stated purpose of Gorky Park when it was opened in 1928

skating rink is the main winter attraction. There is also a roller coaster, boating lake, and magnificent ferris wheel.

► ### Ploshchad Gagarina (Gagarin Square) 124A1

Metro: Leninskiy Prospekt
Gagarin Square was formerly known as the Kaluga Gate, part of the outer rampart which used to girdle the city boundary. The present name commemorates the Soviet cosmonaut Yuri Gagarin, who was greeted here by thousands of cheering Muscovites when Leninskiy Prospekt was the official ceremonial route for Soviet heroes.

► ### Teatralniy Muzey im A. A. Bakhrushina (Bakhrushin Theater Museum) 124C2

Ulitsa Bakhrushina 31/12
Metro: Paveletskaya
Open: Wed–Mon 12–6; closed the last Mon of each month
The merchant Alexei Bakhrushin established this theater museum's collection in 1894. There are more than 200,000 photos, posters, tickets, programs, and personal effects illustrating the history of the Russian stage from the 18th century to the present. Unfortunately, the exhibits are chaotically and unimaginatively displayed. Items of special interest include Chaliapin's costume for the opera *Boris Godunov* and Nijinsky's dancing shoes.

Tserkov Muchenika Ioanna Voyna (Church of St. John the Warrior) 124B2

Ulitsa Bolshaya Yakimanka 46
Metro: Oktyabrskaya
Open: daily from 8 AM
The present red stone structure was built in 1709–1717 by order of Peter the Great, who is also said to have contributed to the plans—the design is accredited to I. P. Zarudniy. The church contains the icon of the Savior which used to hang over the Savior's Gate in the Kremlin, and it was one of those Moscow churches which remained open in the 1920s–1930s.

Green belt
One of Moscow's most attractive and historical green spaces, the Neskuchniy Gardens in the southwest corner of Gorky Park, is currently under threat from urban developers who intend to build luxury apartments there. In 1914, Baedeker described the gardens as "the most beautiful and best kept in Moscow." Although much has changed since then, the gardens have been protected as a historical monument. When local residents woke up one morning to find a children's playground and a tennis court under the bulldozer, they occupied the site, putting environmental issues firmly back on the city's agenda.

Space hero
Yuri Gagarin, who made the first manned space flight on April 12, 1961, subsequently became a test pilot but died tragically in an air crash in 1968. His remains were interred with other Communist notables in the Kremlin Wall in Red Square. The symbolism of the soaring monument on Gagarin Square, made from titanium, is obvious enough, but some visitors might miss the replica of the space capsule *Vostok 1* in which Gagarin made his historic journey.

Vasily Surikov's Morning of the Execution of the Streltsy. *Surikov specialized in epic historical canvases*

Modest philanthropist
After working long hours at his factory, the manufacturer Pavel Tretyakov would spend his evenings seeking out the work of talented new young artists. The director Konstantin Stanislavsky noted Tretyakov's unassuming personality: "Who would ever recognize the famous Russian Medici in the bashful, timid, tall, and thin figure with the bearded, priest-like face?" Instead of taking vacations Tretyakov would spend his summers becoming familiar with the pictures and museums of Europe.

▶▶▶ **Tretyakovskaya Galereya (Tretyakov Gallery)** *124B3*

Lavrushinskiy Pereulok 10
Metro: Tretyakovskaya
Open: Tue–Sun 10–7

The Tretyakov Gallery houses the greatest collection of Russian art in the world (some 50,000 paintings in all), which were presented to the city of Moscow by the merchant P. M. Tretyakov in 1892. The building, which dates from 1900–1905 and was designed by Viktor Vasnetsov, closed in 1985 for a comprehensive program of reconstruction; this was completed nine years later with the addition of a new annex and the inclusion of several older buildings on the street. The "new" gallery is on a different site entirely: it is the repository of mainly modern art.

The Tretyakov Gallery has an exceptional collection of icons, dating back to the 11th century. There is a marked contrast between the immobile and austere images typical of the early Kiev, Pskov, and Byzantine schools (11th–13th centuries) and the more intimate and fanciful creations of the Moscow school (roughly equivalent to the Renaissance period in Western Europe) with landscapes, ancillary figures, and scenes from daily life. Most rewarding, perhaps, are the masterpieces created by the great trio of Moscow icon painters: Andrei Rublev, Dionysius, and Theophanes the Greek. These include Theophanes' Uccello-like *Battle Between the Novgorodians and Suzdallians*; Rublev's *Zvenigorod Deesis* of 1425, which still retains its vibrant blues, greens, and reds, and Dionysius's magnificent *Christ in Glory* of 1500.

Tretyakov's aim in assembling his vast collection was to tell the complete story of Russian art, but inevitably it is artists from his own century, the 19th, that are most to the fore. The *Peredvizhniki* or Itinerants were rebel artists of the 1870s who turned their backs on the conservative Russian Academy of Arts with the intention of creating a national school which drew on Slavic traditions. The subject matter of the Itinerants, whose founder members include Ivan Kramskoy, Vasili Perov, and Fedor Vasilev, is amazingly broad, ranging from portraits and vast historical canvases to religious paintings, landscapes, and scenes depicting the horrors of war and exposing social conflict and inequality. Watch for some of the great canvases by the prolific Ilya Repin, including *Ivan the Terrible and His Son*, *Religious Procession in Kursk Province*, *They Did Not Expect Him*, and several outstanding portraits, most notably of Tolstoy and Tretyakov. Vasili Perov's revealing portrait of Dostoevsky contrasts with neat vignettes of Russian life like *The Last Tavern*. Of V. I. Surikov's dramatic historical canvases, the most outstanding are *Morning of the Execution of the Streltsy* and *Boyarina Morozova*. Vasili Polenov's *Moscow Courtyard* is a delicate evocation of old Arbat; Isaak Levitan, on the other hand, specialized in serene landscapes. Contrast these with the more somber *oeuvre* of Russia's first war artist, V. V. Vereshchagin.

By the 1890s the Itinerants, once at the cutting edge of modernism, were regarded by the new art-for-art's-sake generation as the Establishment. Among the younger artists were several who would collaborate in the future with Sergei Diaghilev on his Ballets Russes: Valentin Serov, Alexander Benois, and Konstantin Korovin. Among the highlights of Tretyakov's collection are Korovin's beautifully conceived and sensitively executed impressionist studies (*Paris by Night* is a fine example); Serov's charming *Girl with Peaches* (a portrait of the patron Savva Mamontov's daughter, Vera), and darkly fantastic canvases by the spiritually tortured Mikhail Vrubel, including *Pan* and *Seated Demon*.

New Tretyakov
Art from the Soviet era as well as works by contemporary Russian artists are accommodated in the New Tretyakov Gallery (Tretyakovka) in Gorky Park, also known as the Central House of Artists. The exhibition features pieces produced in the immediate aftermath of the Revolution by important avant-garde artists such as Kazimir Malevich, Aleksandr Rodchenko, and the Shternberg brothers. Most of the rooms, however, are devoted to the propaganda art known as Socialist Realism. The titles—*Life Is Getting Better*, *Building New Factories*, *Unforgettable Meeting* (a young woman is introduced to Stalin)—speak for themselves.

129

The model for Valentin Serov's Girl with Peaches, *the daughter of art patron Savva Mamontov, died before reaching adulthood*

The early decades of the 20th century saw Russian painters in the vanguard of European art. For a little while after the Revolution, the work of Natalia Goncharova, Vasili Kandinsky, Kazimir Malevich, and Marc Chagall was tolerated, even encouraged in the Soviet Union; by the 1930s, however, the straitjacket of Socialist Realism had been imposed on art, outlawing experiment and rehabilitating the Itinerants as suitable models for aspiring artists.

The street of churches

■ In prerevolutionary times "Holy Moscow," like Rome, was celebrated for its large number of churches. Today there is nowhere in the city with such a great concentration of churches as the neighborhood of Ulitsa Bolshaya Ordynka. ■

Good works
The Grand Duchess Yelizaveta Fedorovna took the veil following the assassination of her husband, Grand Duke Sergei Alexandrovich, in February 1905 by a Socialist Revolutionary. Yelizaveta later became renowned for her charitable work which included the founding of a hospital. Sent into exile in the Urals along with other members of the Romanov family, Grand Duchess Yelizaveta was murdered by the Bolsheviks at Alapaevsk on July 18, 1918, the day after the Tsar and his family had been put to death at Ekaterinburg.

One of the landmarks of Zamoskvoreche: the bell tower of the Church of St. John the Baptist

The name recalls a time when Russia was subjugated to the Mongol Khans. "Orda" refers to the Golden Horde, and in medieval times this was the road to the Tatar headquarters in the south. The area was defended by the companies of the *Streltsy* guard who were also quartered here. Despite the depredations of Communist planners, many of the old buildings along this narrow, historic street have been preserved.

Tserkov Voskreseniya v Kadashakh (Church of the Resurrection)
2–Kadashovskiy Pereulok 7
This is a fine example of the style known as Moscow baroque. Built in 1687, its most striking feature is the massive central tower, lavishly ornamented and capped with five green domes and gilt crosses. The long nave culminates in a magnificent, tapering bell tower, crowned with a tent roof and dating from 1696.

Tserkov Bogomateri Vsekh Skorbyashchikh Radosti (Church of the Virgin of All Sorrows)
Ulitsa Bolshaya Ordynka 20
The original church dates from 1790, but the Great Fire of 1812 destroyed all but V. I. Bazhenov's bell tower. The yellow "rotunda church" in the Empire style which replaced it was completed in 1836 and is by Osip Bove. The church was reopened as early as 1948; the main Sunday service begins at 10 AM.

Marfo-Mariinskaya Obitel (Convent of SS. Martha and Mary)
Bolshaya Ordynka Ulitsa 24
The convent was founded in 1908 by the Grand Duchess Yelizaveta Fedorovna, and the Church of the Intercession of the Virgin was opened four years later to a design by the architect A. V. Shchusev. The white church with its gray dome is visible through an arch in a white stone wall. The convent was reopened in 1992 in a building nearby; the church continues as the state icon restoration center.

Tserkov Nikoly v Pyzhakh (Church of St. Nicholas in Pyzhi)
Ulitsa Bolshaya Ordynka 27a
This impressive building with its five silver domes is now a working church again: there is a daily liturgy at 8 AM except Mondays, and the main Sunday service begins at 9:30. Napoleonic troops looted the church during the occupation of 1812. In 1934 the building was closed and a celebrated icon moved to the Tretyakov Gallery; the bell was at one time used as a prop by the Bolshoy Theater,

while the building itself was put to a variety of uses during the Communist period.

Tserkov Yekateriny (Church of St. Catherine)
Ulitsa Bolshaya Ordynka 60/2 (on corner of Pogorelskiy Pereulok)
The original wooden church was destroyed by fire in the 18th century. Catherine the Great ordered its reconstruction in 1767, commissioning the design from Karl Blank. The bell tower was added in the 19th century.

Tserkov Ioanna Predtechi Pod Borom (Church of St. John the Baptist)
Pyatnitskaya Ulitsa 4 (this street runs parallel to Bolshaya Ordynka)
There was a monastery close to this site in the 14th century; the present church dates from 1675. Although the main body of the building was originally baroque, its present classical appearance follows alterations undertaken in the middle of the 18th century (both the green bell tower and the refectory date from this period).

Tserkov Klimenta (Church of St. Clement)
Pyatnitskaya Ulitsa 26
This red-brick church was begun in 1742 by Pietro Antonio Trezzini but was not completed for another 30 years. Four sturdy but elegant rounded-off towers with star-covered cupolas complement the majestic central dome, whose cupola, by contrast, is of gold. The church was originally part of the estate of Count Bestuzhev-Ryumin, favorite of the Empress Elizabeth.

Tserkov Troitsy v Veshnyakakh (Church of the Trinity)
Pyatnitskaya Ulitsa 51
This Empire-style church was restored after the Napoleonic invasion and completed in 1826. F. M. Shestakov designed the splendid bell tower in 1826. It takes its name from its founder, another colonel of the *Streltsy* guard named Veshnyakov.

Osip Bove's dome crowns the 19th-century Church of the Virgin of All Sorrows Top, opposite: the chandelier that hangs beneath the dome

City of contrasts
"I do not think there exists a single city which bears the faintest resemblance to Moscow ... Here are luxury and penury, abundance and the most extreme deprivation, piety and atheism, the timeless continuity of our grandfathers' days and an unbelievable frivolity—warring elements which, out of their constant conflicts, create this marvelous, outrageous, gigantic whole which we know by its collective name—Moscow."
Konstantin Batyushkov, *Walk Through Moscow* (1812)

Out of Town

▶ **Bittsa** IFCC1

Metro: Bittsevskiy Park

Not all of Moscow is high-rise apartment blocks, sprawling housing projects, and congested roads. Bittsevskiy Forest Park in the south of the city is an enormous recreational area, stretching from the suburb of Zyuzino to beyond the Express Beltway and the Bittsa River.

The more developed end is to the north, by Chertanovskaya metro station. This is the site of the equestrian complex built for the 1980 Olympics, comprising a show-jumping stadium, indoor exercise ring, steeplechase circuit, and dressage field. Horseback riding may become available; if you are interested, ask your Intourist guide or representative. Facilities for the pentathlon event were also built here, including a gym, swimming pool, and shooting range. Streams dissect the northern end of the park, and footpaths wind through the forest. A pleasant way to spend a hot afternoon—take a picnic!

▶▶▶ **Muzey-Zapovednik XVI–XVII vi "Kolomenskoe" (Kolomenskoe Estate-Museum)** IFCD2

Metro: Kolomenskaya
Open: Tue–Sun 11–5; closed Mon

This open-air museum on the banks of the Moskva River was the favorite country estate of several tsars, including Ivan the Terrible. During the 17th century, Tsar Alexei used the grounds for the growing of flax, fruit, and vegetables. Some of the magnificent oaks still standing today date from the reign of Peter the Great (17th century).

The oldest building on the site is the tent-roofed Church of the Ascension, dating from 1532. The blue-domed Church of the Kazan Icon of the Mother of God, dating from the 17th century, is also part of the original complex.

The park contains some remarkable wooden buildings brought here from all over Russia, including a lookout tower from Siberia (1631) and a four-room cabin once used by Peter the Great which came originally from Archangel. The buildings house an exhibition of Russian folk art including ceramics, woodcarving, and painting.

▶▶▶ **Muzey Keramiki i Usadba Kuskovo XVIII v (Kuskovo Estate-Museum)** IFCE3

Metro: Ryazanskiy Prospekt
Ulitsa Yunosti 2
Open: Wed–Sun 10–7; 10–4 in winter

The influential Sheremetev family built this two-story wooden palace, now a ceramics museum. The building dates from 1777, and the interior is decorated with a striking array of paintings, tapestries, and mirrors. Other structures of note include the Dutch and Italian houses, the hermitage, and the grotto, all in a setting of formally arranged gardens on the lines of Versailles. Sheremetev's celebrated company of serf actors performed in the open-air theater near the orangery.

►► Izmaylovskiy Park *IFCE4*

Metro: Izmaylovskiy Park

A pleasant afternoon out can be spent strolling through one of Moscow's biggest parks, shopping in the outdoor market, and inspecting the remains of one of the tsar's out-of-town estates and hunting lodges. The name still commemorates the original owners of this land, the Izmaylovs, but by the 16th century the estate had already passed into the hands of Russia's ruling dynasty, the Romanovs. Tsar Alexei (1629–1676) put the land to good use, cultivating plants, breeding animals, and developing a variety of cottage industries (including a small glass works). His son, Peter the Great, spent much of his childhood here. The "Grandfather of the Russian navy" is said one day to have come across a half-rotten wooden boat which had been presented to Ivan the Terrible by Elizabeth I of England. He repaired the vessel, sailed it on the pond, and never looked back. This is also where Peter first played soldiers—many years later he christened one of his new guards regiments the Izmaylovskiy.

Most of the estate—which consists largely of half-timbered buildings, churches, and palaces—has long gone, but it's worth exploring the site: a small island set in a pond just on the other side of the Izmaylovskoe Shosse (highway). The buildings which have survived are a set of festive gates which used to lead to the palace, an impressive bridge tower of a type similar to that which used to surround Moscow itself, and the five-domed Cathedral of the Intercession, dating from 1671–1672 and modeled on the Uspenskiy Cathedral in the Kremlin. *(Continued page 134)*

A mystery ...

One of the most enduring and controversial aspects of the murder of Tsar Nicholas II and his family at Ekaterinburg in 1918 was finally resolved in 1994, when DNA tests (using comparative samples donated by members of the British royal family) finally laid the ghost of the tsar's daughter Anastasia, who had reputedly escaped death. Over the years there had been many claimants who talked of miraculous escapes from the hail of Bolshevik bullets, but none more convincing than Anna Anderson, who, between 1920 and her death in America in 1984, led many to believe that she was indeed the tsar's daughter. However, the tests revealed the truth—Anna Anderson had no genetic link whatever with the Romanov family.

The Kazan Church was the Tsar's private chapel on his Kolomenskoe estate and was joined to the palace by an underground tunnel

One of Moscow's best-kept secrets (where tourists are concerned at least) is the beach at Serebryaniy Bor

Izmaylovskiy Park is an enjoyable place to relax with Russians. Sidewalk artists abound, a sign that times have changed. In the old days, all such "degenerate art" was confiscated by KGB agents and the artists victimized.

The area near Izmaylovskiy Park metro station is taken over on weekends by hordes of street traders, many of them black marketeers who have come up from the Caucasus. Izmaylovskiy street market is an ideal place to look for souvenirs—be prepared to haggle and beware of buying works of art and antiques, especially icons which may well have been stolen. There are plenty of other things to choose from: *matryoshka* dolls, lacquer boxes, hand-knitted woolen shawls, fox-fur hats, and embroidered tablecloths. There are also more touristy souvenirs to take home to friends, including "MacLenin" T-shirts, rubber Stalin masks, Soviet army paraphernalia.

►► Ostankinskiy Dvorets–Muzey Tvorchestva Krepostnykh (Ostankino Palace Museum of Serf Art) *IFCC5*

Pervaya Ostankinskaya Ulitsa 5
Metro: VDNKh
Open: Oct–May, Thu–Mon 10–4; May–Sep, Thu–Mon 11–5

This estate, like Kuskovo (see page 132), belonged to the Sheremetev family. The wooden palace was designed and constructed entirely by serf labor between 1792 and 1798. The interior is a magnificent tribute to its serf artists and craftsmen. The parquetry, the decorative carvings, and the finely wrought crystal chandeliers all provide a splendid backdrop to the collection of 18th-century furniture, paintings, porcelain, and crystal. Sheremetev's company of 200 actors, all serfs, performed in the special theater which, thanks to a device which raised the auditorium, also served as a ballroom. You can also enjoy a stroll in the palace grounds and a visit to the Church of the Trinity, commissioned by a previous owner of the estate in 1687. The atmosphere of tranquility is spoiled somewhat by the overwhelming presence of the Ostankino TV mast.

Work-shy?
By the end of the Brezhnev era in the late 1970s, subsequently referred to by President Gorbachev as the era of *zastoy* ("stagnation"), workers had become so cynical about corrupt practices and incompetence in their factories that many of them were regularly to be seen in the bars of Moscow as early as three or four in the afternoon. Hence the proverb: "You pretend to pay us, we'll pretend to work."

► Serebryaniy Bor (Silver Pine Forest)   *IFCB4*

Trolleybus: No. 20 from Red Square (Serebryany Bor)
Many visitors do not realize that Moscow has a beach, "Silver Pine Forest." Muscovites come here by the thousand in summer, so expect a crowd. You can swim, lie out in the sun, go for a stroll, or rent a boat. Vendors keep everyone supplied with food and drink.

► Tekhnopark (VVTs)   *IFCC5*

Prospekt Mira
Metro: VDNKh
The All-Russian Exhibition Center is still often referred to by its old, abbreviated name VDNKh (Vystavka Dostizheniy Narodnovo Khozyaistva SSR). The exhibition, which occupies a 750-acre site, was originally designed as a showpiece of the achievements of Soviet socialism and was therefore an obligatory stop on every tourist's itinerary. The 80 pavilions cover agriculture, industry, science, technology, and much more. Since the collapse of Communism, a variety of commercial enterprises, stock exchanges, and currency shops have shifted the ideological slant from socialism to capitalism. Near the metro station and in the shadow of the 300-foot-high obelisk, the Space Museum (see page 138) also offers cafés, movie theaters, an open-air theater, and an amusement park.

►► Tsaritsyno   *IFCD1*

Metro: Tsaritsyno
Catherine the Great is usually associated with St. Petersburg, but in 1775 she bought some land south of Moscow and instructed one of the great Russian architects, Vasiliy Bazhenov, to build her a summer residence. Originally covering an area of almost 6,200 acres, the site was landscaped with formal gardens, and local rivers were dammed to form an attractive series of ponds. When it came to the buildings, Bazhenov surpassed himself, creating a style which ambitiously blended classical, Russian, and Gothic motifs. Catherine was neither amused nor impressed. She pulled down the palace; its subsequent replacement by Matvei Kazakov was abandoned in 1787.

Love match
Count Nikolai Sheremetev married one of his own serf actresses, Praskovya Kovalyova, a case of intermarriage between classes which caused a sensation in its day.

135

Space travel is one of the scientific and technological achievements celebrated at VVTs

■ **No sooner had the railroads come to Russia than Moscow became the hub of the entire national system—not surprisingly, given its geographical location. In all, there are nine stations in the capital serving destinations from Siberia to the Crimea. But the busiest point on the system is the square where three networks converge.** ■

Misnomer
The story goes that the Russian word for station, *vokzal*, derives from an early visit to Britain by Russian engineers and administrators. Wishing to learn everything they could about the railroad system, they overheard someone refer to the London station they were inspecting as Vauxhall; the name impressed them and it stuck.

Trading bar
"A station is not a market," complained mayor of Moscow Yuri Luzhkov in Moscow's evening newspaper, *Vechernyaya Moskva*. The subjects of his wrath were the street sellers who have until recently made it almost impossible for rail passengers to gain access to the Kursk station. The chaos at Station Square is but one aspect of a free economy gone out of control. As one TV pundit put it: "We have a market, yes, but a productive market, no."

Street trading Komsomolskaya Ploshchad is one of Moscow's liveliest squares and as good a place as any to observe the comings and goings of peasants from the surrounding villages as they come to town to shop and to sell. Traditionally the goods for sale would be foodstuffs and rural handicrafts—wooden dolls, whistles, lacquer boxes—but nowadays the people standing in line outside the station concourses sell everything from stockings to toiletries and packs of cigarettes. Keeping vigil morning, noon, and night, these street sellers make little attempt at a sales pitch and resolutely ignore the signs that tell them to keep a certain distance away from the station. When they finally pack up to go home, they congest the foyers and escalators of the metro stations with their shopping carts (Russian-style, made of iron), bags, and even sacks—one feels for the elderly *babushka* loaded up in this way, her wares slung across her shoulder. Komsomolskaya Ploshchad takes on a decidedly less picturesque appearance after the sun goes down when the marshaling yards, underpasses, and shop doorways provide ideal cover for all kinds of illicit dealings in drugs, alcohol, and prostitution.

Station chaos Russian train stations are bewildering places, especially for foreigners. Signs are exclusively in Russian, the staff are virtually under siege, and the sheer numbers sometimes make even movement difficult. Buying a ticket presents its own problems. Lines are inordinately long and obey a logic known only to the initiated. Even Russians find themselves in the wrong line on occasion, and nothing can be more frustrating than to reach the window just as it closes for the midmorning break. Waiting passengers (and Russians, who are used to long waits) crowd into roped-off sections of vast waiting rooms, where television viewing for a small fee helps to while away the hours.

Three in one Komsomolskaya Ploshchad contains three of Moscow's most important train termini, which serve more than half a million passengers a day. Leningradskiy Vokzal (Leningrad Station—the authorities stubbornly refuse to rename it St. Petersburg) was designed in 1851 in the neoclassical style by K. A. Ton, builder of the Great Kremlin Palace. The corresponding terminal in St. Petersburg is built to a similar design. Plaques and images of Lenin abound in commemoration of the Soviet leader's arrival here from Petrograd on March 11, 1918.

Beside the station is the pretentious portico of Komsomolskaya metro station—the interior, one of the most luxurious in the system, is certainly worth a look (see page 69). On the far side of the metro station is another rail terminus. This is Yaroslavskiy Vokzal (Yaroslavl Station), a wonderful piece of art nouveau fantasy by the brilliant architect Fedor Shekhtel. It was designed in 1902–1904, and there is nothing else quite like it in the world. Passengers from the Trans-Siberian Express get off here, as do visitors from the frozen north.

In designing Yaroslavl Station, Shekhtel presented a challenge which was immediately taken up by his rival, A. V. Shchusev. Building began on Kazanskiy Vokzal (Kazan Station) on the opposite side of the square in 1912 but was not completed until 1926. The 200-foot-tall gate tower is modeled on the *kremlin* of the Volga city of Kazan; the window ornamentation is a borrowing from Moscow baroque, but the overall concept is Shchusev's own. Kazan Station is for destinations east: the Urals, Western Siberia, and Central Asia.

A. V. Shchusev designed Kazan Station (shown here) before going on to more ambitious projects, ultimately the reconstruction of Moscow itself
Top: the Leningrad Station, Moscow

Specialist museums in Moscow

Art for the masses
"Art must not be concentrated in dead shrines called museums. It must be spread everywhere—on the streets, in trams, factories, workshops and in the workers' homes."
—Vladimir Mayakovsky

Moscow has more than 80 museums. Whereas some are merely a relentless accumulation of exhibits without much attempt at explanation, the Kremlin Museums, major art galleries, monasteries, churches, and literary museums are looked after lovingly and with a reverence for culture unique to the Russians.

Recent political changes have led to a comprehensive reappraisal, which has led to a reduction in the number of museums dealing with the Revolution and the achievements of Socialism.

It is important to check every museum's opening times, as they can often be maddeningly eccentric. Also bear in mind that many museums are liable to close at some time in the future for renovation and updating. Entrance charges are still relatively low, but foreigners are generally charged more.

The following seven museums are of minor or specialist interest and have not been referred to elsewhere in the book.

▶▶ **Dom-Muzey Khudozhnika V. M. Vasnetsova (Vasnetsov House-Museum)** *IFCC4*
Vasnetsova Pereulok 13
Metro: Kolkhoznaya
Open: Wed–Sun 10–5
A major figure in the folk art revival of the late 19th century, Viktor Mikhailovich Vasnetsov designed this house for himself in 1893–1894 and had it built by peasant carpenters from Vladimir province. The exterior imitates a typical timber-framed house, while the wooden interior displays some of Vasnetsov's own canvases, including a portrait of his daughter.

▶ **Muzey Istorii Goroda Moskvy (Museum of the History of Moscow)** *84B3*
Novaya Ploshchad 12
Metro: Kitay Gorod
Open: Tue, Thu, and weekends 10–6, Wed and Fri noon–8; closed last day of the month
This museum, which is now arousing more interest, traces Moscow's history by means of archeological and other exhibits, paintings, and the like. It was once the Church of St. John the Divine Under the Elm.

▶ **Muzey Kosmonavtov (Space Museum)** *IFCD5*
Prospekt Mira, Alleya Kosmonavtov
Metro: VDNKh
Open: Tue–Sun 11–5:30
Part of the All-Russian Exhibition Center, the museum is located near the obelisk (see Tekhnopark [VVTs], page 135). There are one or two fascinating exhibits ranging from early satellites to the space suits of Yuri Gargarin, and a number of the dogs (now stuffed) blasted into orbit prior to Gargarin's flight, to the very first satellite, *Sputnik*, and *Vostok 1*, in which Gagarin made the world's first manned space flight in 1961.

Lacquer design by Ivan Fomichov of the Boyarin Orsha, after a poem by Lermontov

▶ **Muzey Prikladnykh Iskusstv**
(Museum of Folk Art) *IFCC4*
Leontevskiy Pereulok 7
Metro: Arbatskaya
Open: Tue–Sun 11–5; closed last day of the month
Founded in 1885 by one of Moscow's great art patrons, Sergei Morozov. The museum is devoted to Russian popular art from the 17th century to the present. Look for blue and white pottery, carved wooden toys, lace, embroidery, and lacquer boxes from Palekh.

▶ **Muzey Vooruzhonnykh Sil**
(Armed Forces Museum) *IFCC4*
Ulitsa Sovetskoy Armii 2
Metro: Prospekt Mira
Open: Wed–Sun 10–4:30
Weapons, models, and artillery pieces illustrate the story of the Soviet armed services since the Revolution.

▶▶ **Muzey V. V. Mayakovskovo**
(Mayakovsky Museum) *84C3*
Lubyanskiy Proezd 3/6
Metro: Lubyanka
Open: Fri–Tue 10–6, Thu 1–9
Office chairs, typewriters, old boots with cut-out eyes, life-size posters, and photomontages are just some of the exhibits in this fascinating museum, which is devoted to the life and times of the revolutionary artist, poet, and playwright Vladimir Mayakovsky. A room on the fourth-floor has been re-created to look as it would have when Mayakovsky was living here in 1919–30.

▶ **Muzey-Kvartira F. M. Dostoevskovo**
(Dostoevsky House-Museum) *IFCC4*
Ulitsa Dostoevskovo 2
Metro: Novoslobodskaya
Open: Tue, Thu, and weekends 11–6, Wed and Fri 2–9; closed last day of the month
Dostoevsky spent the first 16 years of his life here. The museum contains many personal effects, but is no match for its equivalent in St. Petersburg (see page 198).

Exhibition hall of the Space Museum at Tekhnopark (VVTs)

139

Lenin's legacy
Virtually every place Lenin stayed was once preserved as a house museum: many of these are now already neglected and will probably close down. A more significant casualty was the Central Lenin Museum, which closed just as it was in the middle of revising its image—thus denying visitors the chance to see Lenin's jacket, riddled with bullet holes when Fanny Kaplan shot him in 1918, or the 1921 Rolls Royce Silver Ghost in which he was driven around.

Excursions

Abramtsevo, Klin, Sergiev Posad (Zagorsk) and the Golden Ring

Abramtsevo Estate-Museum is located along the **Yaroslavl Highway**, near the town of Sergiev Posad/ Zagorsk, 42 miles north of Moscow. Turn off at the exit for **Khotkovo**. You can get there by train direct from Moscow's **Yaroslavl Station** (metro **Komsomolskaya**). A description of the estate follows on page 141.

Klin is best reached by road—take the **Leningrad/St. Petersburg Highway** for about 50 miles northwest of Moscow. Alternatively, take the train from **Leningrad Station** (Leningradskiy Vokzal, metro **Komsomolskaya**).
Klin is described on page 142.

Sergiev Posad (Zagorsk) is 43 miles northeast of Moscow on the **Yaroslavskoe Shosse** (highway). Its relative proximity, together with the smooth road surfaces, make a trip here a good opportunity to try driving in Russian conditions. Alternatively, take the metro to **Komsomolskaya**,

then the *elektrichka* (electric train) from **Yaroslavl Station**. A full description of Sergiev Posad is given on pages 142–143.

The Golden Ring (Zolotoe Koltso) refers to the ancient historical towns that cluster north and northeast of Moscow along what in the Middle Ages were the trade routes linking Russia's two great centers of civilization, Novgorod to the north and Kiev to the south. Intourist organizes tours to all of the towns of the Golden Ring, which include entrance fees to the various museums (for opening times, also see Intourist and other tour operators).

There are Intourist hotels in three of the six main towns of the Ring: Yaroslavl, Vladimir, and Suzdal. If your time is limited, the trip to Suzdal and Vladimir is the most rewarding, but try to spare a morning for a separate trip to Sergiev Posad.

Rostov, Vladimir, Suzdal, and Yaroslav are described on pages 144–147.

140

The monastic refectory at Sergiev Posad (Zagorsk)

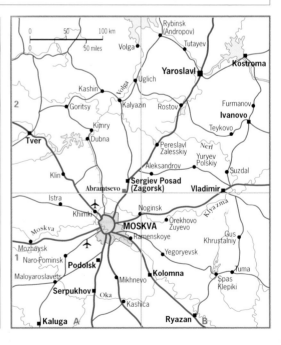

▶▶ **Muzey-Usadba "Abramtsevo"**
(Abramtsevo Estate-Museum) *140A2*

This charming country house set among woods and ponds was bought in 1843 by the great Russian writer, nationalist, and slavophile Sergei Aksakov. After his death, Abramtsevo was acquired by the textile millionaire and art patron Savva Mamontov. Within a few years Mamontov had gathered a colony of artists at Abramtsevo , including Ilya Repin, Vasili Polenov, Valentin Serov, Konstantin Korovin, Mikhail Nesterov, and the brothers Apollinari and Viktor Vasnetsov, whom he inspired to create a new and revitalized Russian art. Some of the designs from Abramtsevo would later turn up in Paris in the guise of theater costumes and stage sets for Diaghilev's Ballets Russes.

Mamontov also opened a school for the local peasant children, which they attended while their parents practiced the traditional crafts of embroidery, woodcarving, ceramics, and icon painting.

The tour of the estate (*Open* Wed–Sun 11–5; closed Apr, Oct, and last Thu of the month) begins with the house, a traditional timber-framed structure said to be the model for the manor house in Chekhov's play *The Cherry Orchard*. The dining room, simply furnished and decorated, has a beautiful tiled fireplace and an easel copy of Serov's engaging portrait of Mamontov's daughter (*Girl with Peaches,* 1887, now in the Tretyakov Gallery). Woodcarving is the predominant theme in the guest cottage: spoons and bowls, lidded boxes, dolls, statuettes, and furniture are all by Mamontov's colony of artists. The studio is most remarkable for its fancy lacework gable—it was designed by the artist V. A. Gartman, whose paintings later inspired Moussorgsky's piano suite *Pictures at an Exhibition*. The chapel was a collaborative effort in the Muscovite and Novgorodian styles, to the design of Viktor Vasnetsov. The iconostasis was designed by several artists including Repin, Vrubel, and Polenov. Many artists came to Abramtsevo seeking inspiration from nature, and not a few Russian landcapes grew out of the magical grounds with their streams, linden trees, and birch groves.

Educated élite
With the rise of a new moneyed class in Russia, many parents are now rejecting state education in favor of private schools. This is not surprising, since the old Soviet-style education system is still reeling after 70 years of regimentation and mass indoctrination. But the new private schools are struggling to survive in an uncertain economic climate and having to cope with spiraling rents, all of which means that prospective parents are often asked to pay large deposits as well as contribute toward the purchase of equipment for the new schools. One of the most exclusive of these new establishments is the "Premier." Its 60 pupils have a staff of seven security men to guard them from potential kidnappings.

19th-century artists came to Abramtsevo seeking inspiration, and many found it there

MOSCOW: EXCURSIONS

►► Klin

140A2

Klin (*Open* Fri–Tue 10–5; closed last Mon of the month) is famous as the rural retreat of Russia's greatest 19th-century composer, Pyotr Ilych Tchaikovsky (1840–1893). The pathologically shy and retiring composer had always valued peace and seclusion. Friends and relatives, notably his famed correspondent Nadezhda von Meck, had long been in the habit of making their country estates available to him when they were in town or abroad. But Tchaikovsky longed for a place of his own and in 1885 acquired Klin: "What a blessing, to know that no one will come, no one will interrupt my work, reading or strolling!" The composer never let a day pass without a long stroll in the grounds, his most favored source of inspiration.

Here at Klin, Tchaikovsky composed the ballets *The Nutcracker* and *The Sleeping Beauty,* and his *Fifth* and *Sixth* symphonies. After his death, the house was converted into a museum by his younger brother, Modest. Twice a year, on the anniversaries of Tchaikovsky's birth and death, composers and musicians come to Klin to play his music.

The gray, timber-framed building is simply but tastefully furnished and reflects Tchaikovsky's delicate sensitivity. The living room opens onto a covered porch and garden and is hung with portraits of musicians, including Beethoven and Anton Rubinstein (Tchaikovsky's teacher at the St. Petersburg Conservatory). The bedroom, warm and intimate, contains a pair of the composer's slippers and a beautifully embroidered coverlet; you can also see the alcoves where Tchaikovsky liked to converse with friends. The wooden study, dominated by a photographic portrait of Tchaikovsky's father, is the room with the greatest atmosphere.

►►► Sergiev Posad (Zagorsk)

140A2

Although Zagorsk has now officially reverted to its prerevolutionary name, **Sergiev Posad,** both names are still in use.

The domes of the cathedrals will orient you toward the center of town, which is situated 44 miles northeast of Moscow. On the way in, stop at the toy museum, a dark red building at **Krasnoy Armiy Prospekt 136**. Each village in the Moscow region specializes in a traditional handicraft or folk art. Since the 17th century Zagorsk's specialty has been wooden toys, including the famous *matryoshka* nest of dolls.

The central attraction of the town is the great **Trinity Monastery of St. Sergius,** founded in 1345 by Russia's patron saint, the scholarly St. Sergius of Radonezh, which looms into view as you approach the town by road. Prince Dmitri Donskoy came here in 1380 to ask the blessing of the already revered monk before the Battle of Kulikovo Field prior to the first Russian victory over the Tatars. Thereafter, the monastery became one of Russia's premier places of pilgrimage and refuge, but it was also of strategic importance as a fortified outpost on the way to Moscow. The Tatars ransacked Sergiev in the 15th century; during the Time of Troubles the monks held out for more than a year while under siege from the Poles. Peter the Great took refuge here during the revolt of the *Streltsy.*

The monastery is surrounded by a massive wall and a series of watchtowers. Pass through the main entrance, known as the **Red Tower**, and adjoining it is the terracotta **Gate Church of St. John the Baptist**, dating from 1693–1699. It was a gift from one of Russia's wealthiest families, the Stroganovs. The stunning **Cathedral of the Assumption**, its five domes covered in blue and golden stars, was built in 1559–1585 by Ivan the Terrible to commemorate the taking of Kazan. The design was inspired by its namesake in the Kremlin. The iconostasis contains a *Last Supper* by the 17th-century master Simon Ushakov.

Outside the cathedral is the **Tomb of Boris Godunov** and his family and a small chapel built in the 17th century on the site of a holy well. Pilgrims still bring bottles to fill with holy water. Opposite the blue and white **bell tower**, dating from 1740–1770, which rises just behind the cathedral, is the **Church of the Holy Spirit**, built by Pskov craftsmen in 1476.

The long building with the brightly painted, checkerboard exterior is the **refectory**, built in 1686 and decorated with carved columns. Beyond the refectory is the **Cathedral of the Trinity**, a plain church built in 1422. The wall paintings are 16th century, but the magnificent iconostasis was created by the great medieval masters Andrei Rublev and Daniil Chorny. Illumination is solely by icon lamps. Rublev's famous icon of the Trinity, painted to commemorate the Battle of Kulikovo, was replaced by a copy and is now in the Tretyakov Gallery (see page 128). The monastery's founder, **St. Sergius**, is buried in a silver sarcophagus donated by Empress Anna in 1730 and adorned by icon lamps. Special permission is needed to visit the nearby **Art Museum**, which houses a collection of embroidered vestments, icons, porcelain, and other treasures.

The Tsar's Chambers, otherwise known as the **Chertogi Palace**, are on the other side of the monastery beyond the main bell tower and are easily distinguishable by their colorfully painted and tiled exterior. They were constructed in the late 17th century for Tsar Alexei.

For centuries the Trinity Sergius Monastery at Sergiev Posad (Zagorsk) was the center of Russian Orthodoxy

Duck!
The tallest of the monastery towers is known as the Utichnaya or Duck Tower, a reference to Peter the Great's predilection for taking potshots at the ducks paddling on the pond below.

Fare-dodging
The cost of a metro token is now more than 24,000 times what it was in Soviet times. Russians have responded by resorting to fare evasion on an unprecedented scale, which is leading to a dramatic shortfall in revenue. A recent five-day survey carried out by the St. Petersburg Transit Authority led to the discovery of 20,000 fare dodgers —more than 1,000 per hour. Of those caught, 863 had shown forged train passes, 7,000 had displayed useless or irrelevant documents such as old Communist Party cards, and more than 10,000 passengers had simply vaulted over the turnstiles. The authorities are now introducing magnetic cards with electronic readers in a desperate attempt to combat the problem.

Bells
One of the most distinctive sounds in Russia is that of its church bells. The art of bell-making is a tradition that stretches back for centuries, and has long been the envy of other nations. In recent times Moscow's Patriarchate has signed a contract with the joint-stock company Expostroymash to cast bells for two Christian Orthodox churches in San Francisco.

►► **Zolotoe Koltso (The Golden Ring)**   140B2

When most towns were founded in the 11th century, Rostov, Suzdal, Vladimir, and Yaroslavl were principalities in their own right, while lowly Moscow was little more than a strategic outpost. By the time of Ivan the Great, Moscow had swallowed up every one of its ancient rivals to make the first Russian superstate, but their proximity to that greatest of waterways, the Volga River, guaranteed them a measure of prosperity through trade.

Visitors are constantly amazed at just how much of old Russia has been preserved here. There are vistas of quite stunning beauty, and each of the settlements has its unique charm: kremlins with churches and monasteries from a variety of periods, preserved wooden houses, and museums displaying the great traditions of icon-painting and handicrafts which still flourish here.

Rostov►► (or Rostov Veliki) "**Rostov the Great**" rose to prominence in the 12th century when it was one of the wealthiest towns in the whole of Russia and an early center of the Orthodox Church. Despite its incorporation into the Muscovite state, it was still wealthy enough in the 17th century to support the building of many cathedrals and churches. Rostov stands on the edge of the serene Lake Nero, and the main sights are within striking distance of its shores. The kremlin was built in the 17th century as a ceremonial residence for the metropolitan.

The five-domed **Church of the Resurrection**, dating from 1670, has two outstanding features: a stone iconostasis and some superb frescos painted by local artists. More artistic masterpieces are in the single-domed **Church of the Savior in the Vestibule.**

Around the kremlin walls are the former servants' quarters of the metropolitan, whose residence, including the remarkable **White Chamber**, has been converted into a museum of sculptures, icons, and enamels. The oldest building in Rostov is the 11th-century **Cathedral of the Dormition**, although little of the original structure survives apart from the lion's-head door handles. Don't leave without having a close look at the belfry, built in the 1680s, which houses some of the most famous bells in Russia.

The single-domed Church of the Savior in the Vestibule— kremlin, Rostov Veliki

The Assumption Cathedral, Vladimir, (right) inspired its namesake in the Moscow Kremlin

Survival of a tradition
Despite the depredations of Communism and the destruction of many historic buildings during World War II, Russia still has an abundance of churches. Novgorod in the 15th century had 150 or so, and even Suzdal, a relatively small settlement, had 50 churches in the 18th century. Compare this to the number of churches one would normally find in a Western town! It is not surprising therefore that the Communists failed to extinguish the Orthodox faith in Russia, which hung on so tenaciously despite the willful neglect of its places of worship.

Vladimir▶▶ This ancient city lies on the Klyazma River, a minor tributary of the Volga, about 115 miles northeast of Moscow. It was founded in 1108 by Vladimir Monomakh, father of Moscow's founder Yuri Dolgorukiy. By the middle of the 12th century, the town was among the most prosperous in northern Russia, and in 1157 Dolgorukiy's son, Prince Andrei Bogolyubskiy, decided to move the Russian capital here from Kiev, which was by then in decline. Craftsmen from all over Russia, as well as Poland and the Holy Roman Empire, subsequently contributed to the beautifying of the new capital. The suitably imposing entry—the **Golden Gates**, erected in 1164 by order of Prince Andrei Bogolyubskiy—paves the way for Vladimir's greatest treasure, the **Uspenskiy** or **Dormition Cathedral**. Rounded golden domes betray its Byzantine origins, while the detail of the stone decoration has a distinctly Romanesque appearance. The interior is equally awe-inspiring, resplendent with icon paintings, some of which date from the 15th century, and is crowned by Andrei Rublev's *Last Judgment* of 1408 which presides over the choir.

Most bus tours take a short detour out of the town to **Bogolyubovo**, to see the remains of **Prince Andrei's palace** and the **Church of the Intercession on the Nerl**. This beautifully proportioned, single-domed church—its walls delicately carved in stone with figures of the Apostles, saints, prophets, and some delightfully outlandish animals—soars toward the vertical, directing hearts and minds to God in peace and tranquility.

Dying tradition
"There will probably be cats and dogs and maybe a goat"—harassed Intourist guide, asked about the animals at the Circus. Foreigners' opinions of the current state of the Moscow Circus vary enormously. Some express great disappointment at the unimaginative and old-fashioned use of animals in the show, while others, mainly people in their fifties and sixties, feel that it continues to reflect circus traditions that are fast dying out in the West.

There are few signs today that Suzdal was once a powerful rival of Moscow

Murder of the princes
The small village of Kideshka, a mile or so from Suzdal, is famous for the Church of SS. Boris and Gleb, built in 1152. On the death of Vladimir of Kiev in 1015, two of his younger sons—Boris and Gleb—were murdered in Kiev on the orders of their ambitious elder brother, Svyatopolk, who wanted their share of the princely territories. Not long after, Svyatopolk himself was killed by his other brother, Yaroslav. While the two innocent victims, Boris and Gleb, were soon canonized by the Orthodox Church, Svyatopolk was dubbed with the enduring epithet "the Accursed."

Suzdal▶▶▶ is the best-preserved town of the entire Golden Ring—a stunning ensemble of domed churches, monasteries, and tent-roofed bell towers, wooden houses, and log cabins. The founder of Moscow, Yuri Dolgorukiy, built the first great fortress here in the middle of a treeless plain surrounded by dense forest. The ancient core of the town nestles in a bend of the gently meandering Kamenka River.

The kremlin has its own architectural jewel: the **Cathedral of the Nativity**, dating in its present form from the early 16th century. A building of perfect symmetry, it is instantly recognizable by its five blue star-spangled onion domes. The interior is decorated with frescoes dating from the early 13th century to the 1630s—a dazzling sequence of blues and golds. The cathedral is also home to the earliest bronze doors in Russia. The archbishop's residence is now a museum of icons painted by artists of the Suzdal school.

Beyond the stalls of the ancient *torg* or marketplace, still lively today, are the **Church of the Resurrection** and the **Church of Our Lady of Kazan**, both dating from the 1730s. Twin churches were common in the region: the small, cozier building was for winter worship, while the larger, more flamboyant church was used in summer.

Two remarkable religious houses on the outer reaches of town face one another across the Kamenka. The 14th-century **Monastery of the Holy Savior and St. Euthymius** occupies the higher bank. It is surrounded by brick walls nearly 20 feet thick, and interspersed with equally formidable watchtowers, the most imposing being the great square entrance tower. Occupying the meadows on the opposite bank is the **Convent of the Intercession**. Its 14th-century origins can still be detected in the architecture—some of the churches have single, rounded domes in accordance with the earlier Byzantine style.

A final port of call might be the **Suzdal Museum of Wooden Architecture (Muzey Drevnosti)**, at the opposite end of town; it brings together wooden churches, windmills, barns, bathhouses, and ordinary dwellings.

Yaroslavl►► As early as 1010 AD there was a settlement at the point where the Kotorosl River flows into the Volga, when Grand Prince Yaroslav the Wise of Kiev renamed it in honor of himself. Yaroslavl's golden age was in the 13th century, but the town enjoyed a revival in the 17th century, when merchants from as far away as England, Germany, and Holland came to buy cloth, leather goods, and silverware.

On the banks of the Kotorosl River is the **Monastery of the Savior**, founded in the late 12th century and for more than 500 years one of the most formidable fortresses in the region (the walls are more than 10 feet thick). The views from the top of the bell tower are well worth the climb. The monks' refectory is now occupied by a museum.

The cream-colored, multidomed **Church of the Prophet Elijah**, dating from 1650, is near the central parking lot. The chapel has one of the last tent roofs erected before the Patriarch Nikon imposed a ban on such "overindulgence" two years later. It was commissioned by a local family of wealthy merchants, the Skripkins. The wonderfully ornate interior includes some magnificent murals which date from the 1680s.

Other churches not to be missed include the **Church of the Epiphany**, with its brilliantly tiled-and-glazed façade, and the **Church of St. John Chrysostom in Korovniki** (1648–1654), noted for its ornate brick window surrounds and glazed tiles.

Strange but true
Legend had it that in the 16th century Solominia Saburova, the divorced and supposedly barren wife of Prince Vasili III, had a child. Fearing for his life, she hid the child with friends, then faked his death and burial. In 1934 a child's coffin was found by her tomb. It contained no bones, just a stuffed shirt.

With more than a hundred varieties of traditional Russian architecture, Suzdal is now an enormous museum town

The Red Arrow

■ Still one of the great Russian experiences, the train journey between Moscow and St. Petersburg beats air and road travel hands down for atmosphere, comfort, and reliability—which is why most visitors continue to opt for Russia's famous train, the *Krasnaya Strela*, Red Arrow. ■

148

Rail first
A merchant traveling to Moscow by train in the early days boarded the train to St. Petersburg by mistake. When he learned of his neighbor's destination he was amazed: "How marvelous! The same train that is taking you to Petersburg is taking me to Moscow. Devilishly clever, these Germans!"

The train departs nightly at 11:55 from Leningrad Station, Moscow. It covers 405 miles in eight hours, arriving at St. Petersburg's Moscow Station at 7:55.

What you need to know Most compartments are two- and four-berth. It's a good idea to book all places to guarantee privacy. Toilet and hand basins are located at the end of each passenger coach. Bring your own food and drink, as buffet facilities are limited. You can ask the guard for boiling water and tea from the samovar. Tickets are sold only for hard currency. Buy them from the Intourist desk in your hotel rather than at the main stations.

Security There *have* been reports of vandals breaking windows and thieves breaking into compartments and robbing passengers. This kind of incident is exceptional. However, for your own peace of mind take strong suitcases with combination locks. Be sure to keep the door of your compartment locked at all times. There is a conductor in each carriage who will listen sympathetically to any complaints you may have about other passengers.

The Nicholas Railroad The day the Moscow to St. Petersburg railroad opened, November 1, 1851, the journey lasted 22 hours because an overzealous official thought to smooth the tsar's progress by greasing the rails along one stretch of track. Nicholas I also insisted on inspecting the line at regular intervals. The railroad took only eight years to build, thanks partly to American technical expertise provided by Major George Washington Whistler, with the labor of more than 50,000 serfs, who worked around the clock in all weathers using only picks, shovels, and wheelbarrows.

Above and below: the Red Arrow in Moscow

■ **Too much advertising, too many game shows, too many imported programs, too little choice, and too much political interference—the complaints about Russian TV sound like those leveled at TV in America and Western Europe. The one unquestionably popular genre is the soap opera.** ■

Television is still a powerful weapon in the hands of the government. Left: TV crew on the streets of Moscow. Above: a market stall stacked with TV s and VCRs. Below: Moscow's Ostankino TV tower

World's tallest
Extending the Ostankino TV tower to a height of 1,844 feet will make it, for a time at least, the tallest tower in the world.

Soaps In May 1994 Russia's main television channel, Ostankino 1, began broadcasting a new 190-part soap opera from Mexico called *Wild Rose,* starring the popular Veronica Castro. It was chosen to replace the phenomenally successful *Simply Maria,* which had made its star, Victoria Ruffo, a household name. For week after week, up to 140 million viewers (about half the entire population) tuned in to *Simply Maria,* based on the turbulent emotional life of a peasant who makes it to the top as a fashion designer. Despite poor dubbing, dubious acting, and an implausible plot, *Simply Maria* was an unqualified hit, especially with women, who were only too glad to escape, if only for an hour or two, from the unremitting hard labor that is the lot of every Russian housewife and breadwinner. The national TV network has its own productions—among them *The Little Things in Life*—but these have made little impact, presumably because the situations are too close to home.

Escapism probably also accounts for the rapid increase in the number of game shows. These follow a predictable formula, but the prizes, such as food hampers, are generally modest by Western standards. The exception to this is *Polye Chyudes* ("Wheel of Fortune"), hosted by Leonid Yakubovich, which gives away cars and luxury cruises.

Communications explosion Russia experienced a communications explosion in 1995, when Moscow's Ostankino TV tower was equipped with new transmitters which theoretically increased the number of available TV stations to 40. However, more "choice" simply meant more duplication, and in any case most Muscovites still cannot afford post-Soviet television sets.

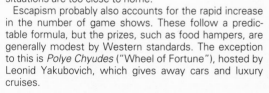

| ПРОСПЕКТ ПРОСВЕЩЕНИЯ |
| Prospekt Prosveshcheniya | **2**

ОЗЕРКИ
Ozerki

Udelnaya УДЕЛЬНАЯ

Pionerskaya ПИОНЕРСКАЯ

Chyornaya Rechka УЕРНАЯ РЕУКА

Petrogradskaya ПЕТРОГРАДСКАЯ

Gorkovskaya ГОРЬКОВСКАЯ

Nevskiy Prospekt
НЕВСКИЙ ПРОСПЕКТ

Mayakovskaya
МАЯКОВСКАЯ

3 | ПРИМОРСКАЯ |
| Primorskaya |

ВАСИЛЕОСТРОВСКАЯ
Vasileostrovskaya

ГОСТИНЫЙ ДВОР
Gostiniy Dvor

Dostoevskaya
ДОСТОЕВСКАЯ

СЕННАЯ ПЛОЩАДЬ
Sennaya Ploshchad

| САДОВАЯ |
| Sadovaya | **4**

Vladimirskaya
ВЛАДИМИРСКАЯ

Tekhnologicheskiy Institut
ТЕХНОЛОГИУЕСКИЙ
ИНСТИТУТ

БАЛТИЙСКАЯ
Baltiyskaya

ПУШКИНСКАЯ
Pushkinskaya

НАРВСКАЯ
Narvskaya

ФРУНЗЕНСКАЯ
Frunzenskaya

КИРОВСКИЙ ЗАВОД
Kirovskiy Zavod

МОСКОВСКИЕ ВОРОТА Moskovskie Vorota

ЗЛЕКТРОСИЛА Elektrosila

АВТОВО
Avtovo

ПАРК ПОБЕДЫ Park Pobedy

МОСКОВСКАЯ Moskovskaya

ЛЕНИНСКИЙ ПРОСПЕКТ
Leninskiy Prospekt

ЗВЕЗДНАЯ Zvezdnaya

1 | ПРОСПЕКТ ВЕТЕРАНОВ |
| Prospekt Veteranov |

| КУПУИНО |
| Kupchino | **2**

©TCS   MC/col   User number 9C02117

Introduction St. Petersburg is a planned city. The focal point is the Admiralty, distinguished by its needle spire and located only a stone's throw from the city's most familiar tourist attraction, the Winter Palace (Hermitage). Radiating like compass points from the Admiralty are three major avenues: Nevskiy Prospekt (St. Petersburg's main shopping street), Gorokhovaya Ulitsa, and Voznesenskiy Prospekt. Crossing these streets from west to east are three famous canals and rivers, the Moyka, the Catherine, and the Fontanka. Dividing the city into north and south is the fast-flowing and majestic Neva River. The main tourist sights on the northern bank of the river are the Strelka, directly opposite the Winter Palace and, just a little farther upstream, the Peter-Paul Fortress.

St. Petersburg has a metro system, but it is not nearly as extensive as its Moscow counterpart, and Petersburgers

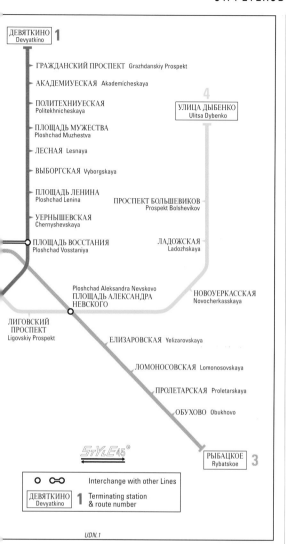

ДЕВЯТКИНО Devyatkino **1**

ГРАЖДАНСКИЙ ПРОСПЕКТ Grazhdanskiy Prospekt

АКАДЕМИУЕСКАЯ Akademicheskaya

ПОЛИТЕХНИУЕСКАЯ Politekhnicheskaya

ПЛОЩАДЬ МУЖЕСТВА Ploshchad Muzhestva

ЛЕСНАЯ Lesnaya

ВЫБОРГСКАЯ Vyborgskaya

ПЛОЩАДЬ ЛЕНИНА Ploshchad Lenina

УЕРНЫШЕВСКАЯ Chernyshevskaya

ПЛОЩАДЬ ВОССТАНИЯ Ploshchad Vosstaniya

ЛИГОВСКИЙ ПРОСПЕКТ Ligovskiy Prospekt

УЛИЦА ДЫБЕНКО Ulitsa Dybenko **4**

ПРОСПЕКТ БОЛЬШЕВИКОВ Prospekt Bolshevikov

ЛАДОЖСКАЯ Ladozhskaya

Ploshchad Aleksandra Nevskovo ПЛОЩАДЬ АЛЕКСАНДРА НЕВСКОГО

НОВОУЕРКАССКАЯ Novocherkasskaya

ЕЛИЗАРОВСКАЯ Yelizarovskaya

ЛОМОНОСОВСКАЯ Lomonosovskaya

ПРОЛЕТАРСКАЯ Proletarskaya

ОБУХОВО Obukhovo

РЫБАЦКОЕ Rybatskoe **3**

STYLE45®

O ⚭ Interchange with other Lines

ДЕВЯТКИНО Devyatkino **1** Terminating station & route number

UDN.1

CITY HIGHLIGHTS ◀◀◀◀◀

ADMIRALTEYSTVO
see page 156

ERMITAZH *see pages 157–165*

ISAAKIEVSKIY SOBOR
see page 169

LETNIY DVORETS
see pages 170–171

KAZANSKIY SOBOR
see page 180

KHRAM SPASA "NA KROVI"
see pages 180–181

MARIINSKIY TEATR
see page 181

RUSSKIY MUZEY
see pages 183–185

ALEKSANDRO-NEVSKIY LAVRA
see page 197

PETROPAVLOVSKAYA KREPOST *see pages 216–218*

153

Canal traffic
At the beginning of the 19th century the waterways of St. Petersburg were the city's main thoroughfare. In 1815 Petersburgers owned 520 boats, 295 skiffs, and 268 whaleboats. One traveler described the sights on the canals thus: "The Russian gondoliers deck their boats and their persons in rich and fantastic colors … occasionally there is an accompaniment to the voice of the *rojok* or reed pipe, tambourine, and two wooden spoons with bells at each end."

rely on the excellent trolley, bus, and trolleybus services. For how to use public transportation see page 268.

The gazetteer, which follows, is divided into areas that, roughly speaking, emanate from the Admiralty outward.

Few Communist symbols remain in a city returning to its imperial traditions

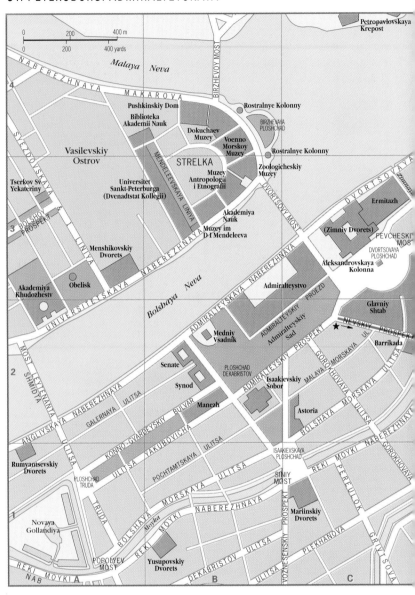

Admiralteyskaya

The Admiralty district is characterized by a single architectural ensemble, astonishing both in size and conception and dominating the waterfront from the Summer Palace to Senate Square. The imperial grandeur testifies to the Admiralty's importance as the administrative headquarters of the Russian Empire, but also emphasizes the Western-facing ethos which gave St. Petersburg its *raison d'être*—not a tiered bell tower or onion dome in sight! The Admiralty was not originally the focal point of

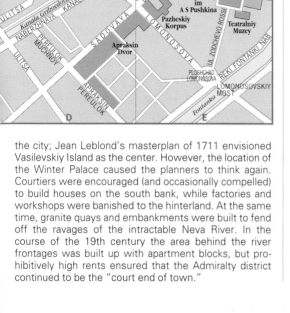

Venice of the North

In the 16th century the French astrologer Nostradamus predicted that "Venice will rise in the North Sea. The City will emerge from the dead water," an uncannily accurate prediction when one considers the bleak and inhospitable spot chosen by Peter the Great for his new city. Yet here, on a wild, flat, boggy marsh that was lost in swirling, freezing mists in winter and where the winds howled in from the Gulf of Finland, Peter had a vision of a great city. Legend has it that on May 16, 1703, when his workmen cut the first strips of turf, Peter placed two of them in the form of a cross, saying "Here shall be a town."

the city; Jean Leblond's masterplan of 1711 envisioned Vasilevskiy Island as the center. However, the location of the Winter Palace caused the planners to think again. Courtiers were encouraged (and occasionally compelled) to build houses on the south bank, while factories and workshops were banished to the hinterland. At the same time, granite quays and embankments were built to fend off the ravages of the intractable Neva River. In the course of the 19th century the area behind the river frontages was built up with apartment blocks, but prohibitively high rents ensured that the Admiralty district continued to be the "court end of town."

The Admiralty Spire
Four elements rule us, and
their rule is benign,
But then man made a fifth,
for man is free.
Does this ark perhaps, with
its austere design,
Deny to space its old
supremacy?
—From *The Admiralty* by
Osip Mandelstam

▶▶▶ Admiralteystvo (Admiralty) 154B3

Admiralteyskiy Prospekt
Bus: 10

A superb neoclassical building designed by A. D. Zakharov
in 1806–1823, the Admiralty is instantly recognizable by its
gilded spire, which is crowned by a weathervane in the
shape of a sailing ship. It stands on the site of Peter the
Great's first shipyard, constructed in 1704 at the same time
as the founding of the city. By 1713, it employed more than
10,000 workers—ten times the number of the city's sec-
ond-ranking employer, the Arsenal. The air was filled with
the smell of tar, and the skies bristled with the masts of
wooden ships. By the end of the 18th century the complex
was enormous—the Admiralty itself was surrounded by
nine shipyards, and contemporary paintings show huge war
galleys under construction on the riverside. When shipbuild-
ing activity was phased out after 1844, the Admiralty building was handed over to the Russian Navy.

▶▶▶ Dvortsovaya Ploshchad (Palace Square) 154C3

Trolleybus: 1, 7, 9, 10. Bus: 10

Palace Square, the focal point of St. Petersburg, is dominated by the magnificent façade of Rastrelli's Winter
Palace (see pages 157–160). It was laid out in its present
form by Carlo Rossi in the 1820s. Russia's triumph over
Napoleon is commemorated by the Alexander Column,
erected in the center of the square in 1834. The victory
theme is continued on the southern side of the square by
the former General Staff Building of the Russian Army,
actually two buildings linked by a gigantic double arch that
wheels toward Nevskiy Prospekt for a distance of 2,000
feet. The first arch is crowned by a superb sculpture of
the Chariot of Victory escorted by warriors.

Before the Revolution, military parades were held on
Palace Square, led by the tsar on horseback and sometimes accompanied by visiting heads of state. In January
1905 the square was the scene of a massacre, known as
Bloody Sunday, which sparked off the revolution of that
year. On November 7, 1917, Bolshevik forces began their
attack on the Winter Palace from this same square,
although there was no mass assault of the kind portrayed
by Eisenstein in the motion picture *October*.

*In its scale alone,
Petersburg can
hardly fail to impress.
The Alexander
Column in the center
of Palace Square
commemorates the
victory over
Napoleon*

▶▶▶ Ermitazh (Hermitage)   *154C3*

Dvortsovaya Naberezhnaya 34
Open: Tue–Sun 10:30–6

There can be no better reason for coming to St. Petersburg than to visit the Hermitage. Renowned as one of the world's leading picture galleries, it is also a treasure house of ancient cultures. In addition, the Hermitage is an extension of the Winter Palace, former residence of the Russian imperial family, and provides a setting of unparalleled opulence for the various dazzling collections. But the experience can be overwhelming: there are 12 miles of galleries, more than three million exhibits, and 1,000 rooms in the Winter Palace alone. Intourist provides a half-day tour with guide, but it is more rewarding (and a good deal cheaper) to arm yourself with a plan of the museum (of which an English-language version is available) and cover the territory at your own pace. There's little point in even trying to do the Hermitage in one day; far better to concentrate on one part of the collection at a time. If your stay in St. Petersburg is limited, try at least to see the priceless collection of 19th- and 20th-century French Impressionist and Post-Impressionist art (see page 163), in particular the recently revealed group of 74 lost masterpieces, which had been languishing in a storeroom since 1945.

The main entrance is on the north side of the building, overlooking the river. There are cloakroom and restroom facilities (typically Russian) inside the main entrance. Tickets are also sold here—there is a special rate for foreigners, and a single payment covers virtually everything in the museum. The sales points inside the museum are surprisingly poorly stocked—the best selections are to be had in major bookstores like Dom Knigi on Nevskiy Prospekt. The Hermitage now has its own marketing company and its official products carry the Scythian stag.

The Hermitage consists of three connecting buildings: the Winter Palace (Zimniy Dvorets), the Small Hermitage (Maliy Ermitazh), and the Large Hermitage (Bolshoy Ermitazh). The present Winter Palace is the fourth on this site (the sixth by some calculations). It was designed by

The Winter Palace exudes imperial grandeur, but few Russian tsars warmed to it. Nicholas II, for example, preferred Tsarskoe Selo

House rules
Catherine the Great created the Hermitage for relaxation. To encourage informality she attached a series of rules to the entrance for the guidance of her guests. Among them Rule 9 stated: "To eat of the sweet and the savory, but to drink with moderation, that each may always find his feet on going out of the doors."

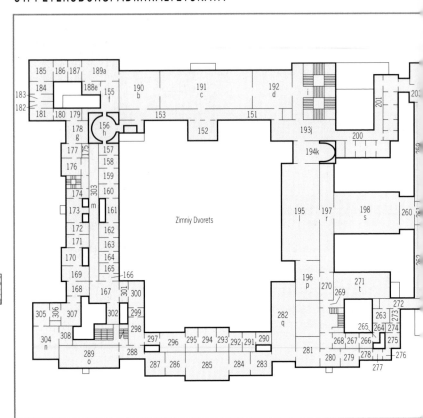

Zimniy Dvorets

Bartolommeo Rastrelli in the baroque style for Empress Elizabeth in 1754–1762. The thousands of peasant laborers, skilled masons, and soldiers who were employed in its construction set up camp in a neighboring field. Rastrelli conceived of a series of immense façades, each broken by even groupings of columns on two superimposed levels. The balustrade and the entrance pediments carry classical urns and sculpted bronze figures. The color scheme has always been a movable feast: ice-blue was the original choice; then, in the 19th century and up to the time of the Revolution, the walls were painted dark red. Catherine the Great preferred the neoclassical style to the baroque and ordered the interior to be redesigned accordingly. In 1837 the Palace was gutted by fire and many people died trying to salvage the treasures. Nicholas I immediately ordered the palace's reconstruction. The architect in charge of the project, V. P. Stasov, showed commendable restraint in re-creating the designs of his distinguished predecessors; he is also credited with introducing a number of fire precautions including brick partitions.

The **Small Hermitage** of 1764–1767 was built for Catherine the Great by Vallin de la Mothe (responsible also for the Gostiniy Dvor, see page 179) as a private retreat; at one time the only point of access was through her personal apartments. The Small Hermitage became the repository

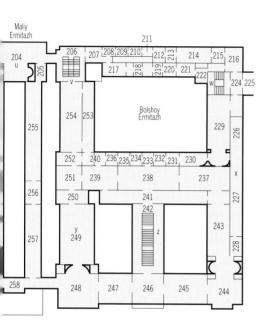

Maliy
Ermitazh

Key to plan of the Winter Palace (Zimniy Dvorets) and Large Hermitage (Bolshoy Dvorets) Second Floor

a Malachite Hall
b Concert Hall
c Nicholas Hall
d Fore Hall
e White Dining Room
f Moorish Dining Room
g Library of Nicholas II
h Rotunda
i Jordan Staircase
j Hall of Field Marshals
k Peter the Great's Throne Room
l Armorial Hall
m Dark Corridor
n Gold Drawing Room
o White Hall
p Picket Hall
q Alexander Hall
r Gallery of 1812
s Hall of St. George
t Cathedral
u Pavilion Hall
v Council Staircase
w Theater Staircase
x Loggia of Raphael
y Tent Room
z State Staircase

The "Bridge of Sighs" spanning the Winter Canal is one reason why St. Petersburg is called the Venice of the North

for the Empress's collection of Dutch and Flemish masters, the origins of the present gallery. The hanging garden, which connects it to the palace, still exists.

The **Large Hermitage** was built in stages and took almost a century (1770–1860) to complete. Y. M. Velten and Giacomo Quarenghi oversaw the original designs, but the interior is the work of A. I. Stakenschneider. A small bridge reminiscent of the Bridge of Sighs in Venice spans the Winter Canal and links the Large Hermitage with Quarenghi's Theater (closed to the public).

Winter Palace (Zimniy Dvorets) Second Floor

To embark on a tour of the second floor of the Winter Palace (see plan above) is to journey into the prerevolutionary past. The cycle of state rooms begins with the magnificent Jordan Staircase from where each year, on January 6, the tsar and his retinue would process down to the Neva for the ceremony of the Blessing of the Waters. Designed by Rastrelli and restored by Vasiliy Stasov after the fire of 1837, the approach is dominated by twin sets of marble pillars, surmounted by arches liberally endowed with gilt stucco. Windows, some real, some painted to create a *trompe l'oeil* effect, are brilliantly reflected in the mirrors opposite, while the ceiling is "supported" by painted classical figures. The steps are of white Carrara marble, the handrails ornamented with gilded moldings.

ST. PETERSBURG: ADMIRALTEYSKAYA

Taking the plunge
The ceremony of the Blessing of the Waters on January 6, from which the Jordan Staircase takes its name, often included infant baptisms, sometimes with unfortunate results. "It has happened," wrote one witness, "that the shivering priests let the unfortunate little creatures slip through their fingers under the ice: 'But what bliss for the baby to go straight to paradise' was the consoling reflection of the superstitious."

There are so many artistic treasures in the Hermitage, sculptures as well as paintings, that it is essential to be selective

The Jordan Staircase was the scene each year for the season's inaugural ball. Here, as many as 8,000 guests would assemble and ascend the staircase, which was guarded by lines of impeccably presented officers in their various dress uniforms, their breastplates and helmets gleaming in the candlelight. Greeting the visitors at the top of the steps were ranks of lackeys, dressed in frock coats trimmed with gold lace, and the Master of Ceremonies wielding an ebony cane. At his signal the orchestra took up a march and all eyes turned to a point in the far distance—a suite of rooms away, in fact—where the imperial couple were awaiting their guests.

Just beyond the Jordan Staircase is the Fore Hall (**Room 192**), where diners would gather for a preliminary glass of champagne before proceeding to the Hall of St. George (see below). The Nicholas Hall (**Room 191**) with its massive Corinthian columns and chandeliers, was decorated by Stasov for Nicholas I, whose portrait hangs here. This is where the most formal of the imperial balls took place.

Historic events Beyond the Concert Hall is the Malachite Hall (**Room 189**), designed by Bryullov but refurbished for Nicholas II's wife, Alexandra. (The green malachite pillars are the outstanding decorative feature.) This room is redolent with quite different and more dramatic historical associations. It was here that Alexander Kerensky's Provisional Government convened for the last time on the night of November 7, 1917. At 11:40 precisely a shell fired from the Peter-Paul Fortress shattered a fourth-floor window just above the Malachite Hall, forcing the ministers to withdraw next door, where they were eventually arrested. The clock on the mantelpiece in the White Dining Room (**Room 188**) was stopped at 2:10 on the morning of November 8—the moment when the Provisional Government finally relinquished power to the insurgent forces. "Bayonet all the sons of bitches on the spot," someone shouted, but in the event the ministers were led peacefully out of the building and frogmarched to the Peter-Paul Fortress.

The suite of **Rooms 168–187** is closed to the public.

Nothing wasted
In the hours following the fall of the Winter Palace on the night of November 7, 1917, the American journalist John Reed managed to get into the building. He reported afterward: "In a room where furniture was stored we came upon two soldiers ripping the elaborate Spanish upholstery from chairs. They explained it was to make boots with ..." Need was hardly the excuse, however, for the raiding of the imperial wine cellars!

Military heroes Return now to the Jordan Staircase and to the second suite of state rooms which has a distinctly martial flavor: the Hall of Field Marshals (**Room 193**), for instance, where portraits of Russian military heroes used to hang. Peter the Great's Throne Room (**Room 194**) leads to Stasov's Armorial Hall (**Room 195**), which bears the coats of arms of Russia's former provinces. Martial figures and battle standards guard the doors. The Picket Hall (**Room 196**), where the palace sentries were mustered, provides an appropriate backdrop for the splendid Gallery of 1812. Designed by Carlo Rossi as a tribute to the victors in the war against Napoléon, the stately barrel-vaulted hall is dominated by 300 portraits of the leading Russian generals and senior officers, all by the same Englishman, George Dawes (1781–1829), who, appropriately enough, also painted the portrait of the Duke of Wellington. The three allied heads of state, however— Alexander I of Russia, Frederick William III of Prussia, and Francis I of Austria—are the work of different artists. Turning off from the gallery is one of the most sumptuous rooms in the entire Winter Palace. This is the Hall of St. George (**Room 198**), originally designed by Quarenghi and completed on St. George's Day, 1795. Apart from the throne at the far end, the most impressive features are the quadruple-tiered chandeliers. This was the scene of many great historical occasions, perhaps the most memorable being the opening ceremony of Russia's doomed parliament, the State *Duma*, presided over by Nicholas II in May 1906.

Operatic climax
In the final act of Tchaikovsky's opera *The Queen of Spades*, the climactic confrontation between the two lovers takes place on the Winter Canal under the arch which connects the Hermitage and its theater. In despair, the heroine Lisa runs to the Palace Embankment and throws herself into the Neva.

Western European art
The Hermitage's collection of Western European art is legendary. It began with Peter the Great, who acquired works depicting sailing ships and the sea, but was not properly developed until the 1780s, under Catherine the Great.

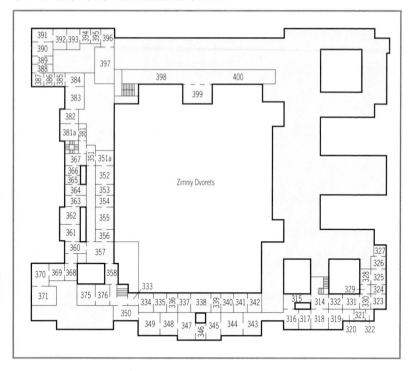

Zimniy Dvorets

Winter Palace (Zimniy Dvorets)—Third Floor

Culture fatigue
There are 400 exhibition rooms in the Hermitage, and to see them all would involve a walk of 12 miles. There are more than 2.8 million exhibits—even to glance at each of them would take nine years. From the original collection of two dozen maritime scenes, the Hermitage has grown to 12,000 sculptures, 15,000 paintings, 600,000 drawings, and 224,000 works of applied art.

She was more systematic, instructing her agents abroad, including Prince Golitsyn and the French encyclopedist Denis Diderot, to keep their ears to the ground for bargains. Money being no object, they were able to buy up entire private collections; it was not an uncommon sight at the Admiralty to see crates packed with canvases being unloaded from foreign ships.

Italian, Spanish, and Flemish art The Italian paintings can be found in **Rooms 207–230** of the **Large Hermitage (Bolshoy Ermitazh)** on the second floor (see plan, pages 158–159). The collection is more impressive in its breadth than in its depth, but there is plenty to savor, from Fra Angelico and Simone Martini through Leonardo and Raphael to Veronese and Titian. There are two Leonardos: the early *Benois Madonna* and the much later *Madonna Litta*. There are a number of works by Veronese in **Room 222**, but the best-represented artist is Titian (**Rooms 219–221**)—his *Portrait of a Young Woman* is a gem.

There are only two rooms devoted to Spanish painting (239, 240), but all the great names are here: El Greco, Velázquez, Murillo, and Goya. More comprehensive is the collection of Dutch and Flemish paintings in rooms 244–258. The Hermitage's superb trawl of Rembrandts, some 25 paintings in all, can be found in **Room 254**. Preeminent are the religious subjects, including *Abraham's Sacrifice of Isaac*, *The Holy Family*, the sublime *Descent from the Cross*, and the intensely moving *Return of the Prodigal Son*. But there are some charming secular paintings too, including one of Rembrandt's own favorites, *Danae* (now restored after a recent slashing), and *Flora*, a

thinly disguised portrait of his beloved wife, Saskia. The collection also includes Rubens, Van Dyck, and Jan Brueghel.

19th- and 20th-century French art Visitors from all over the world come to the Hermitage just to see the outstanding collection of French painting of the 19th and 20th centuries, which is located on the **third floor of the Winter Palace** in the south wing, **Rooms 316–348** (see plan opposite). Gauguin's Tahiti period is well represented with works such as *Eu haere ia oe (Ou vas-tu?)* and, while the Van Goghs are not especially distinguished, there are ravishing exceptions, for example *Les buissons de lilas*. The aficionado of jungles and forests, Henri Rousseau, is here too, with *Combat du tigre et du taureau* among others. **Rooms 318–320** are devoted to an outstanding quadrumvirate of artists: Monet, Degas, Cézanne, and Renoir. Cézanne's arresting self-portrait (*Autoportrait à la casquette*), Monet's scintillating *Dame dans un jardin*, several sensuous pastels by Degas including *Femme se peignant*, and one of Renoir's best-known works, *Portrait de l'actrice Jeanne Samary*, are highlights. Look for the new star attraction, Degas's *Place de la Concorde*; also the 15 "new" Renoirs and four Van Goghs (see page 157). The 35 canvases by Henri Matisse displayed in **Rooms 343–345** are in many ways the pride of the collection: still lifes in a variety of styles, arresting landscapes, studies in the juxtaposition of color such as *La chambre rouge*, and superb examples from the two primitivist cycles, *La musique* and *La danse*. After completing one spellbinding artistic odyssey one embarks immediately on another, as Matisse leads inexorably to Picasso (**Room 349**): *Arlequin et sa compagne (Les deux saltimbanques)*, *L'entrevue (Les deux soeurs)*, a charming gouache entitled *Garçon au chien, Musical Instruments*, and other examples from the Blue, Rose, and Cubist periods.

Those interested in the development of modern art outside France will want to continue the adventure into **Rooms 349, 334** and **333** which contain works by Vlaminck, Derain, Léger, and Vasili Kandinsky.

A visitor pauses to admire one of the baroque masterpieces for which the Hermitage is famous

163

Marketing St. Petersburg's treasure house
During the 70 years of Soviet rule, the Hermitage increased its collections four and a half times over. How to maintain, preserve, display, and promote this vast collection in an unrelenting atmosphere of financial shortages has led the administrators to take advice from the West. Sponsors, such as Coca-Cola, are being sought out; advice is being taken from top-flight American management consultants, and the Louvre is helping to make replicas of popular exhibits so that the tourist market can be fully exploited. If the Hermitage's collection is to be preserved for global posterity, then massive fund-raising will be needed in the West, for as one observer put it: "Those Russians who love the Hermitage have no money."

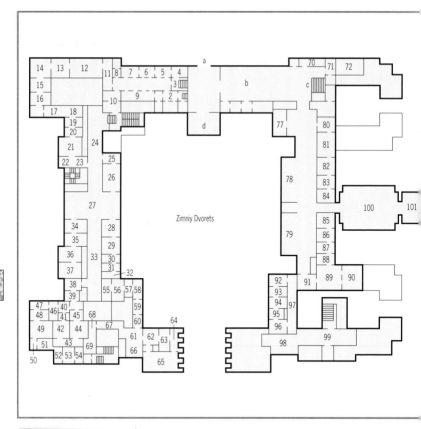

Scythian treasures
If you have joined an Intourist guided tour of the Hermitage, you will be taken to see the Special Collection, which boasts the largest exhibition of Scythian (ancient Russian) art in the world. The gold and jewelry exchanged between the Scythians and the Greek colonies in the vicinity of the Black Sea is unsurpassed.

Russian guidebook, 1874
"For rheumatism, aches and chills try Pine Oil (for rubbing) obtainable from Shtoll and Schmidt on the corner of Kirpichniy Pereulok and the Moyka Embankment."

Architectural elegance

One of the pleasures of the Hermitage lies in discovering some marvelous rooms as you move from one school of painting to the next. Take, for example, the Pavilion Hall (**Room 204**), which serves as a bridge between the Winter Palace and the Large Hermitage. The eye feasts on the interplay of natural light flooding in through the windows and its reflection in the icy chandeliers. Then there is the Tent Room (**249**), with its remarkable pitched roof and coffered ceiling, home to Dutch genre paintings by the likes of Franz Hals and Salomon van Ruysdael. Quarenghi's Loggia of Raphael (**Room 227**) is built in imitation of a Vatican original, though without the Raphaels (the only paintings by this artist are over in **Room 229**). The Alexander Hall (**Room 282**), to a design by Bryullov, is another variation on the theme of "Victory 1812" with bas-reliefs commemorating the various military engagements, an elaborate, high-arched ceiling, and multipatterned parquet floor.

Ancient art

If your thirst for culture still hasn't been quenched, drink your fill of the antiquities housed on the **first floor of the Bolshoy Ermitazh** (**Large Hermitage**, see plan above). The Egyptian artifacts in **Room 100** are greatly overshadowed by the impressive collection of Greek and

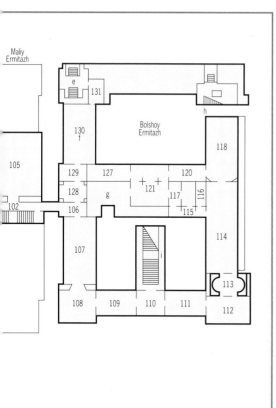

Maliy Ermitazh

e 131

130 f

Bolshoy Ermitazh

118

105

129 127 120

121

128

g 117 116

102 106 115

107

114

108 109 110 111 113

112

Key to plan of the Large Hermitage (Bolshoy Ermitazh) and Winter Palace (Zimniy Dvorets) First Floor
a Main Entrance
b Rastrelli Gallery
c Jordan Staircase
d Ticket Office
e Council Staircase
f Hall of Twenty Columns
g Special Collections
h Theater Staircase
i State Staircase

Something borrowed
In the early 1980s it emerged that the head of the Communist Party in Leningrad, ironically named Romanov, had unofficially borrowed a priceless dinner service from the Hermitage collection for his daughter's wedding. In the course of the celebrations a number of items were smashed. The story was leaked, probably by the KGB, and did little good to Romanov's succession chances.

165

Roman antiquities starting at **Room 106** and including sculptures, wall paintings, busts, and mosaics. One highlight is the superbly decorated Hall of Twenty Columns with its magnificent collection of Etruscan bronzes and ceramics and Roman vases, some dating from the 7th century BC.

There cannot be a more splendid backdrop to a museum collection than the Winter Palace

■ During the 19th century, artistic patronage in Russia was passing from privileged, aristocratic families such as the Stroganovs, Orlovs, and Golitsyns into the hands of the Moscow bourgeoisie. The greatest representatives of this new class of patron were Sergei Shchukin and Ivan Morozov. ■

Master of portraiture
Ilya Repin (1844–1930) is one of Russia's most eminent artists. He trained originally as an icon painter and then studied at St. Petersburg's Academy of Fine Arts. After traveling in Europe he returned to concentrate on painting epic canvases depicting great moments in Russian history. But his greatest skill was as a portraitist, and he painted Tolstoy several times. Some of these portraits can be seen at Tolstoy's country estate, Yasnaya Polyana.

Part of Matisse's ground-breaking Dance *sequence*

Connoisseur Known as "the porcupine" because of his prickly cast of mind, Sergei Shchukin (1854–1937) was both an astute businessman and the finest, most percipient art collector of the age. Well-traveled and fluent in French and German, Shchukin did not begin collecting until he was well over 40, when he purchased Monet's *Argenteuil Lilac*. From that point on he was unstoppable, and by 1914 he had acquired more than 220 paintings of the French Impressionist and Post-Impressionist schools, most notably Cézanne. At his home, the former mansion of Princess Trubetskoy in Moscow, Sergei proceeded to hang his paintings—the dining room alone was covered from floor to ceiling with Gauguins. The Shchukins entertained lavishly, holding parties and concerts in which Chaliapin and Rachmaninov might provide the entertainment; on Sundays Sergei held open house to students and other art connoisseurs, himself taking his visitors on conducted tours. What made Shchukin unique, however, was his championing of Matisse and Picasso when they were still virtually unknown—he continued to back Matisse even after the disastrous Salon d'Automne exhibition of 1910 at which his *Music and Dance* sequence was vilified by the critics. Shchukin ended up with more than 50 paintings by these artists and sponsored a visit by

La Montagne Sainte-Victoire *by Paul Cézanne*

Hidden collections
Despite 70 years of Communist rule, a small group of enthusiastic Russian collectors took considerable risks to build up impressive private art collections, and many of them are now revealing their treasures to the world for the first time. Crammed into every corner of tiny workers' apartments, such collections boast 18th-century Russian furniture, ormolu mounted clocks, works by Fabergé, and many fine examples of Russian avant-garde art that would have been banned in its time. Some of these private collections, such as that of I. S. Zilbersteyn, have already been bequeathed to the Russian nation. The main problem now is to protect them from thieves, who have already robbed several private collectors' apartments.

Matisse to Russia in 1911, a trip which had a profound impact on the development of Russian painting.

Family business Ivan Morozov (1871–1921) came from a family of art patrons—one of his relatives, Savva, put up the money for the Moscow Arts Theater. Ivan's mother, Varvara, was also a noted Moscow philanthropist, who endowed the first public library in the city and held a salon which attracted the likes of Tolstoy and Chekhov. Ivan began collecting paintings by Russian artists, including the modernists Larionov and Goncharova; he was also the first patron to take a serious interest in the work of Marc Chagall. His interest in French painting, however, for which he is now most famous, began only on the death of his brother, Mikhail, in 1904. (Mikhail's own private art collection included works by Bonnard, Degas, and Renoir, most of which his widow donated to the nation.) He would return from regular visits to the Paris auction houses of Vollard and Durand-Ruel with a priceless haul of Renoirs and Van Goghs, Gauguins, and Cézannes, which he duly hung in his mansion on Ulitsa Prechistenka. Portly, with a finely trimmed beard and perfectly tailored clothes set off by a cravat and pearl tie pin, Morozov resembled a typical member of the Establishment; but despite this his taste in pictures was increasingly progressive. From 1908 he started to collect works by Matisse and Picasso, and by the time of the Revolution his collection amounted to more than a hundred Impressionist paintings and more than 450 works by Russian artists.

A question of ownership Shchukin and Morozov both emigrated after the Revolution of 1917 and their collections, amounting to more than 750 paintings in all, were duly nationalized. Since then Madame Irina Shchukin has been trying to claim back or intercept paintings which once belonged to her father-in-law. Her first attempt in 1954, when a number of Picassos were lent to an exhibition in Paris by the Soviet government, was frustrated when the paintings were spirited into the Soviet embassy. Forty years later, in 1994, Madame Shchukin again requested the French courts to impound paintings lent by the Russian authorities (this time the artist was Matisse). But despite letters of protest to Presidents Yeltsin and Mitterrand, she has yet to be successful.

The prescience and taste of collectors like Sergei Shchukin (shown here) gave Russia a head start in acquiring masterpieces of 20th-century art

Walk The Moyka

This is a delightful walk alongside St. Petersburg's most historic and picturesque canal, the Moyka. Start at **Panteleymon Bridge** at the confluence of the Moyka and Fontanka rivers and end at the Narodniy or People's Bridge.

On the right are the magnificent **Summer Gardens**, on the left, the imposing but rather severe **Engineers' Castle** (see pages 170 and 173). Flowing along one side of the gardens, and separating them from **Mars Field**, is one of St. Petersburg's lesser known waterways, the **Swan Canal**.

Continue westward past **Mars Field** where the Moyka River originally rose as a swamp. On the left are the **Mikhailovskiy Gardens and Palace**, now the **Russian Museum**. The handsome neoclassical pavilion on the canal front is by architect Carlo Rossi and dates from 1825.

Clearly visible beyond Potseluyev Bridge, at the junction of the Moyka and Catherine canals, are the twisting towers and spires of the **Cathedral of the Savior on the Blood**. The cathedral was built over the spot where Alexander II was assassinated on March 1, 1881.

The Moyka is full of military associations from the tsarist past, such as place names like Large Horse Guards Bridge (Bolshoy Konyushenniy Most), and Horse Guards Square (Konyushennaya Ploshchad).

Before the bridge, on the left, is the former **Imperial Riding School** and stables, rebuilt by V. P. Stasov in 1817–1823. The **Equerries' Church** in the school was where Pushkin's funeral took place in 1837.

As the canal bends, the beautiful **Winter Canal** with its series of bridges appears on the right. The canal divides the Hermitage and Winter Palace from the Hermitage Theater. Opposite, at Reki Moyki Naberezhnaya 12 (Moyka Embankment) is **Pushkin's house**, now a museum (see page 182). Farther on, on the same side (No. 20), is the former home of the 18th-century court choir, now known as the **Glinka Kapella**. Choral associations gave the nickname "singers" to the bridge here.

The Moyka Canal now crosses **Nevskiy Prospekt** by the **Narodniy or People's Bridge**, one of the first iron bridges in the city (1806–1808). The walk comes to an end here, but not the canal, which eventually leads past Isaakievskaya Ploshchad (St. Isaac's Square) and the Siniy or Blue Bridge to the Mariinskiy Theater.

Quarenghi's round market graces the Moyka Canal

ISAAKIEVSKIY SOBOR

K. P. Bryullov's sumptuous painting of the Virgin Mary with saints decorates the dome of St. Isaac's Cathedral

▶▶▶ Isaakievskaya Ploshchad (St. Isaac's Square)   154C1

Bus: 10. Trolleybus: 5, 22

There are several points of interest in the vicinity of St. Isaac's Square. At the corner of Bolshaya Morskaya Ulitsa is the recently restored Astoria Hotel. Built in the *style moderne* in 1910–1912 to a design by Fedor Lidval, former guests have included the American chronicler of the Revolution, John Reed, and fellow journalist Louise Bryant, as well as anarchist Emma Goldman.

On the opposite side of the square is the former German Embassy, designed in 1912 by Peter Behrens and Mies van der Rohe of the Bauhaus movement. Just behind St. Isaac's Square is Peter Klodt's statue of Nicholas I, erected in 1859.

▶▶▶ Isaakievskiy Sobor (St. Isaac's Cathedral)   154B2

Isaakievskaya Ploshchad
Bus: 10. Trolleybus: 5, 22

The present St. Isaac's Cathedral dates from the early 19th century. The competition for the design was won in 1818 by an inexperienced young architect, Auguste de Montferrand. Construction took 40 years and Montferrand only just survived the official opening in 1858. Intended to match the impressive proportions of the neighboring Admiralty and Winter Palace, the cathedral is enormous, and can accommodate 14,000 worshippers. Building materials were brought from Finland by ship and by a specially constructed railroad. No expense was spared—one estimate of the cost was in excess of 23 million silver rubles—which accounts for the prodigious quantities of gold, bronze, malachite, jasper, and mosaic, not to mention the 14 varieties of marble. The cupola is decorated with a painting by K. P. Bryullov of the Virgin Mary surrounded by saints and angels—Bryullov also had a hand in the iconostasis. A giant pendulum demonstrating the earth's rotation, a relic of the 1930s, when the building was used as a "Museum Against Religion," hung from the dome until recently, when the cathedral was returned to the Orthodox Church. Climb the dome (200 feet high) for a magnificent panorama of the city, as well as a close-up of the 220 pounds of gold leaf that cover both the dome and the rooftop statues.

Tickets are on sale inside the building. Photography is not permitted.

169

Time to chime
The chimes of the Admiralty clock in St. Petersburg can now be heard again after a silence of more than 50 years. The original bells were installed during the lifetime of Peter the Great in 1721. In 1869 a new clockwork mechanism was installed which survived until World War II, when the Admiralty was damaged by enemy bombardment. The clock was repaired, but the bells were only restored in 1996. Visitors can hear the chimes hourly, much as the tsar himself once heard them.

Plans for St. Isaac's
Alexander I studied 24 different plans before the foundations of St. Isaac's Cathedral were laid in 1818. This may have been partly owing to nervousness over the almost complete inexperience of the French architect, Auguste De Montferrand (1786–1858). Nevertheless, the result was spectacular and the cathedral gained renown for the beauty of its candlelit Easter service when, as its bells rang out across the city, its congregation spilled out into the square outside.

While the décor of the Summer Palace is lavish by modern standards, its size gives it quite a homey appearance

Fatal miss
In April 1866 a deranged Polish student, Dmitri Karakazov, took a shot at Alexander II near the main gate of the Summer Gardens after he had been taking a walk there. He missed, but this did not save him from the gallows.

▶▶▶ **Letniy Dvorets i Letniy Sad (Summer Palace and Gardens)**   *155E4*

Bus: 14
Open: Summer Palace, Wed–Mon 10–5; Summer Gardens, daily 8 AM–11 PM

This most unpalatial of palaces is one of the hidden delights of St. Petersburg and reveals the remarkable unpretentiousness of Peter the Great. The simple two-story house of stuccoed brick was designed in the unassuming Dutch style by Domenico Trezzini, architect of the Peter-Paul Fortress. The only external ornament is a series of terra-cotta bas-reliefs. Peter confined himself to six rooms on the ground floor. The heavy oak Admiralty Chair in the reception room is where the tsar presided over meetings. It was specially designed for his enormous frame (he was 6 feet 9 inches tall). Peter collected classical sculptures as well as models and paintings of ships. In his study he pored over volumes on horticulture, medicine, and mathematics and still found time to edit St. Petersburg's first newspaper, *The News*. More often, however, visitors were ushered into the workshop, where the tsar, in a leather workman's apron, would receive them among the mechanical lathes, presses, tools, and measuring instruments. The dining room table could accommodate no more than eight guests; Peter left lavish ceremony and entertaining to his noble subjects, most notably his friend Prince Menshikov. A hatch leads through to the kitchen with its stone-paved floor, hooded stove, earthenware storage jars, and copper and iron cooking pots. Peter's bedroom contains a beautiful oak four-poster bed hung with crimson velvet. The second floor of the palace was occupied by Peter's second wife, Catherine, and their children—visitors can still see the cradle in the nursery.

The Summer Gardens were among the first and loveliest attractions to grace St. Petersburg. Peter I himself laid them out, and was active in planting and tending the trees and shrubs. Now covering about 230 acres, the gardens were originally much larger, stretching across into Mars

Field. The *allées* were planted with imported elms and oaks and graced with classical statues that had to be boxed in winter to protect them from the cold. There was a hothouse for exotic plants, an aviary for rare birds, and a grotto laced with mother-of-pearl. The superb gates were added by Velten in the 1770s. At that time, entertainment was provided by a "horn orchestra, the musicians dressed in bright huntsmen's garb."

▶▶▶ Marsovo Pole (Mars Field)   155E3
Tram: 2, 12, 32

Originally a marsh, Mars Field was drained by Peter the Great to serve as a military parade ground. Later it was used for fairs and other celebrations and was popularly known as the "Petersburg Sahara" because of its dusty, windswept appearance. The existing square's formal and somber character dates from March 1917, when the dead of the first Russian Revolution were buried here in mass graves. Later, the Bolsheviks adapted the memorial to honor their dead from the civil war, erecting the granite Monument to Revolutionary Fighters in the center of the field. Occupying almost the entire western side is the former barracks of the Pavlovskiy Regiment, constructed in 1817–1819 and designed by V. P. Stasov. These troops were the first to mutiny during the March Revolution.

▶▶ Millionnaya Ulitsa
(Millionaires' Street)   155D3

Before the Revolution this was one of the most fashionable streets in St. Petersburg—hence the name, which translates as "Millionaires' Street." No. 10 was designed by one of the architects who worked on the Winter Palace, A. Stakenschneider, for his own use. The French writer Honoré de Balzac courted the Polish countess Eveline Hanska in this house in 1843. On March 16, 1917, the Grand Duke Mikhail Alexandrovich, brother of Nicholas II, renounced his right to the throne from the house at No. 12, so bringing the Romanov dynasty to an end. No. 26 Palace Embankment was the home of another Grand Duke, Vladimir Alexandrovich, whose wife, Maria Pavlovna, was a well-known patron of the arts. Their house became a magnet for the glitterati when the tsar and his family retired to Tsarskoe Selo before the Revolution.

Forbidden pleasures
During the reign of Nicholas I (1825–1855) a special decree was issued restricting the use of the Summer Gardens to officers and "the decently dressed." The gardens remained the exclusive preserve of the aristocracy—this was the poet Pushkin's favorite spot in all St. Petersburg. Even today rules persist, and a modern notice at the entrance to the Summer Gardens outlaws the following: bicycling, motorcycling, skating, ball games, jogging, walking dogs, fishing, feeding the swans, and street trading.

The Pavlovskiy barracks dominates Mars Field; to the left is the Church of the Savior "on the Blood"

■ St. Petersburg is often called the Venice of the North, but a more likely model for the city's picturesque network of canals was Peter the Great's favorite European city, Amsterdam, which he visited in 1697–1698 and again in 1716–1717. ■

Bridge over the Fontanka Canal

Great palaces During the 18th century some of the wealthiest families in the Russian Empire—the Yusupovs, Sheremetevs, and Naryshkins—built their palaces and homes along the granite embankments.

The principal canals and rivers The 4-mile-long Fontanka Canal takes its name from the fountains of the Summer Gardens. The Griboedov (formerly Catherine) Canal (3 miles long) is called after the 19th-century comic dramatist A. S. Griboedov (1795–1829), who lived close by. Following the course of a small stream, it was enlarged in the late 18th century. The granite embankment was completed in 1800. The 3-mile-long Moyka River originally flowed from a swamp in the vicinity of Mars Field. The smallest canal is the Zimnaya or Winter Canal, which flows just to the east of the Hermitage and Winter Palace. Not far away is another delightful waterway, the Lebyazhnaya or Swan Canal, which separates Mars Field from the Summer Gardens.

Bridges There are 332 bridges spanning St. Petersburg's waterways, including 21 drawbridges. The earliest

172

Fashionable hotel
By far the most popular St. Petersburg hotel in Pushkin's day was Demuth's (founded 1770), which occupied a row of houses stretching along the Moyka embankment toward Konyushennaya Ulitsa.

The Church of the Savior "on the Blood" overlooks the Griboedov Canal, the former Yekaterinskiy Canal

bridges were known by the bright colors in which they were painted: "Blue," "Green," "Red," etc. The Green Bridge on the Moyka, near Nevskiy Prospekt, was a simple wooden drawbridge. In 1777 it was renamed the Politseyskiy Bridge, because the home of the Chief of Police was nearby. In 1883 a floating power station, the first in the city, began operating from a barge alongside the bridge; it was used to illuminate Nevskiy Prospekt. The Anichkov Bridge (1839–1841) is famous for its sculptures of four bronze horses and their trainers by Peter Klodt. The widest bridge in St. Petersburg, the Siniy Most (Blue Bridge) crosses the Moyka Canal near St. Isaac's Square. The Lomonosov Bridge (1785–1787), crossing the Fontanka, is one of the oldest in the city. Originally known as the Chernyshev Bridge, it is a severe stone drawbridge with four squat rectangular towers. The engineer J. Perronnet designed seven similar bridges to cross this canal. The Bankovskiy Bridge (1825–1826), designed by W. Traitteur to cross the Griboedov Canal near the Gostiniy Dvor, is one of the most attractive. The cables of the suspension footbridge are supported by pairs of golden-winged griffins.

Unsightly canals Pollution became a problem from the 1830s onward as factories began discharging effluent into the canals, notably the Fontanka. The effect was disastrous, as one observer noted in 1910: "All of them, without exception, are the receptacles of all possible filth—dirt from the factories of every tinge, and from the common sewers, pours into them. From morning until night, washing is going on in them and drinking water taken out close by ... Frequently in summer did I meet the nightmen's carts which discharged their filthy cargo into the Fontanka so that the very air was poisoned."

Cholera With pollution came disease. Right up to the Revolution, cholera notices were posted at bridges, warning inhabitants not to drink the canal water. Even so, many peasants and workmen ignored the injunction. The most famous cholera victim was Tchaikovsky (see pages 176–177). His mother had died of the same disease soon after the family moved to St. Petersburg in the 1850s.

City bypass To alleviate congestion, a new canal, the Obvodniy Bypass, was constructed around the southern boundary of the city in 1834. Docks were built at one end and the canal carried a great deal of barge traffic, notably transports of firewood in winter.

Canal boat trips For those who wish to explore the city's canals, small motorboats leave from the Anichkov Bridge on the corner of Nevskiy Prospekt and the Fontanka (every half hour from 11 AM–9 PM from the end of May to the beginning of Oct); some have English-language commentary. The usual route is westward along the Fontanka to the Kryukova Canal, then turning past the Mariinskiy Theater as far as the Moyka. The final stretch follows the Moyka eastward to the Engineers' Castle and the Summer Gardens, before turning back onto the Fontanka.

Rainy night on the Fontanka

"It was an awful November night—wet, foggy, rainy, snowy, teeming with ... all the gifts of a Petersburg November. The wind howled in the deserted streets, lifting up the black water of the canal above the rings on the bank, and irritably brushing against the lean lampposts which chimed in with its howling in a thin, shrill creak, keeping up the endless squeaky, jangling concert with which every inhabitant of Petersburg is so familiar. In the stillness of the night ... there was the dismal sound of the splash and gurgle of water, rushing from every roof, every porch, every pipe, and every cornice, onto the granite of the pavement."
—from *The Double* by Fedor Dostoevsky

173

A local artist seeking inspiration on the Moyka embankment

The Senate and Synod buildings were designed to harmonize with the Admiralty

Legendary statue
Etienne Falconet won the commission to execute a statue of Peter the Great through the offices of Denis Diderot, the French writer who negotiated a fee for him with Catherine the Great. The statue took almost 12 years to finish, during which time Falconet visited the Riding School and the Imperial Stables to study the movement of horses and riders. The statue of the Bronze Horseman was finally installed in 1782, on a type of Finnish granite known to the peasants living where it was found as "thunder stone," because it had supposedly been split by lightning.

▶▶▶ **Ploshchad Dekabristov (Decembrists' Square)** 154B2

Tram: 31

Decembrists' Square commemorates the liberal guards officers who mutinied against Nicholas I in December 1825. The revolt came at the end of a three-week inter-regnum caused by confusion over the succession after the death of Alexander I. On the morning of December 14, 1825, as 3,000 soldiers from various guards regiments began to assemble on the square to acclaim Nicholas tsar after the swearing of the oath of allegiance, a group of officers staged a mutiny after failing to persuade the Senate to impose a constitutional monarchy on Nicholas. The crowd that had orginally gathered to witness the fes-tivities shouted encouragement to the rebels and even threw stones at Nicholas's commander, General Voynov. Meanwhile, the insurgents, who were concentrated around the statue of Peter the Great, had allowed them-selves to be surrounded. After an intervention by the arch-bishop failed to dissuade them, Nicholas brought several cannon onto the square. Four times during the afternoon the cavalry tried to disperse the rebels, but without suc-cess. The best view of the unfolding drama was from the scaffolding of St. Isaac's Cathedral, then under construc-tion—the builders sympathized with the rebels and hurled poles and debris onto the heads of the soldiers below. Then, in the confused and highly volatile atmosphere, someone on the loyalist side gave the order to fire; the conspirators panicked and eventually broke up in disarray. By evening the leaders were under arrest, and order had been restored. Each conspirator was interviewed person-ally by the tsar, who also decided on the punishment. Five were hanged and 130 others exiled to Siberia, where many of them were joined voluntarily by their wives. This act of retribution set the tone for the entire 30-year reign. Subsequently, the Decembrists came to be venerated as heroes, while the rebellion itself is seen as the beginning of the revolutionary movement in Russia.

Decembrists' Square was laid out in its present form by Carlo Rossi in the 1830s. Etienne Falconet's superb statue of Peter the Great, known as the "Bronze Horseman," occupies a central position. The inscription on the base, in Latin and Russian, reads "To Peter the First from Catherine the Second. MDCCLXXXII." An ensemble of magnificent neoclassical buildings fronts the square. Occupying the western side are the former Senate and Synod buildings (the latter the governing body of the Orthodox Church). Next to them, on the far side of Konno-Gvardeyskiy Bulvar (Horse Guards Boulevard), is the Manège (military riding school). The statues on either side of the entrance are of the Dioskouroi—the heavenly twins, Castor and Pollux.

▶ Rumyantsevskiy Dvorets (Rumyantsev Palace)   154A1

Angliyskaya Naberezhnaya 44
Trolleybus: 5, 22
Open: Thu–Mon 11–6

Built in 1826–1827, the palace is named after N. P. Rumyantsev, the son of a famous field marshal, who bought this house from a British merchant in 1802. The Rumyantsev Museum was originally devoted to art, manuscripts, and coins, and moved to Moscow in 1861, where it was eventually to become the Lenin Library. Nowadays the museum is dedicated to the History of Leningrad, that is to St. Petersburg in the period after the Revolution, although at the time of writing several sections are closed for reevaluation. When this is complete, the core of the exhibition will still be the section dealing with the German army's Siege of Leningrad during 1941–1944, which claimed the lives of nearly 700,000 people, or about one-fifth of the population. The rest lived through bombardment, subfreezing temperatures, and starvation. Dioramas illustrate the often ingenious methods of survival: in winter, for example, water was drawn through holes in the ice. There is a reconstructed air raid shelter and numerous artifacts relating to everyday life. When the Seige was all over, Leningrad was given the honorary title "Hero City." The episode is of such psychological significance to the inhabitants that there is a second museum devoted just to the Defense of Leningrad (see page 206).

Haunted
Alexander Pushkin's celebrated poem *The Bronze Horseman* immortalizes Falconet's statue. Set in 1824 during the worst floods St. Petersburg ever experienced, it tells the story of Yevgeni, who imagines he is being pursued by the statue of Peter the Great come to life: "How terrible he was in the surrounding gloom! What thought was on his brow, what strength was in him! And in that steed what fire!"

Petersburgers love their open spaces: a park near Decembrists' Square

175

The death of Tchaikovsky

■ **Blackmail, hypocrisy, homosexuality, and some of the most sublime music ever to emerge from Russia form the background to events which were ultimately to deprive the world of one of its great composers.** ■

From the score of Tchaikovsky's Symphony No. 6, *the "Pathétique"*

Elusive patron
In 1877, on the brink of mental collapse after the trauma of his disastrous marriage, Tchaikovsky was taken under the patronage of a wealthy widow, Nadezhda von Meck, who had long been an admirer of his work. Thanks to her financial support, Tchaikovsky gave up his teaching post and was able to devote himself to his composing. Over the next 13 years they conducted an intense liaison by letter. But it was to be a relationship on paper only; one of the stipulations of Nadezhda's patronage was that they should never meet.

In the autumn of 1893 Pyotr Ilych Tchaikovsky was at the height of his fame. *Romeo and Juliet*, the ballets *Swan Lake*, *The Sleeping Beauty*, and *The Nutcracker*, violin and piano concertos, several operas, among them *Eugene Onegin*, not to mention five symphonies, were all behind him. He was respected by his contemporaries and revered by a new generation of composers, including Sergei Rachmaninov and Alexander Glazunov, while this music was becoming well known abroad. Only recently he had been awarded an honorary doctorate by Cambridge University, shared the concert platform with other musical giants of the age such as Brahms and Dvořák, and become the toast of America following a triumphant tour. He had been decorated by the tsar and was on nodding terms with several grand dukes.

A cloud on the horizon But Tchaikovsky carried his fame like a heavy burden. Morbidly neurotic and painfully sensitive, he was unable to reconcile his desire for respectability with the demands of his homosexual nature. From the days when he was a law student at the School of Jurisprudence in St. Petersburg, Tchaikovsky had been forming emotional attachments with young men. During the time he was a professor at the Moscow Conservatory, he seems to have had a number of clandestine relationships and risked his reputation in casual sexual encounters. His disastrous marriage to Alexandra Milyukova in 1877, intended to allay these suspicions of his homosexuality, backfired horribly. The ill-matched partnership ended in a nervous breakdown for Tchaikovsky and the onset of madness for his wife.

Last days Yet despite the enormous emotional pressures that Tchaikovsky imposed on himself, there is no evidence of any special anxiety in that fatal autumn of 1893, when he arrived in St. Petersburg from his rural retreat at Klin. Uppermost in his mind was the première of a new symphony, the Sixth, known to the world as the "Pathétique." But he was also busy renewing musical acquaintances at his brother Modest's apartment on Malaya Morskaya Street, where he invariably stayed when in the capital, overseeing rehearsals and taking an interest in Modest's own career as a popular playwright. The night before he was taken ill, he went to see one of Modest's plays, afterward joining in the celebrations in Leiner's Restaurant on Nevskiy Prospekt. None of the guests noticed anything untoward in Tchaikovsky's behavior. According to Modest (the only witness to subsequent events), Pyotr Ilych drank water from the carafe on the dining room table at lunch the following day. Shortly afterward he was taken ill, and cholera was diagnosed. He died several days later.

Photo-portrait of Tchaikovsky taken in Prague in 1888

No sooner had Tchaikovsky been interred with full honors in the Alexander Nevskiy Monastery than rumors about his death began to circulate. Why, wondered the composer Rimsky-Korsakov, had the cholera-infected body been allowed to lie in an open coffin for visitors to kiss, in defiance of all the health regulations then in force? And why, in a city where the water supply was known to be infected, had Modest allowed unboiled water to be served at his table in the first place? There were many inconsistencies in the official account, but it was not until 1978 that a radically different version of events was presented to the world by researcher Alexandra Orlova. Although the true circumstances of Tchaikovsky's death remain a mystery, the burden of her story is this: a high-ranking member of the aristocracy had learned of a liaison between his young nephew, Vladimir, and the composer. To prevent news of this from becoming public, Tchaikovsky was called to appear before a Court of Honor, convened by former colleagues of his from the School of Jurisprudence which, after several hours of deliberation, pronounced a verdict of death. By taking poison—the cholera story was nothing more than a red herring—the composer ensured not only that the affair would remain secret but that his memory and reputation would survive untarnished.

Premonition
Conceived in 1892 and completed in August 1893, Tchaikovsky's *Symphony No. 6 in B Minor*, the "Pathétique" (the title was Modest's) was a programmatic work, the finale of which, in a bold break with convention, was to be an adagio. Tchaikovsky rightly regarded the work as his masterpiece, into which he had poured his deepest feelings. In a moment of prescience he had prefaced the score with the note: "Death—result of collapse."

Kazanskaya

Exotic market
The famous Gostiniy Dvor, which in the 1840s housed thousands of merchants and dealers, once resembled the legendary bazaars of the Orient with its exotic wares, oriental perfumes, and fine antique textiles. It was here that Diaghilev purchased the exquisite embroidered headdresses (*kokoshoniki*) and brightly colored traditional costumes (*sarafani*) for a production of the opera *Boris Godunov*.

Densely populated before the Revolution, this part of St. Petersburg was an area of contrasts. To the east of Nevskiy Prospekt and Horse Guards Square were the elegant homes of aristocrats, guards officers, and senior civil servants; farther west, notably between the Moyka and Catherine (Griboedov) canals, were teeming apartment blocks—the preserve of artisans, sweatshop workers, and shop assistants. After 1917 the Communist authorities moved working-class families in with the rich, before turning their grand apartments into communal dwellings, many of which survive today. Tourists passing these homes little suspect the fast-deteriorating conditions within: whole rooms have been boarded up pending urgently needed repairs, while it is not uncommon for 15 to 20 families to share a single kitchen and bathroom.

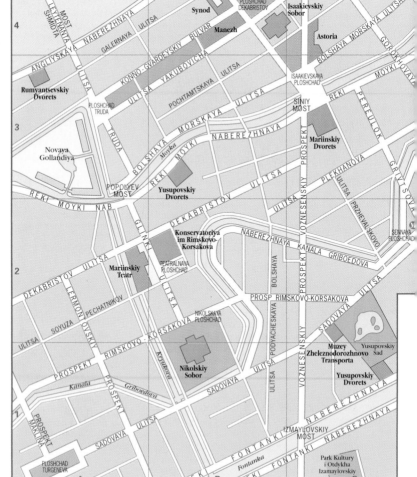

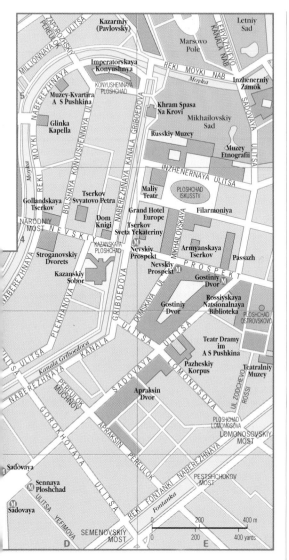

Selling flowers in the shade opposite the Kazan Cathedral

▶▶▶ Gostiniy Dvor (Merchant's Yard) 179E4

The Merchant's Yard, with its distinctive white-and-yellow façade, was completed in the reign of Catherine the Great by Vallin de la Mothe to plans by architect Rastrelli, but without his rich façade. Originally a coaching inn, the *dvor* became a bazaar during the 19th century. The city's most famous shopping arcade has now been renovated.

▶▶▶ Grand Hotel Europe 179E4

Ulitsa Mikhaylovskaya 1/7
Metro: Nevskiy Prospekt
The building dates from 1873–1875 but substantial alterations were made in this century. Now refurbished from top to bottom, the Europe is now arguably Russia's premier hotel, resuming a tradition that goes back to the 1860s.

High society
Back in the 1860s the restaurant of the Grand Hotel Europe was a favorite gathering place for intriguers in the Foreign Office and Secret Police, and a fund of high-society gossip. The restaurant also claimed to have the finest choice of champagne in the world.

One-upmanship

In Gogol's story *The Nose*, a civil servant goes in search of his nose which has taken on a life of its own after being severed at the barber's. At one point he finds it at prayer in the Kazan Cathedral, wearing the uniform of a civil servant. The nose is unco-operative: "I don't see that we can have anything in common. Judging from your uniform buttons, I should say you're from another government department."

▶▶▶ Kazanskiy Sobor (Kazan Cathedral)   179D4

Kazanskaya Ploshchad
Metro: Nevskiy Prospekt
Open: Mon–Fri 11–5, Sat 12:30–5; closed Wed and Sun
The serf-born architect Andrei Voronikhin designed the Kazan Cathedral in 1801. Modeled on St. Peter's in Rome, it was completed ten years later. The massive bronze doors are a copy of Ghiberti's doors for the Baptistery in Florence. The height of the dome is 265 feet, making it a considerable landmark in this low-lying city. The building is dedicated to Our Lady of Kazan and the reputedly miraculous icon that brought the Russian forces victory over the Poles during the Time of Troubles. The martial theme prevails throughout: Marshal Kutuzov, the hero of the Napoleonic Wars, is buried in the cathedral, while much of its silver was recaptured by Cossacks during the Napoleonic retreat from Moscow in 1812. In the 1930s the Communists turned the cathedral into a Museum of Atheism, but it has recently been reconsecrated.

The colonnade on the square is still a favorite meeting place for students and intellectuals, having first become a venue for political demonstrations in the 1870s. In those days agents of the secret police kept an eye on the proceedings from the comfort of a restaurant opposite. Protests continued through the revolutions of 1905 and 1917 and on into recent times.

▶▶▶ Khram Spasa "Na Krovi"
(Church of the "Savior on the Blood")   179E5

Naberezhnaya Kanala Griboedova 2
Metro: Nevskiy Prospekt
The Church of the Resurrection, more appositely known as the Church of the Savior "on the Blood," stands over the spot where, on March 1, 1881, Alexander II was assassinated by members of Russia's first terrorist organization, *Narodnaya Volya* (The People's Will). The Tsar had already survived at least half a dozen attempts on his life. On that fateful Sunday morning, Alexander was returning to the Winter Palace, having just carried out a troop inspection at the Mikhailovskiy Riding School. As his carriage turned onto the canal embankment, one of the terrorists rolled a bomb underneath it, but the Tsar was only slightly injured. He then made the

One of the unmistakable landmarks of St. Petersburg, the Kazan Cathedral, presides over Nevskiy Prospekt

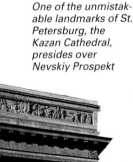

fatal error of leaving the carriage to inspect the damage and to try to help wounded passersby. Seizing on this un-looked-for second opportunity, Ignaty Grinevitskiy threw a second bomb, which mortally wounded the tsar. His body was taken back to his private apartments in the palace where he died shortly afterwards. All the assassins were captured and hanged except Grinevitskiy, who died of his injuries.

A temporary wooden shrine was erected on the site almost immediately, but the ornate and colorful building visitors see today was not completed until 1907. The design, in the neo-Russian style, is by I. V. Malyshev and A. A. Parland. The superb mosaic decoration is by a team of artists led by Viktor Vasnetsov, and the interior is now restored.

► **Mariinskiy Dvorets (Mariinsky Palace)** *178C3*

Isaakiyevskaya Ploshchad
Trolleybus: 5, 22

The Mariinskiy Palace was built by A. I. Stakenschneider for the daughter of Nicholas I, the Grand Duchess Maria. It has a colorful history. From the late 19th century it was used for a variety of political purposes: the tsarist State Council met here, also the Council of Ministers. In April 1902 a student, Stepan Balmashov, entered the palace in the uniform of a guardsman and stabbed to death the Minister of the Interior, D. S. Sipyagin. Later, in 1917, the Provisional Government convened here and, subsequently, the Leningrad City Council. Today the flying of the Russian flag indicates that the Mariinskiy has retained its function as St. Petersburg's town hall.

Vasnetsov's mosaics give the Church of the Savior "on the Blood" its colorful appearance

► ► ► **Mariinskiy Teatr (Mariinskiy Theater)** *178A2*

Teatralnaya Ploshchad
Bus: 22, 322. Tram: 1, 5, 11, 31, 33

Still known abroad as the Kirov, the Mariinskiy (Maria) Theater was designed by A. K. Kavos and named after the wife of Alexander II. It stands on the site of an earlier theater destroyed by fire. Famous for its superb blue and gold interior, the Mariinskiy can hold nearly 2,000 spectators. Before the Revolution all eyes would have focused on the imperial box, which was crowned by large golden eagles. Famous premières here have included Moussorgsky's opera *Boris Godunov*, Tchaikovsky's ballets *The Sleeping Beauty* and *The Nutcracker*, and Prokofiev's *Romeo and Juliet*. The illustrious list of ballet dancers to have made their debuts on this stage includes Anna Pavlova, Tamara Karsavina, Vaslav Nijinsky, and Mikhail Baryshnikov. Also on Theater Square is the St. Petersburg, or Rimsky-Korsakov, Conservatory, founded in 1862 by the pianist Anton Rubinstein. Among the composers to have graduated from here are Tchaikovsky, Prokofiev, and Shostakovich. Rimsky-Korsakov taught here for many years.

In front of the theater is a statue by R. R. Bach, dating from 1906, of another composer, Mikhail Glinka. Glinka's patriotic opera *A Life for the Tsar* (sometimes known as *Ivan Susanin*) always opened the Mariinskiy season.

Old warrior
Thousands of Petersburgers lined the streets on June 13, 1813, for the burial of Marshal Kutuzov in the new Kazan Cathedral. On its walls were hung 107 captured standards from the Napoleonic campaign besides the ceremonial keys to various fortresses and other trophies. Kutuzov had led Russia's army against Napoleon at the Battles of Austerlitz and Borodino and was renowned as a humane leader who did all he could to avoid unnecessary battles and the needless suffering of his soldiers.

The house on the Moyka where Pushkin spent the last months of his life

Bomb under the table
Perhaps the boldest attempt on the tsar's life occurred in February 1880 when a terrorist disguised as a carpenter managed to plant a bomb directly underneath the imperial dining room in the Winter Palace. The blast inflicted a number of deaths and injuries, but the tsar, who was not living in the building at the time, evaded death yet again.

Fateful day
News of Alexander II's terrible fate was brought to his favorite grandson, the future Nicholas II, who recounted: "We drove down the Nevskiy at top speed to the Winter Palace. As we went up the stairs, I saw pale faces everywhere. On the carpet, there were deep red stains. My grandfather was bleeding to death from his terrible wounds as he was carried upstairs."

▶▶▶ **Muzey-Kvartira A. S. Pushkina (Pushkin House-Museum)**   179D5

Reki Moyki Naberezhnaya 12
Trams: 12, 32, 53
Open: Wed–Mon 11–6

There is something affecting about a visit to Pushkin's last apartment; perhaps it is the tragically wasteful manner of his death, perhaps the reverence with which Russians treat both his memory and his work—even today, on the anniversary of his death, floral tributes are left outside the door. The poet lived in these wonderfully evocative rooms from the autumn of 1836 until the fateful day just a few months later when he fought his duel with Baron d'Anthès (see page 191) and was brought back to the house to die.

The museum has been renovated now, and period furnishings and many of Pushkin's personal possessions are on display. The highlight is the poet's study, containing a library with more than 4,500 books in a staggering 14 languages, a desk with a blackamoor paperweight to remind him of his Abyssinian grandfather, and a clock which was stopped at the precise moment of Pushkin's death (2:45 AM).

▶ **Nikolskiy Sobor (St. Nicholas Cathedral)**   178B1

Nikolskaya Ploshchad
Trolleybus: 2. Trams: 1, 5, 11, 31, 33
Open: daily 7–12 and 3–7 for services

The slim golden domes and cupolas of the Cathedral of St. Nicholas, long known as the Sailors' Church, are clearly visible from the Mariinskiy Theater, while the tiered bell tower presides over the Kryukov Canal. This exquisite baroque church was built in 1753–1763 to a design by S. I. Chevakinskiy; its interior, richly decorated with icons, is especially impressive during religious services.

▶▶▶ **Ploshchad Iskusstv (Arts Square)**   179E4

Metro: Gostiniy Dvor

Arts Square, one of the finest in the entire city, was laid out by Carlo Rossi in the 1830s to set off the Mikhailovsky

Palace (now the Russian Museum). Besides the museum, the square also contains the Philharmonic Hall, named in honor of Dmitri Shostakovich, and the Maliy, or Small, Theater, which is the second stage in the city after the Mariinskiy. The design is by A. Kavos, architect of the Bolshoy Theater in Moscow (see page 96). In the 19th century the theater was known for its presentations of French drama. In 1934, Shoshtakovitch's opera *Lady Macbeth* was premièred here. The Shostakovich Concert Hall, on the corner of Ulitsa Mikhailovskaya, was designed in the 1830s by P. Jacot and originally belonged to the élite Club of the Gentry, where aristocrats lost vast fortunes at cards and climbed drunk onto window ledges to satisfy a bet. The club was taken over by Anton Rubinstein's Russian Musical Society in 1859, where guest appearances were subsequently made by a number of distinguished foreign composers, including Berlioz, Wagner, and Liszt. The society was the precursor of the St. Petersburg Conservatory.

▶▶▶ Russkiy Muzey (Russian Museum)   179E5

Inzhenernaya Ulitsa 4
Metro: Nevskiy Prospekt /Gostiniy Dvor
Open: Wed–Mon 10–6. Admission charge; free on Wed
Unlike the Hermitage, the Russian Museum specializes in Russian art. The works are mainly from the 18th century onward, although there is a section devoted to icons. If you missed the Tretyakov Gallery in Moscow for any reason, you should certainly spend some time here: there are well over a hundred rooms in all, and a total of 315,000 paintings to look at.

The museum began life as the Mikhailovsky Palace, home of the Grand Duke Mikhail Pavlovich, brother of Alexander I and Nicholas I. It is one of Rossi's finest creations in the Empire or neoclassical style. To appreciate the full effect, circle the entire building, for it was Rossi's intention that the palace, with its magnificent central portico of eight Corinthian columns, should harmonize not only with the square itself but with the

Madhouse
"Above the yellow loom of government buildings The swirling snow fell thick all through the day; Pulling his overcoat close, a law student swings His arm out wide, and settles back in his sleigh."
—From *Petersburg Stanzas* by Osip Mandelstam
It became the custom in the course of the 19th century to paint institutions and state-owned buildings yellow; the term "yellow house" later became a euphemism for an insane asylum.

Until the 1950s, Arts Square was known as Mikhailovskiy Square after the palace of that name (now the Russian Museum)

ST. PETERSBURG: KAZANSKAYA

Architect Carlo Rossi equated imperial grandeur with the Roman classical style

Art bargains
Russian paintings on sale at a recent auction at Alpha-Art (Central House of Artists) included a canvas of Yasnaya Polyana by Nikolai Ge, valued at $3,000–4,000, a landscape drawing of the Crimea by Vasili Polenov ($400–600), and a sketch made by Nikolai Roerich for the stage set of Rimsky-Korsakov's opera *The Snow Maiden* ($9,000–12,000).

gardens to the rear, where a façade of even grander proportions overlooks the gentle waters of the Moyka.

Icons and the West The second floor of the palace embraces medieval icon paintings on the one hand (Rooms 1–4, including some rare works by the medieval master Andrei Rublev) and examples of the emerging Russian school on the other. The obvious Western influences in paintings by the likes of Ivan Nikitin and "the Russian Gainsborough," Dmitri Levitskiy (Room 19), is due to Peter and Catherine the Great's policy of sending artists abroad. Room 11, known as the *beliy zal* or White Hall, is the only one to have preserved Rossi's original décor. Even the furniture is by the architect, although the murals are by a much less distinguished artist, A. Vighi. Room 15 contains works by Karl Bryullov—his dramatic canvas, *Last Days of Pompeii*, won him international recognition and the Grand Prix at the Paris Salon in 1834.

The Itinerants The work of the Itinerants (see pages 128–129) begins on the first floor with canvases by Perov (Room 23), Savrasov (Room 24), Kramskoy (Room 25), and Nikolai Ge (Room 26)—some of whose work is reminiscent of the English Pre-Raphaelites, for example *Christ and His Disciples in the Garden of Gethsemane*. Ilya Repin (1844–1930) is by far the best-known Itinerant and the best-represented here (Rooms 33–35). His *Barge Haulers on the Volga* exposes the cruel way in which peasants could be treated even after the abolition of serfdom. Repin will also be remembered for his superb series of portraits of great contemporaries, among them the composers Rimsky-Korsakov and Glazunov. Vasili Surikov (Room 36) and Viktor Vasnetsov (annex, Room 40) painted some memorable historical canvases: Surikov's *Stenka Razin* and Vasnetsov's *After Igor Svyatoslavich's Battle with the Polovtsiy* are typical examples.

Rooms 37 and 38 in the main gallery contain works by three highly individual artists: Mikhail Vrubel, Isaak Levitan, and Viktor Borisov-Musatov. Vrubel was plagued by mental illness, and many of his canvases reveal a tortured soul and a visionary cast of mind. Levitan, a close friend of Chekhov's, was the finest landscape artist of his generation, exemplified by such works as *Tishina* ("Quiet"). Borisov-Musatov is most akin to the French Impressionists, although he later branched out into a Symbolist style which greatly influenced younger artists like Larionov and Goncharova (see below).

Russian 20th-century art The Rossi Wing is currently closed. A long corridor leads to the Benois Wing, where Russian 20th-century art is located. This was a period of frenzied experimentation and unending quests for innovation, partly inspired by contemporary Western movements such as Cubism and Futurism, but equally by indigenous sources of inspiration, Russian folk art being the most important. The paintings on exhibition are snapshots of the artists' work at particular stages in their careers. Mikhail Larionov's *A Corner of the Garden* (1905) is a Neo-Impressionist work; compare this with the Rayonist *Landscape* (1913). Rayonism was a style akin to Futurism which emphasized movement and the cult of the machine; an excellent example is Natalia Goncharova's *The Cyclist* (1913) in which the rider is seen speeding past shops and bars—note the mug of beer and the tram number T–402 reflected in the window of the bar. Both Larionov and Goncharova later contributed set and costume designs for Diaghilev's Ballets Russes. Vladimir Tatlin's *The Sailor* (1911–1912), a self-portrait, is also in the Rayonist mold—note the angled lines or rays from which the style takes its name. The Russian Museum has more than 130 paintings by the inventor of Suprematism, Kazimir Malevich, although visitors are unlikely to see more than a handful at any one time. As is self-evident from works like *Suprematism Yellow and Black*, *Black Circle* and *Black Cross* the emphasis is on the stark juxtaposition of apparently simple geometrical shapes. Vasili Kandinsky, who became an exile for much of his long career when his paintings fell from favor, can now be seen again in his homeland. Some of his *Impressions* and *Improvizations* are on show in the museum.

Talented designer
In 1915 the artists Natalia Goncharova and Mikhail Larionov left Russia and settled in Paris together. In Moscow Goncharova had been highly regarded for her costume and set designs for the Kamerny Theater. She continued this work in Paris, designing for Diaghilev's Ballets Russes. Her distinctive Byzantine designs for *The Golden Cockerel* and *The Firebird* attracted much critical acclaim. A large number of her ballet designs are in the collection at the Victoria and Albert Museum in London.

185

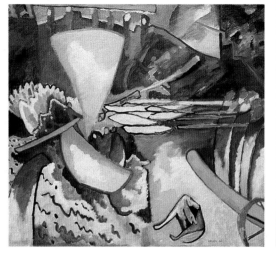

Improvization *by Vasili Kandinsky (1910). Kandinsky was one of many artists out of favor in the Soviet era*

■ **In June 1994 Air France sponsored the first Paris fashion show in Moscow by Printemps, presenting the summer collection of Kenzo and Louis Féraud. But Russia now has its own independent fashion houses which are eager to compete on the international market.** ■

Extravagance

Russian fashion design of the 19th century was influenced in particular by the *haute couture* of the English designer Charles Frederick Worth, who opened a fashion house in Paris in 1857. He was patronized by most of Europe's aristocracy, including Empress Eugénie of France. It was not unknown for wealthy Russian ladies to purchase dresses and cloaks from him in quantities of 12 or 15 in one visit. But soon they had their own designers in Russia, like Madame Olga, who specialized in extravagant full-dress costumes for ladies at court.

Fashion-conscious window shoppers outside GUM

Clothing capital Moscow has been the clothing capital of Russia since at least the 16th century. By 1900, 150,000 Moscow workers were employed in the clothing and textile industries, producing ready-made clothes for the fashionable stores of Kuznetskiy Most, which Baedeker was recommending to visitors as early as 1914. But most of the designs were foreign—the most talented seamstresses were sent abroad to Paris twice a year to keep abreast of the latest developments, while the buyers trawled the fashion houses for the most chic and expensive dresses, which later turned up in Moscow shop windows. Even ordinary Muscovites (excluding the working classes) dressed in the Western style, as ready-to-wear stores copied patterns from foreign fashion journals.

Fashion Renaissance After 70 years of a nationalized clothing industry and standardized and uninspired designs, fashion-conscious Muscovites and Petersburgers are, not unnaturally, looking once more to Italy and France for inspiration. But Russian designers have begun to hit back and are themselves attracting a small but loyal and well-heeled clientele.

The House of Fashion at 24 Kuznetskiy Most was renowned as early as the 1900s for its fashionable imported and hand-made clothes. Today politicians rub shoulders with actresses and top business executives, all anxious to own a suit or a fur coat with the prestigious Kuznetskiy Most label. The emphasis is on classical elegance: ballgowns and evening dresses in silk and taffeta, suits made of the finest blended tweeds, and real furs—coats, hats, stoles, and wraps. You can pick up a fur jacket for around 1,200,000 rubles, but the price tag can be well in excess of 4 million.

"Fashion as theater" One of House of Fashion's former top designers, Slava Zaitsev, has now branched out and is in a league of his own. His spring collections have been shown in such major cities as Paris, New York, Milan, Tokyo, and Seoul. The reviews were effusive: "among the world's best," "a phenomenon," "*haute couture* at its best." Thanks to new Russian fashion magazines like *On-Ona* ("He-She"), Zaitsev is also able to promote both his clothes and himself to Moscow's *nouveaux riches*. A poet, a painter, and a journalist as well as a fashion designer, he is a self-made man who hasn't always found working with others easy. The clothes speak for themselves: they're showy, extravagant, and bold—"fashion as theater" in Zaitsev's words. In his recent shows with a *grezy* ("daydreams") theme, models paraded on the cat-

Fashion

walk with fantastic rococo costumes to the accompaniment of music by Tchaikovsky.

"Beautiful clothing at reasonable prices" The first privately owned fashion house in St. Petersburg, Tatyana Parfionova's Rabalder Foundation, is banking on East–West collaboration. Her new boutique and studio on Nevskiy Prospekt is jointly owned by partner Erik Warming of the Rabalder Clothing Company. New boutiques offering Parfionova's creations have already opened in Stockholm, Oslo, and Copenhagen. Like Zaitsev, Parfionova prides herself on her artistic credentials—in her case formal study at art school and the St. Petersburg Textile Institute. She created her first collection at the age of 28 and after seven years considers that she has created her own style: "I'm naturally influenced by my roots, but I don't do Russian souvenirs. Russian women have become more cosmopolitan, like women in other countries ... Fashion reflects cultural change. I feel a part of the development." Parfionova uses natural fabrics, mostly wool, silk, and cotton. The lines are classical, leaning more toward the styles found at the House of Fashion than Zaitsev's exuberant modernism. Even the colors are restrained. Parfionova the artist is surprisingly down-to-earth in her ambitions: "to create beautiful clothing for women at reasonable prices." Who could ask for more?

Rules of fashion
In 1834, Tsar Nicholas I, ever a stickler for formality and convention, issued an edict which lay down precise rules about the type of dress to be worn by ladies at court, including the style, color, and fabric of garments. These were to accord with traditional Russian dress and featured the *kokoshnik*, an elaborate headdress made in velvet and studded with jewels: blue velvet for the empress and imperial family; crimson for the maids of honor, and green for ladies-in-waiting.

187

Haute couture
Moscow-style. A boutique on Kuznetskiy Most

Spasskaya

At the heart of Spasskaya is Sadovaya or Garden Street, which developed in the 1730s at a time when the area was characterized by its suburban estates. The Sadovaya later became an important shopping street with two of St. Petersburg's busiest markets—the Apraksin and the Haymarket—growing up near by. By the middle of the 19th century, the once fashionable apartment blocks around the Haymarket had become slums, the streets were full of refuse from the nearby market, and the area had the highest number of brothels in the city.

►► Apraksin Dvor (Apraksin's Yard) 189D3

Sadovaya Ulitsa
Metro: Sadovaya
This elegant arcade was named after the aristocratic Apraksin family, who owned a house here. The first street market appeared at the end of the 18th century; by1900 there were more than 600 stalls selling everything from food, wine, and spices to furs, haberdashery, and furniture. Today Apraksin Dvor has the look of a place that has seen better days; nevertheless it has retained much of its exotic

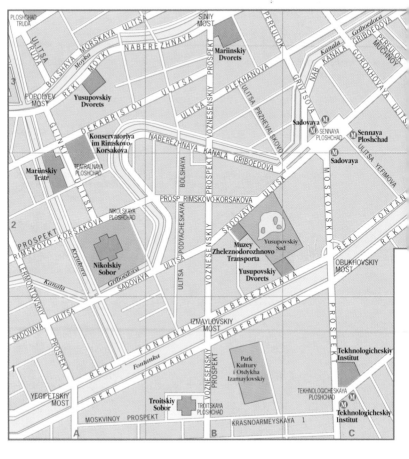

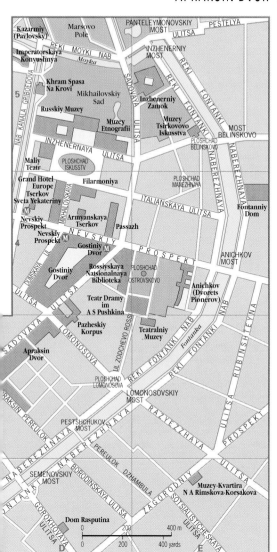

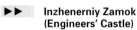

Artistic failure

The Engineering Academy was a suitably authoritarian institution which refused to accept students of weak health, as well as outlawing the wearing of eyeglasses and galoshes! Among the alumni, wearing the familiar black uniform with red epaulettes, was the young Fedor Dostoevsky. His decision to leave may have been prompted by a visit by Nicholas I in 1844. On being shown a drawing by the future writer of a fortress without doors, he commented, "What idiot drew this?"

Paranoid tsar

Tsar Paul I surrounded the Engineers' Castle with a moat, portcullis, and even an underground passage linking it with the Pavlovskiy Barracks on Mars Field. In the event, these elaborate precautions did not protect him for long. Six weeks after he moved in, on the night of March 11, 1801, a group of conspirators led by the governor of St. Petersburg, Count Pahlen, entered the castle. After failing to induce Paul to abdicate, a scuffle broke out during which one of the assailants strangled Paul with a scarf. His son Alexander, who succeeded him, was suspected of complicity and never quite shed the dark taint of parricide.

flavor. Most Petersburgers come for the cheap clothing, but there is also a brisk trade in watches, toys, TV sets, and even guns. This is Russian life in concentrated and, for foreigners, potentially toxic doses.

▶▶ **Inzhenerniy Zamok
(Engineers' Castle)**   *189E5*

Zamkovaya Ulitsa
Tram: 2, 12
Open: picture gallery and small exhibition, Wed–Mon 10–6
Dominating the Moyka and Fontanka canals, the Engineers' Castle is an austere red brick building with a gilded spire, built for Paul I on the site of a former wooden summer palace by Vasiliy Bazhenov and Vincenzio Brenna. In 1823, the palace became part of the Military Engineering Academy.

ST. PETERSBURG: SPASSKAYA

▶ **Muzey Zheleznodorozhnovo Transporta (Railroad Museum)** *188B2*
Sadovaya Ulitsa 50
Metro: Sadovaya
Open: Mon–Thu and Sun 11–5:30; closed Fri, Sat and last Thu of the month
A real treat for train buffs, the Railroad Museum contains more than 6,000 dusty but fascinating exhibits. Items include such gems as models of an armored train used in the defense of Petrograd during the Civil War in 1919; an engine built by the Cherepanovs for the Tsarskoe Selo railroad in 1836; carriages bearing the livery of the first St. Petersburg–Moscow railroad; and a walk-through section of a traditional first-class sleeping compartment, complete with velvet upholstery and *style moderne* accessories.

▶ **Pazheskiy Korpus (Corps des Pages)** *188D3*
Sadovaya Ulitsa
The most select military school in the Empire, the Corps des Pages occupied one of the handsomest buildings in the city, the Vorontsov Palace, built in 1749–1757 for Prince M. I. Vorontsov by the architect of the Zimniy Dvorets, Bartolommeo Rastrelli. Originally a mansion with its own extensive grounds, the palace is now the Suvorov Military Academy and is closed to the public.

▶▶ **Ploshchad Ostrovskovo (Ostrovsky Square)** *189E4*
Metro: Gostiniy Dvor
This beautiful square was renamed in the Soviet period after the 19th-century playwright A. N. Ostrovsky (1823–1886). It was designed by Carlo Rossi in the 1820s and 1830s and named Aleksandrinskaya Ploshchad after the wife of Nicholas I. The neoclassical building in the center is the Pushkin Theater, sometimes known as the Aleksandrinskiy. This, the oldest dramatic company in Russia, can trace its history back to 1756. Among the plays to have been premièred here was Gogol's *The Government Inspector* in 1836. Outside is a statue of Catherine the Great surrounded by a group of her favorites, including Count Potemkin, Princess Dashkova, and the famous General Suvorov. While you're in the area, have a look at the most perfectly proportioned street in St. Petersburg—the colonnaded Ulitsa Zodchevo Rossi (Rossi the Architect Street), which extends behind the theater.

▶▶ **Sadovaya Ulitsa (Garden Street)** *188B2*
After Nevskiy Prospekt, Sadovaya, or Garden Street, is the most important and best-known thoroughfare in the city. The northern end was developed later, in the 18th century, and the buildings that grace it—the Engineers' Castle, the Mikhailovsky Palace, and the Summer and Marble Palaces—give it a stately appearance. Cross Nevskiy Prospekt, and the character of the street changes abruptly from the grandiose elegance of the 18th century to the atmosphere of petty commerce, established in the 19th. Trading activity is focused on the Haymarket and in and around the Apraksin Dvor where you will find a maze of shops, market stalls, and kiosks.

The national pastime. Russians play chess everywhere, as here on Ploshchad Ostrovskovo, now renamed Aleksandrinskaya Ploshchad

Pushkin's duel

■ **Every year on the anniversary of his death, ordinary Russians lay wreaths at poet Alexander Pushkin's former home in St. Petersburg. For many Russians, his verses are the embodiment of the national spirit and are committed to memory** ■

Fatal attraction In January 1837, an anonymous letter implying an adulterous relationship between Pushkin's wife, Natalia Goncharova, and a cavalry officer, Georges D'Anthès, provoked the poet into challenging D'Anthès to a duel. It was the second such letter that Pushkin had received; the dispute had actually been simmering for nearly three years. After the first letter admitting Pushkin to the "Most Serene Order of Cuckolds," a compromise had been patched together by D'Anthès's adopted father, Baron Haeckeren, to prevent a scandal. Now, despite his wife's protestations of innocence, Pushkin decided there was only one honorable way out.

Duel at Black River On Friday, January 27, at Wulf's pastry shop on Nevskiy Prospekt, Pushkin met his second, a former classmate from the Alexander Lycée, Konstantin Danzas. They left at about 4 PM and traveled by sleigh to some woods north of the city near Chyornaya Rechka. When D'Anthès appeared with his second, an attaché at the French embassy, Vicomte d'Archiac, the party proceeded to a clearing where, after measuring out the paces and laying out coats as barriers, the two protagonists took up their positions. When Danzas gave the signal both men took careful aim, but only D'Anthès fired. Pushkin fell to the ground fatally wounded but, leaning on his arm, took aim at his opponent—a shot rang out and D'Anthès fell but did not die. As soon as the news that Pushkin was dying leaked out, crowds began to assemble outside his house in St. Petersburg. Having taken leave of his wife and children, Pushkin wrote a letter of apology to the tsar. He died in the early hours of January 29, 1837.

Pushkin's death mask, in the Pushkin Museum

Epilogue
Konstantin Danzas was given two months' guard-room arrest for his part in the duel; he died penniless in 1871. Natalia Goncharova remarried in 1844, and she and her husband, another guardsman and a friend of D'Anthès, were received in society and favored by the tsar; Natalia died in 1863. Georges D'Anthès was demoted to the ranks after the duel and deported. Unrepentant, he continued to live a pleasure-seeking life until his death from old age in 1895.

Secret burial
So worried were the authorities about the crowds gathering to mourn Pushkin's death that they sealed his rooms, collected his papers, and canceled the funeral service at St. Isaac's. His body was later removed from the Equerries' Church and taken secretly to his country estate at Mikhailovskoe for burial. Pushkin's popularity with the Russian people was confirmed by a rush on the bookstores in St. Petersburg for copies of the pocket-sized edition of *Eugene Onegin*.
In 1937 an obelisk was erected on the site of the duel, near Chyornaya Rechka metro station.

191

Alexander Pushkin: a supreme talent so tragically cut short

First cattle, then hay, and now cigarettes and bootleg liquor. The merchandise has changed but the commercial instinct lives on in the Haymarket

AIDS awareness
Bands like A-Ha, White Snake, and Falco took part in the 1994 White Nights International Culture Festival, the proceeds of which went to AIDS Awareness. For Russia, like America and Western Europe, is now having to combat a spiraling drug abuse and AIDS problem.

▶▶ **Sennaya Ploshchad (Haymarket)** 188C3

Metro: Sennaya Ploshchad

Dirt, squalor, crime, and vice are the attributes traditionally associated with the Haymarket; it began to acquire its reputation in the 1840s, when the original cattle market developed into a general center of petty commerce. The sights, the smells, the too proximate human contact were all more than enough to put off the contemporary traveler. A German visitor described seeing "every kind of filth and garbage ... sheep's eyes, fish tails, crab shells, goats' hairs, fragments of hay, dung and other matters." In the 1860s the novelist Fedor Dostoevsky moved into rooms on the notorious Stolyarniy Pereulok (Joiner's Lane), the only accommodations the impoverished writer could afford. A newspaper of the day, the *Petersburg Newsheet*, described it thus: "There are 16 houses, eight on either side, and in these 16 houses are located 18 drinking establishments, so that anyone seeking pleasure and diversion in liquid refreshment has no need to look for pub signs—go into any house, even any doorway, and there you'll find drink." Gambling, prostitution, and thieving all flourished in the vicinity of the Haymarket. Yet there was also a more colorful side; out on the street there were dolled-up peasant girls dancing to the accompaniment of a fiddle, concertina, or hurdy-gurdy.

The Haymarket was given a complete overhaul in the 1930s when the stallholders were banished, new apartment blocks constructed, trees planted, and the square renamed Ploshchad Mira (Peace Square). The Haymarket's main landmark, the imposing Church of the Assumption, was also demolished to make way for a new metro station. Despite this, locals are still able to point out to any visitor familiar with Dostoevsky's novel *Crime and Punishment* the attic window where the student murderer Raskolnikov lived (Grazhdanskaya Ulitsa 19, on the corner of Ulitsa Przhevalskovo, the modern Joiner's Lane), and the home of his victim, the pawnbroker Alyona Ivanovna (now Griboedova Kanala Naberezhnaya 104). And as the square reverts to its original name, its character as a marketplace has also been restored, though by custom rather than administrative *diktat*. However, where once there were market stalls, there are now corrugated metal kiosks.

► **Teatralniy Muzey (Theater Museum)**   *189E3*

Ostrovskovo Ploshchad
Metro: Gostiniy Dvor
Open: Wed 1–6, Thu–Mon 11–6

The Theater Museum, located just to the rear of the Pushkin Theater, traces the evolution of the Russian stage from the early 18th century onward with photographs, playbills, costumes, and numerous other artifacts. Unfortunately, the exhibition seems to have slept through *perestroika*, and the presentation, although broadly chronological, is dry and dusty to the point of eccentricity. This is a pity, as there is much in the museum to recommend it, including one of the costumes worn by the famous bass Fedor Chaliapin as Boris Godunov; the dress Chekhov's wife, Olga Knipper, wore as Ranevskaya at the première of *The Cherry Orchard*; and some colorful set designs by the great 20th-century theater director Vsevolod Meyerhold.

Chaliapin was celebrated for the power of his characterizations as much as for his voice. Above: in the robe of Mephistopheles in Gounod's Faust *Left: the costume Chaliapin wore in* Boris Godunov

► **Yusupovskiy Sad (Yusopov Gardens)**   *188B2*

Metro: Sennaya Ploshchad

These fine gardens once formed part of the grounds of the Yusupov Palace, which faces the Fontanka Canal. They have changed little since Dostoevsky's day, when they were a highly valued retreat for the impoverished artisans condemned to live in the congested streets nearby. In the 1860s, a local newspaper reported a scheme to construct a system of fountains here which Dostoevsky's hero, Raskolnikov, alludes to in *Crime and Punishment*: "On his way past the Yusupov Gardens, he began to be thoroughly taken up with an imaginary plan of his own: the construction of tall fountains and the way in which they would properly refresh the air on all the city's squares. Little by little he moved on to the conviction that if the Summer Garden were to be extended the entire length of Mars Field and even possibly connected with the gardens of the Mikhailovskiy Palace, this would be an attractive improvement that would also be of benefit to the city."

Stray Dog
Plans are afoot to revive one of St. Petersburg's most notorious prerevolutionary nightspots, the Stray Dog (Brodyachaya Sobaka)—a café founded by actor Boris Pronin in 1912 in a cellar on the corner of Ploshchad Iskustv and Italyanskaya Ulitsa. It was closed down three years later when rumors of orgiastic goings-on threatened to cause a scandal. In its short heyday, the Stray Dog attracted the cream of the literary and artistic avant-garde. The new generation of *sobachniki* hopes to re-create the original atmosphere by staging impromptu poetry recitals, cabaret acts, and other events of an artistic nature.

Walk Nevskiy Prospekt

Russia's most famous street stretches 3 miles from the **Admiralty** to the **Alexander Nevskiy Monastery**. All the major stores are located here, as well as a wide range of cafés, theaters, and movie theaters.

Starting from the **Admiralty** end, the first street to the right is **Malaya Morskaya Ulitsa,** formerly Ulitsa Gogolya in honor of the author Nikolai Gogol, who lived at **No. 17. Number 13** was the last residence of the composer Pyotr Ilych Tchaikovsky (see page 176). The wall near **No. 14 Nevskiy Prospekt** still carries a blue and white warning sign dating from the time of the Siege (1941–1942); it reads: "Citizens! During artillery bombardment, this side of the street is very dangerous."

The premises of the famous jeweler Fabergé were located near the next crossing of Nevskiy Prospekt at **Bolshaya Morskaya 24.**

The pink building on the right-hand side with the large neon sign (No. 15) is the **Barrikada Cinema,** formerly the Noblemen's Club. Opposite, by the Moyka Bridge at No. 18, is a fine

The Narodniy Most on Nevskiy Prospekt was the first iron bridge in the city

colonnaded building in the Empire style; this is the **Literaturnoe Café,** formerly the highly fashionable Café Wulf et Béranger where the poet Alexander Pushkin met his second before heading off for his fatal encounter with Baron D'Anthès (see page 191). The service is poor and the prices are steep, but few visitors can resist paying a call at a landmark so hallowed by Russians.

Cross the **Narodniy Most** (People's Bridge) and on your left is the **Dutch Church,** one of a number of foreign churches on Nevskiy Prospekt, whose presence earned the thoroughfare its one-time nickname, "Toleration Street." The green and white building on the opposite corner is the **Stroganov Palace** (reputed to be one of the finest in St. Petersburg), now a restaurant . The twin-towered Lutheran **Church of St. Peter** is set back from the street at No. 22–24. Opposite is one of St. Petersburg's most distinctive landmarks, the **Kazan Cathedral** (see page 180). Across the way, occupying the former premises of the Singer Sewing Machine Company, is the city's main bookstore, known as **Dom Knigi** (House of Books)—note the distinctive globe on the roof.

On your left as you cross the **Kazan**

Bridge, No. 32–34 is the Roman Catholic **Church of St. Catherine**, a yellow building with a green dome and high rounded arch; it was designed by Vallin de la Mothe in 1763. Across the street are the former jewelers' stalls known as "Silver Row"—the architect is Quarenghi (1784–1787). The unusual five-sided tower formerly belonged to the **town hall** or *Duma*. One of the Nevskiy's most famous landmarks, it was built by another Italian architect, Ferrari, in 1802. In the mid-19th century, semaphore telegraph equipment was installed above the tower to connect the imperial residences of the Zimniy Dvorets (Winter Palace), Gatchina, Kronstadt, Vilnius, and Warsaw, while balloons served as a flood warning. A little farther up, on the right-hand side, is the long façade of **Gostiniy Dvor** (see page 179) and opposite, on the corner of Ulitsa Mikhaylovskaya, is the **Grand Hotel Europe** (see pages 179–180).

Number 40 Nevskiy Prospekt is **Dr. Oetker's** café and restaurant. The building dates from 1794–1798. In the 19th century it was the premises of the baker T. Abrikosov, purveyor to the tsars, and it has recently been faithfully restored to its former glory, with wooden walls and ceiling, bamboo décor, silk paintings, and crystal mirrors. Next door, being restored, is the blue and white **Armenian Church**, followed by the famous department store known as **Passazh**;

The Lutheran Church served the sizable German community

one of St. Petersburg's most famous theaters, also called Passazh, was once in the arcade. A little higher up, at No. 52, is **Yeliseev's** food store, which still retains something of its prerevolutionary opulence. The stained-glass windows, marble counters, chandeliers, and relatively abundant supplies of food imports are worth a look.

The walk ends at a splendid square, **Ostrovskovo Ploshchad** (see page 190) dominated by the **Pushkin Theater** (Teatr Imeni A.S. Pushkina) and the **Russian National Library**. (Rossiyskaya Natsionalaya Biblioteka).

"Heard melodies are sweet but those unheard are sweeter."
—Nevskiy street lamp

What's in a name?
Moskovskiy Prospekt has undergone more name changes than most thoroughfares, even by Russian standards; it has been known at various times as Zabalkanskiy (Trans-Balkan) Prospekt, Mezhdunarodniy (International) Prospekt, and Prospekt I. V. Stalina.

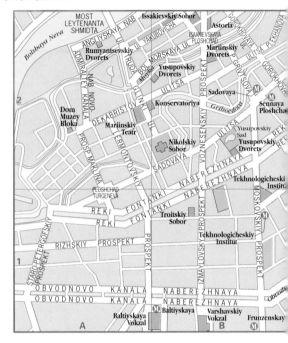

Big idea
Farther south along the Moscow Highway and closer to the airport is an enormous square: Moskovskaya Ploshchad. In the 1930s there were plans to shift the entire axis of the city southward, with this as the new administrative center. The plans were abandoned after World War II.

Nevskiy strollers
"If you wish to meet a friend you stroll up and down the Nevskiy and sooner or later you will probably see him doing the same, sauntering in the broad, animated, pleasant thoroughfare."
—W. B. Steveni,
Petrograd Past and Present

Moskovskaya

If you enter or leave the city via Pulkovo airport, you will pass through the Moskovskiye Vorota (Moscow Triumphal Arch) into the Moskovskaya district. Located on the main southern highway to Moscow, now known as Moskovskiy Prospekt, the arch was built in 1834 to a design by V. P. Stasov but is closely modeled on Berlin's Brandenburg Gate. Once the largest cast-iron structure in the world, it actually commemorates a series of minor and highly questionable military triumphs over the Poles.

Medieval folk hero Alexander Nevskiy provided inspiration for film director Sergei Eisenstein and composer Sergei Prokofiev—but it was Peter the Great who founded the monastery in his honor

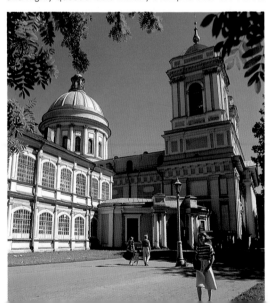

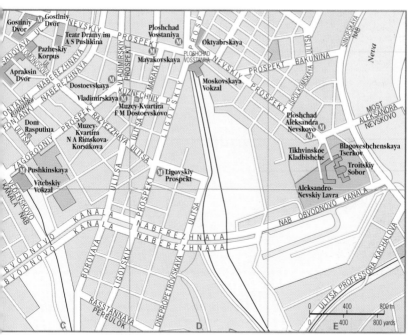

▶▶▶ **Aleksandro-Nevskiy Lavra**
(Alexander Nevskiy Monastery) *197E2*

Reki Monastyrki Naberezhnaya 1
Metro: Ploshchad Aleksandra Nevskovo
Open: Fri–Wed 11–6; closed first Tue of the month

The Alexander Nevskiy Monastery was founded in 1710 by Peter the Great. Believing he had located the exact place where the famous warrior prince and saint had triumphed over the Swedes in 1240, Peter personally chose the site of the first wooden church erected here in 1713. Alexander's remains were transferred to the monastery in 1724 but were later removed to the Hermitage. In June 1989 the body was returned with great ceremony to the silver reliquary in the Trinity Cathedral, where it is an object of veneration to Russian Orthodox Christians.

The Tikhvin Cemetery on the right-hand side is where many Russian cultural figures are buried (there is a small separate charge to enter). A cluster of graves and tombstones near the northern corner is of most interest to Westerners; here are buried the novelist Dostoevsky and the composers Tchaikovsky, Borodin, and Rimsky-Korsakov. (For further guidance, see the custodian at the gate.) The Blagoveshchenskaya Tserkov (Church of the Annunciation), across the Small Monastyrka River, is now a Museum of Town Sculpture.

Beyond the Dukhovskoy Korpus at the heart of the monastery is the **Troitskiy Sobor** (Cathedral of the Trinity). Built in classical style by I. Ye. Starov between 1776 and 1790, it is recognizable by its yellow dome and square bell towers. The church conducts services on Sunday mornings to the accompaniment of marvelous choral singing. The reliquary of Alexander Nevskiy is to the right of the splendid gilded iconostasis.

For more than 30 years composer Nikolai Rimsky-Korsakov was director of the St. Petersburg Conservatory

To help him work through the night, Dostoevsky always made sure he had a glass of strong tea beside him at his writing desk

Courtesy call
In the reign of Alexander I, newly appointed ambassadors and diplomats were expected first to call on his foreign minister, Count Nesselrode, who lived on Nevskiy Prospekt, next door to the Anichkov Palace. Only when their credentials had been verified were they allowed to be presented to the tsar at court.

▶▶▶ **Muzey-Kvartira F. M. Dostoevskovo (Dostoevsky House-Museum)** 197D2

Kuznechniy Pereulok 5
Metro: Vladimirskaya
Open: Tue–Sun 10:30–5:30; closed last Wed of the month
In this corner apartment, Dostoevsky (1821–1881) spent the last three years of his life and wrote the final part of his masterpiece, *The Brothers Karamazov*. Just as Tolstoy's house in Moscow (see page 112) provides an excellent idea of how the gentry lived in the 19th century, so Dostoevsky's rooms afford a glimpse of a typical middle-class existence.

In the hallway are several of Dostoevsky's personal possessions: his umbrella, walking stick, and hat. The nursery, with its dolls, rocking horses, maps, and school books, is especially evocative; the writer would come here to read Pushkin's fairy tales to his beloved young children, Fedor and Lyuba.

Dostoevsky's wife, Anya, turned her room into a study because she was also his secretary and amanuensis. This job entailed not only copying out sections of his work by hand but also keeping the family accounts, no easy matter given Dostoevsky's spendthrift habits—even though by that time he had conquered his near-disastrous addiction to gambling.

Like the other rooms in the house, the dining room has been carefully restored. Dostoevsky took tea here with the family before retiring to the drawing room, where he liked to entertain guests. When the family had gone to bed, Dostoevsky would write throughout the night in his study. On the wall is a reproduction of Raphael's *Sistine Madonna*, a painting that haunted him. On the desk, re-created from photographs taken on the day of his death (from natural causes), are his diary, glass of tea, and some works by Pushkin, his favorite author. The clock on the table has stopped at 22 minutes to nine and the date shows Wednesday, January 28 (1881). On the bottom of a tobacco box which has survived, 12-year-old Lyuba wrote "Daddy died today."

Dostoevsky's St. Petersburg

■ **Dostoevsky's St. Petersburg is at once as real and as fantastic as Joyce's Dublin, Dickens' London, and Victor Hugo's Paris. It is as if the writer needed the city for creative inspiration: of more than 30 literary works from his pen, over two-thirds are set in the capital.** ■

The Crystal Palace Hotel on the corner of Zabalkanskiy Prospekt, Vyazemskiy's (a collection of pubs, gambling dens, and brothels between the Haymarket and the Fontanka), the hay barges on the Neva where tramps and down-and-outs slept in the summer—the locations in Dostoevsky's novels could hardly be more precise. For the writer, St. Petersburg was a real, "half-demented" being: "Rarely does one find so gloomy, harsh, and strange influences on man's soul as in St. Petersburg."

A city for all seasons Dostoevsky came to St. Petersburg when he was 16 and lived here off and on for the better part of 30 years. He changed addresses more than 20 times—five times in the relatively short space of six years (1861–1867). He favored certain areas: in his youth, Vasilevskiy Island; in his middle years, Sennaya Ploshchad (the Haymarket); in his advancing years, Vladimirskaya Ploshchad. He liked corner houses with a view, preferably at an intersection or crossroads, all the better if they were close to a church—the Kazan Cathedral, for example, or St. Isaac's, or the Lutheran Church on Vasilevskiy Island. And he had his favorite seasons. Although he was fond of spring, he liked the fall most of all, when the setting sun caused "the gray, yellow, and dirty green of the houses to light up as if their souls are beginning to shine."

Back from the dead When Dostoevsky returned to St. Petersburg at the end of 1859 after serving ten years' penal servitude in Siberia for alleged involvement in a political conspiracy, penury forced him to settle in the slum quarter known as the Haymarket. After six years of unremitting literary toil, he was forced to leave Russia to escape his creditors. Only in 1871 did he feel secure enough to return. He resumed his literary career, and his crowning achievement, *The Brothers Karamazov*, was completed in his last St. Petersburg home, at Kuznechniy Pereulok 5.

Finger on the pulse An assiduous reader of newspapers, Dostoevsky based many of his stories on actual incidents: the plot of *A Gentle Creature* is drawn from a report in the St. Petersburg newspaper, *New Times*, of the suicide of a seamstress, Maria Borisova, in October 1876. (She threw herself out of the garret window of an apartment block on Galernaya Ulitsa.) The crime in *Crime and Punishment*, the murder of an old moneylender, is based on a similar one committed by one Gerasim Chistov in St. Petersburg in January 1865; the novel's publication the following year was blamed for a series of subsequent copy-cat killings.

Plaque on the Dostoevsky House-Museum

Mock execution
St. Petersburg was the setting for the most traumatic event in Dostoevsky's life. On the night of April 23, 1849, he was arrested and charged with taking part in a conspiracy and transferred to the "secret house" of the Peter-Paul Fortress. After eight months of solitary confinement, he was made to suffer the terrifying ordeal of a mock execution, a gruesome spectacle which took place on the parade ground of the Semyonovsky Regiment.

199

Serov's perceptive portrait of Dostoevsky painted in 1872

Leaving permission
"To leave Russia one has to advertise three times in the twice-weekly *Government Gazette*, stating name, address and intention of leaving the empire," according to J. L. Stephens in *Incidents of Travel in the Russian and Turkish Empires*, published in 1839.

Things were only slightly easier in 1914 when Baedeker advises the traveler to "report his intentions to the Police Authorities, handing in his passport and a certificate from the police officials of the district in which he has been living, to the effect that nothing stands in the way of his departure."

► **Ploshchad Vosstaniya (Uprising Square)**   197D2

Metro: Ploshchad Vosstaniya

Ploshchad Vosstaniya is where the fate of the Romanov dynasty was sealed in March 1917. After a week of bread riots, strikes, and other disorders, demonstrators seized control of this strategically important square, originally named after the Monastery of the Sign which stood on the site of the present metro station, Ploshchad Vosstaniya. For several days Cossacks and mounted police tried repeatedly but vainly to disperse the protestors. Finally, one of the soldiers sided with the crowd and killed a policeman, sparking off a mutiny which eventually spread to the entire garrison. The focal point of the square was "the hippo," a statue of Alexander III on horseback which was ridiculed when first erected. The design was the subject of a competition that had been entered by a number of distinguished sculptors, but was won by Prince Pavel Trubetskoy. Despite the negative public response, it was well-received in art circles, and one art critic described it as the forerunner of modern sculpture, despite its unflattering portrayal of Alexander III. It was removed in 1937 and stored in the Russian Museum. The obelisk that replaced it was erected in 1985. The building occupying the southern side, and the one most familiar to tourists, is the Moscow (formerly Nicholas) Station. The green and white façade, the only part of the original structure to survive, is by K. A. Ton, who also designed the Great Kremlin Palace. Another historic building, on the corner of Ligovskiy Prospekt, is the Oktyabrskaya (October) Hotel, known in pre-revolutionary times as the Severnaya or Hotel du Nord.

► **Dom Rasputina (Rasputin's apartment)**   197C2

Gorokhovaya Ulitsa 64

Although this is not a museum, many foreigners will feel that their tour of St. Petersburg is incomplete without some reference to the "mad monk." When Rasputin was at the height of his fame and influence, ladies of the court would visit the all-powerful figure in his apartment on the fourth floor. Rasputin owed his powerful position to his apparent ability to control the tsarevich's hemophilia with hypnosis. When Nicholas II left the capital to assume his duties at the front as Commander in Chief of the Russian army in 1915, Rasputin transformed himself from a *starets*, or wandering holy man, into an unofficial head of government, influencing everything from the appointment of court officials to the management of the food supply. Blamed, with some justification, for the continued deterioration in Russia's military fortunes, he was finally murdered in December 1916 by an aristocratic cabal led by Prince Felix Yusupov. Poisoned in the cellar of Yusupov's Palace and then shot, he was said to have been still alive when his body was taken out to the Malaya Nevka and dumped over the Bolshoy Petrovskiy Bridge.

▨ **Tekhnologicheskiy Institut (Technological Institute)**   196B1

Metro: Tekhnologicheskiy Institut

The Technological Institute might sound an unlikely destination for a tourist, but this imposing building played an important part in the revolutionary movement. From at least the 1880s onward, radical students would meet workers here, and sometimes illegal political parties, like Lenin's Social Democrats, held their committee meetings on the premises. It is no accident therefore that in October 1905, during the general strike that eventually led to the granting of Russia's first constitution, the Soviet (Council) of elected Workers' Deputies met here to coordinate both the strike and the campaign to bring about political change. Three months later, the Executive of the Soviet, among them Leon Trotsky, was arrested on the premises of the Free Economic Society opposite (33 Moskovskiy Prospekt).

▶ Troitskiy Sobor (Trinity Cathedral) 196B1

Tram: 18

The deep-blue dome of the Trinity Cathedral is a local landmark. Commissioned by Maria Feodorovna, consort of Paul I, the cathedral was built in 1828–1835 to a neoclassical design by Stasov. Closed in the 1930s, and not reopened until 1990, it is overdue for restoration, although religious services are being held here once again.

The cathedral stands on the corner of Izmaylovskiy Prospekt. The barracks of the Izmaylov Regiment (founded by Peter the Great) were at one time located on the streets off the avenue, and they are still known by their Company names—1st Company Street and so on.

Character of a city
"St. Petersburg ... with its architecture borrowed from Italy, its amusements from Paris, and its pretentiousness from Berlin ..."
—Hon. G. N. Curzon from his book *Russia in Central Asia*, published in 1889

The Trinity Cathedral: Peter the Great is said to have married his consort Catherine in the wooden chapel which it replaced

■ **Since the Paris World Fair of 1900 the Fabergé trademark has been a byword for masterpieces of precision jewelry, gold, and silverwork. In 1990 the Fabergé Arts Foundation was established as a joint Russian-U.S. venture with the prime purpose of restoring the master's workshops and showrooms at Bolshaya Morskaya 24.** ■

Avid collectors
Fabergé's workshop is known to have produced 55 imperial Easter eggs, of which 44 survive. Eleven of these are in the collection of *Forbes Magazine* in New York City. An obsessive collector of Fabergé eggs, the late Malcolm Forbes was determined to go one better than the Soviet Union, and in 1985 he achieved his goal by purchasing the cuckoo egg. In Britain, the royal family also has an extensive collection of Fabergé's works held at Sandringham.

Enamel box presented by Nicholas II to Grand Duke Mikhail Mikhailovich to mark the tercentenary of the Romanov dynasty

When Carl Fabergé took over his father's business in 1872 at the age of 26, the firm's reputation was confined to its conventional jewelry and silver and gold work produced in the popular Louis XV style. The development of a new, more original style was due partly to the imagination of the Fabergé brothers (Agathon had joined the firm in 1882) and also to a brilliant succession of head workmasters including Mikhail Perkhin, Franz Birbaum, and Henrik Wigström. Under their influence Fabergé designs underwent a succession of phases through art nouveau, classicism, and something approaching art deco. With the opening of a Moscow workshop on Kuznetskiy Most in 1887, a division of labor became possible: while Moscow concentrated on gold and silverware—mainly dinner services—St. Petersburg branched out into jewelry and *objets d'art*. The range of items was astonishing: cigarette cases and snuff boxes, clocks, *bonbonnières*, pencil cases, letter openers, bell pushes, necklaces, brooches, and rings.

Royal eggs The real breakthrough for the firm came in 1885 with a commission from Alexander III for a commemorative Easter egg of gold and white enamel, containing a golden hen. The idea caught on: when Nicholas II came to the throne it became his habit to commission two Easter eggs annually from Fabergé, one for his wife, the other for his mother. Each year the design, decoration, and surprise became more elaborate and

sophisticated, culminating in the famous 15th Anniversary eggs of 1911. In that year the tsarina's egg was decorated with ivory inlays containing portraits of herself and the tsar and scenes of the coronation; the dowager empress was presented with an orange tree egg complete with golden trunk, foliage of nephrite concealing clusters of diamonds, topaz, amethysts, and rubies and, at the summit, a feathered golden bird which sang at the press of a button before disappearing.

Months, even years were spent in designing Fabergé objects. Young peasant apprentices worked under the direction of specialist masters often in their 70s who taught them the intricate skills of enameling, engraving, gilding with bronze (ormolu), stone cutting, and jeweling. Great technical know-how was also required in constructing the mechanisms for the surprises—springs, levers, and hinges, often of microscopic size. Some of the pieces produced for the royal family were of astonishing complexity—a model of Gatchina Palace complete with trees, lampposts, and statues, or a miniature coronation coach with working door handles each smaller than a grain of rice and complete with leather straps to replicate the rolling movement.

International reputation By the turn of the century, Fabergé was held in the same regard as Lalique, Tiffany, and Cartier; his stand at the Exposition Universelle in Paris in 1900 finally put the firm on the map. The London branch was patronized by Edward VII's wife, Queen Alexandra, and Fabergé's fame extended to America thanks to purchases by the Vanderbilts and other wealthy dynasties. Some of the most sought-after jewels were the flower sprays: cornflowers made from sapphires, scarletinas of ruby, lilies of the valley in pearl and emerald, forget-me-nots of turquoise with rose diamond centers, the stalks and leaves in gold. By 1914 it is calculated that there were more than 150,000 Fabergé objects in circulation, the cheapest of which cost the equivalent of a night at the Ritz Hotel. Fabergé left Russia soon after the Revolution and died in Switzerland in 1920; the company was disbanded in November 1918.

Where you can see Fabergé work today in Russia The largest collection by far is in the Armory of the Kremlin in Moscow, while in St. Petersburg, Fabergé objects are sometimes on display in the Yelagin Palace Museum, the Hermitage, and the imperial palaces at Peterhof and Pavlovsk.

Table manners
As the new Russia struggles to rid itself of its old Communist identity, those with the time and money are eager to equip themselves with the Western European social graces. The new gospel of *Komilfo* (*comme il faut*) is now being preached via magazines like *Domovoi* ("house sprite"), how-to books and TV shows. Aside from advising on matters like how to hold your knife and fork and what to wear for formal engagements, they advise Russians not to "spit out bones and other things onto your plate" or "spear your bread with a fork"!

The mystery of Fabergé's Easter eggs was the secret inside

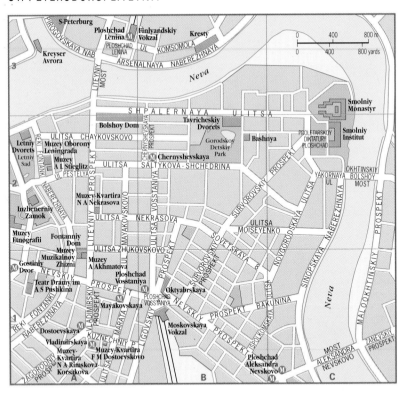

Liteyniy

The name refers to the "Smelting House," a cannon foundry which had been established on the left bank just a few years after the founding of the city. The military presence, always very marked in St. Petersburg, was nowhere more in evidence than in the Liteyniy district, where many of the units that made up the 40,000-strong garrison were stationed.

► **Bashnya (The Tower)** 204B2

13 Tavricheskaya Ulitsa
"The Tower" was the fanciful name given to the apartment where, in the first decade of the 20th century, avant-garde writers and artists used to meet every Wednesday, among them the poets Osip Mandelstam, Anna Akhmatova (see opposite), Alexander Blok, and Vyacheslav Ivanov, to whom the apartment belonged.

►► **Fontanniy Dom (Fontanka House/ House on the Fontanka)** 204A2

Reki Fontanki Naberezhnaya 34
Metro: Gostiniy Dvor
This was the main Petersburg residence of the Sheremetevs, at one time the richest landowners in the country. S. I. Chevakinskiy and F. S. Argunov were the original architects, but the design was altered many times over the years by such distinguished figures as

Quarenghi, Stasov, and Voronikhin. The Sheremetevs were in the vanguard of St. Petersburg's cultural life in the 18th and 19th centuries, especially in the musical sphere. They were also prominent patrons of the arts, turning their house into a museum that boasted a wealth of precious items. In January 1918, the heir to the Sheremetev estate donated the entire collection to the Soviet government. In 1990 the house was returned to the service of musical culture and reopened to the public as a museum in 1994. One wing of the residence is the Anna Akhmatova Museum (see below).

▶▶ Muzey Anny Akhmatova (Anna Akhmatova Museum) 204A1

Entrance: Liteyniy Prospekt 53
Open: Tue–Sun 10:30–6:30; closed last Wed of the month
One of the greatest Russian poets of the 20th century, Anna Akhmatova lived in the Sheremetev Palace, from 1933–1941 and 1944–1954. Born in Odessa but brought up in Tsarskoe Selo, Akhmatova's reputation was already established before World War I. The tragic pattern of her life began with the arrest and subsequent execution of her husband, the poet Nikolai Gumilev, in 1921. During the purges of the 1930s, she lost her son, Lev, and her lover, Nikolai Punin. Her experiences in attempting to track down her son inspired one of her most famous poems, *Requiem*.

▶▶ Muzey Muzikalnoy Zhizni (Museum of Musical Life) 204A1

Entrance: from the Fontanka
Open: Wed–Fri 2–6, weekends noon–6; closed last Wed of the month
The Museum of Musical Life celebrates the significant contribution of the Sheremetevs. In the 18th century concerts and amateur dramatics were performed here by serf composers, musicians, and actresses. In the 19th century the Sheremetev choir was noted for its professionalism— among those to sing its praises were the composers Glinka and Liszt.

Poet Anna Akhmatova. A long-running state campaign of vilification against her culminated in 1948, when party boss Andrei Zhdanov described her as "part nun, part whore"

The Sheremetevs willed their private collection to the state in 1918—one of the few aristocratic families to do so voluntarily

▶▶   **Liteyniy Prospekt**   *204A2*

The tall ornate apartment blocks on this, one of St. Petersburg's main thoroughfares, became a nest of the cultural élite in the later 19th century. The plaque at No. 36 commemorates the poet and publicist Nikolai Nekrasov, whose home, now open to the public, became the editorial offices of the famous radical journal *Sovremennik* ("The Contemporary"), which campaigned for women's rights and the abolition of serfdom. The great impresario Sergei Diaghilev launched another influential magazine, *Mir Isskustva* ("World of Art"), from premises at No. 45 in 1898. Among the visitors to this house were the artists Alexander Benois, Nikolai Roerich, and Leon Bakst. The journal survived only until 1904, but by then its philosophy of "art for art's sake" had changed the face of Russian culture. Diaghilev went on to found the Ballets Russes.

Liteyniy Prospekt also has a more sinister side. The so-called "big house" (Bolshoy Dom, No. 4) was the local headquarters of the secret police during the purges. Its predecessor on the same site, the St. Petersburg regional court, was the scene of several famous trials in tsarist times, including those of the assassins of Alexander II and of Lenin's brother, Alexander Ulyanov, executed for his part in a conspiracy to murder Alexander III. Not far from here, at Shpalernaya Ulitsa 25, was another prison, the House of Preliminary Detention, known as the *predvarilka,* where Lenin was held for 15 months in 1895–1896 before being exiled to Siberia.

▶   **Muzey Oborony Leningrada (Museum of the Defense of Leningrad)**   *204A2*

Solyanoy Pereulok 9
Metro: Chernyshevskaya
Open: Thu–Tue 10–5
The Museum of the Defense of Leningrad tells the dramatic story of the 900-day siege by the German army in 1941–1944. In a single large room, posters, photographs, a reconstructed apartment, and artifacts illustrate artistic life at the time, which continued despite appalling hardships and living conditions. The Communist authorities later awarded St. Petersburg the title "Hero City."

▶▶   **Smolniy Institut**   *204C2*

Proletarskoy Diktatury Ploshchad
Bus: 14, 22, 58, 136. Trolleybus: 5, 15, 16
Situated next door to the Smolniy Convent (see below), this handsome yellow classical building was designed by Quarenghi to accommodate a boarding school for daughters of the nobility, founded by Catherine the Great. It became the girls' equivalent of St. Petersburg's prestigious Alexander Lycée for boys, its pupils wearing a distinctive uniform of white starched apron and linen shoulder cape. Prominent in the girls' curriculum were dancing, music, and drama.

The statue of Lenin in the garden recalls Smolniy's greater claim to fame. In 1917, this building became the headquarters of the Petrograd Soviet and of the Bolshevik Central Committee. Plans for an insurrection were already underway when Lenin arrived at around midnight on the night of November 6 to stiffen the resolve of his troops. At the gate he was turned away by the sentries because his pass was

Russian leaders
"It is a key to Russian psychology, that there have never been any leaders at the right time and in the right place."
—Alexander Tsipko, head of political department of the Gorbachev Foundation, speaking about Solzhenitsyn.

Bust of Karl Marx outside the Smolniy Institute. Ironically, the founder of Communism made few references to Russia in his writings

out of date, but he managed to slip past. The rest, as they say, is history. When the government moved to Moscow in March 1918, Smolniy was handed over to the Leningrad Communist Party. On December 1, 1934, the party chairman and Stalin's great rival, Sergei Kirov, was assassinated in his office here—the incident that sparked off the purges.

► Smolniy Monastyr (Smolniy Convent) 204C3

Open: Tue–Sun 11–4

The magnificent blue, white, and gold convent and cathedral was founded by Empress Elizabeth in 1748. But by the time the empress died in 1761, the building was far from complete, and lack of funds and the departure abroad of the architect Rastrelli led to the project being put on ice. By the time V. P. Stasov finished the convent in 1832–1835, it had become a home for widows. His neoclassical contribution, a departure from Rastrelli's more flamboyant rococo, fails to honor the original intention to add a bell tower which would have been taller than the spire of the cathedral in the Peter-Paul Fortress. The convent was the subject of one of the first photographs ever taken in Russia, in 1852; the cameraman, Roger Fenton, later went on to record the Crimean War.

►► Tavricheskiy Dvorets (Tauride Palace) 204B2

Shpalernaya Ulitsa
Metro: Chernyshevskaya

Catherine the Great ordered the building of the Tauride Palace in 1783 to reward her lover, Prince Grigori Potemkin, for masterminding the Russian annexation of the Crimea. It was completed six years later by I. E. Starov and, as one of the first neoclassical buildings in Russia, was used as a model by architects too numerous to mention. Catherine's son, Paul, avenged himself on his mother's favorite by quartering a regiment of the Horse Guards in the palace and by turning the marvelous colonnaded hall into stables. It was restored after his death, but was used only occasionally by members of the imperial family. The gardens, on the other hand, became a favorite rendezvous of the well-to-do. It is difficult to imagine today, but in the 19th century there were hothouses, vines, an orangery, flower beds, vegetable patches, and 15,000 pots of strawberry plants!

In 1905 the impresario Sergei Diaghilev staged a memorable exhibition of Russian paintings in the Tauride Palace. A year later it became the home of the *Duma*, Russia's first parliament. In March 1917, the Provisional Government was formed in one wing of the palace, while in another wing a Soviet of Workers' and Soldiers' Deputies was convening—the literal origins of the "dual power" which held sway until the second revolution in November.

Disgusted
Not everyone found the Tauride Palace appealing. In 1809 the British traveler Sir Robert Ker Porter complained that mingled in with the classical statues were "the monstrous associates of modern ill-fashioned cupids, negroes, fantastic heads, and hideous whirligig pedestals of 50-colored marbles ... my disgust at this sight can only be compared to your sensations should a group of asses burst in with their horrid brayings, amidst the soul-entrancing sounds of spheric harmony."

The Cathedral of the Resurrection in the Smolniy Convent was commissioned by Empress Elizabeth. Her extravagance was legendary—she spent 1½ million rubles on the Winter Palace alone

Sports

■ **Since the Revolution, Russia has been one of the world's leading sporting nations. Whether your interest lies in spectator sports such as soccer, field hockey, ice hockey, and basketball—all Russian favorites—or whether you prefer to take part yourself, there is no shortage of opportunities in Moscow or St. Petersburg. All you need to know is where to look.** ■

Spectator sports You can order tickets through the service bureau of your hotel.

Moscow sports stadiums: Luzhniki, Vorobyovie Gory, tel: 201 09 55. Olympiyskiy, Olympiyskiy Prospekt 16, tel: 288 37 77. Dinamo, Leningradskiy Prospekt 36 (Petrovskiy Park) tel: 212 70 92.

St. Petersburg sports stadiums: Stadion im. Kirova, Primorsky Park Pobedy, tel: 250 00 30. Petrovskiy Stadion, Petrovskiy Ostrov 2, tel: 238 41 29. Dvorets Sporta Yubileyniy, Dobrolyubova Prospekt 18, tel: 238 40 17.

The soccer season runs from spring to fall, and games are usually held on Saturday afternoons. The top team at the time of writing is Moscow Spartak; its main rival is Moscow Dinamo.

Chess Moscow: Central Chess Club, Gogolevskiy Prospekt, Metro Kropotkinskaya, tel: 291 85 95.

St. Petersburg: City Chess Club, Bolshaya Konyushennaya Ulitsa 25, tel: 314 75 61. You can book a lesson or watch the masters play.

Cycling St. Petersburg: You can rent bicycles from Burevestnik Cycling Club, Engelsa Prospekt 81, tel: 554 17 41.

Golf Moscow: Moscow Country Club, Krasnogorskiy District, Makhabino, tel: 564 34 67. Russian champion golfers with international experience have built an indoor driving range near the Swedish embassy and offer lessons for golfers of all ages and skill levels, tel: 147 07 57. Tumba (Finnish) Golf Club, Ulitsa Dovzhenko 1, tel: 147 83 30.

Horseback riding Moscow: the best place to head for is Bittsa, Balaklavskiy Prospekt 33, tel: 318 07 44. One- to two-hour rides in the woods are available, and there are lessons for children and adults.

St. Petersburg: horse-and-carriage rides are available outside the Hermitage during the summer.

Hunting Rifle-hunting enthusiasts generally head for Leonid Brezhnev's old hunting lodge to kill reindeer, wild boar, and birds. Guns and ammunition are provided by the lodge. Contact the Moscow Society of Hunting and Fishing, tel: 930 49 78, or Greenfield, tel: 924 40 58 or fax: 975 21 69.

St. Petersburg is eager to promote itself as an international sporting venue. The city's cycling club is called "Stormy Petrel"

Sports

Pool Moscow: Armadillo Club, Khrustalniy Pereulok, behind the Rossiya Hotel, tel: 298 50 91.

Rowing Moscow: Rowboats can be rented by taking the metro to Rechnoy Vokzal and then a hydrofoil via Aksakova to Solnyechnaya Polyana. Hydrofoils leave hourly after 7:35. The last boat leaves Solnyechnaya Polyana at 8:28. Phone Rublevo Boat Rentals, tel: 414 10 04, or Torpedo-Zil Water Sports Facility, tel: 277 89 42.

Skating Numerous outdoor neighborhood rinks are flooded in winter.

Moscow: Luzhniki Ice Rink in the Central Stadium, Metro Sportivnaya, tel: 201 14 13; Ostankino, 1-ya Ostankinskaya Ulitsa 7a, tel: 181 55 11.

St. Petersburg: Yubileyniy Palace of Sports is indoors. Skates can be rented. Dobrolyubova Ulitsa 18 (*Open* 11–6, tel: 238 40 17).

Swimming Moscow: The cleanest of the city's indoor pools is the Chayka, metro Park Kultury, tel: 246 13 44. For the serious swimmer there is the world class, indoor Olympic pool on Prospekt Mira 18, tel: 369 10 86; open to all.

St. Petersburg: The best indoor pools are in the hotels, but many are too small for serious swimmers.

Try also the swimming pool of the Army Sporting Club, Litovskaya Ulitsa 3, tel: 542 01 62.

Tennis Moscow: There are both indoor and outdoor courts at Chayka, Korobeynikov Pereulok 1/2, tel: 202 04 74; Luzhniki Sports Center, metro Sportivnaya, tel: 201 16 55.

St. Petersburg: Lawn Tennis Sports Center (outdoor courts), Metallistov Prospekt 116, tel: 540 75 21.

Yachting Moscow: Klyazma Reservoir (*Open* 10–5, tel: 947 43 72). Yacht Club Aurora rents out 35-foot redwood yachts, and provides a captain and sailor for trips from one hour to overnight. Aurora also offers 2–10 person yachts at $70–230 per day.

Picnics are available for $20 a head including shashlik, fruit, and beer. The reservoir is on the Dmitrovskoye Shosse, 3 miles past the beltway.

St. Petersburg: Baltic Shipping Company Yacht Club, Martynova Naberezhnaya 92, tel: 235 43 50; Central Yacht Club, Martynov Naberezhnaya 70, tel: 235 61 02.

Sport
The wide-open spaces in the many parks of Moscow and St. Petersburg are great places to join in some informal game with locals—especially if you have children with you. In summer, the parks are the scene of countless games of soccer, basketball, and volleyball, while in winter there might be a chance to ride shotgun on a toboggan. Some larger parks even have cross-country skis to rent.

Poster advertising the St. Petersburg Goodwill Games, summer 1994

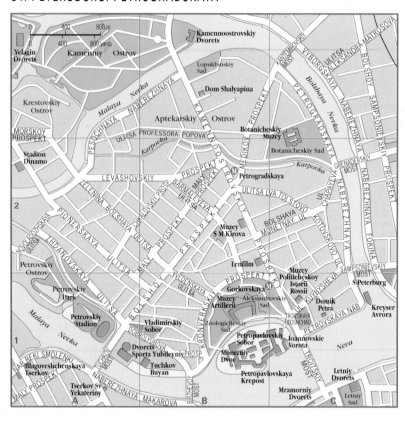

Petrogradskaya

The unmistakable features of opera singer Fedor Chaliapin

The Petrograd Side avoided being incorporated into the early schemes for a planned city, growing up instead as an untidy assortment of suburban settlements occupied by Russian and Tatar workmen. During the 19th century the less developed northern end of the district filled up with wooden *dachas*, the country cottages to which Petersburgers flocked in the summer to avoid the heat.

► **Dom Shalyapina (Chaliapin's House)** *210B3*
Grafito Ulitsa 26
Metro: Petrogradskaya
The great Russian bass Fedor Chaliapin (1873–1938) lived in this apartment from 1914 to 1922 before emigrating to France. Born in great poverty in the Volga city of Kazan, Chaliapin worked as a stevedore while looking for walk-on parts with a variety of private theaters and opera companies. After some time with Tiflis (Tbilisi) Opera, he was taken on by the Mariinskiy but found the atmosphere stifling. In 1896 the great impresario and patron Savva Mamontov signed him up with his own opera company. Over the next few years, Chaliapin developed into one of the greatest dramatic actors and singers of the day, creating roles like Boris

Godunov and Ivan the Terrible and infusing them with his own dynamic personality. When Mamontov's theater collapsed, Chaliapin joined the Bolshoy, the company with which he is most closely associated. In 1909 he received international acclaim as one of the stars of Diaghilev's touring opera company which paved the way for the Ballets Russes.

The apartment, which is currently closed for restoration, contains some of the original furnishings including a walnut chair presented by the writer Maxim Gorky, signed photographs of Chekhov, Tolstoy, and Rimsky-Korsakov, and paintings by Konstantin Korovin, as well as a famous life-size portrait by Boris Kustodiev. To see Chaliapin's costumes, however, you will have to visit the Theater Museum (see page 193).

▶ Domik Petra (Peter's Cabin) 210C1
Petrovskaya Naberezhnaya 6
Metro: Gorkovskaya
Open: Wed–Mon 11–6; closed last Mon of the month
From this simple log cabin, Peter the Great supervised the construction of his new city in 1703–1709. The museum consists of a study and dining room with early 18th-century furnishings. Also on display are Peter's frock coat and rowboat.

▶ Kamennoostrovskiy Prospekt and Bolshoy Prospekt (Stone Island Avenue and Great Avenue) 210B2
Metro: Gorkovskaya, Petrogradskaya. Trolleybus: 10, 128
The two enormous avenues that crisscross the Petrograd Side are undistinguished in themselves but contain a number of interesting sights. On Kamennoostrovskiy Prospekt (Stone Island Avenue), near Gorkovskaya metro are Nos. 1–3, a *style moderne* apartment block designed in 1902 by Fedor Lidval; No. 5, the former villa of Nicholas II's prime minister, Count Sergei Witte; Nos. 10–12, the Lenfilm Studios, formerly the Aquarium Theater, where the first moving picture was demonstrated by the Lumière brothers on May 4, 1896.

On Bolshoy Prospekt (Great Avenue), from the waterfront, are the Tuchkov Warehouse by Rinaldi; the Yubileyniy and Petrovskiy sports stadiums where the Goodwill Games were staged in 1994; and the Vladimirskiy Sobor, a grandiose 18th-century cathedral designed by Trezzini and Rinaldi.

▶▶ Kreyser Avrora (Cruiser *Aurora*) 210C1
Petrogradskaya Naberezhnaya 4
Metro: Ploshchad Lenina. Tram: 6
Open: Tue–Thu and weekends 10:30–4
At 9:40 exactly on the night of November 7, 1917, the cruiser *Aurora* fired a single blank round from its bow gun in the direction of the Winter Palace, where the besieged members of the Provisional Government were still holding out. It was the signal for the insurgents to storm the Palace, arrest the ministers, and hand over power to the Bolsheviks. The *Aurora* was built in 1903 and saw active service during the Russo-Japanese War of 1904–1905; it was one of the few ships of the Baltic Fleet to survive the Battle of Tsushima Straits.

Petersburg Side
"Describing a funeral arc in the sky, a dark ribbon, a ribbon of soot, rose from the chimneys; and it tailed off onto the waters."
—Andrei Bely, St. Petersburg.

211

Communist icon. Stained-glass window featuring Vladimir Ilych Lenin in the Museum of Russian Political History, formerly the Museum of the Revolution

ST. PETERSBURG: PETROGRADSKAYA

At the time of the Revolution, she was in port for a refit, so her place in history is somewhat accidental, but she does symbolize the disproportionate role played by the Baltic Fleet in the Russian Revolution. From mid–1917 onward the sailors made regular forays from the Kronstadt naval base into Petrograd where they invariably made a nuisance of themselves. When General Lavr Kornilov attempted a coup against the Provisional Government, the sailors rallied to its defense; by fall the Baltic Fleet had become closely identified with the Bolshevik cause, which is why sailors in their distinctive black uniforms receive such a high profile in the propaganda paintings of the postrevolutionary period: Lenin himself called them the "pride and glory of the Revolution." The honeymoon did not last long, however. In March 1921, under the slogan "All power to Soviets not to parties," Kronstadt declared itself independent. Immediately Lenin ordered the storming of the fortress by 50,000 soldiers of the Red Army. Kronstadt fell, but only after great loss of life on both sides—a classic case of the Revolution devouring its own.

The cruiser *Aurora* was deliberately sunk in shallow water in 1941 during the Siege of Leningrad, to be later refloated and converted into a museum. You can visit the crew's living quarters and learn more about the ship's fascinating history in an exhibition below deck.

►► Muzey Artillerii (Artillery Museum)   *210B1*
Aleksandrovskiy Sad 7
Metro: Gorkovskaya
Open: Wed–Sun 11–5; closed last Fri of the month
The Artillery Museum moved into this enormous horseshoe-shaped building in 1868; for more than 100 years before that date it had served as an arsenal. Of particular

Flagship of the Revolution—visitors roam the decks of the Cruiser Aurora, *now a naval museum*

Meditating on past glories? A Russian senior citizen inspects the firepower in the grounds of the Artillery Museum

interest is the prerevolutionary collection of small arms, period uniforms, and artillery pieces. Moving into the modern era, there are examples of the distinctive Red Army uniforms worn by soldiers during the Civil War and, more predictably, a detailed account of the Soviet army's performance during World War II—exhibits include a Katyusha rocket launcher and a diorama illustrating the greatest tank battle ever, at Kursk in 1943. Also of interest is the armored car from which Lenin addressed the crowd immediately after his arrival at Finland Station on April 3, 1917.

▶▶ Muzey Politicheskoy Istorii Rossii
(Museum of Russian Political History) *210C1*

Ulitsa Bolshaya Dvoryanskaya 2/4
Metro: Gorkovskaya
Open: daily 10–6

The Museum of Russian Political History occupies the former home of one of the greatest prima ballerinas of the imperial era, Matilda Kschessinska (1872–1971), whose other claim to fame was her affair with Nicholas II while he was still tsarevich. The house, in the *style moderne*, was designed by A. I. Gogen and completed in 1906. The interior is sparsely furnished in accordance with a neo-classical revival, which was fashionable at the turn of the century. Downstairs is a small exhibition on the life and dancing career of Kschessinska, including programs, costumes, ballet shoes, and other ephemera.

In March 1917, Lenin's Bolshevik party commandeered the palace as its headquarters. Kschessinska instigated legal proceedings to get the Bolshevik squatters removed, but to no avail. The mansion became the Museum of the Great October Socialist Revolution, and was one of the great ideological shrines until being undermined by *perestroika*. Since the demise of Communism just two of the Bolshevik offices have been preserved, including Lenin's study.

A further exhibition downstairs entitled *Russia: Terror or Democracy?* attempts to document the political alternatives to Communism that were swept away in 1917 but that are now being reappraised. Among the brochures, party programs, and newspapers are some more arresting artifacts, such as the uniform of a secret police-man, handcuffs, assorted bomb-making equipment, and terrorist death threats (mimeographed handbills and handwritten notes).

Security risk
Photographs of President Bill Clinton and his wife Hillary have appeared in a number of St. Petersburg's bars and restaurants following his official visit to the city in 1996. During the trip, the President created panic among Russian and U.S. security chiefs when he suddenly decided to abandon his limousine and walk the short distance from the Russian Museum to the Church on the Spilled Blood. After a great deal of persuasion, his aides managed to confine him to his limousine while Secret Service personnel, fearful of the security risk, unceremoniously evicted businessmen and their secretaries from their offices on the Griboedov Canal. Were they reminded of the fate of Tsar Alexander II?

Law on facial hair
In the reign of Alexander I, a law was introduced confining the wearing of mustaches and sideburns to military men bearing arms. The regulation was precisely observed so that military doctors and even bandsmen were forbidden the facial decoration.

■ **For nearly a century, ballet has been one of Russia's most reliable exports. However, problems linked to the demise of Communism have threatened standards and exposed decades of complacency and lack of innovation.** ■

Balletomane
After Taglioni's farewell performance in Russia, an admirer bought a pair of her ballet shoes, cooked them in a special sauce, and served them to his friends at a balletomanes' supper held in her honor.

Vaslav Nijinsky dancing in Le Spectre de la Rose *(1911)*

Peter the Great introduced the pleasure of ballroom dancing to Russia and with it created a demand for foreign dancing masters. Among them was the Frenchman Jean-Baptiste Landé, who in 1738, under the patronage of Empress Anna, founded Her Majesty's Dancing School, the future Imperial Ballet. Thirty-five years later, in 1773, a similar school was attached to the Moscow Orphanage; this was the precursor of the Bolshoy.

Petipa St. Petersburg owed its early ascendancy to another Frenchman, Charles-Louis Didelot, who gave the Russian ballet a distinctive style as well as a systematized method of training dancers. But Russia was still dependent on visiting prima ballerinas; no one was more successful than Marie Taglioni, who triumphed in 1837 with *La Sylphide*—even the straitlaced Nicholas I was moved to present her with a cape made from Siberian sables.

By far the most significant arrival in Russia was that of Marius Petipa in 1847. Already famous in France as a performer and choreographer, Petipa took over the Imperial Ballet in St. Petersburg (now the Mariinskiy or Kirov) for whom he created more than 60 ballets before his retirement in 1903. Despite the fact that he was regarded by some as a despot, Petipa's importance is undeniable, for he produced Russian prima ballerinas who were a match for any in the West. He also raised the standard of the *corps de ballet* and, with the help of his exceptionally talented assistant, Enrico Cecchetti, who created the role of Carabosse in *The Sleeping Beauty*, trained a cohort of male principals at a time when many foreign companies used women to play the male roles.

Petipa was also fortunate in his choice of composers. His earliest collaborators, Pugni and Minkus, were mere functionaries. Tchaikovsky, on the other hand, composed scores like *Swan Lake*, *The Sleeping Beauty,* and *The Nutcracker*, which not only enhanced the dancing, but were pieces of music in their own right.

Diaghilev Among the audience at the première of *The Sleeping Beauty* in 1890 were two young enthusiasts, Sergei Diaghilev and Alexander Benois. For the next 15 years Diaghilev, the budding impresario, was preoccupied with the art world, but in 1909 he promoted the first European tour by members of the Imperial Ballet—the origin of perhaps the most famous theatrical venture of all time, the Ballets Russes. Diaghilev was fortunate enough to inherit a new generation of dancers trained by Cecchetti, among them Anna Pavlova, Tamara Karsavina, and Vaslav Nijinsky. Diaghilev's vision and his dancers' prodigious talents were backed up by a galaxy of collabo-

rators: the choreographer Michel Fokine, who created *Les Sylphides*, *Daphnis and Chloë*, and *Prince Igor*, the designers Alexander Benois, Léon Bakst, Nicholas Roerich, and Natalia Goncharova, and the composer Igor Stravinsky, whose three ballet scores, *Petrushka*, *The Firebird*, and *The Rite of Spring*, astonished the ears of Europe in the period leading up to World War I.

Vaganova Emigration of many artists after the Revolution deprived Russia of every principal dancer except Agrippina Vaganova, prima ballerina and graduate of the Mariinskiy Theater School. She alone preserved the Russian ballet tradition, becoming principal of what was eventually known as the Vaganova School. Thanks to her, the Soviet Union was for decades able to play the Bolshoy and Kirov companies as an ace whenever its cultural policies were denigrated by the West. Unfortunately, so successful were the tours of the 1950s and 1960s and so popular were the dancers that defections were virtually inevitable. The trend set in motion by Rudolf Nureyev in 1961 is still going on today—witness the poaching of Irek Mukhamedov by the British Royal Ballet in 1990. The flow will be staunched only when the underlying problems of financial underfunding, limited repertoire, and unequal allocation of roles are addressed.

British bulldog
The prima ballerina Anna Pavlova was born in St. Petersburg, trained at the Mariinskiy, and later toured with the Ballets Russes. An anglophile, Pavlova set up a dance school in Hampstead, London, in 1915. Her home there became famous for its ornamental lake and her pet swans and gazelles. She is also said to have introduced the first thoroughbred English bulldogs into Russia.

Top: detail, the Bolshoy Theater, Moscow
Below: the Bolshoy Company doing what it does best— classical ballet with a popular appeal

Brass monkeys
While Russian army officers enjoyed many privileges during the reigns of Alexander I and Nicholas I, regulations were unimaginably severe and enforced often with sadistic punctiliousness. For example, only if the temperature in St. Petersburg dropped to below 15°F were guardsmen allowed to wear greatcoats on parade.

Distant voices
When the famed Male Choir of St. Petersburg gave a concert in the Maliy Zal of the Philharmonic in 1997 as part of the Mravinsky Festival, it was an unaccustomed treat for the local audience. Russia is famous for its *a capella* singing—a tradition dating back to the 1500s when it was nurtured by the Orthodox Church. The style is now experiencing a revival, but unless more state funding or private Russian sponsorship becomes available, the Male Choir, like so many other first-class performers, will be forced to spend most of its time abroad.

For many revolutionary opponents of the tsarist government, the benign façade of the entrance to the Peter-Paul Fortress concealed the harshest of penal regimes

▶▶▶ Petropavlovskaya Krepost (Peter-Paul Fortress)   210B1
Metro: Gorkovskaya
Open: Thu–Tue 10–6; closed last Tue of the month.
Admission free to Fortress grounds

The foundation stone of the Peter-Paul Fortress was laid on May 27, 1703. The hexagonal fortifications were designed on the traditional Renaissance model, with two perimeter walls incorporating five pentagonal bastions. At first these were hastily constructed from timber and earth using the time-honored Petrine device of slave labor; by 1740, they had been replaced by brick. The construction of the bastions was entrusted to the tsar's leading generals, in whose honor they are named: Trubetskoy, Menshikov, Golovkin, Zotov, and Naryshkin. On the northern side of the fortifications, separated by a moat, a secondary line of defenses was built, known from its crown shape as the Kronwerk. Almost from its inception the fortress had a more sinister purpose—the interrogation and incarceration of political prisoners—thus it became known as the "Russian Bastille." It continued to be used for this purpose until after the Revolution, when the fortress was turned into a museum. One of the great monuments and landmarks of St. Petersburg, it is also one of the top tourist sites, attracting more than two million visitors each year. The ticket office is near the Ioann Gate and admits visitors to the cathedral and Trubestkoy Bastion museum only. Tickets for other parts of the fortress open to the public, including the Commandant's House and Engineer's House, are sold on the spot.

The main entrance is across the bridge leading from the corner of Troitskaya Ploshchad (Trinity Square) to the

Ioannovskie Vorota (St. John's Gate). This yellow classical arch bears the date 1740 and the imperial coat of arms. The gate leads directly to the larger and more ornate Petrovskie Vorota (St. Peter's Gate), designed by the architect of the fortress, Trezzini. Above the Romanov double eagle is an elaborate relief allegorizing Peter the Great's defeat of Charles XII of Sweden. The single-story building with the steeply pitched roof dressed in yellow-and-white brick is the Engineer's House. Adjacent to it is the two-story Commandant's House, where the interrogation of political prisoners took place. Both houses are now devoted to exhibitions on 18th- and 19th-century St. Petersburg life, and display architectural drawings, contemporary street signs, music boxes, statuettes of street traders and other colorful characters, painted dinner services, lithographs, model boats, ball masks, theater programs, quill pens, duelling pistols, uniforms and court dress, visiting cards, and even old chocolate tins.

Outside is a controversial statue of Peter the Great, presented to the city in 1990 by Mikhail Shemyanka.

The first wooden church of SS. Peter and Paul, distinguished by three spires, was founded in June 1703, only a month after the fortress itself. It was soon replaced by a more suitable stone monument; the tall belfry, crowned by its magnificent golden needle, was built first to test the foundations. The Cathedral of SS. Peter and Paul was completed to Trezzini's design in 1733. With great panache, laced with a dash of arrogance, it rejects the traditional Russian design in favor of the European baroque style. The highlight of the interior is the marvelous iconostasis, made of gilded wood and decorated by a real master of the art, Ivan Zarudny. The main focus of attention, however, is the cluster of marble tombs of the tsars and tsarinas. Those of Peter the Great, dignified by a bronze bust and vases of fresh flowers, and of Catherine the Great are to the right of the iconostasis. The remains of the last Romanov tsar, Nicholas II, murdered with his family in Yekaterinburg in 1918, may be interred in the Grand Ducal Mausoleum on the east of the cathedral, built in 1915.

The writer Dostoevsky was one of many alleged subversives whose trial took place in the Commandant's House of the Peter-Paul Fortress

Saints
There are calls from some quarters for Nicholas II to be canonized. Postcards showing an icon of the tsar, his wife, and children, all with halos, are currently on sale. The icon hangs in an American church, the Russian Orthodox Church Abroad, which has already canonized them. In Moscow, the Church of All Saints also has an icon image of the tsar.

Modern visitors contemplating conditions in the cells of the Peter-Paul Fortress

Great flood
On November 6, 1824, it rained incessantly in St. Petersburg and there was a sharp cold wind. At 7 PM the lamps were lit on the Admiralty and Strelka lighthouses to signal warning. During the night the wind strengthened, bringing in floodwaters from the Gulf of Finland. The islands were the first part of the city to be submerged. By the following morning the torrent was such that the granite embankments gave way in places, breaking into pieces or crumbling. This was only one of the 200 major floods that have beset the city since its foundation.

Just beyond the cathedral, on Cathedral Square, is an elegant pavilion with white-columned porticoes. This is the *botniy-dom* or boathouse, where Peter's private vessel was stored. A little further away is a restrained yellow brick building dating from 1805 and bearing the inscription Monetniy Dvor (Mint).

The Trubetskoy Bastion of the Peter-Paul Fortress became a place of confinement in 1718. Its first resident was Peter the Great's own son, Tsarevich Alexis. (It is said that the tsar strangled the youth with his own hands after finding him guilty of conspiring against him.) For a period of more than 150 years, most prisoners, including the Decembrist rebels, were housed elsewhere in the so-called Secret House of the Alekseevskiy Ravelin (no longer standing but situated near the Vasilevskiy Gate). A new prison, comprising 69 isolation cells, was opened in the Trubetskoy Bastion in 1870 and served as a place of detention for the revolutionary opponents of the tsars until 1917. Among those imprisoned here were the anarchist Prince Kropotkin, Lenin's elder brother Alexander Ulyanov, and Leon Trotsky. After the Revolution it was the turn of their oppressors, including several grand dukes. Visitors can inspect a long line of cells running off a central corridor. Each wooden door has a slat for observing the prisoner and for passing through food. Plaques recall the more famous occupants. The interior of each cell—stifling in summer, cold and damp in winter—contains only a simple iron bedstead and a pull-out table attached to the wall. In the windowless punishment cell, prisoners lived on a diet of bread and water for 48 hours at a time. Once every two weeks, each detainee was taken outside to the bathhouse in the exercise yard, which was also where prisoners were put into irons before being taken into servitude.

If you have time, you could take a circuit of the fortress walls. A cannon on top of the Naryshkin Bastion used to fire a regular signal at noon. Inside the Neva Gate a series of markers indicates the levels reached by floodwater at various times; the most famous inundation of all, that of 1824, is described by Pushkin in his famous poem *The Bronze Horseman*. At the southern end of the fortress, at the Commandant's Pier, a boat was kept constantly at the ready for the tsar's personal use.

■ **A visit to the Russian *banya*, baths, should not be missed. Part of the national culture for centuries, the *banya* is quite distinct from the Finnish and Turkish sauna. It is uniquely invigorating, and is said to draw out toxins and improve circulation.** ■

Taking the plunge Bring a towel, shampoo, plastic shoes, sandals, and, if you want, a shower cap. Don't go after drinking, on a full or empty stomach, or if you are feeling tired. After paying your admission charge, hand your valuables to the attendant in the changing room. You may be given a plastic bathing robe and offered a *venik*, the bundle of birch twigs without which no visit to the bath is complete. The bathing area, usually one immense room lined with benches, has metal hand basins for soaking the *venik*. When washing, keep your head dry and don't use soap because it closes the pores. Do gentle exercises to keep the circulation going. In the sauna, sit first on the lowest, coolest ranks of raised benches. Spend no more than four or five minutes here before returning to the bathing room for a respite and a warm shower. It is not advisable to take more than three turns in the sauna. If you want to use the *venik*, first brush it lightly across your body, then strike more boldly. Most Russians finish with a glass of tea or water or even a shot of vodka (be careful not to overindulge, and sip, don't gulp, any liquids). You should now feel the full benefits of the *banya's* theraputic properties.

Moscow baths Sandunovskaya Sauna, 1e Neglinniy Pereulok 1a (*Open* Wed–Mon 8 AM–10 PM, tel: 925 46 31); Krasnopresnenskie Baths, Stolyarniy Pereulok 7 (*Open* Tue–Sun 8 AM–10 PM, tel: 255 53 06. *Admission charge*).
St. Petersburg baths Banya, Olgi Forsh Ulitsa 6 (*Open* Wed–Sun 8 AM–10 PM, tel: 592 76 22); Nevskie Banie, Marata Ulitsa 5/7, no telephone (*Open* Wed–Sun 8 AM–10 PM; closed Mon and Tue).

Yegorov's
The bathhouses of Moscow and St. Petersburg were once the last word in luxury. Yegorov's in St. Petersburg, for example, had a tented disrobing room, decked out in Moorish style with cushions and settees, and a swimming pool traversed by a grottolike bridge and rockery, classical-style statues, and trailing greenery.

*The neogothic interior below is Moscow's Sandunov Baths
Top: Moscow's Krasnopresnenskiy Baths*

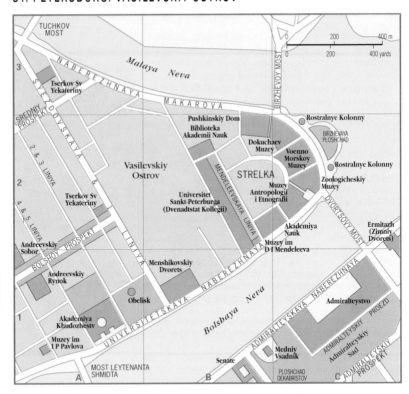

Vasilevskiy Ostrov (Vasilevskiy Island)

Vasilevskiy Island is named after Vassiliy Korvmin, an artillery lieutenant charged with defending it in Peter the Great's day. It lies between the great (Bolshaya) and small (Malaya) branches of the Neva, which divides at the southeastern tip, known as the Strelka or Spit. This was the site of the port, intended by Peter to be the focal point of the city. A Stock Exchange and a Customs House were built here almost immediately, as were the first government buildings in St. Petersburg, known as the Twelve Colleges. The city's first governor, Prince Alexander Menshikov, chose it as the site for his palace, which outshone anything built by his royal master. Even after the center of the city had shifted to the Admiralty, Vasilevskiy Island continued to be important as a commercial and financial center. It was also the focus of some notably forward-looking academic institutions, among them the Institute of Geography, the Library, the Observatory, and, from 1819, the University. Industry encroached during the 19th century, but even as late as 1914 the northern half of the Island comprised little more than woods, wasteland, and kitchen gardens. By that time, there was a large foreign contingent—mainly of Germans—living on Vasilevskiy Island, with their own schools and shops, a Lutheran church, and even German beerhouses.

To find your way around, it is useful to know that all the streets running north to south on the Island are called lines and are numbered—rather like the streets of New York City.

► Akademiya Khudozhestv (Academy of Arts) 220A1

Universitetskaya Naberezhnaya
Trolleybus: 1, 9, 12, 46. Bus: 6, 7, 47
Open: Wed–Sun 11–7

Vallin de la Mothe's noble Academy of Arts was founded in 1757 on the initiative of Count Shuvalov, a favorite of Empress Elizabeth. By the mid-19th century, however, the training had become so formal and stultifying that it provoked a rebellion; this was the origin of the breakaway art movement known as the Peredvizhniki or Itinerants (see page 128). In front of the building are two sphinxes, brought to Russia from Luxor, Egypt, in 1832.

► Churches 220A2

There are two churches dedicated to St. Catherine (Tserkov Sv. Yekateriny) on Vasilevskiy Island. The Lutheran church on the corner of Bolshoy Prospekt was built by Yegor Velten and is recognizable from its four-columned portico and cupola. Near the start of Sredniy Prospekt is Andrei Mikhailov's Orthodox church, marked by its tall bell tower of 1811–1823, which is something of a local landmark. The imposing Andreevskiy Sobor (Cathedral of St. Andrew), situated on the corner of the 6th Line, was built in the 1760s. Also on the 6th–7th Line is St. Andrew's Market (*Open* Mon–Sat 8–7, Sun 8–4). Merchants once lived in apartments above the arcades dating from the 18th century. The most interesting church is the Blagoveshchenskaya Tserkov (Church of the Annunciation) which, with the exception of the 'Church of the Savior on the Blood' (see page 180), is one of the few religious buildings in St. Petersburg built on traditional Muscovite lines.

► Dom Savicheva (Savichev House) IBCB3

Bolshoy Prospekt 6/13

This apartment block was the home of "St. Petersburg's Anne Frank," Tanya Savicheva, an 11-year-old schoolgirl who lived here at the height of the Siege. Between December 1941 and May 1942 Tanya recorded in her diary the deaths of her sister, grandmother, brother, uncles, and mother. The last entry is a heart-rending one: "The Savichevs have died. They have all died. Only Tanya remains."

► Dom I. V. Stalina (Stalin's apartment) IBCB3

Sredniy Prospekt 46

This is where Stalin lived after returning from exile in Siberia in March 1917. Old friends from the Caucasus, the Alliluyevs, helped him find the apartment. He was eventually to marry their youngest daughter, Nadezhda.

► Menshikovskiy Dvorets (Menshikov Palace) 220B1

Universitetskaya Naberezhnaya 15
Tram: 37, 63. Trolleybus: 1, 9, 10, 12, 46. Bus: 6, 7
Open Tue–Sun 10:30–4:40

The handsome yellow-and-white Menshikov Palace (can only be viewed as part of a guided tour—in Russian) was

Angelic sculpture decorating one of St. Petersburg's rostral columns

Protocols of Zion
The notorious *Protocols of Zion* frequently invoked during the tsarist campaign to discredit Russia's Jewish population have finally been exposed. They were in fact written by agents of Nicholas II's secret police, who based them on an anti-Semitic tract published earlier in France. Purporting to be an agreement drawn up by a group of Jewish elders, who met in Switzerland in 1897 and plotted to destroy Christian civilization and impose Jewish world control, the "document" has finally been declared a forgery in a Russian court.

Dwarfs

A favorite distraction at Prince Menshikov's dinner parties was the antics of Peter's dwarfs—two of whom was once induced to celebrate a mock wedding. In the 17th century both dwarfs and giants were a familiar feature of royal and noble households. They were considered to be good-luck mascots and were kept as human pets. Peter the Great even had his placed inside huge pies at banquets and they would leap out as the pies were cut open.

built in 1710–1716 by Giovanni Fontana and Gottfried Schädel for Peter the Great's leading adviser, Alexander Menshikov (1673–1729). The humbly born Menshikov became a bosom companion of the tsar, one of the few capable of sustaining the pace of Peter's frantic social round. Menshikov's extraordinary venality and corruption finally caught up with him after the tsar's death. In 1727 he was accused of treason and exiled to Siberia with his family after being deprived of all his possessions.

The interior of the palace, which has seen a great deal of alteration over the years, is open to the public as a museum, focusing more on 18th-century life than on Menshikov himself, and with disappointingly little—except the marvelous tiled suite of private rooms—to remind one of the original furnishings and décor. Exhibits include lathes and other instruments owned by Peter the Great and some items of his clothing.

Ostrov Dekabristov (The Outer Island)   IBCA4

The northern part of the island was developed after World War II and consists mainly of apartment blocks built in the 1960s–1970s. South of Ulitsa Nakhimova is the Gavan or Harbor district leading to the Sea Terminal on Ploshchad Morskoy Slavy. Many visitors to the city come to know the western part of the island well by staying at the Pribaltiyskaya (Baltic Shore) Hotel, which has rooms with splendid views overlooking the Baltic. There is also a beach of sorts, but it's strictly for walking—it is not unknown for dead seals to be washed up here.

▶▶   Strelka   220B2

The two russet-colored rostral columns (Rostralnye Kolonny) which stand guard over the old harbor were originally lighthouses guiding ships safely into port. An Ancient Roman custom was to adorn rostral columns with the prows of enemy vessels captured at sea, and the custom is alluded to here in the decoration. The figures at the base represent Russia's four great rivers—the Neva, the Volga, the Dnieper, and the Volkhov. The classical theme contin-

Granite embankments protect St. Petersburg from the potential ravages of the majestic Neva River

Originally the center of Peter the Great's administration, by 1835 the Twelve Colleges had been handed over to St. Petersburg University

Curiouser and curiouser
During his first whistle-stop tour of Holland in 1697, Peter the Great attended lectures given by Frederik Ruysch, the most celebrated anatomist of the day. He was also invited to see the scientist's famous collection of anatomical preparations—the so-called Chamber of Wonders. He was so impressed with these curiosities (which included the pickled hand of a child, decorously trimmed with lace) that he later bought the entire collection for 30,000 Dutch guilders. Anyone with a sufficiently sturdy constitution can view some of these choice items in St. Petersburg's Museum of Anthropology and Ethnology.

ues in the building immediately to the rear. Modeled on a Greek temple, this is the old *birzha* or Stock Exchange; it was completed in 1810 to a design by the Swiss architect Thomas de Thonon. The Exchange is now the **Central Naval Museum** (*Open* Wed–Sun 10:30–5). The star exhibit here is the *botik*, the boat in which Peter the Great learned to sail. Most of the other items relate to the Revolution and World War II or to the various rebellions in the Baltic and Black Sea fleets.

The columned buildings on either flank, once warehouses, are now, respectively, the Museum of Soil Science and the Zoology Museum. The latter, one of the largest museums of its kind in the world, with more than 100,000 specimens, was renowned for its collection of mammoths. Many of these are now touring abroad, but not the Siberian mammoth, more than 44,000 years old, which was uncovered in 1902. This can be viewed Sat–Thu 11–5.

The building with the dome on the northern side is the former Customs House, now the **Literary Museum**. To the south and facing the Admiralty are the **Museum of Anthropology** (formerly the Kunstkammer, founded by Peter the Great to house a bizarre collection of curios. *Open* Sat–Wed 11–4:30) and the Academy of Sciences, opened in 1725 with Peter's enthusiastic support and the assistance of German academics and scholars. The architect of the present building (erected in the 1780s) was Quarenghi. Immediately beyond **Mendeleevskaya Liniya▶** is the extraordinary complex known as the **Twelve Colleges**. The sequence of brick red buildings (¼ mile in length) was erected to house Peter's ministries (colleges). These now belong to St. Petersburg University. Dmitri Mendeleev, the famous chemist who invented the periodic table of elements, taught here. A little farther on, the Academicians' House (originally a professors' guest house) commemorates another scientist associated with the university, Ivan Pavlov, of salivating-dog fame.

Wolves
In histories of St. Petersburg the accent has usually been on the unbelievable pace at which the city has developed. This often overlooks the extremely primitive conditions under which most of the inhabitants were expected to live. In 1715 for example, a woman was devoured by a wolf in broad daylight right outside Prince Menshikov's palace on Vasilevskiy Island, while the nearby Vyborg forests were infested with the creatures.

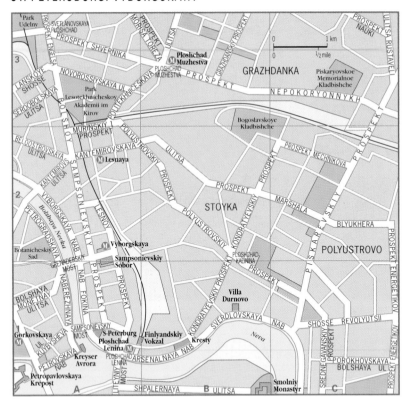

Vyborgskaya
(Vyborg Side)

One of the least visited parts of St. Petersburg, the Vyborg Side played an important role in the Russian Revolution. Sparsely inhabited until the mid-19th century, it grew quickly to be the city's largest factory district. During the revolutions of 1905 and 1917 the workers of the factories here were invariably the most militant in St. Petersburg—on more than one occasion the authorities had to raise the bridges over the Neva to prevent them crossing into the city center. With its cramped working-class housing and narrow lanes, the Vyborg Side was also ideal for revolutionaries holing up before escaping to the relative safety of Finland, then an autonomous province of the empire.

Flood control
There appears to be no end to Russia's environmental doldrums. A 17-mile barrier across the entrance to the Neva River (under construction in December 1993) was unfortunately found to trap sewage in St. Petersburg Harbor, causing a major pollution problem.

▶ **Bolshoy Sampsonievskiy Prospekt**
(Great Samson Avenue)   *224A2*

Once known as Prospekt Karla Marksa in deference to its revolutionary pedigree, this long featureless avenue is the main route through Vyborgskaya. Just to the west is one of the city's best-known hotels, the St. Petersburg (formerly the Leningrad). The Bolsheviks held their first legal political meeting following the collapse of tsarism at No. 37, then a temperance hall. Just opposite was the Nobel factory, established in 1849 and now known as Russian

Diesel. A little farther on is the Sampsonievskiy Sobor (see page 226). Opposite No. 77 were the quarters of the notorious First Machine Gun Regiment, one of the most reliable supporters of the Bolsheviks during the turbulent days of 1917. Serdobolskaya Ulitsa 1, another Communist shrine, is where Lenin stayed on the night of the Revolution itself before traveling to the Smolniy Institute (see page 206).

▶ Finlyandskiy Vokzal (Finland Station) 224A1

At 11:10 on the night of April 3, 1917, Vladimir Ilych Lenin and his shabby-looking band of fellow exiles arrived in St. Petersburg at Finland Station. A large crowd, alerted by handbills announcing Lenin's arrival, had gathered outside the station, and sailors from the Baltic Fleet formed a guard of honor as Lenin was escorted to the former imperial waiting room near platform 1, where he made his first speech since arriving back on Russian soil. Then he was carried outside on the shoulders of soldiers and sailors, and he made another short speech before the procession moved off to Bolshevik headquarters at the Kschessinska Mansion (see page 213). In 1926 the first Soviet statue of Lenin was unveiled near the station. In a large glass case on platform 5 is Locomotive No. 293, which took Lenin into hiding in Finland after the Bolsheviks had been outlawed for their role in the "July Days," then brought him back again to the outskirts of Petrograd by the same route on October 7. The present Finland Station was constructed in the 1950s, but parts of the smaller yellow building that Lenin would have known can still be seen to the sides.

▶ Kresty (Prison of the Crosses) 224B1

Ulitsa Komsomola

The Prison of the Crosses, so called because of its ground plan, was first built in the reign of Catherine the Great. One of the first acts of the revolutionaries after the collapse of tsarism was to free the prisoners here after setting fire to the prison buildings—thus the Kresty had a significance not dissimilar to the Bastille in Paris.

Men only
In the early 19th century only ten percent of the population of St. Petersburg was female, largely because male factory workers and artisans from the rural hinterland came without female dependents. Single males usually lived communally in *artels*, each *artel* comprising men from the same rural province or district. The men would be expected to send at least part of their wages back to their village to support the family and would often return with presents like fountain pens and even umbrellas. A young man who had not worked in the city could never be regarded as a good catch.

225

Lenin once stood on the footplate of this locomotive, posing as a fireman in order to evade capture

▶ **Piskaryovskoe Memorialnoe Kladbishche**
(Piskaryovskoe Memorial Cemetery)   *224C3*

Prospekt Nepokoryonnykh
Metro: Ploshchad Muzhestva, then bus No. 123
Open: daily 9–6

The Piskaryovskoe Memorial Cemetery is dedicated to the 670,000 Leningraders who perished, mostly from disease and starvation, during the siege of 1941–1944. Nearly 500,000 of them were interred in great haste in mass graves here, the present mausoleum dating from the 1950s. Two memorial halls lead to the Eternal Flame and at the end of the long central avenue is *The Motherland*, a statue by Vera Isayeva and Robert Taurit. Solemn music by Shostakovich plays in the background. Until recently, Piskaryovskoe was a favored Intourist excursion, intended to remind Westerners of the enormous sacrifices made by the Soviet people during what they know as the Great Patriotic War. The cemetery is difficult to get to for the tourist, but Piskaryovskoe is still a place of pilgrimage for the citizens of former Leningrad, most of whom lost relatives during those desperate times.

▶ **Sampsonievskiy Sobor**
(St. Samson's Cathedral)   *224A2*

Bolshoy Sampsonievskiy Prospekt 41
Metro: Vyborgskaya

Work began on the Cathedral of St. Samson as early as 1728, making this one of the oldest monuments in the city. It was opened in 1740 on the feast of St. Samson (June 27). This attractive church with its fine baroque iconostasis, its bell tower, and five cupolas is said to have been where Catherine II married Prince Potemkin in secret in 1774.

▶ **Villa Durnovo**   *224B1*

Sverdlovskaya Naberezhnaya 22

This imposing columned mansion, built in 1813–1814 by Andrei Mikhailov, was later occupied by the wealthy senator and minister L. P. Durnovo. At the outbreak of the March Revolution the villa was commandeered by the Petrograd anarchists who, after a series of gun battles, were ousted by the Bolsheviks.   •

It is difficult to imagine nowadays that the stately Villa Durnovo was once the scene of a shootout between Bolsheviks and anarchists

■ **Price and availability of food, lack of housing and jobs, the rise in violent crime, deteriorating standards in the health service, and pollution are the topics exercising Russian journalists today.** ■

Judging by the titles of Russian newspapers alone, little seems to have changed. *Pravda*, once the official organ of the Communist Party, *Izvestiya* and *Komsomolskaya Pravda* are still there, albeit with altered editorial perspectives. For example, *Moskovskiy Komsomolets*, which once spoke for the Moscow branch of the Communist Youth Wing, is now a thrusting investigative paper with a radical reputation. The most fearless paper of all, however, is new: *Nezavisimaya Gazeta* ("Independent Newspaper"). Having begun life as a Yeltsin supporter, it has recently become disillusioned, reflecting the trend in the population generally.

Tabloids The appearance of sensation-seeking tabloids, often with promising titles like *Top Secret*, is a relatively recent phenomenon, as is the growth of pornographic publications, pop magazines like *Rovesnik* ("Your Age"), and lavish glossies aimed at the newly rich.

Pop magazines Pop magazines are also mushrooming. *Rovesnik* has articles about the likes of Mick Jagger, George Michael, and Iron Maiden.

Corruption is the scourge of today's media; it is claimed that 80 percent of all reports appearing in the Russian press are written "to order." Journalists can apparantly receive offers of up to $100 a time to write a favorable movie review, to boost a particular computer company, or to profile an up-and-coming politician.

Pravda
Founded by Lenin as the mouthpiece of the Bolshevik (Communist) Party in 1912, the newspaper *Pravda* ("truth") has never come closer to closing than in the last few years, when its huge publishing debts have left it without the wherewithal to cover printing costs. So far it has survived. An old dissident joke runs: "In Truth (*Pravda*) there is no News (*Izvestiya*) and in News there is no Truth."

227

Popular reading
One particularly popular tabloid is *Skandaly* which takes most of its stories from abroad: everything from flying saucers to the Bermuda Triangle. The advertisements in papers like this also reveal changing social trends— Russians look to the classifieds if they want to buy a gun or require the services of private detectives.

The Botanical Gardens. St. Petersburg's islands are a haven of peace and tranquility

The Islands (Ostrova)

There are more than 100 islands strewn across the Neva Delta. But when Petersburgers refer to "the islands" (*ostrova*) they are usually talking about a small cluster to the north of the city. They are still charming today: green and romantic, full of undiscovered corners, forgotten monuments, and once grand but now sadly neglected country houses.

Traditionally the islands were the summer refuge of the very wealthy, who built or rented out *dachas* among the parks and lakes, and dined in fashionable restaurants like Cubat Frères on Kamenniy Island or the Krestovskiy Restaurant, where late-night suppers were accompanied by wild gypsy music.

Lucky escape
Aptekarskiy Island was once the summer home of Nicholas II's most controversial prime minister, Pyotr Stolypin. On August 12, 1906, a suicide squad of Socialist Revolutionary "Maximalists" managed to break through the tight security surrounding the *dacha* to blow it up. Stolypin escaped but 32 others were killed, including the terrorists themselves.

► **Aptekarskiy Ostrov (Apothecary's Island)**　　　*IBCC5*

Metro: Petrogradskaya. Bus: 128
"Apothecary's Island" is separated from the Petrograd Side by the attractive Karpovka River, where pleasure boats ply the waters in summer. Just to the north of Grenaderskiy Bridge is the island's main attraction, the Botanical Gardens (Botanicheskiy Sad). The gardens (*Open* Sat–Thu 1–4; 11–5 in summer) were founded by Peter the Great in 1713 for the cultivation of medicinal herbs. Covering an area of 40 acres, they are resplendent with trees, shrubs, flowers, and plants (some 36,000 varieties in all). The gardens offer an excellent opportunity to relax for an hour or two. (The main entrance is on Ulitsa Professora Popova 2; the Botany Museum is open Sat–Thu 11–4.)

The dominant landmark in this area is the TV transmitter (1,037 feet high), completed in 1965. Not far away, on Ulitsa Grafito, is the former apartment of the great Russian bass Chaliapin (see page 210). A walk through the delightful Lopukhinskiy Sad will take you onto Kamenniy Island.

▶▶ Kamenniy Ostrov (Stone Island)   *IBCC5*

Bus: 134

Perhaps the most beautiful of all the islands, Stone Island is famous for its old *dachas*, many of them concealed within the park. Among those with residences here were Peter the Great's chancellor Alexander Golovkin (the original owner of the island), Alexei Bestuzhev-Ryumin, and the Princes Dolgorukov. On the eastern tip is Stone Island Palace, built in 1776–1781 by Catherine the Great for her son Paul. Yegor Velten designed the palace to drawings by V. I. Bazhenov. A handsome building of white and yellow stucco, it is now a sanatorium. At the western end of the island is the wooden Kamennoostrovskiy Theater, first erected in 1827 but redesigned shortly afterward by the architect of the Bolshoy Theater in Moscow, A. Kavos.

▶ Krestovskiy Ostrov (Krestovskiy Island)   *IBCB5*

Bus: 71. Tram: 17, 21, 26, 33

This, the largest of the islands, has a number of important sporting venues, including the rowing center and the Kirov Stadium, dating from immediately after World War II when volunteer labor laid out the enormous Primorskiy Park Pobedy (Seaside Victory Park). The stadium has a capacity of 100,000 and was renovated for the 1994 Goodwill Games. The Dinamo Sports Center, on the other side of the island, was built in the 1920s.

▶ Yelagin Ostrov (Yelagin Island)   *IBCB5*

Trolleybus: 9. Tram: 17, 26

Cars are banned on this island, which takes its name from I. P. Yelagin, a courtier of Catherine the Great who owned a mansion here in the 1770s. Appointed a "Central Park of Culture," the island becomes busy at weekends and public holidays. In 1817 Alexander I bought the island from Count Orlov and commissioned a new palace (*Open* Wed–Sun 10–6) by Carlo Rossi, which he presented to his mother. The palace contains a number of fine rooms, including the Porcelain Room, beautifully decorated with painted stucco by Antonio Vighi, and the Oval Hall. If you walk along Primorskiy Prospekt for about half a mile to a point called *strelka* ("spit"), you can catch a view of the sunset over the Gulf of Finland.

Temple
The Buddhist temple in Staraya Derevnya (north of Yelagin Island) was built on the initiative of the Dalai Lhama in 1915. A modernist flavor was provided by designer, Nikolai Roerich, who decorated the building. Roerich is better known for his stage designs for Diaghilev's ballets.

Two sphinxes, guarding the southern embankment of Kamenniy Ostrov, overlook the Malaya Nevka, a tributary of the Neva River

Specialist museums in St. Petersburg

► **Dom Muzey Bloka (Blok Museum)**   196A2

Dekabristov Ulitsa 57
Tram: 31, 33. Bus: 22
Open: Wed–Mon 11–5, Tue 11–4

This was the apartment of the Russian symbolist poet Alexander Blok (1880–1921), most famous for his poem *The Twelve*, a mystical celebration of the Revolution. Quickly disillusioned with Communism, he succumbed to illness and died prematurely. Blok's apartment, which he shared with his wife, is a branch of the Russian Museum.

►► **Mramorniy Dvorets (Marble Palace)**   155D4

Millionnaya Ulitsa 5/1
Metro: Gorkovskaya
Open: Wed–Mon 10–6

Catherine the Great had good reason to present the Marble Palace to her favorite Grigori Orlov. Not only was he her lover for more than 12 years (a record); he also organized both the *coup* that made her empress and the murder of her husband, Peter III. The architect was the Italian Antonio Rinaldi, who had already proved himself at Oranienbaum. Building began in 1768 in Catherine's favorite neoclassical style. The marbles—pink, green, blue-gray, which give the palace its name—were mined in Siberia. Some of the original interiors have been restored and contain exhibitions of Russian painting.

► **Muzey S. M. Kirova (Kirov Museum)**   210B2

Kamennoostrovskiy Prospekt 26/28
Metro: Gorkovskaya
Open: Thu–Tue 11–6

Until recently virtually everything in St. Petersburg was known by the name of the one-time Leningrad Communist Party First Secretary, who was purged by Stalin in 1934. There is yet to be a reappraisal of Kirov, and the museum focuses exclusively on his merits.

Before the Revolution the Marble Palace, with its magnificent façade, was the residence of Grand Duke Konstantin

► Muzey-Kvartira N. A. Nekrasova (Nekrasov House-Museum) 204A2

Liteyniy Prospekt 36
Metro: Vladimirskaya. Trolleybus: 3, 8, 15, 38
Open: Mon, Wed–Fri 11–5; closed last Thu of the month
A poet and progressive journalist, Nekrasov lived here in bourgeois comfort for the last 20 years of his life. The centerpiece is the bedroom reconstructed to look as it did in the final months of his life, with medicines and a servant's calling bell as well as copies of Nekrasov's journal.

► Muzey-Kvartira N. A. Rimskova-Korsakova (Rimsky-Korsakov House-Museum) 197C2

Zagorodniy Prospekt 28
Metro: Vladimirskaya. Trolleybus: 3
Open: Wed–Sun 11–6
This was once the apartment of the composer Nikolai Rimsky-Korsakov (1844–1908). From an aristocratic background, he became professor of composition at the St. Petersburg Conservatory in 1871, where he remained until his death. He is mainly remembered for his operas which include *Tsar Saltan* and *The Golden Cockerel.*

►► Muzey Prikladnykh Iskusstv A. L. Stieglitz (Stieglitz Applied Arts Museum) 204A2

Solyanoy Pereulok 15
Metro: Chernyshevskaya
Open: Mon–Sat 11–5:30
The design of this late 19th-century building by Maximilian Mesmacher is based on the great palaces of the Italian Renaissance. Baron Aleksandr Stieglitz was a patron of the arts who founded the museum and the art school. There are studios here even today, but the attraction for visitors is the stunning interiors, re-created and decorated in a variety of national and period styles from High Renaissance to Louis XIV. The tour concludes with a visit to Mesmacher's Grand Exhibition Hall with its magnificent glass roof.

Muzey Tsirkovovo Iskusstva (Circus Museum) 189E5

Reki Fontanki Naberezhnaya 3
Metro: Gostiniy Dvor
Open: Mon–Fri noon–5 for groups
Addicts of the circus will enjoy this fascinating if rather wooden exhibition comprising more than 80,000 items of circus memorabilia, mainly relating to St. Petersburg's Ciniselli Circus.

►► Yusupovskiy Dvorets (Yusupov Palace) 154B1

Reki Moyki Naberezhnaya 94
Bus: 22
Open: daily 11–5; guided tours only
This splendid palace was built by Vallin de la Mothe in 1760. The highlight is the spectacular Moorish Hall where Islamic arches and motifs are picked out in golds and reds. The walls contain inscriptions from the Koran, while the equally intricate coffered ceiling completes the astonishing effect. The theater interior, equally resplendent but in contrasting rococo style, is still in use today.

End of the "Mad Monk"
It was in the cellars of the Yusupov Palace that the infamous "Holy Man," Grigory Rasputin, was murdered in December 1916. After surviving poisoned cakes at supper and a gunshot wound in the chest, he staggered into the courtyard where Prince Feliks Yusupov battered in his skull with a bronze candlestick. Yet when Rasputin's corpse was dragged from the river two weeks later, there was water in his lungs—indicating death by drowning.

Colorful abstract advertising the Circus Museum

■ **"For us, the cinema is the most important of all the arts."** With this crisp declaration, Lenin justified the nationalization of the Soviet film industry in 1919. Today, Russian film directors are trying to consign to the past a 70-year tradition of "cinema as propaganda" to re-create the industry on a new, commercially viable but creatively independent basis. ■

It was the Lumière brothers who brought the cinema to Russia. The first movie, a documentary featuring the coronation of Nicholas II and Alexandra, was presented in May 1896 at the Aquarium Summer Theater in St. Petersburg—Kamennoostrovskiy Prospekt 10, later to become even more famous as the address of the Leningrad Film Studios (Lenfilm). Before World War I, censorship guaranteed that, artistically speaking, Russian movies were nothing but safe costume dramas like *The Death of Ivan the Terrible* and *1812*. "Decadent" or mystical subjects were a surer box-office draw, but audiences at the first picture houses, the Parisiana in St. Petersburg, for example, came for the French farces and the latest productions from Hollywood.

Art of the film Film as an art form, however, was the child of the Russian Revolution. The propaganda value of movies was immediately recognized by the new government—during the Civil War the famous "agit"-trains showed short but extremely effective movies to peasant audiences all over Russia. But the Revolution was above all the perfect training ground for a new generation of directors, and the first film school in the world opened in the Soviet Union. In 1923 one of them, Lev Kuleshov, the first theorist of Russian film, made *The Strange Adventures of Mr. West in the Land of the Bolsheviks*, a satire about an imaginary American visitor to Soviet Russia. This was the first time Russian audiences had the chance to see "the Kuleshov effect," the technique of montage. Kuleshov's pioneering work inspired two of the great masters of the medium, Vsevolod Pudovkin in Leningrad and Sergei Eisenstein in Moscow.

Although most of Eisenstein's artistic triumphs—*Strike* (1924), *The Battleship Potemkin* (1925), and *October* (1927)—were motivated by propaganda, they were anything but conventional in form; Eisenstein took montage to its limits with a splicing technique which he referred to as "shocks." Other talented directors, including Sergei Yutkevich, Grigori Kozintsev, and Lev Trauberg, were influenced by circus and vaudeville, while the work of Dziga Vertov was a forerunner of *cinéma vérité*. But the era of experiment came to an end with the imposition of Socialist Realism. For ten years not one of Eisenstein's film projects saw the light of day, and when he did finally emerge from the shadows in 1938 it was with the "safe" historical drama, *Alexander Nevskiy*. (The biggest plus was his fruitful collaboration with the composer Sergei Prokofiev.) Ideological conflicts over his next movie,

An actor is made up for a performance at St. Petersburg's Lenfilm Studios. When they were founded in 1918, Soviet Russia was at the cutting edge of the film industry

however, the epic *Ivan the Terrible*, eventually destroyed his health.

Perestroika The shackles of conformity were only finally broken at the fifth congress of the film-makers' union in May 1986, when a director long out of favor, Elem Klimov, was elected first secretary—five of his six films had been "arrested" or banned. But despite the unprecedented artistic freedom which followed, and the release of dozens of long-suppressed films, the Soviet movie industry was plunged into a crisis from which it has still to emerge. A bureaucratic fossil, it has found it harder than most to adapt to the challenges of television, home videos, and the Hollywood blockbuster.

Salvation may come from overseas. In 1993 a French delegation, including leading film-makers Pierre Richard and Gerard Depardieu, visited Russia with the declared aim of combining to fend off the formidable Hollywood challenge. As a result of the agreement, French audiences will soon have the chance to see movies by young graduates of the Russian State Institute of Cinematography, while Russian audiences will be shown French films, some of which, like *Rasputin*, will be shot on location in Russia.

Epic drama
One of the longest and most expensive movies ever made was Sergei Bondarchuk's version of Tolstoy's *War and Peace*. Originally in four parts and with a running time of 8¾ hours, it took five years to make and has some of the most spectacular battle scenes ever created. Over 165,000 military uniforms had to be made and the re-creation of the Battle of Borodino of 1812 involved 120,000 "extras" from the Soviet army.

Scene from Sergei Eisenstein's great epic film Oktyabr (October) *of 1927*

Excursions

Tsarskoe Selo, Pavlovsk, Peterhof, and Oranienbaum

Tsarskoe Selo Tsarskoe Selo (formerly Pushkin) is situated about 15 miles south of St. Petersburg and about 3 miles from Pavlovsk. The easiest way to get there is to take the train from St. Petersburg's **Vitebskiy Vokzal** (Vitebsk Station), Zagorodniy Prospekt (metro: Pushkinskaya), to **Dyetskoe Selo** (the next-to-last stop on the suburban line—see Pavlovsk, page 238). Buses 371 and 382 go directly to the palace, but if you wish to see the other sights first, then it's a comfortable and interesting walk through the town. Avoid coming on Mondays and Tuesdays, however, when many of the sights are closed.

Pavlovsk Pavlovsk is about 20 miles south of St. Petersburg. The easiest and cheapest way to get there is by train; Pavlovsk is about 35 minutes from St. Petersburg's **Vitebskiy Vokzal** (Vitebsk Station), Zagorodniy Prospekt (metro: Pushkinskaya). Trains leave from platforms 1 and 2 and tickets are sold at a separate *prigorodniy kassa* (suburban ticket office) beside platform 1. The service is irregular from St. Petersburg; returning trains are much more frequent, about half-hourly. Pavlovsk (*Open* Mon–Thu, Sat and Sun 10–5:30) is the last stop on the line.

Peterhof Peterhof (Petrodvorets) is situated about 20 miles from St. Petersburg, on the southern shore of the Gulf of Finland. The fastest and most enjoyable route in summer (May–Sep) is by hydrofoil, departing from the **Winter Palace Embankment** in St. Petersburg. The ride takes about 40 minutes and the palace is open Mon–Fri 10:30–6; closed last Tue of the month. Otherwise, trains leave from the **Baltic Station**, Naberezhnaya Obvodnovo Kanala (metro: Baltiiskaya) at regular intervals. Buses No. 350, 351, 352, 356 depart for the palace grounds about every ten minutes.

Oranienbaum (Lomonosov) This is best reached by taking the suburban train from St. Petersburg's **Baltic Station**, Naberezhnaya Obvodnovo Kanala (metro: Baltiiskaya). The trip takes about an hour. The Lower Park is only a short walk from the station.

Left: the imperial station and (opposite, lower left) Catherine Palace at Tsarskoe Selo. Tsarskoe derives not from the Russian word for "royal" but from a Finnish word meaning "island"

235

▶▶▶ Tsarskoe Selo (formerly Pushkin)   234

To see the town properly, you need to spend the whole day here. The main sights are the **Catherine Palace (Yekaterinskiy Dvorets)**, the **Alexander Lycée**, and **Pushkin's** *Dacha*. The town is laid out on a grid pattern and is graced with fine and elegant houses. Just off **Moskovskaya Ulitsa** is the **Market Hall**, a smaller version of St. Petersburg's Gostiniy Dvor.

In tsarist times, Tsarskoe Selo, like Pavlovsk, was a fashionable haunt of the aristocracy, which was anxious to be near the imperial family and to escape the noxious air and oppressive climate of the capital. After the Revolution of 1905 Nicholas II and his family lived here more or less permanently. Tsarskoe Selo Station then would have been bristling with blue-uniformed officers of the *gendarmerie*, the tsar's security service, anxiously on the lookout for revolutionaries and other malcontents. In 1937 it was renamed after the famous poet. Pushkin was overrun by the Germans in 1941; when they left three years later, the palaces were devastated.

Dacha A. S. Pushkina (Pushkin's *Dacha*)▶▶▶

(Pushkinskaya Ulitsa 2. *Open* Wed–Sun 11–6) In 1831, Pushkin and his young and beautiful wife, Natalya, spent the summer here, during which time he wrote a series of short stories, *The Tales of Belkin*. Pushkin was already well known and, while going for walks in the park, would be greeted not only by pupils of his alma mater, the Lycée, but by court officials and other writers.

The rooms retain much of their period furnishings and offer a fascinating look at life in the early 19th century. Most visitors are drawn to the study where Pushkin used to spend his mornings writing. The desk is scattered with the poet's possessions, including a griffin paperweight, an inkwell, quill pens, a calling card, books, and curled-up pages of manuscript, full of crossings out, doodles, and even a sketch of Natalya herself. Two additional rooms created after Pushkin's death are devoted to two of his contemporaries, the poet Zhukovsky and the historian Karamzin.

Curse of the Lycée?
Pushkin's short, unhappy life finds echoes in the fate of other former Lycée comrades: Ivan Pushchin and Wilhelm Kuechelbecker were punished for their involvement in the Decembrist conspiracy by prison and Siberian exile respectively, while fellow poet, Anton Delvig, died prematurely in 1825.

The royal chapel of the Catherine Palace. Much of the interior décor, including the frescoes, was stripped and looted during World War II

Missing masterpiece
One of the greatest art thefts perpetrated by the Germans during World War II was the removal of the exquisite 18th-century amber panels from the Amber Room at Tsarskoe Selo, which had long been prized as one of the finest art treasures in Russia. In 1941, as the Germans advanced across Russia, Erich Koch, Gauleiter of East Prussia, ordered troops to strip the Pushkin palaces of all their works of art. The Amber Room was dismantled and taken to Königsberg Castle, where it was packed into 24 trunks to await transportation to Germany. When the Russians retook the castle in 1945, the amber panels had vanished and have never been seen since.

Aleksandrovskiy Dvorets (Alexander Palace)▶ The yellow-and-white **Alexander Palace** is just a few minutes' walk from Pushkin's *dacha* along **Ulitsa Vasenko**. It was built by Quarenghi for Alexander I when he was still crown prince. Now a little decrepit, it was the preferred residence of Nicholas II and his family in the decade leading up to the Revolution—the pond and playground in particular were a favorite haunt of the children.

Tserkov Znameniya▶ A short walk from the Alexander Palace and visitors are allowed their first glimpse of the blue-white-and-gold façade of its older sister. Before embarking on a tour, however, there are still more treats in store. Next door to the Lycée is the small but attractive **Church of the Sign**, with a spire reminiscent of the cathedral in the Peter-Paul Fortress. It was designed by I. Ya. Blank in 1734–1747. In the garden next door is a statue of Pushkin dating from 1900.

Memorialniy Muzey Litsey (Alexander Lycée)▶▶▶ (Sadovaya Ulitsa 2. *Open* Wed–Mon 10–4) Painted yellow and white, this building is linked to the Catherine Palace by an imposing arch.

The poet Alexander Pushkin was one of the original pupils at this élite educational establishment. Many of the schoolrooms have been beautifully preserved, such as the **Great Hall**, where on June 9, 1817, Pushkin gave a much-acclaimed poetic recital entitled *Recollections of Tsarskoe Selo*. Of the **newspaper room**, Pushkin recalled: "[It] was never empty when we were out of class. Russian and foreign newspapers were read without a break to a background of incessant chatter and argument." The **library** contains works by all the classical authors including Homer and Virgil but also Voltaire. The **physics laboratory** is laid out as a lecture room with banks of wooden desks, a blackboard, teacher's podium, and a globe. Beyond is the **art room**—the drawing class was one of Pushkin's favorites. Most evocative of all are the **students' dormitories**. First comes the simply furnished room of the duty master, complete with pitcher and washbasin, then the bedrooms of the pupils themselves, all perfectly preserved with simple cot bed, washstand, chest of drawers, and writing desk. Above the door is the name of each of the original pupils, and you will see Russian visitors making a beeline for number 14, Pushkin's room.

Yekaterinskiy Dvorets▶▶▶ (Sadovaya Ulitsa 7. *Open* Wed–Mon 10–5; closed last Mon of the month). The **Catherine Palace** is named after Peter the Great's wife, who built a small country house here in 1718. However, it was the combined ambition of Empress Elizabeth and her architect Rastrelli which led to the magnificent ensemble one sees today. The central feature is the stupendous baroque façade, more than 3,000 feet long, decorated with even lines of columns, pilasters, and ornamented window frames and surmounted by a cluster of gleaming golden cupolas. By the time of Catherine the Great, tastes had changed and she ordered the redesign of the interior rooms in the more fashionable neoclassical style. Her architects were the Scotsman Charles Cameron and the Italian Giacomo Quarenghi. Thereafter, it became Catherine's informal summer residence.

To date, 22 of the original rooms have been restored, and the decoration is magnificent throughout. The tour begins in the **southern wing**. Visitors pass through the **Cavaliers' Dining Room** to the sumptuous gilded Great Hall. Designed by Rastrelli, it covers 9,250 square feet and is the largest room in the palace. The huge ceiling fresco, *The Triumph of Russia*, is by G. Valeriani. At this point visitors return via the main staircase, which dates from 1860, to the **north wing** of the palace. The dazzling **Amber Room** was designed by Rastrelli in the 1750s. The original paneling, by the German A. Schlüter, was presented to Peter the Great by the King of Prussia in 1716. With great brilliance Rastrelli incorporated it into his own design, adding decoration in the form of gilded wood carvings, mirrors, and mosaics cut from agate and jasper. The walls of the **Picture Hall** are covered with more than 130 paintings, most of them originals. Exquisite stucco bas-reliefs adorn the **Green Dining Room**, and silks with Chinese motifs give the beautiful **Chinese Blue Drawing Room** its name.

Adjacent to the palace are the **baths** (*thermae*), exquisitely decorated with immeasurable quantities of agate and jasper. The **park**, with its Palladian-style bridge, artificial ruins, and Quarenghi's island concert hall, is delightful.

ST. PETERSBURG: EXCURSIONS

▶▶▶ Pavlovsk

Restoration of Pavlovsk
By the end of World War II, 62 of Leningrad's historic buildings had been damaged or destroyed. The Soviet authorities were faced with the enormous task of reconstruction, a task that called for the invention of many new techniques. Pavlovsk was to become the guinea pig for these new techniques and the experience gained there was to be applied to the subsequent restoration of many of St. Petersburg's other historic monuments.

It was a monumental achievement. During the 25 years it took to restore the palace to its former glory, it was often said that it would have been easier simply to rebuild from scratch. Thankfully, Pavlovsk had been well-documented during its original construction, which was to prove of invaluable help in its restoration.

Landscape gardener Pietro Gonzaga "arranged his trees as a painter arranges his colors on the canvas."
—A. Lunacharsky

Pavlovsk (*Open* Mon–Thu and weekends 10–5) was a gift from Catherine the Great to her son Paul (later Paul I). The palace, designed by the Scottish architect Charles Cameron in 1782, was completed four years later but was heavily altered by V. Brenna in 1797–1799. Pavlovsk was a great favorite with Paul's German-born wife, Maria Fyodorovna, who lived there until her death in 1828.

With the arrival of Russia's first railroad, the town became a resort for the seriously rich, who were joined in the summer by as many as 100,000 day-trippers from St. Petersburg. The original station was just to the northeast of the **Iron Gate**. This was also the site of the *Kurzal* or Vauxhall where bands played and where concerts were held. (Dostoevsky set a number of the scenes in his novel *The Idiot* in the *Kurzal*.) The concerts were sponsored by the Tsarskoe Selo railway company, whose managers persuaded the waltz king himself, Johann Strauss the Younger, to perform here with his orchestra in 1856 and for the next ten seasons. (Strauss even composed a "Pavlovsk Forest Polka.")

Pavlovsk was occupied by the Germans from 1941 to 1944, when it was almost totally destroyed. Restoration work began immediately and is still not complete.

There is a bus service from the station to the palace, but it is much more rewarding to walk through the park. The entrance is directly opposite the station (tickets are sold at the kiosk). Entry to the palace is separate.

Unfolding along the banks of the **Slavyanka River** is a vista of landscaped valleys and hillocks, threaded with rivers, ponds, and lakes, and interspersed with avenues of linden trees. In the vicinity of the palace itself (glimpsed periodically through the trees) the grounds are studded with grottos, pavilions and other flights of fancy, including an aviary, the **Temple of Friendship** (the first Doric-order building in Russia), and a dairy—a pastoral touch inspired by Maria Fyodorovna's meeting with Marie Antoinette at Versailles where there was also a "farm."

The neoclassical façade of the palace at Pavlovsk

Premature burial
One of the composer Shostakovich's favorite anecdotes relating to his experience of the terrible Siege of Leningrad concerns a bizarre funeral procession he saw in the streets. Just as the coffin was being loaded onto an open truck, with the musicians playing the Funeral March, "all of a sudden the corpse gets up from his coffin, and all the relatives and friends fell into a faint. Can you imagine, it wasn't a corpse they were going to bury, but somebody who was in a state of lethargic sleep. Only the musicians kept their wits about them ... and started playing the Internationale."

The most striking feature of the palace is the semicircular **colonnade**, the work of Vincenzio Brenna, who took over from Cameron in 1786. Visitors often note the similarity between Pavlovsk and Thomas Jefferson's buildings, Monticello and the University of Virginia. The likeness is no accident: Jefferson and Cameron used the same model, the Villa Tressino in Italy. Many other distinguished architects later worked on the palace, including Quarenghi, Voronikhin, and Carlo Rossi.

The outstanding rooms are on the second floor. Beneath the palace's central cupola is the **Italian Hall**, conceived as a Roman temple in the manner of the Pantheon. Tsar Paul's **Hall of War** and Maria Alexandrovna's **Hall of Peace** are linked by the magnificent **Grecian Hall**, the white walls and fireplaces fronted by massive green columns of *faux* marble. The **library**, designed by Voronikhin, has a parquet floor inlaid with 12 different kinds of wood. In the **Empress's Dressing Room** are two toilet sets, one of Sèvres porcelain presented to her by her friend Marie Antoinette, the other of gilded steel with bronze and silver inlay by the Tula craftsman S. Samarin.

The southern wing of the palace, designed by Brenna, is on an altogether grander scale. Most imposing are the **Picture Gallery** and the **Throne Room**.

The private apartments on the ground floor are on a more human scale. The highlights are Rossi's **Corner Drawing Room** with its lilac walls of *faux* marble, gold hangings, and elegant fireplace, and two rooms with interiors by Cameron—the austere **White Dining Room** and the more cheerful **Ballroom**.

Nineteenth-century glass tripod from the palace at Pavlovsk

Vases, statues, and gilded stucco adorn Rastrelli's magnificent ceremonial staircase at Petrodvorets

Birth of a city
"The haughty Swede here we'll curb and hold at bay. And here, to gall him, found a city."—Words attributed to Peter the Great by A. Pushkin in *The Bronze Horseman*

Construction addict
"Building is a devilish business. It eats money and the more one builds, the more one wants to build. It's a sickness like alcoholism and also a kind of habit."
—Catherine the Great

▶▶▶ Peterhof (Petrodvorets) 234

Tickets for entry to the Upper Garden and the Lower Park are sold in kiosks in the grounds. Separate tickets for access to the state rooms and apartments of the **Great Palace** (*Open* Tue–Sun 11–6) are sold inside the rear entrance. Entry to Monplaisir and other attractions is by additional ticket.

It was while Peter the Great was overseeing the construction of the naval base at **Kronstadt** (clearly visible from the jetty) that he decided to build a palace overlooking the Baltic. His ambition was to create another Versailles, which he had visited on his grand European tour in 1717. But only the fountains and the charming **Monplaisir Palace** were finished in his own lifetime; the **Great Palace** and the grounds were eventually completed by Catherine the Great. In the process Le Blond's original plans and designs were discarded by his successor, Rastrelli, who added a third story as well as the two magnificent wings with golden pavilions. Much later, the interiors too were remodeled by the German Yegor Velten and the Frenchman Vallin de la Mothe.

Every summer, musicians are drafted into the out-of-town palaces to drum up revenue for restoration

Visitors enter via Rastrelli's **ceremonial staircase** and pass through the **Blue Reception Room** with its remarkable oak parquet floor and damask curtains to the **Chesma Room**, decorated with canvases by German artist F. Gakkert glorifying the defeat of the Turkish fleet at Chesma Bay in June 1770. The **Throne Room** and the **Audience Hall** which follow are distinguished by red velvet hangings over rounded windows with stuccoed white moldings. Displayed in the **White Dining Room** (designed by Velten in 1774–1775) is the 196-piece dinner service made in Staffordshire, England, for Catherine the Great. Two Chinese studies, in breathtaking red, green, and gold lacquer, frame the **Picture Hall**. The 365 paintings, one for each day of the year, are of ladies of the court. Of the rooms comprising the **Imperial Suite**, the most outstanding is the **study**, designed by Le Blond for Peter the Great.

Leading down the hill from the palace to the sea is the terrace containing Peterhof's signature, the **Grand Cascade**. Among the statuary, the central figure of Samson represents Russia's victory over the Swedes. The **Neptune Fountain** in the **Upper Garden** dates from the 1650s and was made to celebrate the end of the Thirty Years War. The **Triton Fountain** in the **Lower Park** honors a naval victory over Sweden. Also noteworthy is the **Chessboard Cascade** with its dragons and checkered chutes.

The Lower Park leads to a series of smaller palaces and pavilions, the most pleasing of which is Peter's own **Monplaisir** (*Open* May–Oct, Thu–Tue 11–6) with its magnificent view of the Gulf of Finland from the **Naval Study**. The main feature of the decoration is the tsar's personal collection of paintings, revealing a predictable taste for seascapes. In **Peter's Bedroom** are his dressing gown and nightcap. Monplaisir is said to be the place where he interrogated his son Alexei before sentencing him to death.

Next to Monplaisir is the **Catherine Wing** (*Open* Wed–Mon 11–6) built in the 1740s. Several rooms are open to the public, and among Catherine's personal effects are a walking stick and ceremonial uniform.

241

View of the Great Palace at Petrodvorets from the Upper Garden

ST. PETERSBURG: EXCURSIONS

▶▶ **Oranienbaum (Lomonosov)**   *234*

Peter the Great's leading minister, Prince Alexander Menshikov, having already built himself a more imperial residence in St. Petersburg than that of the tsar, repeated the performance at Oranienbaum, where the palace was more stately than Peter's imposing residence at Peterhof. But soon after Peter's death the corrupt and venal prince was disgraced and banished to Siberia, where he died penniless. Oranienbaum (named from the orange trees that were planted in the Lower Park—an ostentatious luxury in St. Petersburg's northern European climate) was presented by Tsarina Elizabeth to her nephew (later Peter III) and his German-born wife Catherine (later "the Great"). Their loveless marriage was played out here, where Peter indulged his obsession with things military (his hero was the Prussian King, Frederick the Great). For the members of his court, life was hell. Peter compelled everyone on the estate—courtiers, officials, gentlemen-in-waiting, chamberlains, even the gardeners—to drill daily in the palace grounds. Not content with this extravagance, Peter acquired hoards of lead soldiers which he "exercised" on enormous tables specially constructed for the purpose. Court ritual, as Catherine later recounted with gusto, was so intolerably dull that few guests would come voluntarily. To add to their misery, Peter considered himself a musician and gave regular concerts on the violin. Catherine recalled: "He did not know a single note but he had a good ear, and for him the beauty of the music lay in the force and violence with which he played it." When Tsarina Elizabeth died in 1761, Catherine staged a *coup* with the help of her lover, Prince Orlov, and the weak and ineffectual Peter, for all his military posturing, was swiftly deposed.

Except for the park, Oranienbaum is closed Oct–Apr. Visitors enter via the **Lower Park** and are immediately confronted with the main façade of Menshikov's Great Palace, designed by Fontana. Built above a complex of terraces, it consists of a **central pavilion**, topped by a tiny

Sole survivor
Oranienbaum was the only imperial palace in the vicinity of St. Petersburg to escape German occupation during World War II. It did, however, endure heavy bombardment and looting during the Siege of Leningrad, and was vandalized and looted by the Nazis before their retreat from Russia.

Domed pavilion and lower lake at Oranienbaum Palace

Precious Meissen porcelain on show in Peter III's palace at Oranienbaum

cupola and golden crown and set off by two handsome wings ending in two additional domed pavilions.

The palace has been closed to the public for some time, but sections are reopening after restoration. Visitors may, however, visit the delightful **Palace of Peter III** (*Open* Wed–Mon 11–5; closed last Mon of the month). A simple two-story building comprising 12 rooms in all (six for the servants, six for the tsar and his guests), only the **upper story** is open to the public. The architect was Antonio Rinaldi, who arrived at Oranienbaum in 1756 and remained for more than ten years. The highlight of the interior is the lacquerwork paneling of the **Picture Gallery**, the only example of its kind by Russians to have survived the war.

Equally rewarding is a tour of the **Upper Park**, with its elaborate bridges, ponds, and subtle blend of trees—silver birch, lindens, and oaks. At the lower end is Catherine the Great's **Chinese Palace** (*Open* Wed–Mon 11–5; closed last Mon of the month), also by Rinaldi. For "Chinese" read "exotic"—there is not a hint of *chinoiserie* in the exterior decoration and little enough indoors, apart from the Oriental wallpaper and vases in the large and small **Chinese Rooms**. The overall style is a curious blend of baroque and rococo. Despite its extravagant attractions, the empress spent only 48 days here in her entire 34-year reign.

Catherine also commissioned the extraordinary so-called **Skating Pavilion** (also by Rinaldi), a blue-and-white confection of palatial proportions comprising tiers of columns and balustrades. This was in effect a grandstand for the local sport known as "Russian Mountains" in which sleighs would race down artificial slopes running the entire length of the park.

Lost treasures
After almost 50 years of intrigue and rumor, the Russians finally admitted in 1994 that, tucked away in Moscow's Pushkin Museum, they hold the legendary Schliemann treasure discovered at the site of ancient Troy in 1873. Until 1945 this hoard of golden headdresses, rings, goblets, and necklaces had been the prize exhibit in Berlin's Museum of Pre- and Early History, but it disappeared after the occupation of Berlin by Russian troops in 1945. Russia's belated admission to the treasure's true location has broken the ice in the delicate negotiations over the thousands of artworks looted by both sides during the war. It has been suggested that the "dream swap" would be the Schliemann treasure for the Amber Panels, looted from the Catherine Palace at Tsarskoe Selo.

Shopping

Hopeful artist waiting for customers outside the art market in Moscow's Izmailovskiy Park

Shopping hours in Russia are extremely variable, not to say erratic. Most stores open six days a week, and many food stores are also open on Sundays. There is usually an afternoon break, any time between 1 and 3 PM. However, most Western stores and the larger Russian department stores (GUM, for example) work through the lunch break.

To choose what you want in a Russian shop, ask the assistant to write down the price, then line up at a cash desk (*kassa*) to pay. Finally return to the counter with your receipt and collect your purchase.

Markets Both cities have a large number of colorful markets (29 in Moscow alone), mostly selling fish, fruit, vegetables, and dairy products. Much of the more exotic produce comes from the Caucasus or Central Asia, and for this reason is beyond the average Russian budget.

MOSCOW STORES

Antiques Antikvariat, Bolshaya Yakimanka Ulitsa 56; **Fotina Auction House**, Ulitsa Arbat 6/2; **Kupina**, Ulitsa Arbat 18.

Art Galleries Arbatskaya Sloboda, Arbat Ulitsa 6; **1–0 Gallery**, Ulitsa Bolshaya Yakimanka 6; **Moscow Gallery**, Kuznetskiy Most Ulitsa 11; **Tsentralniy Dom Khudozhnika (Central House of Artists)**, Krymskiy Val Ulitsa 10.

Books and Records Biblio Globus, Myasnitskaya Ulitsa 6; **CD World**, Myasnitskaya Ulitsa 30; **Dom Knigi**, Ulitsa Noviy Arbat 8 (large selection of Russian books); **Disk**, Leninskiy Prospekt 11 (Russian and foreign music); **Melodiya**, Ulitsa Noviy Arbat 22 (large, old-fashioned record store); **Transylvania 6–5000**, Tverskaya Ulitsa 25;

The market traditions of Red Square go back more than five centuries. You can pick up cheap calendars and postcards at bookstalls like this one outside St. Basil's

Youth jamboree
The summer of 1997 saw 4,000 Girl Scouts and Boy Scouts from around the world descend on Moscow for the first international jamboree to be held there since the Revolution. Following a visit by Robert Baden-Powell to St. Petersburg in 1908, Russia became the first country outside the U.K. to form a scouting movement. The organization flourished until 1925, when it was replaced by a new, ideo-logically based movement, the Pioneers. Since the collapse of the Soviet Union, membership of the Pioneers has declined drastically while the Russian scouting movement has prospered. The Moscow organization alone now has more than 4,000 members.

Zwemmer Bookstore, Kuznetskiy Most 18 (English-language books).

Children Detskiy Mir, Teatralniy Proezd 5 (various toy outlets).

Children's clothing Benetton, Ulitsa Arbat 13, also GUM; **Boys and Girls**, Sadko Arcade; **Grant Clothing Store**, Petrovskiy Passage; **Mothercare**, Noviy Arbat Ulitsa 11.

Department Store TsUM, Petrovka Ulitsa 2.

Fashion Carlo Pazolini, Novinskiy Bulvar 1/2 (Italian fash-ion for men and women); **Kuznetskiy Most**, Kuznetskiy Most Ulitsa 10 (women's fashion); **Salamander**, Leninskiy Prospekt 37a (European footwear and acces-sories); **Slava Zaytsev Showroom**, Prospekt Mira 21 (Russian *haute couture*); **Tretex Salon**, Ulitsa Pokrovka 22 (casual clothes and Italian leather jackets); see also **Shopping Malls** (below).

Food Arbat Irish House, Ulitsa Noviy Arbat 13; **Exposhop Supermarket**, Krasnopresnenskaya Naberezhnaya 14; **Stockmann Grocery Store**, Zatsepskiy Val 4/8; **Garden Ring Supermarket**, Bolshaya Sadovaya Ulitsa 1, Leninskiy Prospekt 146, and Ulitsa Serafimovicha 2; **Olympic-Gulliver Supermarket**, Krasnaya Presnya Ulitsa 23.

Delicatessens Amarkt, Malaya Bronnya Ulitsa 27/14; **Vienna Trade House**, Prospekt Mira 1/91.

Markets Tsentralniy, Tsvetnoy Bulvar 15 (flowers, etc.); **Izmaylovskiy Park** (street market, weekends); **Rizhskiy**,

Books
The first Moscow Book Fair, held in 1979, was attended by publishers from 37 countries including the USA, Europe, Israel, Saudi Arabia, and China. Perhaps this inspired British author John Le Carré to center his popular spy novel *The Russia House* on a Russian book fair. The novel was later made into a film starring Sean Connery and Michelle Pfeiffer and was one of the first big budget Western films to be shot on location in Russia.

"Guards" liquor flasks for sale. Soviet insignia are still popular with tourists

Prospekt Mira 94–6 (farmers' market). There is a good kiosk-market outside **Kiev Station** and a huge flea market at **Luzhniki.**

Shopping Malls GUM, Krasnaya Ploshchad 3 (outlets include Benetton, Braun, Christian Dior, Estée Lauder, Polaroid Studio Express); **Petrovskiy Passage,** Petrovka Ulitsa 10 (L'Oriel, Kodak Express, Sony); **St. George Street,** Radisson-Slavyanskaya Hotel, Berezhovskaya Naberezhnaya 2 (Trussardi Fashion, Gzhel Porcelain Salon, Paco Rabanne, Cartier watches); **Sadko Arcade** (Expocenter), Krasnogvardeyskiy Proezd 1 (Foodland, Pizza Pazza, Top Sport).

Souvenirs In the first instance, see the stores in the shopping malls (listed above). Also worth a look are the street traders concentrated in the Arbat every day and at Izmailovskiy Park on weekends. **Arbatskayaharka,** Ulitsa Arbat 27 (wooden toys); **Boutique,** Rozhdestvenka Ulitsa 3; **Rostov Finift,** Ulitsa Vozdvizhenka 5 (enamel manufactured in Rostov); **Russian Art,** Berezhkovskaya Naberezhnaya 2 (glassware); **Russkiy Suvenir,** Kutuzovskiy Prospekt 9; **Russkie Uzori,** Petrovka Ulitsa 16; **Yantar,** Gruzinskiy Val Ulitsa 14.

ST. PETERSBURG STORES

Antiques Ariadna, Konnogvardeyskiy Bulvar 11 (paintings and antiques).

Art Galleries Blue Drawing Room (Golubaya Gostinaya), Bolshaya Morskaya Ulitsa 38 (Exhibition Center of the Painters' Union of St. Petersburg); **Borey,** Liteyniy Prospekt 58; **Garmonia-Adam,** Kamennoostrovskiy Prospekt 26/8; **Guild of Masters,** Nevskiy Prospekt 82 (oils, graphics, batik, and jewelry); **Iskusstvo,** Nevskiy Prospekt 16; **Palitra Art Gallery,** Nevskiy Prospekt 166 (near Ploshchad Aleksandra-Nevskovo metro station—a new gallery exhibiting work of established and new artists; **Petropol,** Millionnaya Ulitsa 27; **Salon-Shop of Fine Art,** Nevskiy Prospekt 31; **Staraya Derevnya,** Savushkina Ulitsa 72.

Books and Records Bukinist, Liteyniy Prospekt 59 (antiquarian and secondhand books); **Dom Knigi,** Nevskiy Prospekt 28 (largest bookstore in St. Petersburg); **Iskusstvo,** Nevskiy Prospekt 52 (art books); **Severnaya Lira,** Nevskiy Prospekt 26 (sheet music, instruments, and CDs); **Writers' Bookstore,** Nevskiy Prospekt 66.

Children DLT Bolshaya Konyushennaya Ulitsa 21/23 (toys and clothing).

Department Stores House of Petersburg Trade, Bolshaya Konyashennaya Ulitsa 21–3; **Moskovskiy Univermag,** Moskovskiy Prospekt 205 and 220; **Velena,** Nevskiy Prospect 19.

Fashion Alivekt, Nevskiy Prospekt 24 (clothes); **Lolita,** Nevskiy Prospekt 11 (women's clothing); **Nevskiy,**

Surplus to requirements In 1994, President Boris Yeltsin opened an élite military academy, harking back to imperial traditions, in a desperate attempt to placate the hundreds of thousands of Russian servicemen recently made virtually redundant by the troop withdrawals from Eastern Europe. The cadets will be housed comfortably in specially constructed barracks in Kaluga, south of Moscow, but their eventual role in Russia's now overstaffed army is yet to be made clear.

Nevskiy Prospekt 11 (shoes); **Nevsky Prospekt Fashion House**, Nevskiy Prospekt 21 (Russian fashion house); **Real-Myuzik Clothes Store**, Nevskiy Prospekt 54; see also **Shopping Malls** (below).

Food Kalinka Stockmann Supermarket, Finlandskiy Prospekt 1 (wide selection of food and nonfood products just behind St. Petersburg Hotel); **Produkty**, Nevskiy Prospekt 11.

Delicatessens Yeliseevskiy, Nevskiy Prospekt 56 (famous prerevolutionary food store).

Jewelry Biryuza, Nevskiy Prospekt 69; **Polyarnaya Zvezda**, Nevskiy Prospekt 158; **Samotsvety**, Mikhaylovskaya Ulitsa 4; **Yahont**, Bolshaya Morskaya 24 (in former Fabergé premises).

Markets Kuznechniy Rynok, Kuznechniy Pereulok 3 (the best farmers' market in St. Petersburg); **Ptichiy** (Kondratevskiy) Rynok, Polyustrovskiy Prospekt 45 (known as the bird market, sells pets and clothes); **Veschoviy Rynok**, Sadovaya Ulitsa (behind Apraksin Dvor—flea market).

Shopping Malls Apraksin Dvor, Sadovaya Ulitsa; **Gostiniy Dvor**, Nevskiy Prospekt 35; **Passazh**, Nevskiy Prospekt 48. There is a good kiosk-market outside Sennaya Ploshchad metro station.

Souvenirs In the first instance, see **Shopping Malls**, listed above. **Hermitage**, Nevskiy Prospekt 116 (paintings, tapestry, embroidery, jewelry, Palekh boxes, samovars, china, silver, and ceramics, near Ploshchad Vosstaniya metro station); **Image**, Nevskiy Prospekt 92; **Khudozhestvennye Promysly**, Nevskiy Prospekt 51; **Podarki**, Nevskiy Prospekt 54, or Bolshoy Prospekt 51 (Petrograd Side); **Steklo, Farfor, Khrustal**, Nevskiy Prospekt 64 (glass, china, crystal); **Suveniry**, Nevskiy Prospekt 18; **Vanda**, Nevskiy Prospekt 111.

Sales talk
The jargon of Western salesmanship is creeping into Russia at every corner. Witness the following advertisement from a Russian magazine: "You've decided to sell your apartment? You're doing this for the first time and don't know where to begin? In that case, come to the experts of our organization. Don't turn to people you don't know. Today this is dangerous."

Western fashions have infiltrated even Russia's smaller towns (this is Oranienbaum)

Godzilla comes to town (in this case, Moscow). Dinosaur mania knows no frontiers

Strippers

Young Russian men and women, desperate to chase a lavish lifestyle in the West, are turning up in droves to audition for Moscow's striptease school. Once the students qualify, they are exported to predictably low-life bars and clubs, mainly in Germany, Italy, and Turkey. Needless to say, few will ever fulfill their expectations, but current conditions will drive some Russians to any extreme.

Meanwhile, at Moscow's exclusive strip club Dolls, professional strippers from the United States are earning up to $2,000 a night for entertaining the capital's flashy new class of young businessmen.

Under Communism, nightlife in Russia used to end at about 10:30 when the theaters closed. Nowadays, you can have a late dinner after a visit to the Bolshoy or Mariinsky, as many restaurants stay open into the early hours, and, while the metro closes down at 1 AM, taxis are available around the clock. Dining out in the company of locals is among the more pleasurable experiences of visiting Russia, and one which many foreigners miss out on, preferring the familiar hotel restaurant. A night out at the theater invariably brings home to foreigners the importance Russians attach to high culture. Drinking into the early hours can only really be done in the restaurants or hotels—Russia still lacks a bar or café culture, although there are signs that this is beginning to change. Nightclubs abound in Moscow and St. Petersburg, but a word of warning is needed here. Clubs with exotic names like Manhattan Express and Night Flight draw a shady clientele, including Mafia bosses and their entourages with dollars to throw away. Prices are set accordingly and, where the Mafia is, prostitutes will never be far behind. As in the West, nightclubs have variable entrance charges, with concessions if you turn up early. Usual dress rules apply, but security is tight and you may need to present your passport or some other form of identity. Nightclubs in hotels often have floor shows, and every major hotel has one or two late-night bars so you can usually get a drink until about 4 AM.

MOSCOW ENTERTAINMENT AND NIGHTLIFE

Concert Halls Moscow Conservatory, Bolshaya Nikitskaya Ulitsa 13, tel: 229 36 87; **Rossiya Concert Hall**, Moskvoretskaya Naberezhnaya 1, tel: 298 55 50; **Tchaikovsky Concert Hall**, Triumfalnaya Ploshchad 4 /31, tel: 299 03 78. Look for concerts in Moscow's churches.

Theater and Ballet Bolshoy Theater, Teatralnaya Ploshchad 1, tel: 292 33 19; **Moscow Circus** (old):

Tsvetnoy Bulvar 13, tel: 200 68 89; (new): Prospekt Vernadskovo 7, tel: 930 28 15; **Palace of Congresses**, The Kremlin 917 23 36; **Pushkin Drama Theater**, Tverskoy Bulvar 23, tel: 203 85 82 (often features modern dance); **Obraztsov Puppet Theater**, Sadovaya-Samotyochnaya Ulitsa 3, tel: 299 23 10.

Tickets for both ballet and theater performances can be obtained from the service bureaus of hotels or alternatively from **IPS Theater Box Office**, Hotel Metropol, Teatralniy Proezd 1/4, tel: 927 69 82. Kiosks at the main metro stations also sell tickets, if you succeed in making yourself understood in Russian.

Movie theaters Americom House of Cinema, Radisson Slavyanskaya Hotel, Berezhkovskaya Naberezhnaya 2, tel: 941 88 90; **Illuzion Cinema**, Kotelnicheskaya Naberezhnaya 1/15, tel: 227 43 53; **Kinocentre**, Druzhinnikovskaya Ulitsa 15, tel: 205 73 06.

Foreign movies are occasionally screened. See listings in *The Moscow Times*.

Exhibitions Central Exhibition Hall (Manezh), Manezhnaya Ploshchad, tel: 202 93 04 (*Closed* Tue); **Central House of Artists**, Krymskiy Val Ulitsa 10, tel: 238 98 43; **Phoenix Cultural Centre**, Kutuzovskiy Prospekt 3, tel: 243 49 58.

Casinos Casino Royale, Ulitsa Begovaya 22, tel: 945 19 63 (nightclub, jazz bar, restaurant); **Karusel**, Ulitsa 1-ya Tverskaya-Yamskaya 11, tel: 251 64 44; **Metelitsa**, Cherry Casino, Ulitsa Noviy Arbat 21, tel: 291 11 70 (roulette, blackjack, poker, Oasis stud poker, baccarat); **Metropol**, Teatralniy Proezd 1/4, tel: 927 60 67.

Buffet
Russians introduced the idea of buffets—a selection of snacks to be enjoyed before the sit-down meal. It lives on in the Russian predilection for *zakuski* (hors d'oeuvres). At times the enjoyment of the *zakuski* can be so protracted that the main meal is delayed for hours!

Nightclubs Arbat Blues Club, Aksakov Pereulok 11, tel: 291 15 46 (jazz club); **Arlecchino**, Ulitsa Druzhinnikovskaya 15, Kinocenter, tel: 265 97 59; **B. B. King**, Ulitsa Sadovaya-Samotyochnaya 4/2, tel: 299 82 06; **Hermitage Club**, Karetniy Ryad 3, tel: 299 11 60 (all-night disco, Fri–Sun); **Karo-Utopia**, Pushkinskaya Ploshchad 2, tel: 229 00 03; **Manhattan Express**, Rossiya Hotel, tel: 298 53 54 (*Open* seven days a week for dinner and dancing); **Moscow Hill Nightclub**, Trubnaya Ploshchad 4, tel: 208 33 41; **Night**

Nightclubs cater exclusively to Russia's new jet set

Flight, Tverskaya Ulitsa 17, tel: 299 41 65 (disco: men over 30, women over 21, doormen sometimes insist on passports); Nostalgic Art Café, Chistoprudniy Bulvar 12, tel: 916 94 78; Pilot, Tryokhgorniy Val 6, tel: 252 27 64 (all-night disco Thu–Sat from 11 PM); Russkaya Troyka, Orlyonok Hotel, Ulitsa Kosygina 15, tel: 939 86 86; Up & Down, Zubovskiy Bulvar 4, tel: 201 50 70; Zhar-Ptitsa, Kudrinskaya Ploshchad 1, tel: 255 42 28; Zolushka, Ulitsa Novosushchovskaya 26, tel: 972 14 50.

Bars Artists Bar and Chaliapin Bar, Hotel Metropol, Teatralniy Proezd 1/4, tel: 927 60 65/4; Hermitage Bar, Savoy Hotel, tel: 929 85 77; Jacko's Piano Bar, Leningradskaya Hotel, Kalanchovskaya Ulitsa 21/40, tel: 975 19 67; Moose Head Canadian Bar, Bolshaya Polyanka Ulitsa 54, tel: 230 73 33; News Pub, Ulitsa Petrovka 18, tel: 230 73 33; Remy Martin Piano Bar, Sadko Arcade, Expo Center, tel: 940 40 65 (and other bars in the Expo Center); Rosie O'Grady's, Zamenka Ulitsa 9/12, tel: 203 90 87; Shamrock Bar, Arbat Irish House, Ulitsa Noviy Arbat 13, tel: 291 76 41.

ST. PETERSBURG ENTERTAINMENT AND NIGHTLIFE

Concert Halls Bolshoy Zal Filarmonii, Bolshoy Philharmonic Hall, Mikhaylovskaya Ulitsa 2, tel: 110 42 78 (booking office tel: 311 73 33); Glinka Kapella (former Imperial Chapel Choir), Reki Moyki Naberezhnaya 20, tel: 314 11 53; Maliy Zal, Glinka Chamber Hall, Nevskiy Prospekt 30, tel: 312 83 33.

Theater and Ballet Aleksandrinskiy (Pushkin) Theater, Ploshchad Ostrovskovo 2, tel: 312 15 45; Bolshoy Drama Theater, Nabevezhnaya veki Fontanki 65, tel: 310 04 01; Maliy Drama Theater, Ulitsa Rubinshteyna 18, tel: 113 20 78; Maliy Opera and Ballet Theater, Ploshchad Iskusstv 1, tel: 219 19 88; Mariinskiy (Kirov) Theater of Opera and Ballet, Teatralnaya Ploshchad 1/2, tel: 114 44 41; Music Hall, Park Lenina 4, tel: 232 94 66; St. Petersburg State Ice Ballet, Dvortsovaya Naberezhnaya 120/2, tel: 315 20 75.

Tickets for both theater and ballet performances can be obtained from the service bureaus of hotels (expensive) and also from Central Box Office No. 1, Nevskiy Prospekt 42, tel: 311 31 83.

Movie theaters
Avrora, Nevskiy Prospekt 60, tel: 315 52 54; Barrikada, Nevskit Prospekt 15, tel: 315 40 28; Khudozhestvenniy, Nevskiy Prospekt 67, tel: 314 00 53; Kolizei, Nevskiy Prospekt 100, tel: 272 87 75; Kosmonavt, Bronnitskaya Ulitsa 24, tel: 316 20 40; Spartak, Ulitsa Saltykova-Shchedrina 8, tel: 272 78 97.

For details of programs, see listings in *St. Petersburg Press*.

Exhibitions Smolniy Cathedral, Ploshchad Rostrelli 3, tel: 311 36 90; St. Petersburg Art Union of Russia, Union of Artists, Bolshaya Morskaya Ulitsa 38, tel: 314 30 60.

Jazz has been popular in Russia at least since the 1920s, when even classical composers like Shostakovich used it as a source of inspiration

250

A productive market?
Discussions about the nature and effectiveness of the Russian economic market are virtually endless in Russia's media today, but few meaningful conclusions are drawn and the arguments usually go around in circles. Virtually every politician and economist has his own notion of the market and applies it accordingly. Moscow mayor Yuri Luzhkov, for example, while having a reputation in the West as a progressive, is criticized at home for running the economy of the city like a tsar.

Casinos Casino Admiral, Hotel Astoria, Malaya Morskaya Ulitsa 20, tel: 210 59 06; **Casino Hotel Pribaltiyskaya**, Korablestroiteley Ulitsa 14, tel: 356 41 53; **Premier**, Nevskiy Prospekt 47 (Titan Cinema), tel: 315 78 93; **St. Petersburg Palace Casino**, Aleksandrovskiy Park 4, tel: 233 05 42 (bar with free coffee and soft drinks).

Nightclubs Jazz Philharmonic Hall, Zagorodniy Prospekt 27, tel: 164 85 65; **Kradrat Jazz Club**, Pravdy Ulitsa 10, no telephone; **Money Honey**, Apraksin Dvor 14, tel: 310 01 47; **Olbi Jazz Club**, Shpalernaya Ulitsa 33, tel: 272 98 50; **Pereval**, Bolshaya Monetaya Ulitsa 31/3, no telephone; **Planetarium (Star Dust Night Discothèque)**, Alexandrovskiy Park 4, tel: 233 49 56 (restaurant, stage show, disco Russian-style); **Pub Corsar**, Bolshaya Morskaya Ulitsa 14, tel: 219 41 82; **Rotterdam Club**, Prospekt Veteranov 69, no telephone; **Tam Tam Club**, Maliy Prospekt 49/16 Line (Vasilevskiy Island), no telephone (rock and punk, basic. *Open* Wed and weekends); **Tunnel**, Lyubyanskiy Pereulok (between Blokhina Ulitsa and Zverinskaya Ulitsa), tel: 238 80 75 (techno music in an old bomb shelter. *Open* Thu and Sat); **Wild Side**, Bumazhnovo Kanala Naberezhnaya 12, tel: 186 34 66.

Bars Angleterre, Hotel Astoria, Bolshaya Morskaya Ulitsa 39 (*Open* to 1 AM, tel: 210 50 09); **Astoria Night Bar**, live music and dancing (*Open* to 5 AM); **Bier Stube**, Nevskiy Prospekt 57, Nevskiy Palace Hotel, tel: 275 20 01; **Chayka**, Griboedova Kanala Naberezhnaya 14, tel: 312 46 31 (Western-style bar); **Dr. Oetker**, Nevskiy Prospekt 40, tel: 311 90 66 (bar-restaurant. *Open* till midnight); **Grand Hotel Europe**, Mikhaylovskaya Ulitsa 1/7, tel: 119 60 00; **John Bull English Pub**, Nevskiy Prospekt 79, tel: 164 98 77; **Mollie's Irish Bar**, Rubinshteyna Ulitsa 36, tel: 319 97 68; **Rose Pub**, Liteyniy Prospekt 16, tel: 275 35 54; **Shamrock**, Ulitsa Dekabristov 27, tel: 219 46 25; **The Beer Garden**, Nevskiy Prospekt 86, tel: 275 76 20 (outdoor bar, live music); **Tribunal**, Angliyskaya Naterezhnaya (near Bronze Horseman), tel: 311 16 90; **Warsteiner Forum**, Nevskiy Prospekt 120 (near Ploshchad Vosstaniya), tel: 277 29 14.

All change
"Everything is changing: the times, the government, the rate of exchange. But the value of real estate never changes." This piece of Moscow metro advertising graphically reflects the rapid growth of a capitalist mentality in the new Russia.

It could be anywhere, but this one is in St. Petersburg—an open-air pop concert

The dining out revolution began here, in the elegant surroundings of Moscow's Kropotkinskaya 36 Restaurant

Bistro
The Russians are responsible for introducing the word "bistro" to international usage. In Russian it means "quickly." It is said that the term arose during the Russian occupation of Paris in 1815, when troops would shout "bistro" to waiters in restaurants.

See pages 280–283 for listings of hotels and restaurants.

EATING OUT

The advent of private restaurants in the late 1980s has changed the dining out scene in Moscow and St. Petersburg radically—Moscow, however, offers by far the greater choice. The old state-run restaurants, infamous for their inefficient service and mediocre quality, have now all but disappeared. Prices elsewhere tend to be broadly in line with those of Western Europe, and standards are by and large up to the mark. Western-style cafés and fast-food outlets (Russian and international) are on the increase in both cities, but are still largely confined to the central districts. The selection on pages 281–283 takes account of this.

While it is not strictly necessary to make an advance reservation, booking is advisable (use the travel reps at your hotel). Opening times vary, but many restaurants nowadays stay open very late, especially on weekends. English is usually found on menus, and an increasing proportion of staff are familiar with European languages.

ACCOMMODATIONS

No longer the nightmare it once was, choosing accommodations is now up to you and is not dictated by Intourist. The main criticism nowadays is the preponderance of very expensive hotels, like the Metropol, the National, and the Savoy in Moscow and the Grand Hotel Europe and Astoria in St. Petersburg. These cater unashamedly to the luxury end of the market, with deluxe and even presidential suites. Refurbishment has itself created a problem, namely the upgrading of more and more hotels, taking them beyond the confines of the average budget. What remains is the traditional Soviet-style tourist hotel (the Cosmos in Moscow and the Moskva in St. Petersburg, for example), much improved but overly large, inconveniently located, with widely varying services and facilities. Bear in mind that the old Intourist star ratings, now unreliable, are sometimes still used. These hotels are still expensive for what they offer, but you can at least expect the following: a money exchange and bank, a post office, book/souvenir shop, cafés, restaurants, and bars, one of which at least should be open around the clock. Most major hotels are equipped with business centers but not all offer a comprehensive service. For excursions, restaurant bookings, and other information, make use of the service bureaus. Most rooms have cable and satellite TV and their own shower/bath. Package tourists traveling with Intourist should expect this class of hotel. There are plenty of budget options in both cities but with serious drawbacks. Locations can be remote, standards of cleanliness, service, and security may all leave something to be desired, and rooms will not always include bathroom or shower; breakfast too will probably be an optional extra. However, there are some bargains to be found, especially in St. Petersburg—see pages 280–281.

To summarize, Russia still has a long way to go where tourist accommodations are concerned, but standards are improving all the time and, broadly speaking, value for money should be expected. Most staff in the larger establishments are now learning to speak English and other foreign languages, but training in customer relations does not always produce the desired results. Although some reception staff are still inclined to be surly, brusque, and uncommunicative (sometimes comically so), within the confines of the same hotel you are almost certain to find helpful and friendly individuals who will go out of their way to make your stay enjoyable.

Security Security in the larger hotels is more than adequate, but if you're worried you can always leave valuables in the hotel safe. Complaints should be made in the first instance to the *dezhurnaya* or floor manager, an official worth keeping on the right side of. She is the person to go to if the light or television isn't working, if you need water for tea, or if you're not happy with the cleaning. Leave your key with her whenever you leave the hotel.

Return flight
German amateur pilot Mathias Rust, imprisoned in Russia for landing a plane in Red Square and for invading Soviet airspace, is now back in Moscow working in a German-owned restaurant.

253

School inspection
Discipline in schools under Nicholas I was strict, and the tsar acted as his own inspector. On one visit, he was scandalized by the sight of a student sitting in rapt attention but with an elbow placed on his desk. The teacher was severely reprimanded and threatened with dismissal.

In recent years there has been a marked return to pre-revolutionary standards of comfort and service. The newly refurbished Hotel Baltschug Kempinski overlooks the Moskva River

With the Russian and Western sources of information now available, independent travel is at last becoming a reality

Grapevine
Reflecting the rush to acquire Western business skills and the privileged careers they're expected to give access to, Moscow's State Academy of Management currently has four applicants for every place; its reputation has spread purely by word of mouth, as it eschews advertising.

Visiting the former Soviet Union used to be something of an endurance test. Tourists, having been consigned to a catch-all hotel entirely populated by foreigners, would spend the whole duration of their vacation here being shepherded around by pressingly knowledgeable Intourist guides who unerringly knew the correct ideological line on any given subject. The tour destinations were chosen with a view to revealing the achievements of the Communist regime, so that, for example, a trip to the Exhibition of Economic Achievements in Moscow or to the Lenin Museum in St. Petersburg (then Leningrad) were *de rigueur.*

Optional extras included such thrilling outings as a trip to look around a school or collective farm—needless to say these were showcase institutions, the pupils being the sons and daughters of Soviet diplomats or ministers; the collective farm chairman, too, was invariably a fully paid-up Party member.

Confined to barracks in the evenings, tourists and any stray Soviet visitor who happened to drop in were carefully segregated, using the highly effective barrier of hard currency. Indeed, open fraternization between tourists and locals was frowned upon. On the flight home a cheer would go up when the pilot announced that the plane was leaving Soviet air space. The best one could say was that visiting the country had been an "experience."

Gorbachev's policy of *glasnost* in the 1980s proclaimed a new era in Soviet tourism whereby foreigners were welcomed rather than simply tolerated; however, only since Communism itself has been swept away has real and lasting change become possible. Having said that, it will clearly take decades for the old habits and attitudes to be thoroughly eradicated, and for visitors to regard the prospect of a journey to Moscow or St. Petersburg with the same degree of equanimity and even enthusiasm as a trip to Paris or Rome.

Using the hotels Intourist still enjoys a large share of the hotel business. Despite a recent overhaul, imperviousness to criticism seems to be endemic so that changes are introduced when the tourist agency sees fit, not when visitors would like them. Guides are invariably courteous and knowledgeable as far as the history and the institutions of the country go, but they are often amazingly behind the times and ill-informed—don't ask them for the address of a good nightclub, for example. Many visitors to Russia still seem to be under the misapprehension that they must comply with the Intourist itinerary. In order to make the most of a visit to Russia, it is absolutely essential to cut loose from these apron strings and to see the country without constraints. By all means take advantage of the highlights available—tickets to the Bolshoy, for example—as you won't easily be able to pick these up elsewhere. But you can get around Moscow and St. Petersburg quite comfortably by yourself, and if you are worried about the language or security you can always team up with other foreigners and explore the cities together. Make full use of the service desk at your hotel for booking a table at a restaurant, tickets to the theater, unusual excursions, train reservations, or general information. You may have to speak to more than one individual before you find the person with the relevant expertise, but persist and don't be discouraged by excuses—you have the right to these services, after all you have paid. If your hotel is not equipped to deal with your requests, try a larger or more central one. If the doorman stops you, simply say you are a foreigner and show him your hotel card. Invariably there are moments when you will miss the simple Western comforts—but a coffee in the Metropol in Moscow or the Grand Hotel Europe in St. Petersburg or even a McDonald's will quickly recharge the batteries and you will be ready once more to cope with the vagaries of life in Russia.

Health hazard
Since Western tobacco firms have been severely restricted in their marketing by antismoking legislation, they have moved their sights onto countries desperate enough for financial investment to encourage them. Most people smoke in Russia, and the authorities have always adopted an ambiguous attitude at best to the health issue. In Soviet times the health warning on cigarette packets was sponsored not by the health ministry but by the ministry for food and tobacco.

Take coffee in the luxurious surroundings of the Hotel Metropol

255

Orientation Getting acquainted with Moscow and St. Petersburg is much easier nowadays than it used to be—some of the major street signs are in English as well as Russian. Generally speaking, people are friendlier and more used to foreigners. They will help out—provided you can make yourself understood fairly quickly. Knowledge of English is increasing day by day, especially among young people; the older generation is more likely to know German. If you don't know Russian, it's a good idea before setting off to ask someone who does to write down your destination, metro station, etc., then at least you can point to the relevant information.

It is essential nowadays to have an **up-to-date** map as the names of a great number of streets (and metro stations) have been changed. To add to the complication, many Russians still refer to places by their old names. Before setting off, take time to organize your itinerary. Check you have your map and that the museums you intend to visit are open. No place in the world works to such eccentric hours as Russia. Every museum, for example, closes not only one or two days a week, but once a month (at least) for cleaning, etc. Also bear in mind that any number of places of interest are liable to close for restoration. To be sure, ask your hotel to phone the venue on your behalf. Maps are sold at hotel shops, major bookstores, and by street vendors.

Information on Moscow and St. Petersburg is at last becoming more available thanks to the appearance, none too soon, of English-language newspapers containing listings. Many of these, *Moscow News* for example, are free and you can pick up a copy in the hotel lobby. If you need more detailed information, there are one or two Western-produced directories now available (see page 274 for details).

Transportation The public transportation system in Moscow and St. Petersburg is more comprehensive than any comparable city in Europe. For details see pages 268–269.

The Moscow metro is much more extensive than the St. Petersburg equivalent. If you don't know Russian,

Potato-rustling
One of Russia's most valuable commodities during times of food shortages throughout history has been the humble potato. Never more so than now, for it is still a staple of the Russian diet. But with the rise in crime of all kinds, Moscow's authorities are now being forced to police their potato warehouses in order to protect them from persistent break-ins. As the director for security of one warehouse put it: "Russia needs its potatoes, Russia cares for its potatoes, nurtures them. Of course, we must protect them too."

No longer a monopoly, the old state firm of Intourist still has the lion's share of the excursion market

*Reading the runes—
Muscovites come
to terms with a
gargantuan train
timetable*

257

allow plenty of time to work things out. Getting lost or confused is never so bad if you're in company, so take a friend underground with you. Trams and buses are easier to use and so cheap that you can afford any number of rides in a day. Make sure you buy a ticket from the driver at the front, as fines have recently been increased.

Personal security Sensational reports in the press about the Mafia, etc., should be put in perspective. While Moscow and St. Petersburg are by no means crime-free, they are still comparatively safe cities for the visitor. From a personal point of view, try not to display your wealth too conspicuously. Watch your valuables at all times, especially in markets, on the metro, and in restaurants. Keep a special eye on cameras, video cameras, etc., as these are prime targets for the thief. Leave what money you don't need (also valuables) behind in the room or hotel safe. Side streets are badly lit at night, so stick to the main highways. Women should never go out alone at night. Report a crime immediately to hotel reception. See page 272.

General health care and restrooms With the rise in poverty and subsequent fall in living conditions in Russia since 1990, there has been an increase in associated diseases. For the tourist, upset stomachs are common, as standards of health and hygiene are low and ecological pollution abounds. Always use **boiled or bottled water** to wash any fresh fruit and to brush your teeth. Avoid ice in your drinks (except in the newly refurbished hotels). Extra care has to be taken in St. Petersburg where the infamous parasite *Giardia lamblia* lurks in the water supply causing severe diarrhea and requiring strong treatment.

Avoid public restrooms like the plague! Even in museums, washroom facilities are often way below Western standards. At every opportunity use the toilets in the Western hotels. In any event, it is always wise to carry a small pack of tissues around with you. And don't expect to find machines dispensing condoms or feminine hygiene products either.

Toilet town
Moscow's Sanitary and Epidemiological Inspectorate (MosSanEpidNadzor for short) is in the process of upgrading the city's noxious and poorly maintained public restrooms. Meanwhile, more than 40 public restrooms in the center of town have been permanently closed. Many of these facilities were built at the time of Stalin's funeral in 1953 to meet the needs of the millions of mourners who descended on the capital from all over the Soviet Union. Mayor Luzhkov has asked the owners of stores now occupying these prime sites to provide toilets for their customers at their own expense—but the appeal has so far fallen on profoundly deaf ears.

Road sense
With the advent of Russia's *nouveau riche* there has been a rush on car purchases. Unfortunately many proud new owners of BMWs and Mercedes are reluctant to equip themselves with the obligatory driver's license. In order to get through a Russian driving test, the learner has to study mechanics and obtain a doctor's certificate confirming that he or she has no history of mental illness. So many drivers, particularly those with gangster connections, prefer simply to buy a license on the black market and drive off—at speed—leaving Russia's traffic police to turn a blind eye.

Survival guide

Shopping You will need to be very hungry to be tempted by the rolls, hot dogs, etc., on sale from street stalls. In any case, avoid the temptation as standards of hygiene leave a great deal to be desired. Kiosks do sell many Western brands of chocolates, soft drinks, cosmetics, and so on. Follow your instincts here, but be aware that there have been a large number of prosecutions recently for tampering with labels and for the adulteration of food and drink. If you need anything, it's best to buy from the hotel shops and Western stores.

If you become ill in Russia you will be reassured to know that central pharmacies nowadays stock leading Western brands of medicines. It should be possible now to buy personal items such as toothpaste and shampoo in department stores and hotel shops, but it is advisable to take your own supply of contraceptives, prescribed drugs, aspirin, antibiotic creams, Band-Aids, sanitary napkins or tampons, etc., and (especially in St. Petersburg in the summer) mosquito repellent. Watch for the sign "Apteka" (**Аптека**) meaning pharmacy.

Dealing with Russians In the bad old days, Russians were suspicious of foreigners and sometimes downright hostile—heads would avert if one so much as asked the way, and it was not unheard of for a girl wearing fashionable Western clothes to receive a public dressing-down on the metro. Thankfully, Russians today would view such attitudes as amusing eccentricities, largely confined, to the very old or to the die-hard Communist—an endangered, but by no means extinct, species. Modern Russians are open about themselves and curious about, though not necessarily envious of, Westerners. They are friendly and mostly helpful, but foreigners should never forget that everyday life in Russia imposes stresses and strains that would try the patience of a saint. Don't judge the people as a whole by the rudeness or indifference of a single individual—you certainly wouldn't at home. At the practical level, don't expect Western standards of service, at least don't expect consistency, even in the major hotels. If you have a complaint or problem, pursue it politely but firmly—Russians have a tendency to wish difficulties away. A smile and a *spasiba* ("thank you") will always be appreciated.

Fragrant pick-me-up
Russia's swank new department stores are seeing some rather odd customers in their cosmetics departments these days. Recent shortages of alcohol have forced St. Petersburg's hardened drinking fraternity off hooch and dubious adulterated forms of booze onto proprietary cleaning fluids, liquid fuels, and now even cheap perfume. The sight of vagrants traipsing up to the beauty counters to buy their favorite scented tipple must be the ultimate paradox.

258

Fast-food Russian-style is available at this snack bar in GUM

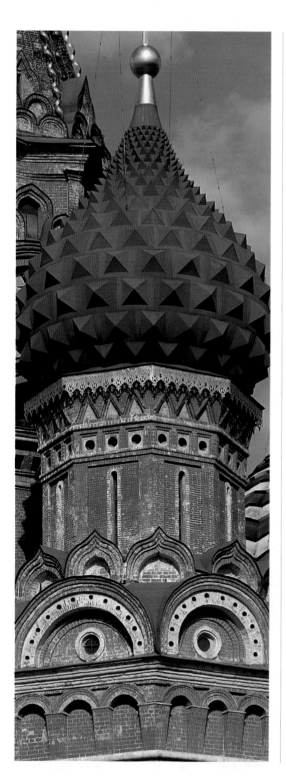

TRAVEL FACTS

Arriving by air
Most major airlines fly to Moscow's international airport, Sheremetyevo 2, and to St. Petersburg's airport, Pulkovo 2. The Russian airline, Aeroflot, operates all major routes into Russia, but safety standards have recently given cause for concern.

Airports
Sheremetyevo 2, Moscow Arrival and departure information—tel: 578 56 14/91 01.
Facilities: Currency exchange (*Open* 9 AM–10 PM); limited duty-free shops (24-hour); bar; restaurant (*Open* 12–midnight).

For accommodations information contact the Russian Japanese Aeroservice desk or the Intourtrans bureau on the second floor. The airport is about 25 miles from the city center. **Bus** to city (1 hour). Bus No. 517 goes to Planernaya metro station; No. 551 goes to Rechnoy Vokzal metro; from there take the metro to the center (bus tickets can be bought from the driver). **Taxis** are abundant, but negotiate a price first. If you have pre-booked a transfer to your hotel, present your voucher at the Intourist desk and they will arrange for a taxi.

Pulkovo 2, St. Petersburg Arrival and departure information—tel: 104 34 44.

State carrier—Aeroflot headquarters, St. Petersburg

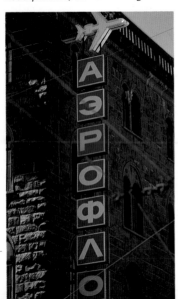

Facilities: There is a small gift shop in the renovated arrivals building; a larger duty-free shop; and a bar serving light snacks in the departure lounge.

There is no efficient system of public transportation from Pulkovo Airport to the city, so a taxi is recommended.

Airline offices
Aeroflot: Moscow—Leningradsky Prospekt 37, tel: 155 50 45.
St. Petersburg—Nevskiy Prospekt 7/9, tel: 314 69 43.

Air France: Moscow—Koroviy Val Ulitsa 7, tel: 237 23 25.
St. Petersburg—Pulkovo 2, tel: 104 24 33/119 82 52.

British Airways: Moscow—Krasnopresnenskaya Naberezhnaya 12, floor 19, office 1905, tel: 253 24 92.
St Petersburg—Bolshaya Morskaya Ulitsa 36, tel: 119 62 22.

Delta Airlines: Moscow—Krasnopresnenskaya Naberezhnaya 12, tel: 253 26 58.
St. Petersburg—Bolshaya Morskaya Ulitsa 36, tel: 311 58 20/58 19.

KLM: Moscow—Krasnopresnenskaya Naberezhnaya 12, floor 13, tel: 253 21 50.
St. Petersburg—Pulkovo 2, Airport Office, tel: 104 34 40.

Lufthansa: Moscow—Olimskiy Prospekt 18/1, Hotel Penta, tel: 975 25 01.
St. Petersburg—Voznesensky Prospekt 7, tel: 314 49 79/59 17.

Swissair: Moscow—Krasnopresnenskaya Naberezhnaya 12, tel: 253 89 88.
St. Petersburg—Pulkovo 2, tel: 314 50 86/311 61 12.

Arriving by train
You can reach Moscow and St. Petersburg by rail from Western Europe. (London to Moscow via Berlin and Warsaw takes about two and a half days; the journey from Helsinki to St. Petersburg is about seven hours). Terminals are generally named after the train's point of departure, so you will arrive at the St. Petersburg (Leningrad) or Kievskiy station in Moscow, and the Moscow, Finland, or Warsaw station in St. Petersburg. Train services operate all year round, but schedules vary. Book seats prior to departure.

Hydrofoils set out from the Winter Palace (Hermitage)

For train information in Moscow, **Moscow**: tel: 921 45 13 (in English). In **St. Petersburg**, tel: 168 01 11 or 162 33 44.

Arriving by road
If arriving by road, check recommended routes with Intourist as there are only a few overland entry points.

Arriving by boat
If you have the time, take the ferry to St. Petersburg from Helsinki. The journey lasts about 13 hours. Ferries also run from Stockholm, Riga, and Kiel. Ferries arrive at the Sea Passenger Ship Terminal, Morskoy Slavy Ploshchad, Vasilevskiy Ostrov (trolleybus 10 and 12).
Sea Passenger Port, Morskaya Slavy Ploshchad 1, tel: 355 13 10.
Sea Commercial Port, Mezhevoy Kanala 5, tel: 114 94 01.

Customs regulations
Passing through customs is no longer the nightmare it used to be, but expect long lines and delays. Read the customs regulations carefully. Before entering the country, you will

be given two **customs declaration forms.** Fill out one, listing how much currency you have (include even small change) and any valuables (include rings, radios, watches, computers, musical instruments, etc.). This form is stamped at customs as you enter the country, and you will not be allowed to leave without it. On departure you complete the second form and hand both to customs with your passport.

Remember—there is no limit to how much **foreign currency** you can take into Russia, but you are not allowed to take any rubles out.

Allowances
You cannot under any circumstances take **antiques, icons, or works of art** out of the country without permission from the Ministry of Culture. There is

Customs will evaluate all art purchases prior to departure

also a limit to the value of souvenirs and gifts you may take out, but currently inflation makes this difficult to enforce. Duty-free allowances are as for all countries outside the EU.

What to bring
Most of the things you will need for your trip are readily available, especially in Western-owned supermarkets—but often at prohibitive prices, as Moscow is one of the most expensive cities in the world. Take all prescribed medicines with you, also contraceptives, first-aid items, laundry detergent, specialist batteries for cameras, shavers, etc., and an umbrella. In winter, bring waterproof shoes, a warm hat, scarf, and gloves (see **What to wear** below).

Travel insurance
It is essential to check your insurance before traveling. Foreign nationals are eligible for free emergency medical care in public hospitals (there is a nominal charge for medicines); however, private clinics are as costly as in the West. Insure against theft of luggage, credit cards, and tickets as well.

Visas
All travelers to Russia need a visa. There are three types of visa: Tourist, valid for a set number of days up to 30; Business, valid for up to 60 days and obtained on presentation of a letter or fax from a Russian firm; and Visitor, for which you need a personal invitation and guarantee of accommodations from a Russian.

Your travel agent will automatically give you an application form for a Tourist visa. Send this, along with three passport-size photographs and photocopies of the first six pages of your passport, to Intourist. If you are traveling independently, apply to the Russian embassy.

Visa extensions, in Russia, can be obtained from the UVIR (department of visas and registration) offices. Lost visas have to be reported to this office too—and quickly. Once in Russia, you cannot leave again without a visa. All visas are registered with UVIR automatically by your hotel. If you are staying in private accommodations, it is not necessary to register with UVIR unless you stay more than a week. The UVIR main office in Moscow is at Ulitsa Pokrova 42, tel: 207 02 39. In St. Petersburg, Saltykova-Shchedrina Ulitsa 4, tel: 278 24 81/273 90 38 (*Open* Mon–Fri 9:30–5:30).

No immunizations are required by the authorities in Moscow and St. Petersburg, but your polio, tetanus (within ten years), and typhoid fever shots should be current. Children should also have diphtheria injections; adults who have not had a diphtheria booster are advised against close physical contact. The risk of catching hepatitis A increases with the length of your stay; vaccination is highly protective and effective for ten years. AIDS, too, is on the increase, and visitors intending to stay for longer than three months may be asked for an HIV certificate.

Hospitals and clinics
Free medical treatment is available to tourists on production of a passport or medical card. The hotel will call a doctor for you. Prescribed drugs must be paid for, so take out a good travel medical insurance that includes evacuation: Russian medical standards are much lower than American. If needed, there are several good private medical centers and polyclinics that charge for their services.
Moscow American Medical Center, 2-Tverskaya-Yamskaya 10, tel: 956 33 66 (general medical care, X rays, tests, pharmacy).
Athens Medical Center, Michurinsky Prospekt 6, tel: 143 25 03.
European Medical Center, Gruzinsky Pereulok 3/2, tel: 253 07 03 (299 78 92 in emergency).
International Medical Clinic, Gorokholsky Pereulok, 10th floor, tel: 280 71 38.
Sana Medical Center (French joint venture) Ulitsa Nizhnaya Pervomayskaya 65, tel: 464 12 54 (*Open* Tue–Sun).
Tourist's Clinic (with AIDS prevention clinic), Gruzinsky Proezd 2, tel: 254 43 96.
St. Petersburg American Medical Center, Reki Fontanki Naberezhnaya 77, tel: 325 61 01. Clinic hours,

Western-owned pharmacies stock most leading brands

Mon–Fri 8:30–6 (Western doctors and registered nurses; 24-hour emergency access for members).
St. Petersburg Policlinic No. 2, Mokovsky Prospekt 22, tel: 316 62 72/110 11 02 (24-hour emergency cover). Clinic hours Mon–Fri 9–9, Sat 9–3.

Pharmacies
Moscow American Drug Store, Shmitovskiy Proezd 3, tel: 956 33 66 (*Open* Mon–Fri 8:30–6, Sat 10–2).
Drugstore at Sadko Arcade, Krasnogvardeyskiy Proezd 1, tel: 253 95 92.
International Pharmacy in European Medical Center, Gruzinskiy Pereulok 3, tel: 253 07 03 (*Open* 9:30–6:30).
Sana Medical Center (French), Ulitsa Nizhnaya Pervomayskaya 65, tel: 464 12 54 (*Open* Tue–Sun).
St. Petersburg Panatseya, Gorokhovaya Ulitsa, tel: 314 05 85.
Petrofarm, Nevskiy Prospekt 22, tel: 311 20 04 (24-hour emergency counter).
Pharmacy Damian, St. Petersburg Policlinic No. 2, Moskovskiy Prospekt 22, tel: 110 17 44; fax: 292 59 39 (Western medicines, personal hygiene products, etc. *Open* 9–8).
Salute, Kamennoostrovskiy Prospekt 38, tel: 234 93 05 (*Open* 9–7).

When to go

May–September marks the height of the tourist season. In April and October you'll save money and enjoy the surprisingly mild climate. Visit during one of the festivals—the Russian Winter Festival (December 25–January 5) or the St. Petersburg White Nights (June 21–9)—and see the Russians in a celebrating mood.

Climate

The weather in Russia is wonderfully invigorating in winter—but it can be *very* cold (expect temperatures well below freezing November–February), and there are frequent heavy snowfalls. St. Petersburg is warmed by the sea, but the cold winds that lash

Summer at Yelagin Island

across the Gulf of Finland often make it seem colder than Moscow. The thaw begins in March, so if you dislike slush avoid this period. Moscow has beautiful spring days with temperatures around 70°F. In the summer, temperatures soar to between 80° and 90°F and it can be humid, especially in Moscow. The wettest months are July and August.

For the Moscow weather forecast, tel: 975 92 22; St. Petersburg, tel: 001.

What to wear

Winter: Warm coats, thick tights, warm pants (jeans are not ideal in the depths of winter), thermal underwear,

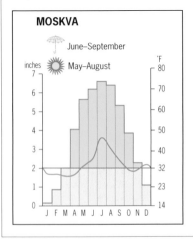

MOSKVA

June–September
inches May–August
°F

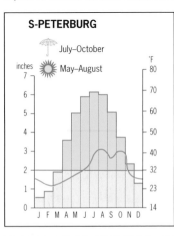

S-PETERBURG

July–October
inches May–August
°F

fleece-lined boots, thermal gloves and—very important—a warm hat (preferably one that covers your ears). Russian central heating systems are all remarkably efficient, so you can dress light indoors.

Summer: Dress as you would in any Western country, but remember to pack a raincoat. Wear modest clothing when visiting churches (a hat or headscarf and covered shoulders for women; shirts and pants rather than shorts for men).

National holidays
All businesses, public services, stores etc., are closed for the following holidays: **January 1**—New Year's Day; **January 7**—Epiphany; **March 8**—Women's Day; **May 9**—VE Day; **June 12**—Independence Day; **November 7**—Day of Reconciliation; **December 12**—Constitution Day. There is also a holiday during the Orthodox Easter.

Time differences
Moscow time (St. Petersburg is in the same time zone) is 11 hours ahead of Los Angeles, eight ahead of New York, three ahead of London, and two hours ahead of Central European Time.

Money matters
The ruble is the official currency of Russia. One hundred kopeks make up one ruble, but inflation has made kopeks almost worthless. After the collapse of Communism there was a frantic rush for hard currency, especially dollars. However, a law passed in 1994 forbids transactions in Western currency and, although many street traders still ask for dollars, restaurants, stores, and bars charge in rubles.

The dollar is king in Russia—you may find it harder to exchange other currencies, even in official exchange offices. Bring all denominations of dollar bills; the smaller ones are useful for tips and small transactions, the larger for exchanging. The bills have to be in good condition—even banks are reluctant to accept soiled money because of counterfeits.

Credit cards (Visa, MasterCard, AmEx, JB, Diner's Club) are accepted in major restaurants and hotels, even for the smallest purchases. They can also be used to get cash from the big banks and hotels, but are not generally accepted elsewhere. A few banks are members of the SWIFT currency transfer system so you can transfer money from an account at home. ATMs are becoming more available, but are still not widespread.

Credit card fraud is increasing, so have your passport ready for identification when using a card.

The Bank of America and the Chase Manhattan Bank have offices in Moscow.

Changing money All Russian banks have exchange counters. The rate fluctuates wildly, so watch the signs. Changing money on the streets is technically illegal and risky, especially with large sums. The traders are out to make big profits and you cannot always tell, under their pressured selling techniques, whether you are getting a good deal.

Traveler's checks can be exchanged for dollars in all major hotels and **American Express offices** (a high commission is charged). If you intend to leave the country with more dollars than you brought in, ask for a *razreshenie* (an official exchange document) for customs.
American Express Moscow, Sadovo-Kudrinskaya Ulitsa 21a, tel: 956 90 04, fax: 253 93 72; American Express St. Petersburg, Grand Hotel Europe, Mikhaylovskaya Ulitsa 1/7, tel: 119 60 09, fax: 119 60 11.

Foreign currency exchange is no longer a state monopoly

265

Car rental

There are many private chauffeur firms now in Russia. The cars are not luxurious, but many of the large hotels (and Intourist) offer car rental, with or without a driver. In reality there is little difference between renting a car with a driver and taking a taxi (drivers will take fares by the hour as well as by distance).

Moscow car rental InNis (Nissan/ Russian joint venture, chauffeur service), Bolshaya Ordynka Ulitsa 32, tel: 230 61 60, fax: 230 62 13.

Auto-sun (car rental), Sheremetyevo 2 Airport, tel: 231 91 52, fax: 956 92 60.

Avis, Berezhkovskaya Naberezhnaya 12, Door 15/1, tel: 240 99 32, fax: 240 99 32, and at Sheremetyevo 2 Airport tel: 578 56 46.

Hertz, Chernyakhovskovo Ulitsa 4, tel: 151 54 26, fax: 956 16 21.

St. Petersburg car rental Avis, Konnogvardeyskiy Bulvar 4, tel: 312 63 18, fax: 312 72 92.

Cosmos Travel and Limo Service, 2nd Line 35, Vasilievskiy Island, tel: 327 72 56, fax: 327 74 29.

Eurodollar, Kommunisticheskaya Bolshaya Ulitsa 1/5, tel: 298 61 46, fax: 911 09 59.

Europcar, Krasnopresenskaya Naberzenaya 12, tel: 253 29 74, fax: 151 63 26.

Hertz, Ispolkomskaya Ulitsa 9/11, tel: 277 40 32, fax: 274 25 62

Petrointour, Pirogovskaya Naberezhnaya 5/2, tel: 542 87 35, fax: 542 86 91.

Taxis

The desk at your hotel will book a taxi for you, but make sure you order it at least an hour in advance. If hailing a cab on the street, look for official taxis—yellow with a checkered band on the door. A green light in the corner of the windshield indicates the taxi is available. Many Russians use their own cars as unofficial taxis, so you'll have no problem finding a cab. Whether using an official or a privately owned cab, the fare should be agreed before you begin your ride as very few taxis work by the meter.

Warning: Taking unofficial taxis is common in Russia, but can be more dangerous for visitors. Don't get into a cab with more than one passenger already in it and avoid unlicensed cabs at night.

A 24-hour taxi service is available:
Moscow: Outside the Hotel Intourist on Tverskaya Ulitsa.
St. Petersburg: In St. Isaac's Square, outside the Hotel Astoria.

Roadside service: top off your tank straight from the tanker

Driving tips

Don't! Driving in Russia is every bit as bad as in the busiest of Western capitals, if not worse. All signs are in the Cyrillic alphabet, gas stations are few and far between, the roads are full of potholes, and the whole system is chaotic. The traffic police (GAI) have a reputation for corruption and, by all accounts, enjoy stopping and fining foreigners. It is illegal to drive after drinking any alcohol.

If you do decide to risk driving, you need: an international driver's license, or a national license which must have an insert in Russian; the Intourist booklet *Instructions for Foreign Motorists*; and, if you take your own car, a certificate promising to take it back out of the country with you.

In general Russian traffic laws are in line with the rest of Western Europe and America. If you are driving your own car, you will need to use 95 octane gas (Russian cars take 76 or 93).

Fuel

Moscow: Andropova Prospekt 6, tel: 116 95 11; Kashirskoe Shosse 105, tel: 234 02 33; **Grant**, Malaya Gruzinskaya Ulitsa 38, tel: 252 23 50 (Mon–Fri); **NeftoAgip** station, Leningradskoe Shosse 63, tel: 458 49 57 (24 hours, English spoken).

In **St. Petersburg** the **Neste Petro Service** offers 24 hours gas and travel shops, taking credit cards, at the following sites:
Pulkovskoe Shosse 34a, tel: 122 03 01; Moskovskiy Pr. 100, tel: 298 45 34; Maliy Pr. 68, Vasilevskiy Island, tel: 355 08 79; Avangardnaya Ulitsa 36, tel: 135 58 67; Savushkina Ulitsa 87, tel: 239 04 15.

Car breakdown An emergency service for breakdowns is not easy to find. However, one of the following numbers may be helpful:
Moscow AVTO S.O.S. tel: 256 06 36/64 02 (24 hours). Spare parts are available from **Kalinka Stockmann**, Lyusinovskaya Ulitsa 70/1, tel: 954 82 34.
NeftoAgip Station (foreign makes) Leningradskoe Shosse 63, tel: 458 49 57.
St. Petersburg Hyundai Service,

Bumper to bumper—rush hour free-for-all along the Kremlin embankment

Ulitsa Trefoleva 2, tel: 252 44 29; **Service**, Respublikanskaya 20, tel: 528 57 56 (foreign makes).
TDV-AUTO (Ford dealer), Kommuniy Ulitsa 16, tel: 521 37 20.
Swed Car (Volvo), Energetikov Prospekt 59/3, tel: 225 40 51.

Flying

You may wish to think twice before taking an internal flight: standards, in all respects, may not match up to what you are used to. The airports are often crowded, although preference is given to Intourist travel groups, and facilities fall short of Western standards. Passports and visas are required at check-in. There is only one class and no no-smoking sections. Some flights have numbered seats, others have open seating. Be sure to bring your own food with you.

Metro

Moscow's famous metro is a fast, cheap, and reliable way of getting around the city. Although much more restricted, the St. Petersburg system is just as efficient. A basic knowledge of the Cyrillic alphabet is essential if you are to avoid getting lost.

Each station has its own name—even two stations on the same site but on different lines. So every time you change lines, you have to change stations. Stations are indicated by a large **red neon letter M**. There is a basic flat fare; admission is by tokens which can be bought at the *kassa* (*касса*) in the entrance hall of every metro station. Put the token into the turnstile and wait for the green light. Beware the escalators which are usually deep (especially in St. Petersburg). Indicator boards in the station give exit and transfer information. Other signs on the platform list the stations on the line, and a clock tells you how long it is since the departure of the last train. As the train's doors are about to close, a loudspeaker announces: "*Ostorozhno, dveri zakrivayutsya, sleduyushchaya stantsiya ...*" ("Attention, the doors are closing, the next station will be ..."). If you get a seat, be prepared to offer it to an elderly person; Russians expect that. As the train pulls into a station, its name is announced, followed by information about changing lines, which can be

Advertising, on billboards and over the public address system, is a novelty on the metro

tricky. To know which direction to go in, look for a sign with the word *perekhod* (*переход*) and the name of the station you want. Then check the list of stations on the wall by the train to make sure you are going in the right direction. To get back to street level, look for the sign *vykhod* (*выход*). The metros of both cities are open 5:30 AM–1 AM.

Tickets

To pay your fare on any form of transportation you can buy transportation coupons, *talony* (*талону*), at kiosks, on buses, trams, and in shops. These should be punched in a machine as you board the buses and trams; if you can't reach, pass your coupon along for others to punch and return. Ticket checkers at the metro will not let you through unless your *talon* is punched in the machine in the entrance hall. Transportation cards valid for a month for any form of transportation are called *ediniy bilet* (*единый билет*).

Bus, trolleybus, and tram

Buses, trolleybuses, and trams operate in both cities. All transportation in Moscow runs between 5:30 AM and 1 AM, and in St. Petersburg between 5:30 AM and half past midnight. Yellow boards show bus route

Metro ticket and tokens

numbers and the terminus. "A" represents a bus, "T" a trolleybus. Tickets for all three overground networks can be bought from the driver at a flat rate for any ride. Tram signs hang on wires over the street adjacent to the tram stop.

Trains

Electric commuter trains get very crowded but have the advantage of being extremely cheap. The long-distance trains offer more in the way of comfort; on longer rides, it is usual to book the whole compartment to avoid sharing. Keep close guard on your valuables. At night, for extra security, tie the door shut from the inside.

Tickets can be purchased on the day of departure at the "same-day window"—*sutochnaya*, (*суточнал*). **Tickets in advance** (from one to 45 days before traveling) can be bought from: Moscow: **Central Railway Agency**, Kharitonyevskiy Malyy Pereulok 6, tel: 262 03 19; **Interrail (BCT)**, Chistoprudniy Bulvar 12a, tel: 916 93 64; **Intourtrans**, Ulitsa Petrovka 15/13, 1st Floor (international); Ulitsa Griboedova 6/4 (domestic); St. Petersburg: **Central Railway Agency Office**, station inquiries tel: 168 01 11; ticket ordering tel: 162 33 44.

Foreigners have to buy their tickets from Intourist at the station or at their hotels, because they are expected to pay more and usually in dollars.

Train stations

Moscow has nine main train terminals, all easily reached by metro. For trains to Minsk and Western Europe—**Belorusskiy Vokzal**; eastward to Kazan, the Urals, and Central Russia—**Kazanskiy Vokzal**; west to Prague, Budapest, Belgrade, Bucharest, and Kiev—**Kievskiy Vokzal**; south to Ryazan, the Crimea, the Caucasus, and Kharkov—**Kurskiy Vokzal**; or to Kharkov, Simferopol, Yerevan, and Baku—**Paveletskiy Vokzal**; north to St. Petersburg, Murmansk, and Finland—**Leningradskiy Vokzal**; for Riga and Volokolamsk—**Rizhskiy Vokzal**.

For excursions northward to Sergiev Posad (Zagorsk) or beyond to Yaroslavl, or to catch the Trans-Siberian Express—**Yaroslavskiy Vokzal**. **St. Petersburg** has five main train terminals. For trains to Gatchina, Oranienbaum/Lomonosov, and Peterhof/Petrodvorets—**Baltiyskiy Vokzal**; Helsinki, Vyborg, Repino, and Lake Ladoga—**Finlyandskiy Vokzal**; Moscow, Caucasus, Crimea, Georgia, and Central Asia—**Moskovskiy Vokzal**; Smolensk, Novgorod, Kiev, Odessa, Pavlovsk, and Tsarskoe Selo/Pushkin—**Vitebskiy Vokzal**; Pskov, Poland, Eastern Europe, and the Baltic States—**Varshavskiy Vokzal**.

The St. Petersburg metro system is far from comprehensive, so learn to make use of the buses and trams

The media

Radio and television There are two main Russian TV channels as well as a local station and an education channel. European programs are imported to Russia via cable and satellite. Most of the main hotels offer **cable TV** with **CNN**. Channel 3 broadcasts the CBS evening news at 7:30 and also BBC and ITN bulletins dubbed into Russian.

Radio Moscow has an English-language service and broadcasts news every hour throughout the day. Radio 7 (73.4 and 104.7 FM) broadcasts news in English on the half hour. Radio Maximum (103.7 FM) broadcasts pop and rock music interspersed with English-language discussions of cultural events, current affairs, etc.

The Voice of America and BBC World Service also broadcast programs to Russia.

Newspapers International newspapers and magazines are available in all the main Russian hotels, including the *International Herald Tribune*, *The Times*, the *Guardian*, the *Daily Mail* and *Daily Express*, *Die Welt*, *Le Monde*, *PC World*, *Reader's Digest*, *Time*, and *Newsweek*. Occasionally international newspapers are on sale in kiosks and bookstores in central areas.

Local English-language newspapers are available in both cities and provide useful listings as well as interesting articles on local life: they include the dailies (*Moscow Times* and *Moscow Tribune)* and the weeklies (*Moscow News*, *St. Petersburg Press* and *Neva Week)*.

Post offices

Mailboxes are blue and white. Airmail to the USA and the UK is reliable, but takes about three weeks; incoming mail is less reliable and can take even longer.

Post offices are usually open between 8 and 10 AM to 7:30 PM.

The main post offices provide all the usual services; branch post offices will accept international letters but not packages. Packages must be taken unwrapped to the main office, where they will be officially inspected and then wrapped for you.

There are limited postal services in the major hotels.

Moscow Central Post Office, Myasnitskaya Ulitsa 26, tel: 923 36 83; **International Post Office**, Varshavskoe Shosse 37, tel: 114 46 45.

St. Petersburg Central Post Office, Pochtamtskaya Ulitsa 9, tel: 312 83 02; **Peter T.I.P.S.**, Nevskiy Prospekt 86, tel: 279 00 37 (offers postal services via Finland and courier services within the city).

From computer courses to apartment swaps—advertisements on a public bulletin board

Telephone and fax

Moscow area code 095; St. Petersburg area code 812. Telephone booths for calls within Russia can be found throughout the cities. For international calls, faxes, and telexes, go to your hotel desk, an intercity pay-phone center, or a main post office.

Faxing would appear to be a better option than relying on the mail service, but fax lines are busy and a shortage of fax paper means that machines in Russia are often not in working order.

Moscow Central Telegraph Office, Tverskaya Ulitsa 7, tel: 925 15 88; 924 90 04 (public fax and telex service).

St. Petersburg Center of Business Communication, Bolshaya Morskaya Ulitsa 3–5 (*Open* daily 9–9, tel: 119 03 32/312 20 85).

Business centers

Most of the hotels now offer a range of business services including international telephone lines and fax. The most efficient are at the **Hotel Metropol** and the **Radisson-Slavyanskaya Hotel** in Moscow and the **Grand Hotel Europe** in St. Petersburg.

Moscow business centers
Americom Business Center, Radisson-Slavyanskaya Hotel, tel: 941 84 27, fax: 941 84 27; **Business Center**, Rozhdestvenka Ulitsa 3, tel:

Most modern hotels are equipped with business centers

928 37 80, fax: 929 75 71; **GUM Business Center**, Krasnaya Ploshchad (Red Square) 3, tel: 921 09 11, 921 88 73, fax: 921 46 09; **Metropol Business Center**, Hotel Metropol, tel: 927 60 90, fax: 927 60 10.

St. Petersburg business centers
American Business Center, Nevskiy Palace Hotel Arcade, Nevskiy Prospekt 57, tel: 275 44 24; **Business Center**, Grand Hotel Europe, tel: 312 00 72, fax: 119 60 01; **Ipris**, (copy center), 2 Shvedskiy Pereulok (Nevskiy Prospekt), tel: 315 57 82; **Pribaltiyskaya Business Center**, Korablestroiteley Ulitsa 14, tel: 356 02 63; **St. Petersburg Hotel**, Vyborgskaya Naberezhnaya, tel: 542 94 11.

Translation service

Guide and interpreter services are expensive but efficient, providing skilled interpreters and translators for business meetings and written translations of documents. In addition, guides will not only accompany you on excursions, but will also organize them on your behalf.

Moscow Americom, Berezhkovskaya Naberezhnaya 2, tel: 941 86 41.

St. Petersburg Znanie, Ulitsa Kavalergardskaya 10, tel: 275 61 09.

Emergency telephone numbers
Fire—01
Police—02
Ambulance—03
Gas leaks—04

Moscow Ambulances from the
American Medical Center, tel: 256
82 12.
Hospital information, tel: 208 75 84.
To trace people taken to the hospital,
tel: 924 31 52 or 208 91 57.
American Medical Center, 2
Tverskoy-Yamskoy Pereulok 10, tel:
956 33 66.
St. Petersburg Ambulances for
foreigners (better equipped and
English spoken): **Policlinic No. 2**
ambulance tel: 110 11 02.
Accident information, tel: 273 30 55
(for people transported by
ambulance).
Traffic police information, tel: 315
00 19 (for people involved in
accidents).

Contact lenses
Moscow Optic Moscow, Ulitsa
Arbat 30, tel: 241 15 77 (*Open* 10–7);
Optiks Medical Center (Finnish joint
venture), Frunzenskaya Naberezhnaya
54, tel: 242 30 69.

Dentist
Moscow Sofitel Dental Clinic,
Korovinskoe Shosse 10, tel: 488 82
79.
Med Star, Lomonosovskiy Prospekt
43, tel: 143 60 76.

*The GAI (traffic police) at work.
Roadside supervision is strict in
Russia*

The Dental Clinic, Pullman Iris
Hotel, tel: 488 82 79 (*Open* 10–5).
St. Petersburg Dental Clinic Medi,
Nevskiy Prospekt 82, tel: 275 35 89
(*Open* 24 hours).
Nordmed (private dental clinic),
Tverskaya Ulitsa 12/15, tel: 110
06 54 (*Open* 9–5:30, Thu 9–8;
evenings and weekends, tel: 110
04 01).

Crime and police
The citizens of Moscow and St.
Petersburg can no longer boast that
their streets are free from muggings.
As "wealthy Western visitors" you
are bound to attract a lot of attention,
some of it unwelcome, especially if
you throw your money around, so
the advice is to dress down, be wary
of groups of young vagrants, and
keep jewelry, watches, and cameras
out of sight. In other words, take as
much care of your property as you
would in New York, London, or any
other big city.
   Carry photocopies of your passport
and visa, leaving the originals in your
hotel safe. Keep the numbers of
your traveler's checks and credit
cards. Car theft is increasing; radios,
luggage, and valuables left in view in
a car are prime pickings.
   If you are the victim of crime,
inform your hotel (and ask for an

interpreter), the police, and the embassy as soon as possible. Most hotels have their own militia department attached to them, so reception can put you in touch directly with the police.

Known as the *Militsia*, the police wear blue-and-gray uniforms with red lapels and cap bands. The GAI or traffic police also wear gray uniforms. There is something of a trend for uniform-wearing nowadays—not only off-duty soldiers and sailors but bouncers in restaurants often dress in combat jackets and fatigues. Don't be alarmed!

Embassies and consulates

Embassies offer a number of services to their nationals (including passport replacements, postal voting, assistance in the event of a death or other emergency). Some desks operate 24 hours a day.

Moscow
U.S.A.: Novinskiy Bulvar 19/23, tel: 252 24 51, fax: 956 42 61.

St. Petersburg (consulate)
U.S.A.: Furshtadtskaya Ulitsa 15, tel: 274 82 35, fax: 213 69 62.

Lost and found
Moscow
Lost property in the metro, tel: 222 20 85. Lost property in taxis/ public transportation, tel: 923 87 53.
St. Petersburg
Lost property departments (*Byuro Nakhodok*): Sredniy Prospekt 70 or Zakharevskaya Ulitsa 19. Lost on public transportation, Zakharevskaya Ulitsa 19, tel: 278 36 90.

Restrooms
Russian public restrooms are rare and dreadful; use those in hotels, restaurants, and museums where possible. But if you find yourself miles from a decent one and have to use a public restroom, take your own supply of toilet paper or tissues.

Restrooms may be marked WC or *Туалет* (*tualet*). Men's rooms will have an "*М*" and women's a "*Ж*."

There are "automated toilets" at Paveletskiy Station in Moscow and on St. Petersburg's Nevskiy Prospekt. If you are *really* desperate, there are also primitive restrooms at all main train stations.

American embassy in Moscow

Maps

It is essential to take with you a good clear map. Make sure it is up to date, as names of streets, metros, and even theaters are changing very quickly. Russian maps can be bought at kiosks or in bookstores.

Other sources of information

Moscow *Moscow Times* (English-language daily); *Time Out in Moscow* (weekly); *Where Moscow* (directory including maps, telephone listings, services); *Moscow Business Telephone Guide; Traveler's Yellow Pages and Handbook for Moscow* (with map).

St. Petersburg *The St. Petersburg Times* (English weekly); *St. Petersburg News* (English weekly); *Traveler's Yellow Pages and Handbook for St. Petersburg* (also includes good city map); *Where in St. Petersburg* (directory with maps).

Camping and rental accommodation organizations

Camping: Campsites must be booked in advance—you will be issued with a camping pass which confirms your booking and supports your visa application. Costs include electricity and cooking facilities, but because of

Moscow is surprisingly well-endowed with green spaces, such as the Kolomenskoe Estate

possible shortages, take your own equipment.
Moscow Mozhayskiy Shosse 165 (10 miles west of the city); **Butovo**, Bolshaya Butovskaya Ulitsa 5, tel: 548 79 00 (15 miles south of the city).
St. Petersburg Retur Camping (campers, chalets, sauna, bars, etc.), Primorskoe Shosse, 19 miles, tel: 237 75 33, fax: 273 97 83; **Olgino Motel Camping** (camping; chalets not recommended), Primorskoe Shosse 11 miles, tel: 238 35 50, fax: 238 39 54.

Staying with a family

You will be warmly welcomed, comfortable, and well fed. A good arrangement will provide the invitation necessary to obtain a visa, a private room, and meals. You may also find a family that will act as your guides and interpret for you. However, you may be out of the city center. Check the address carefully before booking. The room can be booked through accommodation agencies. For Moscow, St. Petersburg, and other Russian cities, contact **Host Families Association**, Tavricheskaya Ulitsa 5, kv 25, St. Petersburg, tel/fax: 275 19 92.

Private accommodations

Rented accommodations are cheaper, but it helps to know the system in shops and to speak the language. Official agencies offering apartments for long- or short-term leases are:
Moscow Home Sweet Home, Kutuzovskiy Prospekt 14, tel: 255 46 59; **New Solutions**, Volodarskaya 38, tel: 915 67 22 (hotels, bed and breakfast and apartments).
St. Petersburg Peter T.I.P.S., Nevskiy Prospekt 86, tel: 279 00 37, fax: 275 08 06 (apartments, family stays, guesthouses).

Visitors with disabilities

Traditionally, the Russians have paid scant regard to the needs of the disabled. It is impossible to use public transportation with a wheelchair, and the crowded metros and buses would not be easy for anyone with visual impairment to negotiate either. While theaters and museums generally have no access for wheelchairs, the new international hotels do offer assistance to disabled people, but in

CONVERSION CHARTS

FROM	TO	MULTIPLY BY
Inches	Centimeters	2.54
Centimeters	Inches	0.3937
Feet	Meters	0.3048
Meters	Feet	3.2810
Yards	Meters	0.9144
Meters	Yards	1.0940
Miles	Kilometers	1.6090
Kilometers	Miles	0.6214
Acres	Hectares	0.4047
Hectares	Acres	2.4710
U.S. Gallons	Liters	3.7854
Liters	U.S. Gallons	0.2642
Ounces	Grams	28.35
Grams	Ounces	0.0353
Pounds	Grams	453.6
Grams	Pounds	0.0022
Pounds	Kilograms	0.4536
Kilograms	Pounds	2.205
U.S. tons	Metric tons	0.9072
Metric tons	U.S. tons	1.1023

MEN'S SUITS

U.S.	36	38	40	42	44	46	48
U.K.	36	38	40	42	44	46	48
Rest of Europe	46	48	50	52	54	56	58

DRESS SIZES

U.S.	6	8	10	12	14	16
U.K.	8	10	12	14	16	18
France	36	38	40	42	44	46
Italy	38	40	42	44	46	48
Rest of Europe	34	36	38	40	42	44

MEN'S SHIRTS

U.S.	14	14.5	15	15.5	16	16.5	17
U.K.	14	14.5	15	15.5	16	16.5	17
Rest of Europe	36	37	38	39/40	41	42	43

MEN'S SHOES

U.S.	8	8.5	9.5	10.5	11.5	12
U.K.	7	7.5	8.5	9.5	10.5	11
Rest of Europe	41	42	43	44	45	46

WOMEN'S SHOES

U.S.	6	6.5	7	7.5	8	8.5
U.K.	4.5	5	5.5	6	6.5	7
Rest of Europe	38	38	39	39	40	41

St. Petersburg only the **Grand Hotel Europe** allows full wheelchair access.

Opening times

Store opening times vary from around 8 to 9 or even 10 in the morning. Closing times are just as haphazard—between 6 and 8 Mon–Sat, with a lunch break between noon and 3. Western stores and supermarkets usually dispense with a lunch hour. Some food stores and post offices are also open on Sunday. **Kiosks** stay open until nearly midnight, especially near hotels and tourist areas.

Banks *Open* Mon–Fri between 9 and 10 and closing between 1 and 6 in the afternoon. Main post offices open daily, 9–9.

Museums are usually open from 10 or 11 to 6 or 7. Most close at least one day a week and another day at the end of each month for cleaning and maintenance. Check with your hotel and Intourist before going out.

Parks and gardens

Moscow Botanical Gardens, Botanicheskaya Ulitsa 4; **Gorky Park**, Krymskiy Val Ulitsa 9; **Izmailovskiy Park**, Narodniy Prospekt 17; **Kolomenskoe**, Proletarskiy Prospekt; **Novodevichiy Convent**, Novodevichiy Proezd 1; **Sokolniki Park**, Sokolnicheskiy Val.

St. Petersburg Botanical Gardens, Professora Popova Ulitsa 2; **Kirov Central Park**, Yelagin Ostrov 4; **Garden of the Anichkov Palace**, Nevskiy Prospekt 39; **Summer Gardens and Palace of Peter I**, Letniy Sad; **Moskovskiy Park Pobedy**, Kuznetsovskaya Ulitsa 25; **Park Babushkina**, Obukhovskoy Oboroniy Prospekt 149; **Tauride Gardens**, Saltykova-Shchedrina Ulitsa 50.

Photography

Photographic supplies are expensive in Russia, so you may like to bring your own film and spare batteries. Western-brand films are sold in hotel shops and other outlets. If you buy Russian film, get it processed in Russia. Many museums allow photography, but you have to buy a special (sometimes expensive) permit at the *kassa* as you enter.

275

Stone carvings on the Cathedral of St. Demetrius, Vladimir

Places of worship

Churches are reopening all the time in Moscow and St. Petersburg, following an extensive restoration program. A selection of those open for worship at the time of writing follows.

When entering a church, women should cover their heads, men should remove their hats. Shorts and sleeveless shirts should not be worn (cover bare shoulders). Flash photography is usually forbidden.

Moscow Russian Orthodox: **Danilovskiy Monastery**, Danilovskiy Val 22, tel: 235 07 08 (Sunday liturgy 7, 9); **Novodevichiy Convent**, Church of the Assumption, Bolshaya Pirogovskaya Ulitsa 2, tel: 245 31 68 (Sunday liturgy 7, 10); **Yelokhovskiy Cathedral**, Spartakovskaya Ulitsa 15, tel: 267 79 51 (Sunday liturgy 7, 10). **Baptist:** Maliy Vuzovskiy Pereulok 3, tel: 917 08 62 (Sunday services 10, 2, 6; Thursdays 6). **Buddhist:** Ostozhenka Ulitsa 49, tel: 245 09 39. **Mosque:** Vypolzov Pereulok 7, tel: 281 38 66 (services Friday 1 PM). **Roman Catholic:** St. Louis, Lubyanka Malaya Ulitsa 12, tel: 925 20 34 (Sunday Masses: 8 [Latin], 11, 6:30 [Russian], 12:30 [English or French]; weekdays: 9, 6:30). **Synagogue (choral):** Arkhipova Ulitsa 10, tel: 923 96 97; Maria Roshcha Synagogue, 2-e Veshlavtsev Pereulok 5a, tel: 289 23 25.

St. Petersburg Russian Orthodox: **Alexander Nevskiy Monastery**, Reki Monastyrki Naberezhnaya 1, tel: 274 04 09 (Sunday liturgy 10). The **Kazan Cathedral**, Kazanskaya Ploshchad 2, has recently reopened for worship. For service times tel: 311 04 95. **Baptist:** Bolshaya Ozernaya Ulitsa 29a, tel: 553 45 78. **Buddhist:** Primorskiy Prospekt 91, tel: 239 13 41. **Mosque:** Kronverkskiy Prospekt 7, tel: 233 98 19. **Roman Catholic:** Our Lady of Lourdes, Kovenskiy Pereulok 7, tel: 272 50 02. **Synagogue and Jewish religious center**, Lermontovskiy Prospekt 2, tel: 114 11 53.

Student and youth travel

Russia now has its own **Youth Hostel Association**, affiliated to the International Youth Hosteling Association. RYH can help visitors with visa processing, clean and inexpensive hostel accommodations up to Western standards, travel information, and tickets for domestic train travel both within Russia and for trans-Siberian and trans-Mongolian services.

Russian Youth Hostels (Russia): St. Petersburg 193312, 3-ya Rozhdestvenskaya Ulitsa 28, tel: 277 05 69, 329 80 18, fax: 277 51 02. In the USA contact **Russian Youth Hostels**, 409 N. Pacific Coast Highway, Building 106, Suite 390, Redondo Beach, CA 90277, tel: 310/379-4316, fax: 310/379-8420. Otherwise contact your national Youth Hostel Association.

Hostels

Moscow Travelers Guest House, Bolshaya Pereyaslavskaya Ulitsa 50, tel: 971 40 59; **St. Petersburg International Hostel** (American-Russian Joint Project), 3rd Rozhdestvenskaya Ulitsa 28, tel: 277 05 69, fax: 277 51 02. **Hostel Holiday**, Mikhailova Ulitsa 1, tel/fax: 542 73 64.

Tipping

As in other countries, it is traditional to tip waiters and taxi drivers. Porters, too, will expect a tip for helping with luggage. Watch for a service charge (between 5 and 15 percent) that may be added to bills on top of the 20 percent value-added tax.

Intourist

Intourist, the former state travel organization, has now been privatized. The new company and its affiliates cooperate with travel agencies abroad, which act on its behalf. It continues to run numerous hotels, motels, campgrounds and restaurants in Moscow and St. Petersburg, and Intourist retains the lion's share of the travel market.

Moscow Head office: Ulitsa Petrovka 13, tel: 927 11 79 (*Open* 9–6).

Intourist desks can also be found in these hotels:

Belgrade, Smolenskaya Ploshchad, tel: 248 16 76.

Cosmos, Prospekt Mira 150, tel: 217 07 85.

Intourist, Tverskaya Ulitsa 3/5, tel: 956 84 00.

Mozhayskaya, Mozhayskaya Shosse 165, tel: 447 34 34.

St. Petersburg Head office: Isaakievskaya Ploshchad 1, tel: 210 09 05 (*Open* 9–6).

Petrointour, Pirogovskaya Naberezhnaya 5/2, tel: 542 87 35, fax: 542 86 91; can also be found in St. Petersburg hotels, including the Grand Hotel Europe, Astoria, Nevskiy Palace, Pribaltiyskaya, Pulkovskaya, St. Petersburg, Moskva, and Karelia.

Intourist travel agencies overseas

U.S.A.: Rahim Tours, 12 South Dixie Highway, Lake Worth, Florida 33460, tel: 407/585-5305, fax: 407/582-1353; Intourist Promotion Office, 630 Fifth Avenue, Suite 868, New York, NY 10111, tel: 212/757-3884/5, fax: 212/459-0031.

Canada: Intourist, 1801 McGill College Ave, Suite 630, Montreal, Quebec H3A 2N4, tel: 514/849-6394/5, fax: 514/849-6743.

London: Intourist Travel Ltd., Intourist House, 219 Marsh Wall, London E14 9FJ, tel: 0171-538 8600, fax: 0171-538 5967.

Australia: Intourist Australia Ltd., Underwood House, 6th Floor 37–49 Pitt Street, Sydney, NSW 2000, tel: 02 247 7652, fax: 02 251 6196.

Other travel agencies

Moscow: American Express, for air tickets and business travel, Sadovo-Kudrinskaya Ulitsa 21a, tel: 956 90 00; **Barry Martin Travel**, Malaya Kommunisticheskaya Ulitsa 3/4, tel: 956 12 13; **Service Globus**, Bolshaya Kommunisticheskaya Ulitsa 1/5, tel: 298 61 90 (also has a desk at Sheremetevo 2, tel: 578 75 34).

St. Petersburg: City Excursion Bureau, Angliyskaya Naberezhnaya 56, tel: 311 40 19; **Central Travel and Tour Agency**, Bolshaya Konyushennaya Ulista 27, tel: 315 30 14; **American Express Travel Service**, for air tickets, business travel, foreign exchange, Mikhaylovskaya Ulitsa 1/7, tel: 119 60 09, fax: 119 60 11; **Griphon Travel USA**—St. Petersburg representatives, for low-cost air tickets, Moskva Hotel Service Bureau, tel: 274 00 22; **EPOL**, specializing in custom tours of Russia, also St. Petersburg, Moscow, Kiev, and the Baltics, Liteyniy Prospekt 6/1, tel: 279 50 60, 278 09 52, fax: 279 50 66.

Tourist information is improving all the time, but slowly

Language guide

A few hours spent mastering the Russian alphabet before you go will be amply rewarded. Being able to decipher names of streets, metro stations, etc., will give you the freedom to wander around by yourself rather than being shepherded about in a group.

hello	zdrávstvuytye	*здравствуйте*
goodbye	dasvidániya	*до свидания*
good morning	dóbraya útra	*доброе утро*
good evening	dóbry viécher	*добрый вечер*
goodnight	spakóyni nóchi	*спокойной ночи*
please/you're welcome	pazhálsta	*пожалуйста*
thank you	spasíba	*спасибо*
yes	da	*да*
no	niét	*нет*
excuse me	izvinítye	*извините*
where?	gdyé?	*где?*
when?	kagdá?	*когда?*
how many?	skólka?	*сколько?*
how much?	skólka?	*сколько?*
I	Ya	*Я*
we	mwee	*мы*
left	naliéva	*налево*
right	napráva	*направо*
straight on	pryáma	*прямо*
I don't speak Russian	ya nye gavaryú parússki	*Я не говорю по русски*
can you speak English?	vy gavarítye pa-anglíyski?	*Вы говорите по-английски?*
write down please	napishíte eta, pazhál sta	*Ипишите это, пожалуйста*
one	adín	*один*
two	dvá	*два*
three	trí	*три*
four	chitírye	*четыре*
five	pyát	*пять*
six	shést	*шесть*
seven	siém	*семь*
eight	vósim	*восемь*
nine	dyévit	*девять*
ten	dyésit	*десять*
twenty	dvátsat	*двадцать*
thirty	trítsat	*тридцать*
forty	sórok	*сорок*

fifty	pyátdesyat	*пятьдесять*
sixty	shéstdesyat	*шестьдесять*
seventy	siémdesyat	*семьдесять*
eighty	vósimdesyat	*восемьдесять*
ninety	devyanósta	*девяносто*
one hundred	stó	*сто*
one thousand	tísicha	*тысяча*

Useful signs

entrance	*вход*
exit	*выход*
no entrance	*нет входа*
free entrance	*вход свободный*
toilet	*туалет*
gentlemen	*мужской*
ladies	*женский*
stop	*стой, стойте*
go	*идите*
crossing	*переход*
closed	*закрыто*
open	*открыто*
cashier	*касса*
occupied	*занято*
vacant	*свободно*
no smoking	*нелъзя куритъ!*
information	*справочное бюро*
restaurant	*ресторан*
elevator	*лифт*
telephone	*телефон*
taxi	*такси*
buffet	*буфет*
bar	*бар*
pharmacy	*Аптека*

Cyrillic alphabetic pronunciation

А	ah	*Б*	b
В	v	*Г*	g
Д	d	*Е*	ye (yellow)
Ё	yaw	*Ж*	zh
З	z	*И*	ee
Й	i (boil)	*К*	k
Л	l	*М*	m
Н	n	*О*	o (ought)
П	o	*Р*	r
С	s	*Т*	t
У	ooh	*Ф*	f
Х	ch (loch)	*Ц*	ts
Ч	ch (chain)	*Ш*	sh
Щ	shch (Ashchurch)		
Ъ	(hard sign)	*Ы*	i (sin)
Ь	(soft sign)	*Э*	ay
Ю	yooh	*Я*	yah

278

HOTELS AND RESTAURANTS

МАКДОНАЛД

HOTELS AND RESTAURANTS

The following recommended hotels and restaurants in Moscow and St. Petersburg have been divided into three price categories:

- budget ($)
- moderate ($$)
- expensive ($$$)

ACCOMMODATIONS

MOSCOW

Baltschug Kempinski Hotel ($$$) Ulitsa Baltschuga 1 (tel: 230 65 00). This old, restored hotel with all modern facilities including small business center, swimming pool, gyms, and sauna is handy for the Tretyakov Picture Gallery and not far from Red Square.

Belgrade Hotel ($$) Smolenskaya Ploshchad 8 (tel: 248 16 76). A modern high-rise with adequate facilities, the Belgrade is located near the Garden Ring. Metro: Smolenskaya.

Budapest Hotel ($$) Petrovskiye Linii 2/18 (tel: 924 88 20). Good value, not far from the Kremlin. Cable TV. Metro: Kuznetskiy Most.

Cosmos Hotel ($$) Prospekt Mira 150 (tel: 217 07 86). A very large, modern hotel (1970s) opposite the VVTs. Popular with Intourist, the facilities are more than adequate, but the big drawback is the half-hour ride from Red Square.

Danilov Hotel ($$$) Bolshoy Stary Danilov Pereulok (tel: 954 05 03). Built to accommodate guests of the Danilovskiy Monastery in the south of the city. Metro: Tulskaya.

Intourist Hotel ($$$) Tverskaya Ulitsa 3/5 (tel: 956 84 26). For its price and location near the Kremlin, a bargain. Several restaurants and a lively, slightly tacky nightlife.

Marco Polo Presnya Hotel ($$$) Spiridonevskiy Pereulok 9 (tel: 956 30 10). This Russian-Austrian joint venture has just 68 rooms and caters mainly for business travelers: it offers a translation service and business center.

Metropol Hotel ($$$) Teatralniy Proezd 1/4 (tel: 927 60 00). Designed by a British architect, this is one of the most expensive hotels in Moscow, but also one of the most luxurious. Recently renovated and centrally situated with every facility.

Mezhdunarodnaya ($$$) Krasnopresnenskaya Naberezhnaya 12 (tel: 253 13 91, 253 10 72). Built with the financial backing of American industrialist Armand Hammer, "the Mezh" is part of the World Trade Center. Lacking in atmosphere, but with comprehensive facilities.

Moscow Travelers Guest House ($) Bolshaya Pereyaslavskaya Ulitsa 50, floor 10 (tel: 971 40 59). A modern youth hostel

recently affiliated to the International Youth Hostel Federation. Located a little beyond the Garden Ring. Book early. Metro: Prospekt Mira.

National Hotel ($$$) Okhotniy Ryad 14/1 (tel: 258 70 00). Fine centrally located hotel which has just been modernized and upgraded.

Novotel Hotel ($$) Sheremetyevo 2 (tel: 578 94 01). Rather pricey, and within a stone's throw of the international airport.

Olympic Penta Hotel ($$$) Olympiyskiy Prospekt 18/1 (tel: 971 61 01). This Russian–German joint venture has 486 double rooms and 12 de luxe. Excellent business facilities, restaurants, nightclub, health club. Metro: Prospekt Mira.

Orlyonok ($$) Kosygina Ulitsa 15 (tel: 939 88 45). A comfortable hotel in the pleasant suburb of Sparrow Hills, attracting mainly business people.

Pullman Iris Hotel ($$$) Korovinskoe Shosse 10 (tel: 488 80 00). An out-of-town environment with garden, sports facilities, and a first-class French restaurant. Metro: Petrovsko-Razumovskaya.

Radisson-Slavyanskaya Hotel ($$$) Berezhkovskaya Naberezhnaya 2 (tel: 941 80 20). This prestigious (and very expensive) American-run hotel has 430 rooms and first-class facilities (shopping arcade and business center). Metro: Kievskaya.

Rossiya ($$) Ulitsa Varvarka 6 (tel: 232 50 50). The advantage of "the Russia" is its location just beyond the far side of Red Square; the disadvantage is its size. Relatively cheap but soulless, although the service is improving.

RusOtel ($) Varshavskoe Shosse (tel: 382 14 65). Not very accessible (on the southern outskirts of the city), but pleasantly situated. A U.S. joint venture featuring sauna, small swimming pool, and bar. Metro: Yuzhnaya, then bus.

Savoy Hotel ($$$) Ulitsa Rozhdestvenka 3 (tel: 929 85 00). A Russian–Finnish joint venture, this small luxury hotel has 86 rooms in a protected neoclassical building. It is in a very central location. Metro: Lubyanka.

Sovetskiy Hotel ($$) Leningradskiy Prospekt 32/2 (tel: 250 72 55). A Russian–French joint venture. This small hotel (60 rooms) is reasonably priced, but not centrally situated. Nearest metro: Belorusskaya.

Ukraina Hotel ($$) Kutuzovskiy Prospekt 2/1 (tel: 243 28 95). The Ukraina dates from 1957. Situated just opposite the White House and overlooking the Moskva River, it has comfortable rooms at a very reasonable price but the facilities are Soviet. Metro: Kievskaya.

ST. PETERSBURG

Astoria ($$$) Bolshaya Morskaya Ulitsa 39 (tel: 210 50 09). This turn-of-the-century protected building overlooks St. Isaac's Cathedral. Luxurious and expensive.

Grand Hotel Europe ($$$) Mikhaylovskaya Ulitsa 1/7 (tel: 119 60 00). This beautifully restored hotel is ideally situated just off Nevskiy Prospekt. Facilities include business center, banks, and Amex office.

Kievskaya Hotel ($) Dnepropetrovskaya Ulitsa 49 (tel: 166 04 56). Cheap, but a bus ride (No. 14) away from Ligovskiy Prospekt metro. Restaurant, bar, and friendly staff.

Mercury Hotel ($$$) Tavricheskaya Ulitsa 39 (tel: 278 19 77). Pleasantly located near the Tauride Gardens, this small expensive hotel caters mainly to foreign business travelers. Bar, restaurant, Winter Garden.

Mir Hotel ($$) Gastello Ulitsa 17 (tel: 108 51 66). Clean, comfortable, and good value, set in the southern suburbs. Metro: Moskovskaya.

Moskva Hotel ($$) Aleksandra Nevskovo Ploshchad 2 (tel: 274 30 01). This ugly high-rise has one advantage only—it's near Ploshchad Aleksandra Nevskovo metro.

Neptune Hotel ($$) Obvodnovo Kanala Naberezhnaya 93a (tel: 210 18 04). This self-styled "business hotel" is comfortable but very inconveniently located—a good walk south of Pushkinskaya metro.

Nevskiy Palace ($$$) Hotel Nevskiy Prospekt 57 (tel: 275 20 01). Dating from 1861 and now restored, this hotel has the perfect location on Nevskiy Prospekt. Facilities include whirlpool, sauna, and massage. Nice—if you can afford it. There are 287 rooms and suites.

Okhtinskaya ($$) Bolsheokhtinskiy Prospekt 4 (tel: 227 37 67). New with good facilities. Fine view across the Neva to the Smolniy Convent but difficult to reach (Bus: 174 from Novocherkasskaya metro).

Oktyabrskaya Hotel ($) Ligovskiy Prospekt 10 (tel: 277 63 30). This Soviet-style hotel has a historic location, opposite the Moscow train station. Metro: Ploshchad Vosstaniya.

Pribaltiyskaya Hotel ($$) Korablestroiteley Ulitsa 14 (tel: 356 02 63). A favorite with Intourist, this hotel has fine views overlooking the Baltic, but the location (a bus ride from Primorskaya metro) is inconvenient. Facilities: business center, bowling, swimming pool, bars, restaurants, nightclub.

Pulkovskaya Hotel ($$) Pobedy Ploshchad 1 (tel: 264 51 22). Handier for the airport than the center of town, this modern Finnish–Russian venture has good facilities including tennis courts. Short walk from Moskovskaya metro.

Rus Hotel ($$$) Artilleriyskaya Ulitsa 1 (tel: 279 50 03). A modern Russian–Italian hotel, convenient for Chernyshevskaya metro and downtown. Bars, café, sauna, hairdresser, currency exchange.

St. Petersburg Hotel ($$$) Vyborgskaya Naberezhnaya 5/2 (tel: 542 94 11). Now reopened after a major refit, this hotel is located just opposite the Cruiser *Aurora*, on the Vyborg Side. The facilities are first-class. Metro: Ploshchad Lenina.

St. Petersburg International Hostel ($) 3–ya Rozhdestvenskaya Ulitsa 28 (tel: 277 05 69). A member of the International Youth Hostel Federation. This is an American venture aimed at youngsters and backpackers. Not far from Ploshchad Vosstaniya metro, this is unusually central for a youth hostel.

Sovetskaya Hotel ($$$) Lermontovskiy Prospekt 43/1 (tel: 259 34 42). Awkwardly located a walk away from Baltiyskaya metro. Good facilities including three restaurants, business center, Bavaria pub.

RESTAURANTS AND CAFÉS

MOSCOW
Russian
Atrium ($$) Leninskiy Prospekt 44 (tel: 137 30 08). Contemporary Russian cuisine in an intimate setting.

Boyarskiy ($$$) Hotel Metropol, Teatralniy Proezd 1/4 (tel: 927 60 63). Dishes cooked according to old Russian recipes, accompanied by a small folk orchestra.

Glazur ($$$) Smolenskiy Bulvar 12 (tel: 248 44 38). Danish as well as Russian cuisine in a luxurious 18th-century mansion.

Kropotkinskaya 36 ($$$) Prechistenka Ulitsa 36 (tel: 201 75 00). The first cooperative restaurant in Moscow. Deserved reputation, courteous service, piano entertainment.

Razgulyai ($$) Spartakovskaya Ulitsa 11 (tel: 267 76 13). Plain Russian fare, good service. Gypsy music on weekends. Nearest metro: Baumannskaya.

Russkiy Traktir ($) Ulitsa Arbat 44 (tel: 241 98 53). Handy for the Arbat.

Stanislavskovo 2 ($$$) Leontevskiy Pereulok 2 (tel: 291 86 89). A beautiful restaurant in a 19th-century house. Traditional Russian dishes, well presented.

Yar ($$$) Leningradskiy Prospekt 32/2 (tel: 250 74 49). On the site of one of Russia's most famous prerevolutionary restaurants. Rasputin was once thrown out of here. Yar specializes in dishes such as roast pig gourmand and veal Orlov.

Zaidi i Poprobuy Café ($$) Prospekt Mira 124 (tel: 286 75 03). A popular restaurant near the Cosmos Hotel—reservations are essential. Not far from VVTs.

American
American Bar & Grill ($$) Tverskaya Yamskaya Ulitsa 2 (tel: 251 28 47). A home away from home for U.S. visitors. The restaurant offers reliable food and excellent service. No credit cards. Open 24 hours.

Azteca ($$) Intourist Hotel, Tverskaya Ulitsa 3/5 (tel: 956 84 89). Mexican food by an American chef.

La Cantina ($$) Tverskaya Ulitsa 5 (tel: 292 53 88). Ideal location and friendly service are the main recommendations—Tex-Mex.

HOTELS AND RESTAURANTS

Pizza Hut ($$) Tverskaya Ulitsa 12 (tel: 229 20 13) and Kutuzovskiy Prospekt 17 (tel: 243 17 27). A familiar name for Americans and Europeans alike.

The Exchange ($$$) Radisson-Slavyanskaya Hotel, Berezhkovskaya Naberezhnaya 2 (tel: 941 80 20). Steak house. New special menu each week.

European

Anchor ($$$) Moscow Palace Hotel, Tverskaya-Yamskaya Ulitsa 19 (tel: 956 31 52). A new restaurant. Seafood from the U.S.A.

Golden Ostap ($$$) Schmidtovskiy Proezd 3 (tel: 259 47 95). Georgian and European cuisine. Jazz piano and small casino.

Le Café Français ($$$) Pullman Iris Hotel, Korovinskoe Shosse 10 (tel: 488 80 00). Stylish French setting and food.

Patis Pasta ($$) Tverskaya Yamskaya 1/3 (tel: 251 58 61). Open 24 hours. Large helpings of home-made pasta, and excellent service.

Patis Pizza ($$) Tverskaya Ulitsa 4 (tel: 292 08 91). A new glass-roof pizza joint outside the Hotel Intourist and within a stone's throw of Red Square.

Strastnoy 7 ($$) Strastnoy Bulvar 7 (tel: 299 04 98). One of the early private restaurants. European cuisine, and Russian specialties. The live music can be intrusive.

Greek Restaurant ($$) Krasnopresnenskaya Naberezhnaya 12 (tel: 255 92 84). Boat restaurant serving traditional Greek dishes, moored opposite Expocenter.

Teatro Mediterraneo ($$$) Metropol Hotel, Teatralny Proezd 1/4 (tel: 927 60 69). Delicious Mediterranean dishes; a favorite of Moscow's in-crowd.

Writers' Union Restaurant ($$) Povarskaya Ulitsa 52 (tel: 291 21 69). Where the literary élite dined in palatial surroundings in Soviet times.

Yakimanka Cafe ($$) Bolshaya Polyanka Ulitsa 2/10 (tel: 238 88 88). Once had a reputation for traditional Uzbek cooking, but the menu is now changing to a broader European cuisine. Nearest metro: Polyanka.

Fast Food:

McDonald's ($) Bolshaya Bronnaya Ulitsa 29 (tel: 200 16 55). The first in Moscow (off Pushkin Square); Gazetniy Pereulok 15 (tel: 956 98 18), off Tverskaya Ulitsa, near Intourist Hotel; Ulitsa Arbat 50/52 (tel: 241 36 81).

Pizza Hut takeout. See above.

Jewish

U Yuzefa ($$) Dubininskaya Ulitsa 11/1 (tel: 238 46 46). Moscow's only kosher restaurant known for good food and service. Metro: Paveletskaya.

Seafood

Pescatore-90 Prospekt Mira 36 (tel: 280 24 06). Delicious Italian fish dishes. Italian television and papers available.

Sirens ($$$) Ulitsa Bolshaya Spasskaya 15 (tel: 208 14 12). Near Sukharevskaya metro. Delicious seafood at a price, including Norwegian salmon with caviar sauce and fried shark.

The Lobster Grill ($$$) Metropol Hotel, Teatralny Proezd 1/4 (tel: 927 60 69). The finest seafood in an elegant setting.

Southern Republics

Farkhad ($$) Bolshaya Marfinskaya 4 (tel: 218 41 36). Excellent Azerbaijani cuisine. Bring your own wine.

Guria ($) Komsomolskiy Prospekt 7/3 (tel: 246 03 78). Georgian food. Nearest metro: Park Kultury.

Kolkhida ($$) Sadovaya-Samotechnaya Ulitsa 6 (tel: 299 67 57). Excellent Georgian cuisine. Bring your own wine. Nearest metros: Sukharevskaya /Mayakovskaya.

Sayat-Nova Café ($) Ulitsa Yasnogorskaya 17 (tel: 426 85 11). Cheaper range of Armenian food.

U Pirosmani Café ($$) Novodevichiy Proezd 4 (tel: 247 19 26). Superb Georgian food and regional wines in this restaurant near the Novodevichiy Monastery.

Other Cuisines

Dragon na Ordynka Restaurant ($$$) Bolshaya Ordynka 59 (tel: 231 92 51). Chinese cuisine. Open until 5 AM.

Golden Lotus ($$) Krasnopresnenskaya Naberezhnaya 12 (tel: 255 25 00) (Expocenter). Recipes from Szechuan province with Chinese mood music.

Korea House ($$$) Volgogradskiy Prospekt 26 (tel: 270 13 00). Korean cuisine in pleasant setting.

Manila ($$$) Vavilova Ulitsa 81 (tel: 132 00 55). A bright Filipino restaurant.

Mei-Hua ($$) Rusakovskaya Ulitsa 2/1 (tel: 264 95 74). Excellent Chinese food and pleasant atmosphere. Metro: Krasnoselskaya.

Moscow Bombay ($$) Glinishevskiy pereulok 8 (tel: 292 97 31). An unusual menu comprising Indian, Chinese, European, and vegetarian dishes. Exotic dancing/piano.

Tokyo Restaurant ($$$) Hotel Rossiya, Varvarka Ulitsa 6 (tel: 298 53 74). Original Japanese cuisine.

ST. PETERSBURG
Russian

Austeria ($$$) Petropavlovskaya Krepost (tel: 238 42 62). Located in one of the bastions of the Peter-Paul Fortress, the Austeria serves 18th-century and modern Russian dishes. Friendly and efficient.

Dom Arkhitektora ($$$) Bolshaya Morskaya Ulitsa 52 (tel: 311 45 57). Classic Russian cuisine in elegant surroundings.

Imperial ($$$) Kamennoostrovskiy Prospekt 53 (tel: 234 17 42). Tsarist nostalgia and music in traditional palm court. Metro: Petrogradskaya.

Le Café ($$$) Nevskiy Prospekt 142 (tel: 271 28 11). A bakery, restaurant, and café at the upper end of Nevskiy.

Literary Café ($$) Nevskiy Prospekt 18 (tel: 312 60 57). Go for the splendid interior décor and literary associations (Russian poet Alexander Pushkin once dined here)—food, drink, and service leave much to be desired.

Saigon ($$) Ulitsa Plekhanova 33 (tel: 315 87 72). Don't be misled by the name: this restaurant serves standard European Russian fare. Nearest metro: Sadovaya.

Staraya Derevnya Café ($$$) Ulitsa Savushkina 72 (tel: 239 00 00). A restaurant with a prerevolutionary flavor. Gypsy music on Fridays and Saturdays. Metro: Chernaya Rechka, then bus 32, 166. It might be worth getting a taxi.

Troika ($$$) Zagorodniy Prospekt 27 (tel: 113 55 19). Traditional Russian cuisine with a variety show.

European

Afrodita ($$$) Nevsky Prospekt 86 (tel: 275 76 20). Caters to a sophisticated clientele, and offers good international fare—menu alternates between 17 different cuisines. Fresh seafood a specialty.

Ambassador ($$$) Fontanka Naberezhnaya 14 (tel: 272 91 81).Luxurious setting and candlelight—and you pay for it.

Angleterre ($$$) Hotel Astoria, Bolshaya Morskaya Ulitsa 39 (tel: 210 59 06). A sophisticated restaurant in a prerevolutionary hotel.

Antwerpen ($$$) Kronverskiy Prospekt 13 (tel: 239 97 46). Popular with tourist groups, so reservations essential. Busy. Flemish and European cuisine.

Beer Garden ($) Nevskiy Prospekt 86 (tel: 273 31 89). Set back off the main street, the terrace is a haven for the weary sightseer. Situated next door to Afrodita (see above).

Bella Leone ($$$) Vladimirskiy Prospekt 9 (tel: 113 16 70). A small, smart Italian restaurant. Service is sometimes a little too pressing.

Brasserie Grand Hotel Europe ($$$) Mikhaylovskaya Ulitsa 1/7 (tel: 119 60 00). Dine in the elegant surroundings of the Grand Hotel, with quality French cuisine at affordable prices.

Chayka ($$) Griboedova Kanala Naberezhnaya 14 (tel: 312 46 31). Much frequented by tourists, the centrally located Chayka offers standard German cuisine and beer.

Daddy's Steak Room ($$) Moskovskiy Prospekt 73 (tel: 298 77 44). This restaurant boasts "the best steaks in St. Petersburg," but the competition is limited. Also serves pizzas.

Dr. Oetker ($$) Nevskiy Prospekt 40 (tel: 312 24 57). A beautifully redecorated pub-restaurant, convenient for sightseeing. Serves snacks as well as main meals.

Domenico's ($$$) Nevskiy Prospekt 70 (tel: 272 57 17). Night spot and restaurant for the well-heeled.

Pietari ($$) Moskovskiy Prospekt 222 (tel: 293 18 09). A modern restaurant serving mainstream European dishes at surprisingly moderate prices.

Schwabski Domik ($$$) Krasnogvardeyskiy Prospekt 28/19 (tel: 528 22 11). German beer, schnitzel, würst, etc. Folk ensemble.

Shamrock ($$) Dekabristov Ulitsa 27 (tel: 219 46 25). Friendly Irish bar serving home-style food, handy for the Mariinskiy Theatre.

Fast Food

Carrols ($) Ulitsa Vosstanya 5 and Nevskiy Prospekt 45. No phone. Unpretentious burgers, apple pie, ice cream, etc.

Gale ($) Nevskiy Prospekt 108 (tel: 222 76 81). Fried chicken, salads, sandwiches, and other snacks.

Seafood

Demyanova Ukha ($$) (Demyan's Fish Chowder) Kronverkskiy Prospekt 53 (tel: 232 80 90). Russian seafood.

Ocean ($$) Primorsky Prospekt 31b (tel: 239 63 05). Boat restaurant offering seafood, traditional Russian cuisine, and folk music.

Southern Republics

A Thousand and One Nights ($$$) Millionnaya, 21/6 (tel: 312 22 65). Uzbek and international cuisine.

Bagdad ($$) Furshtadtskaya Ulitsa 35 (tel: 272 35 33. Uzbek (Central Asian) cuisine. Metro: Chernyshevskaya.

Fortetsiya ($$) Ulitsa Kuibysheva 7 (tel: 233 84 88). Cozy but the food is nothing special.

Pirosmani ($$) Bolshoy Prospekt 14 (tel: 235 64 56). Georgian cuisine in artistic surroundings.

Tbilisi ($$) Sytninskaya Ulitsa 10 (tel: 232 93 91). Very friendly atmosphere and good value. Metro: Gorkovskaya.

Other Cuisines

Golden Dragon ($$) Dekabristov Ulitsa 62 (tel: 114 84 41). Near the Mariinskiy Theater, this restaurant offers more than 120 Chinese and Southeast Asian dishes prepared by top chefs.

Hebei ($$$) Bolshoy Prospekt 61 (tel: 233 20 46). Chinese cuisine from Hebei province.

Korean House ($$) Reki Fontanki Naberezhnaya 20 (tel: 275 72 03). Excellent Korean cuisine.

La Cucaracha ($$) Fontanka Naberezhnaya 39 (tel: 110 40 06). The first Mexican cantina in St. Petersburg. There is live Latin music at weekends.

Senat Bar ($$$) Galyernaya Ulitsa 1–3 (tel: 314 92 53). President Clinton's visit here is the stuff of legend, but the quality of the food does not always live up to its reputation.

Index

Principle references are given in **bold**.

INDEX

INDEX/PICTURE CREDITS/CONTRIBUTORS

Picture credits

The Automobile Association thanks the following photographers and libraries for their assistance in the preparation of this book.

BRIDGEMAN ART LIBRARY 115 Portrait of Leo Tolstoy, 1887, by Ilya Efimovitch Repin (1844–1930), Tretyakov Gallery, Moscow, 128 The Morning of the Streltsi's Execution by Vasily Ivanovich Surikov (1848–1916), Tretyakov Gallery, Moscow, 129 Woman with Pomegranates by Valentin Alexandrovitch Serov (1865–1911), Tretyakov Gallery, Moscow, 199b Portrait of Fedor Dostoevsky, 1872, by Vasili Perov (1834–82), Tretyakov Gallery, Moscow, 202/3 Necklace of miniature eggs by Fabergé, Werner Collection, Luton Hoo, Bedfordshire, 202b Enamel box with miniatures of Nicholas II & Alexandra of Russia by Fabergé, Private Collection, 203 The Nicholas II equestrian egg, jeweled & guilloche enamel with silver gilt & gold mount by Carl Fabergé (work master Victor Aarne), Christie's, London.
MARY EVANS PICTURE LIBRARY 30a, 30b Ivan the Terrible. **J. FREEMAN** 42/3 Mayakovskaya Metro, 75 Moscow, Terem Palace, 99 Moscow Arts Theater, 111 Moscow, Melnikov House, 130a, 131 Moscow, Church of the Virgin of All Sorrows, 219b Moscow, Sandunov Baths. **RONALD GRANT ARCHIVE** 233 "October." **HULTON DEUTSCH COLLECTION LTD** 40b Stalin, Lenin & Kalinin, 44a St Petersburg, anti-aircraft gun detachment, 45 Yalta conference, 82b Beria. **THE MANSELL COLLECTION LTD.** 31a Map of Moscow, 31b Ivan the Terrible & Son by Repin, 32b C18 Map St. Petersburg, 36/7 Napoleon's retreat from Moscow, 36b Burning of Moscow, 37b Marshall Kutozov, 38b Women at work, 39 Russian poor, 55 C19 View of Kremlin,177 Tchaikovsky, 191b Pushkin, 214 Nijinsky. **J. MASSEY STEWART** 12a Kirov Ballet perfomance, 34/5 Departure of Empress Catherine II, 35 Catherine the Great, 38a prerevolutionary currency, 41 dismantling Alexander III's statue, 83 Dzerzhinsky statue. **PICTURES COLOUR LIBRARY LTD.** 214/5 Bolshoi Theater. **RANGE/BETTMAN/UPI** 44b Red Army. **REX FEATURES LTD.** 10/11 Moscow coup 1991, 10 Moscow election, 11 Moscow coup 1991, 13b Solzhenitsyn, 46/7 army parade, 46 Tanks parade, 47Mikhail Gorbachev, 62 Kremlin, Palace of Facets, 71 Russian Government. **RUSSIA & REPUBLICS PHOTOLIBRARY** 13a Bolshoi Theater, 21 Chef & shashlik, 67 Cathedral of Assumption & Patriarch's Palace, 92 Pushkin Fine Arts Museum, 95 Petrovsky Passage, 215 Bolshoi Ballet perfomance. **SPECTRUM COLOUR LIBRARY** Spine, Russian dolls, 17 Red Square excavating, 33a St Petersburg, Petrodvorets Summer Palace, 40 St Petersburg, *Aurora*. **TRIP** 103 Vodka vendor (A. Kuznetsov), 144 Rostov-Veliki, Church of the Savior in the Vestibule, Kremlin (J. Wiseman). **ZEFA PICTURES** 20b Caviar and champagne, 146, 147 Suzdal.

All other pictures were taken by Ken Paterson and are held in the Association's own library (AA PHOTO LIBRARY).

Contributors

Revision copy editor: Janet Tabinski   **Original copy editor:** Helen McCurdy
Revision verifiers: Christopher and Melanie Rice